PENNSYLVANIA

Philadelphia •

NEW JERSEY

Potomac R.

MARYLAND

ODSTOCK ⚔

⚔ ALDIE
Washington •
⚔ WARRENTON

ONBURG ⚔
CEDAR MOUNTAIN ⚔⚔ ⚔ BRANDY STATION
⚔ FREDERICKSBURG
BARNETT'S FORD ⚔

Richmond ○

James R.

VIRGINIA

NORTH CAROLINA

SOUTH CAROLINA

Atlantic Ocea

N

CIVIL WAR THEATER

Locations and Dates of General Joseph Kargé's
Principal Engagements with Confederate Forces

In the EAST with 1st New Jersey Cavalry:

Date	Place
June 2, 1862	Woodstock, Va.
June 6, 1862	Harrisonburg, Va.
August 8, 1862	Barnett's Ford, Va.
August 9, 1862	Cedar Mountain, Va.
August 20, 1862	Brandy Station, Va.
September 29, 1862	Warrenton, Va.
October 31, 1862	Aldie, Va.
December 11-13, 1862	Fredericksburg, Va.

In the WEST with 2nd New Jersey Cavalry:

Date	Place
February 22, 1864	Okolona, Miss.
May 2, 1864	Bolivar, Tenn.
June 6, 1864	Rienzi, Miss.
June 10, 1864	Brices Cross Roads, Miss.
July 16, 1864	Grand Gulf, Miss.
December, 28, 1864	Egypt Station, Miss.
April 5-12, 1865	Siege of Mobile, Ala.
April 17—May 20, 1865	March thru Alabama

Star on Many a Battlefield

Colonel Joseph Kargé as Brigade Commander. COURTESY OF LIBRARY OF CONGRESS.

Star on Many a Battlefield

Brevet Brigadier General Joseph Kargé
in the American Civil War

Colonel Francis C. Kajencki
U.S. Army Retired

Rutherford • Madison • Teaneck
Fairleigh Dickinson University Press
London: Associated University Presses

Associated University Presses, Inc.
Cranbury, New Jersey 08512

Associated University Presses
Magdalen House
136-148 Tooley Street
London SE1 2TT, England

Library of Congress Cataloging in Publication Data

Kajencki, Francis C
   Star on many a battlefield, Brevet Brigadier General Joseph Kargé in the American Civil War.

   Bibliography: p.
   Includes index.
   1. Kargé, Joseph, 1823-1892. 2. United States—History—Civl War, 1861-1865—Campaigns and battles. 3. United States—History—Civil War, 1861-1865—Biography. 4. Generals—United States—Biography. I. Title.
E467.1.K2K34   973.7'3   77-89781
ISBN 0-8386-2149-X

PRINTED IN THE UNITED STATES OF AMERICA

To the Memory of
Virginia T. Kajencki

Contents

List of Photographs, Maps, and Other Illustrations 9

Preface 11

Acknowledgments 15

Prologue 19

  1. Gallant Son of Liberty 20
  2. New Citizen Turns Volunteer 28
  3. In Pursuit of Stonewall Jackson 39
  4. Bayard's Cavalry Holds Off Jackson 56
  5. Charges against the Commander 71
  6. Clash of Cavalry 75
  7. Return to Action 97
  8. Sherman's Meridian Expedition 113
  9. Kargé Beats Forrest 136
10. Battle of Brice's Cross-Roads 147
11. Higher Command and More Frustration 168
12. Gallant Victory at Egypt Station 186
13. Alabama Campaign 206
14. Soldier Becomes Educator 219

Epilogue 230

Appendixes
  A: Kargé's Congratulatory Order,
     14 January 1865 237
  B: Letter of General Grierson
     to Colonel Kargé, 28 July 1865 238

Notes 239

Bibliography 259

Index 267

Illustrations

Photographs and letters

Colonel Joseph Kargé as Brigade Commander — 2
Letter of General C. C. Washburn to President Lincoln, 22 January 1865 — 12
Brigadier General George D. Bayard — 40
A Cavalry Column Crosses Rappahannock River on Pontoon Bridge — 41
Lieutenant Colonel Joseph Kargé with Brigadier General Samuel W. Crawford — 59
Colonel Kargé's Recruiting Notices — 99
Letter of Secretary of State to Governor of Illinois, 6 July 1863 — 105
Lieutenant General Nathan Bedford Forrest — 114
Brigadier General William Sooy Smith — 122
Benjamin H. Grierson as Colonel — 123
Major General C.C. Washburn — 139
Brigadier General Samuel D. Sturgis — 141
Site of Camp Winfield Scott, Nevada — 223
Professor Joseph Kargé, Ph.D. — 225
In Memoriam Joseph Kargé — 231, 232, 233

Maps

Civil War Theater — Endpapers
In Pursuit of Stonewall Jackson — 42
Guarding the Rapidan River Line — 58
First Line of Defense at Battle of Cedar Mountain — 65
Engagement at Brandy Station — 78
Scouting the Movements of Lee's Army — 84
March of Kargé's Second New Jersey Cavalry against General Forrest — 115
Sherman's Meridian Campaign — 117
Kargé's Raid to Rienzi and Reconnaissance to Corinth — 150
Battle of Brice's Cross Roads — 156
March of Colonel Kargé's Cavalry Brigade with General Slocum — 171
General Washburn's Plan to Trap Forrest — 180
Kargé Overwhelms Rebels at Egypt Station, Mississippi — 191
Ground Plan of Camp Winfield Scott, Nevada — 223

Preface

Brevet Brigadier General Joseph Kargé almost single-handedly contributed two-thirds of the cavalry effort of the state of New Jersey to the winning of the Civil War. Of the three volunteer cavalry regiments fielded by the state, Kargé trained and commanded the First New Jersey Cavalry, originally recruited as "Halsted's Horse," and led the regiment in campaigns in Virginia. At Brandy Station, he suffered a serious battle injury that forced his subsequent resignation from the service on 22 December 1862.

Kargé recovered from his wound by the spring of 1863. Eager to return to action, he obtained the backing of Governor Joel Parker and the authority of the War Department to organize and recruit the Second New Jersey Cavalry Regiment. General Robert E. Lee's dramatic invasion of Pennsylvania in June 1863 temporarily diverted Kargé from his objective. Governor Parker called on the citizens to join the militia to fight the rebels, and he appointed Kargé the state's Chief of Cavalry. Following Lee's defeat at Gettysburg, Kargé resumed his goal of recruiting and training the Second New Jersey Cavalry, which he then led against the enemy in Tennessee, Mississippi, and Alabama. When he stepped up to the command of a cavalry brigade, the Second New Jersey always served in his brigade. The First and the Second New Jersey Cavalry Regiments became known for their disciplined behavior and gallant performance, strongly reflecting the attributes of their commander. Both of these regiments established enviable reputations in their areas of fighting.

Star on Many a Battlefield is not a biography of Joseph Kargé, although biographical data are included to describe the man. Nor is it a history of the two regiments he commanded. The account may properly be called a military biography that attempts to portray Joseph Kargé's leadership and to assess his contribution to the overall war effort. Accomplishing these two objectives called for a review of the battles and campaigns in which Kargé took part, as the setting for a better understanding and evaluation of the role he played. His actions are then woven into the battles and campaigns.

Head Quarters District of Vicksburg,

Vicksburg Miss., January 22ᵈ, 1865.

His Excellency,
Abraham Lincoln.
President,
Sir.
It affords me great pleasure to recommend for promotion Col. Joseph Kargé, of the 2ᵈ New Jersey Cavalry. I have known Col. Kargé long and well, and I regard him as one of the most dashing and valuable officers in the Cavalry service. He has earned a star on many a battle field, and I know of no one whose promotion is more deserved

I have the honor to be

Your Obdt Servt
C. C. Washburn
Maj Genl

Letter of General C. C. Washburn to President Lincoln, 22 January 1865. COURTESY OF NATIONAL ARCHIVES.

Regrettably, Joseph Kargé left no written accounts of his eventful life. The tale of his exciting youth as a Polish revolutionary was fortunately published in Princeton's *Nassau Literary Magazine* in 1887, after he had agreed to an interview by one of his students. That European experience strongly influenced the future naturalized American, who answered President Abraham Lincoln's call for volunteers in 1861. Kargé's role as a cavalry leader is reflected in his reports and correspondence contained in the *Official Records of the Rebellion*. Newspapers, especially those of New Jersey, also recorded the activities of his regiments. I believe that no substantial account of Kargé's military life has been presented before and the man who first beat General Nathan Bedford Forrest has gone unrecognized.

Some historians of the Civil War misrepresent Kargé's ethnic identity, perhaps inadvertently, for lack of more substantial research. Mark M. Boatner III in *The Civil War Dictionary* gives his place of birth as Germany. Earl Schenck Miers implies that Prussia was his country of origin, when he refers to Kargé's Prussian military background in *Ride to War: The History of the First New Jersey Cavalry Regiment*. Both historians are technically correct, but in reality Joseph Kargé was a proud son of Poland.

The surname Kargé is of French origin, although the family resided in the Polish province of Poznan for generations. At the time of Kargé's birth in 1823, Poland had ceased to exist as an independent country. She had been dismembered by Prussia, Austria, and Russia in the infamous partitions of 1772, 1793, and 1795. One of the main difficulties in establishing the identity of Poles, in the Civil War and in other activities as well, is that they are often listed as Prussians, Austrians, or Russians.

How did Kargé identify himself? The United States Census for 1870 and 1880, when he lived in the Borough of Princeton, lists Poland as his place of birth. This was technically incorrect, but Kargé never recognized the partitions. In official correspondence to the War Department, Kargé stated repeatedly that he was "a native of Poland." His friends and associates knew his origin well. A colleague on the Princeton faculty said that Kargé fondly and proudly cherished his memories of Poland and the use of the Polish language.

Joseph Kargé never ceased to work for the cause of Polish independence. When the Poles challenged the Russian Tsar in the bloody uprising of January 1863, Kargé joined his fellow Union officer Brigadier General Wladimir Krzyzanowski and civilian leaders of Polish descent to organize the Central Polish Committee in the United States.[1] The American Committee established a bond of sympathy for the National Central Committee in Poland, and tried to rouse American public opinion in favor of the insurrection. Kargé saw a close relationship between his position as an American citizen and his membership on the Central Polish Committee in the United States. At home "the Union was fighting to prevent the dismemberment of a nation, while in Poland a nation was fighting to throw off the shackles of dismemberment."[2] In this respect the Polish insurrection substantially helped the international position of the United States and adversely affected that of the Confederate states. The uprising created for Great Britain and France the specter of a confrontation with Russia and Prussia, and thereby weakened the attempts of the two Western powers to recognize the Confederacy.[3]

Although Joseph Kargé was proud of his Polish origin, he was equally devoted to his adopted country. He was one of the first to answer President Lincoln's call to arms and, at age thirty-eight, gave up a successful school of modern languages for the hard and dangerous life of a combat soldier. Joseph Kargé was of the same mold as the Marquis de Lafayette and General Thaddeus Kosciuszko.

Acknowledgments

My beloved wife, Virginia, who died in 1969, was my motivation over the years to write this book. She created the kind of family environment conducive to achieving this goal, and she became a staunch supporter of my writing project. During years of intermittent research on Kargé, I had opportunities for official government visits to Washington, D.C., and to Army agencies on the East Coast. Invariably, I arranged for a couple of days of leave, following the completion of my official business, to do research at the National Archives and the Library of Congress. Virginia encouraged me, notwithstanding the prolongation of my absences from home that left her with the cares of the family. She was proud of my project. Oftentimes at close gatherings, and springing from her unbounded loyalty, she intimated that the book was about ready for the publisher, when in fact I had yet to write the first page. Having finally completed the book, I dedicate it to her memory.

I am indebted to Victor A. Wojciechowski of Trenton, New Jersey, for biographical information on Joseph Kargé, and to the efforts of his fellow citizens to revive the memory of that gallant Pole. I wish to mention Henry Archacki of New York, who as National Chairman of the American-Polish Civil War Centennial Committee conducted several observances in Kargé's honor. Representing the Committee as Regional Chairman for the Washington, D.C., area, I was proud to be associated with Archacki in the conduct of Centennial tributes to Poles in the Civil War.

I wish to express my appreciation to Dr. Albert Elsasser, retired professor of English at Princeton University. Dr. Elsasser showed great interest in Joseph Kargé and cooperated wholeheartedly with Wojciechowski in arranging memorial services at the Kargé gravesite in Princeton Cemetery. Dr. Elsasser also reviewed an early draft of my manuscript and offered many valuable comments. I thank him for his help.

I acknowledge the many hours of assistance from the staffs of the Library of Congress, National Archives and especially Dale E. Floyd of Military Archives Division, the Army Library in the Pentagon, and Library of the State Historical Society of Wisconsin, as well as the significant help of Kenneth W. Richards, former head of Archives and History Bureau, State Library of New Jersey; of Julienne A. Sears, interlibrary loan librarian at El Paso Public Library; and of Mary Lou Valdez and Josephine Melendez at the library of the U.S. Army Air Defense School, Fort Bliss, Texas, and their source of my requests, U.S. Army Military History Institute, Carlisle Barracks, Pennsylvania. L. James Higgins, Jr., curator of manuscripts, Nevada State Historical Society, kindly provided information and photographs of Camp Winfield Scott. Charles and Helen Kilczewski supplied biographical data on Joseph Kargé. They form part of a group of history-minded citizens of Wilmington, Delaware, who have restored a large room at Fort Delaware where, among others, memorabilia of Joseph Kargé are on display. I wish to thank my son, Anthony, for obtaining data from the Library of Congress, and my daughter, AnnMarie, for reviewing and proofreading the manuscript. My cartographers are Edward J. Krasnoborski, Michael Pillow, and Edward Van Reet.

The process of piecing together the events of the past sometimes forces a writer to make historical judgments from conflicting evidence. I have tried to be painstakingly accurate, drawing my conclusions, insofar as possible, from primary materials and notwithstanding what other historians may have said. Biographical data on Joseph Kargé is based on American sources. I alone take responsibility for any errors in this book.

Star on Many a Battlefield

Prologue

In 1864 the success of General William T. Sherman's campaign to capture Atlanta, Georgia, depended on "his lifeline to the rear"—the single-track railroad through Chattanooga and Nashville to the Ohio River. The one Confederate general whom Sherman feared most was Nathan Bedford Forrest, the South's "Invincible Raider." Sherman mounted repeated expeditions to pin down Forrest in Mississippi and thereby keep him from that lifeline in Middle Tennessee. Driven to fury by the Raider's exploits, Sherman called him "That Devil Forrest!" Nonetheless, the federal commander determined to destroy Forrest "if it cost 10,000 lives and breaks the Treasury."

On the second day of May 1864, a force of infantry and cavalry from Memphis marched again to drive Forrest out of Tennessee, chase him if necessary into Mississippi and destroy him. The elusive rebel, however, habitually outmaneuvered his foe. A master tactician, General Forrest had as yet never tasted defeat. On this day he occupied a strong position about one mile west of Bolivar, Tennessee, to protect a key bridge across the flooded Hatchie River. He aimed to deny the bridge to the enemy and keep him at bay while his main raiding force escaped into Mississippi with supplies and recruits from the latest foray into Northern-held territory. The Confederates at Bolivar waited for the Yankees confidently in fortified trenches.

Colonel Joseph Kargé led the Union advance. He commanded a light cavalry brigade of seven hundred troopers on a search mission for the enemy. As he approached Bolivar he scattered the enemy pickets before him to attack Forrest and the estimated eight hundred defenders. In a hard, two-hour battle, Kargé uprooted the Confederates from their earthworks and rifle pits, and drove them back through the town in confusion. The rebels retreated across the river and, destroying the bridge, escaped into the shadows of evening twilight. Thus Kargé handed Forrest his first defeat.[1]

The fighting reputation of Forrest is wellknown, but who was Kargé? As in his fierce attack on Forrest, Kargé had lived through some dangerous adventures, beginning in Europe as a young revolutionary.

19

1

Gallant Son of Liberty

Before escaping to America in 1851, Joseph Kargé had become embroiled in the nationalistic movement that swept across Europe in 1848. He belonged to a secret group of patriots, working for the liberation of Poland. At the same time he served as an officer in the Royal Horse Guard of Prussia. On 15 March of that year, when rioting and street fighting broke out in Berlin, the government authorities ordered the royal cavalry regiment to protect the palace.

Kargé had been ill, and a night-long exposure to wintry weather brought on a relapse. The next day the twenty-four year-old soldier was confined to quarters. Stretching out his lean body on a cot in the guard room, he rested for several hours. His normally dark features were pale, but his eyes flashed excitement as he listened to the uproar in the streets. The young revolutionary felt caged and helpless, yet a fierce determination seared his mind to get away and join the people. The youth refused to consider the double danger of being shot at as a Prussian soldier by the insurgents and as a deserter by the military. When the commander ordered his company to charge the rebel barricades, Kargé could hold back no longer. Grabbing his equipment, he rushed to the muster hall. He forced himself to sit erect in the saddle as he took his place in the line of mounted cavalry. The thoughts of escape, liberty, and vengeance were a powerful motive. The Guard company fired its two cannons, and, on command, the horsemen attacked the insurgents in a furious charge. As they galloped down the street the troopers were enveloped in a hail of bullets fired from every window, housetop, and barricade.

Only three Prussian guards reached that death-dealing obstruction in the street. Kargé was the first. He dashed over the debris and into the core of spewing fire. His horse fell dead, but the wiry, 160-pound rider scrambled forward on all fours and stood up among the battling citizens, a glaring target in his uniform. In a second a dozen weapons were aimed at him, but just as quickly Kargé flung down his helmet and sword and, lifting up his hands, shouted: "*Hoch lebe das Volk! Hoch lebe das Volk!* [Long live the people!]." The insurgents lowered their weapons as they welcomed him and answered with the same cheer. Shouldering a musket, Kargé took his place behind the barricade. Whenever a Prussian uniform appeared in his sight, he fired a deadly complement in return for the harsh and degrading treatment meted out to him by his superiors. Fate had been kind to Joseph. Just one hour before, he had been lying ill in the guardroom, but the chance to fight for liberty had propelled him into headlong action. The young revolutionary had dared and won.

After three days and nights of street fighting, the government withdrew the royal guards and some thirty thousand troops of all arms from Berlin. The King freed political prisoners and granted other concessions. Kargé returned to his native province of Poznan, where the secret Polish Revolutionary Committee assigned him the task of forming a cavalry force. Selecting mostly university students from the more prominent families, Kargé organized an elite battalion of three hundred troopers. Each had had some military service and furnished his own arms and horse. Kargé drilled them almost every day and night for three weeks, but he laid aside his training when the Committee ordered him to conduct an inspection of cavalry units in the other towns of the province. Arming himself with two pistols, Kargé rode off one evening in April. About midnight, within the outer fortifications of the city of Poznan, a Prussian sentry unexpectedly confronted Kargé , took him prisoner, and escorted the unhappy revolutionary to the commandant of the fortress. Kargé's papers and notes gave him away. The commandant charged the youth with being a deserter from the army and a traitor to the Prussian government. The next morning the guards escorted the young Pole down a corridor of the fortress to a narrow, iron cage that stood fastened to the wall. They removed some officers' equipment stored in the cage and thrust Kargé into this converted prison. Almost six feet tall, he could barely stand up. To further humiliate him, the guards fastened a placard to the cage that read: "A Perjurer and a Traitor to the King."

The approaching hour for a parade prompted a flow of soldiers down that corridor and past the cage. Kargé thought he detected sympathy in the eyes of many of them. Although most soldiers passed by in grim silence, some cursed and spat at him. Kargé stood there awkwardly, caged like a wild animal, subjected to this abuse. He grew weak and was soon covered with filth, yet he met every eye firmly. Years later, when he related this incident, he said: "I would have died before letting my pain find expression before them." At one o'clock in the afternoon the commandant came and, after glaring at the prisoner for a few seconds, declared: "Such is the reward meted out to a scoundrel!" Looking back defiantly, Kargé exclaimed: "Do you call this German culture? It is the culture of the Goth and the Vandal! Shoot me if I deserve, but do not torture me." The taunt struck home, for the commandant ordered him released from the cage and confined to a normal prison cell.

No one at the Poznan fortress had the authority to court-martial Kargé . As a royal guard he could be tried only by his peers. The commandant transferred him temporarily to the Glogow fortress, fifty miles from Poznan. Here the commandant proved sympathetic. He assigned the prisoner a pleasant room, provided him with wine and cigars, and ordered the mess to serve dinner. The commandant had no proof of Kargé's treason. His prisoner had simply been engaged in organizing cavalry units; many others, who besides were German, had done likewise. After Kargé had spent two days at Glogow, the commandant offered to let him travel to Berlin without guard if he would promise not to try to escape. Kargé agreed. In Berlin he found the city still in the hands of the people, with no military authority to surrender to. He continued to Potsdam, where he reported to the commandant. Although Kargé's superiors intended to check into the charges against him, they did not take them seriously and restored the young officer to duty with his unit. This good fortune he owed to that daring charge against the barricade and his apparent capture by the insurgents.

Soon the Polish Revolutionary Committee sent word to Kargé to return to Poznan. No longer bound by his parole, Joseph deserted and once again was at the head of his cavalry battalion. He saw the relative freedom in the province come to an end, for the Prussians now determined to break up the Polish military camps by force. One morning young Kargé's battalion came up on a Prussian artillery battery emplaced just beyond a wheat field. An easy target, so it seemed, the Poles charged across the field only to be surprised by a battalion of sharpshooters who lay concealed in a ditch. Their opening fire cut down one-half of Kargé's men. In the savage encounter that followed with a waiting Prussian cavalry force, Kargé's impetuous life almost ended that day. He found himself surrounded by a group of some thirty Prussians, all pressing in for the kill. A pistol shot got Kargé in the hand; a second bullet shattered his knee, then an enemy lancer pierced his ribs. These were followed by a second jarring lance stroke that struck his hip and toppled him from his horse. The enemy left him on the field for dead. He lay unconscious for several hours until a Prussian detail came by to pick up the wounded and to bury the dead. The men carted Kargé to a temporary hospital set up in a nobleman's mansion near the scene of battle. The loss of blood so weakened him that he did not regain consciousness for a week. His strong constitution, however, brought him past the crisis, and he began to recover. The authorities allowed his mother and sister to come to nurse him.

There could be no doubt that Joseph Kargé had deserted the Prussian army, for he had been captured in the very act of rebellion. In June 1848 the army issued orders for his trial, assigning as members of the court-martial the officers against whom Kargé had fought. Although these officers seemed sympathetic, their verdict was a foregone conclusion. The court-martial found the accused, age twenty-four, guilty of desertion and overt acts of conspiracy, and sentenced him to death. They forwarded the sentence to Berlin for approval by the Secretary of War and countersigning by the King. This technicality caused an automatic respite of two weeks. Other conspirators were shot at once.[1]

The condemned patriot spent some time reflecting on his short but eventful life. He had fought to liberate Poland and felt satisfaction for having made this effort. His emotions, though, welled up at the thought of leaving his mother, whom he loved and respected. Joseph was the youngest of seven children, born 4 July 1823 near Poznan, a city that became part of Prussia in 1793, following the second partition of Poland. His parents were landed gentry, highly respected in the community. Although his father's ancestors were French, they had lived in Poland for generations. An accomplished soldier, Joseph's father had served Napoleon as a colonel of cavalry in the invasion of Russia. After the Emperor's disastrous retreat from Moscow, Colonel Jacob Kargé returned to his estate near Poznan. He died before Joseph came of age but lived long enough to impress on his son's mind the example of a high-toned officer and man. Joseph's mother Veronica was of Polish descent. A woman of superior and attractive character, she possessed executive ability and skill. She survived her husband and continued to manage the estate and to care for the family interests to an advanced age.[2]

Joseph felt the strongest affection for both parents, who imbued him with a sense of personal honor and a strong individuality. He developed a fine physique and a courtly bearing. He attended the Gymnasium (high school) in Poznan for a well-grounded course in classical, historical, and literary studies. The youth long remembered the impressive instruction he received in the Catholic religion from a gentle, earnest, and fair-minded professor of that department. His mother's deep devotion to the Roman Catholic faith prompted her to encourage both Joseph and his brother to enter the priesthood, and she guided Joseph's life in that direction. But after a long and conscientious self-examination he became convinced that he did not possess a calling for religious life. With his mother's consent he abandoned this purpose.

Upon completing the Gymnasium in 1844, Joseph took university courses at Breslau (now Wroclaw) in philology and history. In 1845 he enrolled at the College de France in Paris for a full course of Slavic literature, chaired then by Poland's national poet, Adam Mickiewicz. Kargé continued his education during the period of 1846-48, while serving in the Royal Horse Guard. He interspersed these courses with his military duties and secret political activity.[3]

Joseph Kargé's native instincts and soldierly qualities became aroused in the revolutionary atmosphere that then pervaded partitioned Poland and Europe as a whole. He threw himself with patriotic and impetuous ardor into revolutionary movements pointed toward the recovery of his country's independence. While pursuing studies at Breslau University, he joined a secret political society bound to absolute obedience to the Central Polish Committee of Paris. In June 1845 he traveled on a student's passport to Russian Poland for the avowed purpose of studying Slavic folklore among the peasantry, but his mission called for laying the groundwork for an uprising. After an absence of five months he returned to Paris.

In December he set out again, with the specific goal of obtaining the numbers of men and horses the Polish gentry could provide in support of a revolt planned for March 1846. Unfortunately, the authorities became suspicious of all students, following the arrest of a university student in another province. The Tsar's police picked up Kargé as a suspect and imprisoned him in Warsaw. In the absence of direct proof the Russians did not press charges. They simply escorted him to the frontier, where the Prussian officials took custody. Whereas the Russians had treated Kargé courteously, the Prussians imprisoned him as a rebel. They subjected him to solitary confinement and ill-treatment in Poznan for six weeks. Finally, they absolved him of any wrongdoing but ordered him as a Prussian subject of military age to report for duty. Allowed a choice of location, Kargé took Berlin and in 1846 entered the Royal Horse Guard, in which he served for two and one-half years.[4]

The young cavalryman always considered his Prussian military service as the bitterest period of his life. In addition to the hard knocks that recruits usually receive, Kargé had to endure taunts and aspersions upon his birth, character, education, and loyalty. The officers in particular made it a point to provoke him. However, through self-control and obedience he slowly won their respect and that of his comrades. In time his superiors promoted him to drillmaster and placed him in charge of recruits from the Polish provinces who could not speak German. Kargé's strict but considerate treatment and his use of the Polish language won the affection of his charges.

Notwithstanding his military position, Kargé continued his secret membership in the revolutionary group and kept up with plans of the conspirators. The outbreak of the Revolution of 1848 precipitated the series of dangerous activities that had led to his court-martial and the verdict of death.

The short delay between the sentence and expected execution gave the Kargé family time to plan Joseph's escape. Among a number of favorable circumstances, the status of Joseph's sister increased the probability of success. She was the wife of the Prussian *landrath*, or county superintendent, a Pole by birth. Often in the company of Prussian officers at official functions, Kargé's relatives found out certain details about the hospital-prison. During the day a single cordon of guards surrounded the building, which housed between three hundred and four hundred men. At night one line of guards would take stations near the building, another inside the iron picket fence, and a third just outside the fence. As a further measure of security, the officer-of-the-day twice daily checked Kargé's room on the second floor and the guards in the corridor outside. In the room the one window of French design was divided into four sections by a wooden cross at the center, and it measured fifteen feet from the ground. An officer suggested to Kargé's sister that her brother's escape could be made possible by placing trusted men on his side of the prison. This condition favored Kargé , for the guards were reservists, men who had served their time, and they were mostly Poles.

The Kargé family planned well. The mother and sister spun a silk rope and delivered it secretly to Joseph. His brother bribed the sergeant of the guard with six hundred thalers for his promise of cooperation and that of the fifteen-man relief. On the designated night the sergeant posted his men at ten o'clock as usual. At the same time the officer-of-the-day visited Kargé's room and departed. When things quieted down, Kargé removed the rope from its hiding place and fastened one end to the cross of the window. He crawled out on the ledge, becoming acutely aware of his injured hand and knee. He wound the rope around his leg, took hold with his good hand, and began to descend. The exertion proved too much for the convalescing prisoner. He lost his grip, slid down the rope a few feet, and burned his hand so that he let go and fell to the ground. The shock of his injured leg striking the hard surface caused him to black out temporarily. When he regained consciousness he was wracked by a terrific pain over his entire body. Forcing himself to go on, he managed to crawl toward the fence. The guards on the second line were stationed ten yards apart, but in the darkness he rolled between two of them undetected, helped by the shadows of an overcast sky. Having reached the fence, Kargé faced a dilemma. The blackout and pain had caused him to lose his bearings. He did not know whether the gate stood to the right or left of him. If he should move in the wrong direction, he could spend the night crawling around the inner park. He decided to go to the right. Grasping the iron pickets with one hand, he pulled his body along the fence for about fifty yards. The agonizing task took a full hour. Kargé became encouraged when he discovered that he had indeed reached the gate. He groped for the latch and then carefully opened the gate. He crawled past the outer line of guards and across a road into a wheat field. Here he lay awhile, exhausted by the ordeal. Soon he heard a gentle whistle like that of a whippoorwill. When the signal came twice more, he answered it. In a few moments two men approached quietly, picked him up, and carried him several hundred yards to a secluded spot where his brother waited. They placed him gently in a light spring wagon and rode off into the darkness.

The brother, four accomplices, and the wounded Joseph had gone not more than five miles when the sound of cannon firing signaled the prisoner's escape. The driver now lashed the horses to a mad gallop. There was no need to spare the animals, for the Kargé family had arranged for fresh horses every fifteen miles along the route of escape. All during the night the party dashed on. Kargé lost consciousness from the pain and exhaustion. When he came to in the morning, he found himself in Stettin (now Szczecin) on the Baltic Sea, one hundred miles distant from the prison-hospital. He was by no means safe, but a kindly Jewish physician took the hunted youth into his home, thereby endangering his own life and property. Nonetheless, he cared for Kargé until the young man recovered his strength. Six weeks later Kargé continued the journey to Paris, his destination, where he remained a political exile for a time.[5]

In September 1848 the restless Kargé returned to Poland. Posing as a German citizen, he wandered about the country in 1849 and 1850, eluding the police as he maintained his interest in revolutionary activities. Finally, he made his way to Hamburg and there deliberated whether to escape to France or England. Since the London Exposition was set to open in May 1851, Kargé settled on England. One last obstacle stood in his way. He must get aboard an English vessel without capture by the secret police. Late one evening Kargé cautiously entered the office of an English steamship company. The agent could speak neither French nor German, and Kargé knew no English. The young Pole began to feel that his "escape would be foiled at the last moment by the confusion of tongues." Fortunately, the ship's purser entered the office. Noticing Joseph's air of dejection, the purser spoke to him in French. As soon as the Englishman understood Kargé's dangerous position, he offered to help. He placed a cap bearing the ensign of the British navy on Kargé's dark hair and accompanied him to the wharf. Encouraging Joseph, the purser advised: "Come on, and put on a bold face. We will talk and cross the gangplank together."

It was near midnight, the time for the vessel to sail with the tide. Flickering pitch and tar fires dimly illuminated the wharf—a condition of some advantage, but police stood on both sides of the boarding plank to examine each person as he walked by. With a firm, confident step and with head erect, Joseph strode past the police without detection. The ship's crew untied the ropes from the pier and the packet began to move away. Joseph felt joy and relief like heady wine. Describing his emotions, he said: "The moment my foot pressed English oak, I turned, removed my cap, and revealing my face to those whose clutches I had escaped, I bade a defiant farewell to them and to my old life. I was a free man, and free forever."[6]

In London, by mere chance, Joseph met his brother, who had also come to England to seek political freedom. Deciding jointly to go to America, they sailed for New York in 1851.[7]

New Citizen Turns Volunteer

Kargé Trains a Cavalry Regiment Despite Dissension and Opposition

A lone mortar shell pierced the dark skies above Charleston Harbor and traced a high-arching trajectory. Having reached its zenith, the shell came down directly over Fort Sumter. The bright flash of the explosion at 4:30 A.M. on 12 April 1861 signaled the start of the Civil War. All the Confederate batteries ringing the harbor now sprang into action. The Southerners, under the command of General Pierre T. Beauregard, subjected the Union defenders of the isolated fort to an intensive bombardment.[1]

At nearby Fort Moultrie, Private Arthur Grabowski joined his fellow South Carolinians in the attack on Major Robert Anderson's federal garrison. Having enlisted in the First South Carolina Regiment, young Grabowski would be advanced during the war to the grade of colonel. This gallant Pole would later distinguish himself as an educator and then, reaching the age of ninety-three, would enjoy the distinction of becoming one of the few remaining Confederate soldiers.[2] On this historic day he helped his Southern compatriots assert the sovereignty of the Confederate States of America.

The attack on Fort Sumter electrified the North and caused a wave of patriotic fervor to sweep the country. On 15 April, the day following the surrender of the fort, President Abraham Lincoln called for seventy-five thousand volunteers to help preserve the Union. Applicants swamped the recruiting stations. Lincoln's political foe Stephen A. Douglas loyally supported the President's call for troops.[3] Lincoln's appeal likewise evoked a strong response from Joseph Kargé, who for ten happy years in the United States had enjoyed a kind of freedom he had never known in his youth.

On arriving in New York, Kargé immediately declared his intention of becoming a citizen, and after waiting the statutory five years he became naturalized in 1856.[4] Joseph first settled in Danbury, Connecticut, where he found employment as a teacher in a private language school. Here he met and courted a thirty-one-year-old widow, Maria T. Williams, descendant of a Revolutionary War family. They were married in 1852 in New York by Dr. Gardiner Spring of the Brick Presbyterian Church.[5] Moving to New York with his bride, Joseph opened an academy for classical languages. The venture succeeded and the family grew. Kargé became the father of two sons, Ladislaus and Romuald.[6] His peaceful life as an educator ended abruptly with President Lincoln's dramatic call for soldiers. Almost thirty-eight years of age, Kargé volunteered to serve his adopted country with the same deep patriotism and devotion to liberty that he had displayed earlier in behalf of his native land. His military experience gained him a commission as lieutenant colonel of a New Jersey cavalry regiment.

In the Civil War the governors of the individual states conducted the recruiting of soldiers, but the federal government, under the Act of Congress approved 22 July 1861, authorized ordinary citizens to form private bodies of troops for national service. Accordingly, on 4 August 1861 the War Department granted the Honorable William Halsted permission to organize a cavalry regiment. Halsted had become well-known in the state of New Jersey from his service in the Congress and as a prominent member of the Bar. Approaching his seventieth birthday, though, he did not possess the physical stamina for arduous duty with the cavalry, nor did he have the necessary military experience to organize and train a large body of soldiers. Nonetheless, he demonstrated his ability to raise more than eleven hundred volunteers for his regiment, called Halsted's Horse.[7] By 26 August 1861 six full companies of the regiment were ready to leave Trenton for Washington, D.C. On departure, the troopers presented a creditable appearance in full dress uniform, although the march along State Street appeared very informal. Some soldiers carried good-sized hams, and all were noisily exuberant along the route to the depot. A large crowd gathered there to see them off. As the train pulled out, the citizens set off enthusiastic cheers for the cavalrymen of Halsted's Horse.[8] In Washington the companies went into camp on the grounds of the Kalorama district, between the old tomb of Decatur and the steep bank of Rock Creek. Additional companies of the regiment followed in quick order, reaching eleven in number by early September.[9]

In a short time the camp of Halsted's Horse became a scene of disorder and confusion, filled with undisciplined and insubordinate citizen-soldiers. Colonel Halsted knew little, if anything, about drill, camp sanitation, or the need for discipline. The men did nothing except what they were told, and often questioned the orders they received. They neglected the most rudimentary and obvious sanitary measures. Filth accumulated in camp, festered in the sun, and the smell combined with the foul night odors from the creek and river. Officers who tried to live up to their responsibilities, to the extent they understood them, were often ridiculed and compared resentfully with other easy-going superiors. Without firm backing from the regimental commander, the conscientious officers were soon forced to give in to the tide of popular opinion.[10]

The intolerable conditions persisted when the regiment relocated to a camp across the Potomac River, prompting Private F. Rodgers to complain directly to General George McClellan, commanding the Army of the Potomac. Writing from Camp Mercer, Virginia, on 17 October 1861, Rodgers said he wanted to call the General's attention "to the disorganized condition of the 1st New Jersey Cavalry." Rodgers accused Colonel Halsted of forming the regiment for self-gain: "He has come out here with the purpose of making money instead of being a good officer—he has made the Regt. a family affair." Rodgers pointed out that one son held the quartermaster post "and [is] a very incompetent man for the office, as he neglects the men and horses in every respect." Another son was a sutler, and a third, a wagonmaster. In addition, a son-in-law served as captain and a cousin as major in the regiment. Rodgers made a sweeping condemnation: "There is not an officer or man in the Regt- but what is dissatisfied with the Col-."[11]

In this insufferable environment, Kargé soon found himself embroiled in never-ending controversy. An immediate problem centered on the question of the position of lieutenant colonel, the second-in-command of the regiment. For some unexplained reason Kargé and another individual, Julius H. Alexander, were both appointed to this position. The officers soon divided themselves into two opposing groups, supporting Kargé or Alexander. Halsted either did not perceive or was unable to prevent this division of officers. He displayed appalling ineptitude. He could not overcome his own confusion or that in the regiment, and with each passing day he became more confused. Somehow the regiment managed to get by. The War Department shifted the regiment from one camp to another, and finally attached it to a provisional cavalry brigade. The regiment pitched camp about three miles from Alexandria, on the old Mount Vernon Road.[12]

The question of the two competing lieutenant colonels was now settled. Joseph Kargé was mustered in as lieutenant colonel on 18 October 1861, following Alexander's discharge the preceding day. Halsted, exhausted by the rigors of camp life, left for Washington on sick leave, and Kargé assumed command of the regiment. He organized the camp along military lines, stressing sanitation and orderly procedure. He trained the raw troops almost by himself, since he lacked a regimental cadre. Except for a few militia units, the North possessed no cadre for volunteer cavalry. This dearth of trained officers and selected enlisted men made the job more difficult, but Kargé applied himself vigorously to the task. He enforced the strictest discipline and put into practice a military conduct that is normal to every regular unit. His civilian-soldiers, however, had not yet learned to understand or to accept it.[13]

The condition of Kargé's men reflected the poor discipline prevalent at the outset in both the Union and Confederate armies. Even later, the soldiers' tendencies to straggle and to forage were all too common. They often performed outpost duties with indifference and displayed poor fire discipline.[14] On the Confederate side, General Stonewall Jackson, perhaps more than any other general, sought to stem the tide of lax discipline. Especially strict with his officers, Jackson looked to them ''to set an example for unhesitating obedience and the precise performance of duty.'' Although he tolerated the citizen-soldiers' more relaxed attitude toward military behavior, he reacted sternly in cases of flagrant breach of discipline. He had one soldier who committed acts of pillage in violation of his specific order, arrested, court-martialed, and shot to death in twenty minutes. Jackson habitually approved the death sentence for deserters handed down by courts-martial.[15] Straggling too he raged against. On one occasion an angry Jackson ordered his provost marshal to shoot all stragglers who refused to go forward.[16] In general, however, military duties during the Civil War appeared to have been carried out on a more voluntary basis than in modern armies. A commander could never be certain that his subordinates, including general officers, would obey without question.[17]

As a former officer in the Prussian cavalry, Kargé understood the need for organization, training, and discipline. He drilled his regiment hour after hour, and on Sundays too. At times he became exasperated over the reluctance of some men to submit to discipline. He interpreted this attitude as an indication of mutiny against his efforts to establish order. Whipping out his saber on occasion, Kargé would swing it menacingly and threaten to run it through the bellies of laggards, malcontents, or anyone else showing the slightest sign of rebellion.[18] The threat in such cases brought a dramatic response, but, unfortunately, Kargé's blunt and unbending manner sparked a hostile reaction in a good number of the officers. Months later their bitter feelings, having become deep-rooted, would flare up and cause him much pain and embarrassment.

Among his many problems, the lieutenant colonel had trouble with his regimental quartermaster, Colonel Halsted's son, over his failure to obtain needed supplies. It upset Kargé to have these serious shortages while the camp lay in sight of Washington, for the nation's capital, paradoxically, overflowed with food and supplies of all description. To add to the problem, the last company had reported to camp without uniforms, blankets, or tents to shelter the men. Kargé repeatedly warned the supply officer to get the required equipment, but to no avail. Exasperated, he reported the quartermaster's incompetence to the brigade commander, who investigated the matter and found that this officer had entered the service improperly. Kargé at once dropped him from the rolls of the regiment and appointed another quartermaster, who procured the needed supplies and equipment without difficulty. Halsted, still on sick leave in Washington, became indignant when he learned of the removal of his quartermaster. The colonel maintained that the move should have been cleared with him first. In fact, he interpreted Kargé's action as a direct personal attack. Rushing back to camp, Halsted engaged Kargé in a violent quarrel and literally wrested the command of the regiment from his lieutenant colonel. Halsted's behavior threw the regiment into utter confusion.[19]

This deplorable situation went from bad to worse. Halsted sided with the men in their complaints against the executive officer. The old man also frittered away Kargé's hard work of training and disciplining, which had made the regiment over into some semblance of a soldierly organization. The better officers realized that Halsted's conduct undermined the morale of the regiment and would surely lead to its collapse and disbandment. While these officers might question the severity and the authoritarian discipline imposed by Kargé, they nevertheless could see that his military experience, firmness, and consistent leadership would bring about an efficient military unit. The more perceptive officers began to side with and support Kargé. Halsted automatically considered as hostile everyone associating himself with Kargé or sympathetic to his views. Although split by jealousy and dissension, the regiment somehow continued to function from one day to the next.[20]

In November 1861 the Army of the Potomac detached Halsted's Horse from the First Volunteer Cavalry Brigade and assigned it to the division of General Samuel P. Heintzelman. About this time Halsted got into trouble with the War Department over an alleged misuse of government funds. The army preferred court-martial charges against him for drawing both forage and money for two successive months, thus defrauding the government of several hundred dollars. Although technically true, the offense stemmed from carelessness rather than fraud. As brought out subsequently, he had signed requisitions on the Quartermaster Department without bothering to check what he did. The army commander placed the colonel under arrest and removed him from the command of the regiment. Once again Kargé took charge of Halsted's Horse. The lieutenant colonel seized this opportunity to try to mold the regiment into a fighting organization. His fundamental objective aimed to make soldiers out of both the officers and enlisted men. He began by ordering the most inefficient officers to Washington to face the Examining Board, which ruled on their fitness. This action naturally spurred the other officers. Ably assited by Major Myron H. Beaumont, the senior major, Kargé exerted great pressure on the regiment. At every drill or activity of any sort, Kargé or Beaumont supervised in person.[21]

Training recruits to be cavalrymen posed a difficult task. The volunteers faced the double challenge of learning to be horsemen as well as soldiers. The horses had to become accustomed to the firing of weapons, blast of bugles, and other battle noises. Horses must also become familiar with their riders when they fired from the saddle or swung their sabers. Practice and more practice for both man and beast became the daily routine. In time the horses learned the drills as well as, if not better than, the men. The animals soon recognized the bugle calls and responded to "March!" or "Halt!" or "Wheel!" without waiting for their riders to prompt them.[22] As the result of Kargé's intensive efforts during a period of five weeks, the regiment began to look and act like a body of cavalry. Comfortably quartered in camp, the regiment was reported to be "in good drill and discipline—better than most of the volunteer cavalry regiments."[23] Still, many of the men felt bitter toward Kargé over his forceful methods. Trouble would erupt, but first came a pleasant interlude.

Kargé's regiment at Camp Custis lay within a short distance of Fort Lyon. Built on commanding terrain just to the southwest of Alexandria, Fort Lyon formed a part of the defense system of Washington, and at this time also served as the headquarters of the Fifty-eighth New York Infantry Regiment ("Polish Legion"). The regimental commander, Colonel Wladimir Krzyzanowski, invited the Poles in the Army of the Potomac and the German officers of his regiment, about sixty in all, to join him for dinner to commemorate the Polish uprising of 29 November 1830. As a correspondent reported, that date is memorable in the history of Poland, for at 7:00 P.M. on 29 November the students of Warsaw gave the signal of revolt and drove fifteen thousand Russians from the city. The war for independence raged for one year, but Russian superiority crushed the revolt.[24]

At 7:00 P.M. on 1 December, Krzyzanowski's guests, including Joseph Kargé, assembled at Fort Lyon and soon sat down at a table in a large wooden building erected for the occasion. The feast of a dinner and the ample refreshments put the Polish and German officers into a buoyant mood. Presiding, Krzyzanowski toasted the company and the officers who had served in the Revolution of 1830. He offered a special toast that Poland would become independent again. After a Captain Maas responded to the toast, the regimental band played the Polish national anthem, and "the guests chimed in with characteristic vehemence." Following the rendition, "Kriz" called on Captain Gustave Struve, European historian and former representative to the Frankfort Diet, to make a short address. Struve, like Krzyzanowski and the others present, was a zealous freedom fighter who looked upon the Civil War as a "Holy Cause." Speaking in German, Struve said in part:

> Comrades! We meet here tonight to celebrate an heroic event; the great, though, alas, unsuccessful blow for independence struck by the sons of Poland in 1830. We meet, also, as Americans, to sustain the liberties of our adopted land. We meet as men on the proudest battle-field of the world to fight for moral principles and the rights of man.

The host and guests offered additional toasts—to the health of President Lincoln, Generals George McClellan, Franz Sigel, Louis Blenker, who was the division commander, and others. They sang national airs, and then listened to patriotic remarks by the chaplain of the Fifty-eighth Regiment, by a Captain Wittich, former editor of the

Dresden Abend Zeitung, and by Lieutenant Colonel Kargé. It is not known whether Kargé spoke in Polish, German, or English. Promptly at eleven o'clock Krzyzanowski brought the festivities to a close and the company retired.[25]

The evening with Colonel Krzyzanowski and his officers was indeed a pleasant affair. The following morning, as he had done for days, Kargé bore down on the training of his regiment. In the weeks that followed, the opposition to his tough discipline continued to simmer. It broke out into the open on Christmas Day, when Captain Robert N. Boyd, commanding Company D, preferred court-martial charges against Kargé. Boyd was a "Halsted man." Perhaps more than any other officer in the regiment, he resented Kargé's authoritarian conduct and seemed reluctant to obey orders. A week before Boyd drew up the charges, Kargé had accused him of instilling mutiny in his men and placed him in arrest for four days. Thoroughly angered, Boyd penned a long list of charges against his commander. The specifications, to name a few, stated that Kargé worked his soldiers on Sundays from morning until night, that he used profane language, that he threatened to cut down disobedient soldiers with his saber, and that he had confined Boyd to his tent for six hours without allowing the captain "to go out of his tent to discharge the imperative calls of Nature." Furthermore, the specifications read that Joseph Kargé falsely told Colonel Halsted "he had been an officer in the Polish Cavalry Service and that he had commanded a squadron of cavalry of said service."[26]

Boyd's objection to working on Sundays and to training from dawn to dusk stemmed from a feeling shared by most volunteers in the early part of the war. A lieutenant colonel of an Ohio volunteer infantry regiment described his own soldiers' misconception of military service: "Very many of these soldiers think they should be allowed to work when they please, play when they please, and in short do as they please. Until the idea is expelled from their minds, the regiment will be but little if any better than a mob."[27]

As required by regulations, Kargé forwarded the charges to General Heintzelman, the division commander, on 28 December 1861. Recognizing the peevish nature of the accusations, Heintzelman wrote General McClellan on 30 December: "There is an evident combination to get rid of the lieutenant colonel of the regiment." Heintzelman labeled the charges "frivolous." He pointed out that Kargé, having been educated in a foreign service, displayed a more arbitrary manner than was agreeable in the American army, and this gave offense. "I have been endeavoring to get him to soften his manner," Heintzelman wrote. "The few weeks he has had command of the Regiment, there is visible and marked improvement in the discipline of the men and appearance of the horses. The Regiment will now compare favorably with any Volunteer Cavalry I have seen in Service." Expressing confidence in Kargé, the general concluded: "If he has been guilty of any wrong, I do not believe it to have been done intentionally. His whole aim appears to have been for the improvement and benefit of the regiment."[28]

When the charges reached the headquarters of the Army of the Potomac, General McClellan returned them immediately, instructing Heintzelman to dispose of the charges "in such manner as he may deem most conducive to the interest of the Service." Before the papers left army headquarters, they passed through General George Stoneman, Chief of Cavalry. Stoneman ruled the "charges against Lieut. Colonel Kargé are not entertained because of the frivolous nature of some of them and the doubtful spirit in which all of them seem to have been framed."[29] Thus ended the first of several attempts to oust Kargé from this New Jersey regiment. He had placed his trust in the wisdom and sense of fair play of his superiors, and they supported him.

By the middle of January 1862, Halsted settled his troubles with the War Department and resumed command of the regiment, which the department now ordered to a camp in Washington City. The move occurred during a heavy downpour, and the men and horses were soon knee-deep in mud. For two days they bivouacked in the streets of Washington. In time the regiment laid out a new camp near the road leading out of Seventh Street toward Rockville. The men found themselves cramped, uncomfortable, and harassed by heavy levies for guard duty, leaving them little time to engage in worthwhile training. The emotional Halsted, meanwhile, gave vent to his hatred of Kargé. He arbitrarily placed him in arrest, and Beaumont, too, who had assisted the lieutenant colonel so ably in the training of the regiment. Discipline now collapsed. The better officers found themselves in disgrace, and the poorer ones indulged in excessive drinking. Halsted allowed the affairs of the regiment to drift, while he spent most of his time before the Examining Board, pursuing the cases of the officers reported by Kargé.[30]

Following Kargé's arrest, Halsted attempted to have him court-martialed on charges of insubordination. This latest personality clash between the two senior officers occurred in January 1862, after Kargé had led a part of the regiment on a grueling reconnaissance of northern Virginia. The weather turned miserable, and Kargé's exposure for more than thirty-six hours to near freezing rain left him with a severe cold and an attack of rheumatism. The regimental surgeon ordered him to leave camp for the warmth and comfort of a boarding house in Washington, where his recovery could be hastened. This Kargé did. On learning of his departure, Halsted at once dispatched an officer to the boarding house at 390 North Capitol Street, with orders for Kargé's immediate return. Unable physically to comply, Kargé asked for twenty days of sick leave. Halsted refused and, on 27 January 1862, formally notified his second-in-command: "You will consider yourself under arrest. Your limits will be your boarding house until other limits shall be assigned by proper authority." He followed up this action on 8 February with court-martial charges, which he forwarded to Brigadier General I. N. Palmer, commanding the First Brigade of Volunteer Cavalry. Palmer responded by ordering Regimental Surgeon W. L. Phillips to examine Kargé thoroughly at the boarding house. Confirming Kargé's illness, the surgeon recommended the patient remain in the warmth and quiet of his temporary quarters, and Palmer granted Kargé official leave to validate his absence from the regiment. In forwarding the court-martial charges to General Stoneman, Palmer said Halsted had no right to deny Kargé's request for sick leave but should have advanced the request to higher headquarters for decision. Stoneman simply dismissed Halsted's charges as "biased, inconsequential, and of a frivolous character." [31]

Rumors now plagued the regiment that the War Department planned to disband it, as part of a proposed reduction of the cavalry. Men began to desert by the scores. General Stoneman may have lent credence to the rumor by his recommendation to General McClellan "that the Regt. be either mustered out of Service, or that the *officers* be discharged and the rank and file be distributed amongst other Regts." Speaking as the Chief of Cavalry of the Army of the Potomac, Stoneman said on 22 January 1862: " . . . with its present organization it can never become anything but a useless bill of expense upon the service." He condemned the officers as a group whose sole occupation "appears to be to prefer charges against each other and quarrel among themselves." [32]

Notwithstanding the precarious existence of the regiment, Halsted continued to stir up confusion and disorder by his peevish and irrational actions. In early February 1862 he ordered the arrest of the popular Chaplain Henry R. Pyne, whom Halsted labeled uncooperative and insubordinate. The reason for Pyne's arrest appeared to be his loyalty to Kargé. Prior to departing the regimental camp on sick leave, Kargé had entrusted the chaplain with the key to his field desk. In Kargé's absence and without his consent, Halsted decided to go through that officer's private papers. He demanded that Pyne surrender the key, claiming that Kargé's locked desk contained official papers. The chaplain refused. Reacting angrily, the colonel added to the trumped-up charges against Pyne the additional one of drunkenness. Fortunately, Halsted's superiors recognized the emotional nature of the charges and flatly rejected them all.[33]

In mid-February 1862 two decisive actions dramatically reversed the ebbing fortunes of the regiment. First, New Jersey Governor Charles S. Olden recognized the regiment as a state unit. "Halsted's Horse" became officially the "First New Jersey Cavalry Regiment." Next, the Governor mustered out William Halsted and on 19 February 1862 appointed Sir Percy Wyndham to succeed him. Wyndham, an English soldier of fortune, had served in the Sardinian Army and with the Italian patriot Giuseppe Garibaldi. Sir Percy accentuated his flamboyant character with an unusually long mustache. It should have been clear that the new commander would bring valuable and varied experience to the regiment. Yet the state's *New Brunswick Times* asked petulantly: "Have we no material in New Jersey out of which to manufacture competent colonels, without resorting to foreigners to fill up the list?"[34]

Colonel Halsted left camp one morning and that evening Colonel Wyndham arrived quietly. Taking command, he released everyone from arrest. Spirits soared and the future looked promising. The War Department ordered the regiment to return to Camp Custis, Virginia, and placed it again under General Heintzelman. The First New Jersey Cavalry engaged in numerous marches and reconnaissances. With Wyndham, Kargé, and Beaumont providing energetic leadership, the regiment prepared itself for active campaigning. But the men were keenly disappointed to be held back from General McClellan's campaign against Richmond. The Army of the Potomac sailed for Fort Monroe without them.[35]

In Pursuit of Stonewall Jackson

The Trap That Failed

"Clear the way for the advance to Richmond," General Irvin McDowell ordered, and the men of Brigadier General George D. Bayard's Cavalry Brigade crossed the Rappahannock at Fredericksburg on 25 May 1862. Riding with Bayard, the First New Jersey Cavalry penetrated deep into Virginia. They saw no Confederates, but evidence of recent rebel activity stood all around them. Burned-out bridges, still smoking, forced the blue horsemen to ford streams swollen by heavy rains. The task seemed easy to the troopers, who strained to join the Army of the Potomac in the grand assault on Richmond.[1]

President Lincoln had detained McDowell's corps from sailing with McClellan for Fort Monroe. The President believed that his commander had not provided a sufficient number of soldiers to insure the safety of Washington. When McClellan repeatedly asked for McDowell's forty-thousand troops, the President finally agreed to release McDowell, but only for an overland march that would keep him between Washington and the Confederate forces around Richmond. The President showed no interest in "swapping queens," as General Robert E. Lee expressed it on the possible capture of Washington while McClellan took Richmond.[2]

Before McDowell's march began, the First New Jersey Cavalry had left their winter quarters at Camp Custis on 18 April, and had moved south to Falmouth. Along the banks of the Rappahannock they indulged in small arms fire with Mississippi riflemen on the opposite side. At times small Union raiding parties dashed across the river and stirred up some excitement. A Texas regiment that relieved the Mississippians proposed a truce, and the New Jersey troopers promptly accepted it. During the month-long pause along the river, the army banded the regiments of the First New Jersey and the First Pennsylvania to form Bayard's Cavalry Brigade.[3]

Brigadier General George D. Bayard. COURTESY OF NATIONAL ARCHIVES.

The 26-year-old Bayard attained the star of a brigadier general, US Volunteers, on 28 April 1862. The year before, while training West Point cadets to be cavalrymen, First Lieutenant George Dashiell Bayard had received notification of his election as colonel of the First Pennsylvania Cavalry Regiment. Bayard was graduated from the United States Military Academy in 1856, standing number eleven in a class of forty-nine. He gained cavalry experience in Indian wars on the frontier, where he was wounded in the face by a poisoned arrow. Although General McClellan wanted him on his staff, the young officer preferred the command of the Pennsylvania regiment, and now he led the cavalry of General McDowell's corps.[4]

Three days after crossing the Rappahannock, Bayard's command reached a point only eight miles from elements of the Army of the Potomac. Advancing with the spearhead, Kargé reined his horse. Other troopers paused too as they listened to a low, reverberating noise rolling in from the direction of Hanover Court House. The booming sound came from the cannonade of General Fitz-John Porter's artillery, in support of McClellan's attack on the Confederate capital. The First New Jersey Cavalry, however, would not take part, for Stonewall Jackson's thrust into the Luray and Shenandoah Valleys brought an abrupt change in federal plans.[5]

Cavalry Column Crosses Rappahannock River on Pontoon Bridge. U.S. ARMY PHOTOGRAPH.

On 21 May 1862, General Thomas J. Jackson marched on General Nathaniel Banks's Union forces at Front Royal and Strasburg. Banks avoided a showdown battle and possible destruction by retreating to the safety of the north side of the Potomac River. Disappointed by Banks's withdrawal, President Lincoln nevertheless saw Jackson's movement as an opportunity to get behind him with a sizable force and destroy the Confederate Army of the Valley. The President stopped McDowell's planned march to Richmond, instructing him instead to rush two of his four divisions to the Valley. The President's command stunned

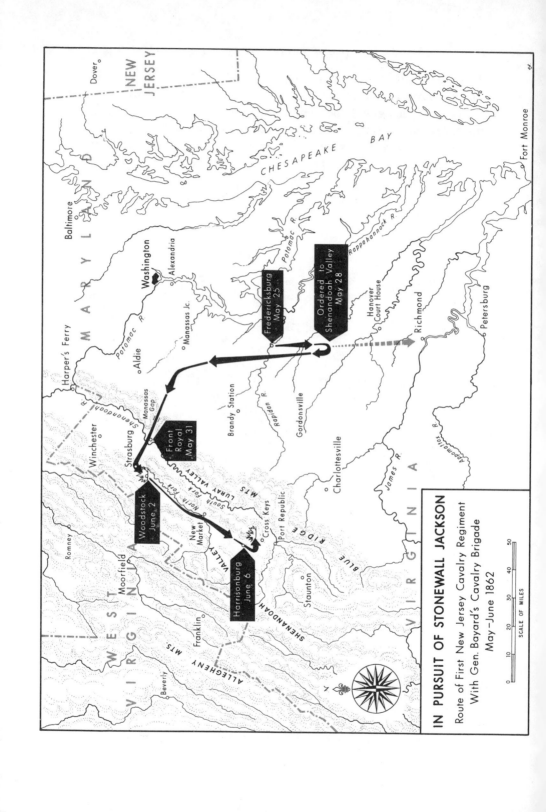

IN PURSUIT OF STONEWALL JACKSON

Route of First New Jersey Cavalry Regiment
With Gen. Bayard's Cavalry Brigade
May–June 1862

SCALE OF MILES

0 10 20 30 40 50

Map labels:

NEW JERSEY

Dover

Fort Monroe

CHESAPEAKE BAY

M A R Y L A N D

Baltimore

Washington

Alexandria

Harper's Ferry

Manassas Jc.

Aldie

Potomac R.

Fredericksburg May 25

Ordered to Shenandoah Valley May 28

Rappahannock R.

Hanover Court House

Richmond

Petersburg

Appomattox R.

Brandy Station

Rapidan R.

Gordonsville

Charlottesville

James R.

B L U E   R I D G E   M T S

V I R G I N I A

Port Republic

Cross Keys

Manassas Gap

Winchester

Strasburg

Front Royal May 31

Shenandoah R.

North Fork

South Fork

LURAY VALLEY

Woodstock June 2

New Market

Harrisonburg June 6

SHENANDOAH VALLEY

Staunton

Ronney

Moorfield

Franklin

Beverly

A L L E G H E N Y   M T S

W E S T   V I R G I N I A

N

McDowell. "This is a crushing blow to us," he telegraphed the Secretary of War. Nonetheless, McDowell immediately ordered the divisions of Generals James Shields and Edward Ord to Strasburg to close the eastern pass over the Blue Ridge Mountains. At the same time, the President ordered General John C. Frémont at Franklin, Virginia, to march his fifteen-thousand troops east to block the southern exit at Harrisonburg. And Banks, meanwhile, would oppose any Confederate movement through the northern exit of the Valley.[6]

McDowell recalled Bayard's brigade from the vicinity of Hanover Court House. The cavalry operations south of the Rappahannock had served their purpose—a feint to mislead the Confederates as to the destination of Shields's and Ord's divisions. McDowell received instructions from the President on 24 May to lay aside the movement on Richmond and "to put 20,000 men in motion at once for the Shenandoah." By noon of 25 May all elements of Shields's division had departed Falmouth, and Ord's division followed. On this same day Bayard crossed the Rappahannock in an ostensible march on Richmond.[7] Three days later the disappointed cavalrymen retraced their route to Fredericksburg. Bayard spurred his men, who covered the thirty miles under a scorching sun. The horses grew tired and listless, having received little feed the day before. At Catlett's Station on the Orange and Alexandria Railroad the cavalry paused long enough to draw one day's rations and some grain for the horses. Additional supplies would follow in wagons.[8]

Near the town of Haymarket a severe thundershower lashed the troops. Their rubber ponchos afforded some relief. Although the storm subsided, the skies continued to threaten. An early dusk began to settle over the soggy earth, when the First New Jersey Cavalry approached the low-lying Bull Run Mountains and rode into Thoroughfare Gap. Shortly Bayard camped the brigade for the night. Except for a small number of wagon teams, which managed to struggle through the mud and keep up with the horsemen, the supply trains had been left far behind. The men would have to get along without them for more than a week. The next morning, 30 May, the brigade continued through the gap on the macadamized road. The hard surface affected the horses, already fatigued by the constant riding of the past five days. Many troopers, dismounting to walk and lead their animals by hand, lagged behind their mounted companions. Thus, hours after the brigade again encamped for the night, stragglers came in by twos and threes and tried to recuperate during the few remaining hours of darkness.

Bayard's cavalrymen reached the Shenandoah Valley on 31 May. Kargé and the entire brigade covered the last mile or two through the Manassas Gap in an excited gallop. They made the dash after the cavalry came upon a large Union force of infantry and artillery soldiers who virtually blocked the road for a considerable distance. The Gap forms a somewhat choked passageway through the Blue Ridge Mountains, whose rock-covered slopes close in on the winding road. Bayard paused for a moment at the sight of the infantry and artillery. With a whoop and a roar, he led the brigade off the road and dashed cross-country—knocking down fences, leaping over obstacles and ditches, scrambling through the brush, and finally emerging from the Gap to see General James B. Ricketts's infantry brigade marching into Front Royal.[9] In reaching the Valley from a point thirty miles south of Falmouth, Bayard's cavalrymen had covered some one hundred miles in three-and-a-half days.[10]

Ricketts's brigade, from Ord's division, was not the first federal unit to enter Front Royal. A day earlier Shields's division had arrived and wrested the town from the Confederates. Had Shields marched immediately to attack the rebel defenders who held Strasburg open for Jackson's retreating army, he might have intercepted Jackson. Strasburg lay some ten miles away by road, but Shields had no specific order to push on and he marked time in Front Royal. Shields explained: "We would have occupied Strasburg, but dare[d] not interfere with what was designed for Frémont." Meanwhile, to the west of Strasburg, Confederate General Richard S. Ewell kept Frémont's troops at bay. Frémont had not followed President Lincoln's instructions. Rather than march east from Franklin to Harrisonburg, Frémont fell back northward on his lines of communication to Moorefield; he then turned east toward Strasburg. He gave many reasons for the change in route. In particular, he wished to avoid the danger of overextending his inadequate supply lines. He also feared the threat of Jackson's army's getting in his rear by a march to the west side of the Shenandoah Mountains.[11] Neither Shields nor Frémont moved aggressively to close the Strasburg corridor, and through that opening Jackson's army poured south in a steady stream.

General McDowell arrived at Front Royal on the evening of 31 May in the midst of a furious storm. The rains lasted several days and flooded the country from the Lehigh to Richmond, carrying away millions of dollars worth of property in Pennsylvania and sweeping away the bridges on the Shenandoah and Rappahannock rivers. For many days all communication across the Shenandoah River was cut off.[12] The morning after his arrival, McDowell ordered Bayard to attack Jackson's supply train, then in retreat through Strasburg. Guided by information that nothing more than Confederate cavalry protected the train, Bayard sent out the First Pennsylvania Cavalry Regiment alone on this mission. He quickly discovered that "heavy masses of infantry, artillery and cavalry were all plainly discernible, drawn up in commanding positions around the town—a force so largely exceeding my own that an attack was utterly out of the question." Confronted by such strong and well-positioned rebel forces, the First Pennsylvania withdrew from the Strasburg side of the Shenandoah. Darkness and a steady downpour of rain settled over the land and stopped further operations.[13]

The First New Jersey spent a wet night in a swampy bivouac area, which the regiment had occupied after dark. Wyndham did not allow any fires lest their position be revealed to the enemy, one-and-a-half miles away in Strasburg. The hungry troopers had to be satisfied with such fragments of wet crackers as remained in their haversacks. The rain continued all night, and the men waited for daylight in abject misery. With the dawn on 2 June came a break in the weather. The clearing skies revealed a beautiful sunrise, and the spirits of the men rose. Immediately after reveille, Kargé with a force of two hundred New Jersey cavalrymen trotted out of the bivouac area. Bayard had assigned him a mission: Take a battalion of the regiment and reconnoiter the vicinity of Strasburg for the enemy. Splashing across the turbulent Shenandoah, Kargé's battalion headed directly for a hill a quarter of a mile from town. From this vantage, Kargé looked for the rebels. Finding none in sight, he promptly ordered Lieutenant Henry W. Sawyer's platoon of Company D into Strasburg. At the same time Kargé fanned out the remaining troopers in a sweep through the neighboring wooded areas. Shortly, he notified Bayard that no enemy remained in the area. The brigade commander instructed Kargé to move his battalion into the town and augmented him with a detachment of Pennsylvania "Bucktails." These were a group of riflemen recruited by Lieutenant Colonel Thomas L. Kane from among the lumbermen of Western Pennsylvania. The nickname originated with the men's wearing of bucktails in their caps.[14]

Kargé had not reached Strasburg when Wyndham joined him. Kargé gave the regimental commander a quick report of his reconnaissance and urged an immediate pursuit of the enemy. Wyndham agreed. Taking charge of the battalion, the colonel started off on the Staunton Road. Kargé meanwhile awaited the arrival of the remainder of the regiment, occupying himself with the evacuation of some forty prisoners captured by Lieutenant Sawyer. In less than an hour the major portion of the First New Jersey appeared, and Kargé led them south at a brisk trot along the Valley Pike. He found the road strewn with arms, blankets, and knapsacks discarded by the retreating rebels. He also noted small numbers of prisoners that Wyndham's advance battalion had captured. In a short time the regiment met Wyndham returning with an escort of about twenty-five troopers. Wyndham wanted to confer with Bayard and had left the battalion in position further up the pike under the command of Major Alexander Cummings. Ordering Kargé to continue the pursuit, Wyndham resumed his search for the general.[15]

Bayard had passed through Strasburg but, learning of General Frémont's approach, the cavalry commander rode out to report to him. Meeting the "Pathfinder's" army for the first time, Bayard noted the large numbers of Germans, a fact that prompted him to say in a letter to his father: "I am now in the Dutch Army."[16] In pursuing Jackson, Bayard's brigade entered Frémont's area of operations, and McDowell agreed to Frémont's assuming control over Bayard's command as a temporary measure of combat necessity. Frémont assigned Bayard the mission of leading the advance of his army, a task already performed by the First New Jersey Cavalry. To put more pressure on the rebels, Bayard deployed the First Pennsylvania Cavalry on the right of the advance. The Confederates, retreating from point to point, took advantage of every favorable location to make a stand and check the Union pursuit.[17]

Upon Wyndham's departure for Strasburg, Kargé brought all available carbineers to the front and marched forward. As the regiment entered a heavy oak woods, he slowed down the advance to a more cautious pace. His instinct for danger proved right. Before the cavalrymen cleared the woods, a Confederate artillery piece barked and a shell buzzed overhead. A second round followed immediately, hitting the ground about fifteen feet to the right of the leading column, scattering its fragments in all directions. Riding up front with Kargé, the regimental bugler suffered a grazing wound in the leg. The enemy artillery engaged the First New Jersey near Woodstock, where General

Ewell, commanding Jackson's rear guard, hoped to delay the federal pursuit for a few hours.[18] Rejoining the regiment at this point, Wyndham halted the advance. He moved the troopers out of range of the Confederate cannon and drew them up in line in a heavy grove of timber, about 150 yards to th left of the road. He called for his artillery. The rebel guns, meanwhile, continued the firing. Shell and shot sliced through the trees and tore down limbs, but the New Jersey soldiers stood safely removed from the target area. Shortly a Union battery of six guns pulled up, took position, and began to return the fire.

Wyndham ordered an attack on the rebel batteries. With lusty hurrahs, his troopers rushed forward, leaping over fences and charging across fields blanketed with exploding shot. Kargé galloped directly for the enemy battery, with elements of the Second and Third Battalions behind him. He could see the battery at some distance away, on a rise of ground near the edge of heavy oak timbers. Major Beaumont, with part of the First Battalion, moved through a ravine in an attempt to fall on the enemy's left flank. As Kargé's men approached the rebel position, they were in imminent danger of being shelled by their own artillery. Rounds fell close to them on all sides, but they kept galloping for the battery. At this point the Confederates decided that the time had come to beat a hasty retreat. "We were not more than 600 yards off," Kargé said, "when the enemy limbered up and moved off with his pieces, being supported by two divisions of cavalry."[19]

The woods swallowed the fleeing enemy, and in less than a minute Kargé lost sight of them. He gave up the chase and returned to the pike with about sixty troopers. Forming his detachment in a gully close to the left of the road, Kargé waited for Wyndham, who soon rode up with the rest of the regiment. The two senior officers conferred for a few minutes, and the commander again moved the regiment forward along the pike, but not for long. Expecting to flush out the enemy, Wyndham plunged into the woods once more with about fifty men of Company D, with Kargé on his heels with the regiment. Some ten minutes later Kargé heard a sharp volley of musket fire ahead, and soon small groups of stragglers emerged. He stopped and rallied them. Just then enemy artillery fire hit the regiment, but supporting Union batteries came up to engage the rebel guns in a duel. Shells shrieked through the air or came down crashing among the trees. The explosions looked startling but proved harmless, except for one dramatic incident. As Kargé stood his place in line, an artillery round struck directly beneath his horse. Bursting between the forelegs, the explosion threw horse and rider into the air. The round tore the animal apart, but Kargé came down unhurt. He emerged from a cloud of smoke, splattered with the blood of his mount.[20]

A severe thunderstorm hit the troops, as if the heavens wished to join the battle. A correspondent reported: "I encountered a more violent thunder shower than is generally laid down in books." He described the hailstones as "nearly as large as hen's eggs."[21] The storm subsided but a drenching rain followed. Wet and panting, Frémont's infantry arrived, too late for further action. As darkness set in, the Confederates withdrew under cover of night. The exhausted troopers of the First New Jersey encamped on their first field of battle, in sight of the town of Woodstock. Kargé reported one trooper killed, five severely wounded, and several horses lost. Frémont gave an overall account of the day's activities in a message to the Secretary of War. He reported pursuing Jackson's army until about 10 A.M., when the enemy made a determined stand of an hour. He attacked the rebels with one thousand cavalry under General Bayard and another six hundred cavalry under Colonel Charles Zagonyi, with artillery support from two batteries of Brigadier General Julius Stahel's infantry brigade. Although the enemy turned to fight repeatedly, Frémont's soldiers often drove him from his position during a running battle of four hours. The federal advance made eighteen miles in five hours. "The pursuit was so rapid," Frémont wrote, "that it was impossible to get the infantry up before he reached for the night the heights beyond Woodstock."[22]

The morning of 3 June Bayard's brigade passed through Woodstock unopposed. Kane's Pennsylvania Bucktails moved right along with the cavalry, and the First Maine Battery brought up the rear. At Edinburg, Kargé found the bridge burned by the retreating Southerners. Though the river flowed deep from the heavy rains, it could be forded, and the pursuers crossed without incident. They transported the ammunition on the backs of horses, and the men skipped over the shaking beams of the ruined bridge like rope dancers. The march continued without meeting the enemy.

Anxious to save the bridge over the Shenandoah near Mount Jackson, Bayard ordered his two regiments to gallop ahead. The Confederates, meanwhile, had ignited the tar-smeared timbers, which gave off clouds of acrid smoke. When the charging Pennsylvanians approached the bridge, rebel artillery fire raked them over and threw them back. Bayard repeatedly pressed his men, but in vain. Wyndham tried crossing the river on horseback but could not force the steed to brave the swollen waters.[23] The cavalrymen watched helplessly as the bridge disappeared. A correspondent described the scene: "The bridge had been fired and blazed like dry tinder. One by one the timbers loosened and tottered, until finally the whole blazing pile gave way, and fell hissing into the river below, that rolled a barrier of deep water between the rebels and further pursuit."[24] Finally, federal batteries reached the site. "Our guns came clattering up," Pyne said, "and opened an angry fire upon the enemy, forcing them to retire out of range, but they did it with an air of triumph that enhanced our mortification...." With the bridge destroyed and the river an impassable barrier, the disappointed First New Jersey Cavalry camped on the bank to await the construction of a pontoon bridge. The next day it seemed that the bridge would be completed, but a fresh flood brought down trees, logs, and pieces of the half-burned trestlework from above. The pontoons were knocked away from their moorings and swept down river.[25] During the forty-eight-hour delay at Mount Jackson, Bayard wrote his father: "I am in good health, although I have not had on dry clothes for three days, and we were two days with nothing to eat but what we picked up on the road."[26]

Not until Thursday afternoon, 5 June, did Bayard's cavalrymen cross the Shenandoah. They continued south for about seven miles and halted for the night a mile beyond New Market. Prior to 6 o'clock Friday morning, the cavalry resumed the march, and Kargé noted: "For the first time we advanced in proper battle array, the artillery and infantry in the center, following the pike, the cavalry on the flanks...." About 3 P.M. the forward troops, having reached the vicinity of Harrisonburg, emplaced artillery in positions to command the surrounding area. Bayard ordered Wyndham and Kargé to take the regiment, reinforced with four companies of the Fourth New York Mounted Rifles, to attack and scatter any enemy cavalry in Harrisonburg, but to fall back if infantry were encountered. Meeting no serious opposition, Wyndham drew up on a rise of ground just beyond the town.[27]

The inhabitants told the cavalry that Jackson's army had passed through Harrisonburg that morning and turned east toward Port Republic, a village twelve miles away. The rebel rear guard marched only an hour or two ahead of the Union advance, and scouts reported finding a body of enemy horsemen on the far side of a wooded area facing the First

New Jersey.[28] The rebels seemed to dare the federal cavalry to pursue them. Wyndham at first resisted the temptation but finally gave the order to go after them. When the troopers had covered about three miles, partly by platoons and partly by fours, as the ground permitted, they approached a forest so thick that trees and brush closed in on the road. Halting briefly, Wyndham ordered Captain John H. Shelmire's Company A to take the advance, and the regiment followed the company into the dark woods. Suddenly, the troopers were startled by fire from the right. Shelmire's company bravely rushed onward. Wyndham pushed on with more men, and Kargé supported him with the rest of the regiment.[29]

The First New Jersey rode into a trap sprung by Brigadier General Turner Ashby, the fearless cavalry chief of Jackson's army. Unexpectedly, the blue horsemen were enveloped in a roar of musketry from screened infantry. "I saw fire in our front and on both flanks," Kargé said. Having panicked, the first two platoons emerged from the forest in a hasty retreat, threatening to throw the rest of the column into disorder. Wyndham made an oblique movement to the left and Kargé followed in the face of deadly fire from a belt of woods. The two officers dismounted to tear down fences that separated them from those woods. In the chaos of the fire fight, Wyndham disappeared and Kargé's horse reared from the impact of a minié rifle ball in the hip.[30] Unable to mount the injured animal, Kargé barely missed being captured, but several of his men came to the rescue. The rebels shot the standard-bearer's horse, and he suffered a face wound, which caused him to lose the regimental standard to the enemy.[31]

With no visible point to rally on, and in the midst of great confusion, each officer sought to find his men. Captain Thomas Haines, while trying to control the excited troopers, became a conspicuous target for a rebel officer. Whipping out his pistol, that officer killed Haines with a single shot. Suddenly, with a fierce yell, a body of Confederate cavalry charged down on the milling New Jerseymen, who broke and fled in disorder. The retreat went pell-mell for about a mile and a half before the regiment could be checked. The Fourth New York Mounted Rifles offered no help. They had not engaged in the fight; but, instead of covering the retreat, they also withdrew.[32] Meanwhile, Bayard came up with the First Pennsylvania Cavalry and four companies of Kane's Bucktails, who attacked Ashby's command shortly before sundown. Kane's small unit of 120 officers and men assaulted the Confederates with such accurate and deadly fire that the Bucktails forced the rebels to give way. Brandishing his sword, the mounted Ashby tried to rally them. A bullet got his horse, and he continued to lead on foot, oblivious of the danger. Another bullet struck him in the chest, and he died almost immediately. The engagement lasted only thirty minutes, but both sides fought with great intensity. The Bucktails suffered heavy casualties, losing forty men killed, wounded, or missing, including their commander, who was wounded and captured. The Confederates withdrew when Colonel Gustave Cluseret's brigade from General Frémont's army arrived in support, and the fighting ended.[33]

The rout of the First New Jersey Cavalry had its moments of heroism. Kargé praised the bravery of Captain John Kester and singled out the cool behavior of Captains Robert Boyd and Virgil Broderick for their part in halting the disorderly flight. In the fighting Boyd's pistol jammed and, drawing his saber, he killed two rebels without receiving a scratch. The individual exploits, though, could not make up for the cost of the ambush. The regiment had lost thirty-two men in killed, wounded, and missing. Besides Wyndham, the rebels had captured Captains John Shelmire and Henry Clark.[34] Dispirited by the rout, the First New Jersey Cavalry did not join the Bucktails in their fight against Ashby. Neither did it take part in the Battle of Cross Keys on 8 June, when Frémont made a halfhearted attack against the Confederate troops under General Ewell. During this battle Bayard's brigade remained at Harrisonburg to protect Frémont's baggage trains. Many of the cavalry horses needed shoeing and were unfit for duty.[35]

While Frémont pursued Jackson's army up the Shenandoah Valley, Shields marched his division on a parallel course along the adjacent Luray Valley. The Massanutten Mountains separated the two federal columns. Shields became frustrated from his attempts to join Frémont. He found that Jackson had destroyed the bridges across the swollen South Fork of the Shenandoah. Nonetheless, one of Shields's brigades under Colonel Samuel S. Carroll rushed south to Port Republic. On the morning of 8 June Carroll's cavalry pursued the rebels across the bridge to the west bank of the river. Although surprised, Jackson easily repulsed the small Union force, which then failed to destroy the bridge on its withdrawal and thus left Jackson with the initiative. The following day Jackson crossed the river to attack the brigades of Carroll and Brigadier General Erastus B. Tyler in the Battle of Port Republic. The five thousand federal soldiers fought tenaciously, but they were no match for the fifteen thousand Confederates who forced them back. Jackson remained in command of the situation, although Shields had not given up. He dispatched a message to Frémont, suggesting they cooperate in a joint attack on Jackson the following day. Shields proposed that he press Jackson directly with his full division of ten thousand soldiers, while Frémont crossed the Shenandoah on his pontoon bridge to attack Jackson's flank. No sooner had Shields made this proposal than he received specific orders from McDowell to return to Luray at once. Frémont, too, got President Lincoln's telegram to halt at Harrisonburg and stop the pursuit.[36]

Stonewall Jackson's rapid marching and hard fighting in the Shenandoah Valley diverted McDowell's strong corps from General McClellan's army near Richmond, and thus Jackson saved the Confederate capital. For the Union commanders, the valley campaign ended on a note of high frustration. The tremendous rainfall at the beginning of the pursuit swept away nearly all the bridges on the Shenandoah. Those that withstood the flooding Jackson destroyed, thereby managing to stay a safe distance from his pursuers. On 5 June, three days before the Battle of Port Republic, Shields lamented: "The rains have saved him at present from annihilation." But Shields failed to keep his division closed up for maximum strength, as McDowell repeatedly cautioned him to do. Shields, therefore, gave Jackson the opportunity to attack and defeat his two exposed brigades at Port Republic. Bitter over the result, Bayard commented:"Shields' force is very much demoralized. We have had none but citizen-generals in command in this valley. Hence the results are inconclusive and nugatory."[37]

Following the end of the valley campaign, the War Department returned Bayard's brigade to General McDowell. Greatly relieved, Bayard told his father: "I am thoroughly disgusted with this department. Frémont's army is a rabble. He is a perfect gentleman but not adequate to such a command. He has been outgeneralled by Jackson who made a splendid retreat . . . . I shall tomorrow [June 16] shake from my boots the dust of his department, and thank God that my service here is over."[38]

In all, the First New Jersey Cavalry Regiment did well in the pursuit of Stonewall Jackson, their first campaign. The one glaring exception was the ambush and rout at Harrisonburg on 6 June 1862. This event demonstrated that the regiment's state of discipline and training had not as yet reached the level of excellence sought by Kargé. A newspaper correspondent who covered the pursuit said that the federal cavalry was "not so efficient an arm of the service as it might be made." He saw no reason why the North could not have "splendid cavalry regiments," and he declared that a "well disciplined one is a terrible bolt to launch on the flanks of the enemy."[39]

Colonel Wyndham's "impulsive bravery" contributed directly to the rout of the First New Jersey Cavalry. Kargé questioned Wyndham's decision to engage the Confederate cavalry that had made such ostentatious demonstration to entice pursuit. Had Kargé been in command, he would more than likely have remained at Harrisonburg to await Bayard's further orders. In describing the incident Kargé said: "The colonel objected (to engaging the enemy cavalry), but finally, through some unexplained reasons, he gave the order forward, and our wearied horses and men took up again the march." As a good soldier, Kargé loyally obeyed the order, but his official report showed his irritation when he added: " . . . and onward we went, 'waddling' through bottomless roads." While he refrained from criticizing his commander in an official report, he expressed himself candidly in personal correspondence. He said that the rout of the regiment could not be charged to any lack of bravery on the part of the officers and men, but, he was "sorry to say, through the want of judgment and common sense of its leader."[40]

Prior to giving "chase," Wyndham swept through Harrisonburg and established a good reconnoitering position a mile beyond the town. He had, in fact, accomplished his assigned mission. The time of day was already mid-afternoon when the scouts informed him of the antics of the rebel cavalry. In the absence of a specific objective, and considering the nearly impassable condition of the soggy ground and the weariness of the troopers and horses, the gains to be achieved by an attack on an enemy detachment seemed nebulous, indeed. The *New York Tribune* charged the rout of the First New Jersey Cavalry to "Colonel Windham's bad conduct, neglect or disobedience of orders." The paper said that Bayard severely censured Wyndham for rashness and unskillful conduct. The *Tribune* added that the regiment, having made a fatiguing march, attacked the Confederates "when the horses were staggering in the ranks from exhaustion, and the men had been without other rations than beef for three days." Bayard's two official reports do not contain any criticism of Wyndham. For the details of the pursuit of Jackson, Bayard refers to the reports of Kargé and Colonel Owen Jones, First Pennsylvania Cavalry. Bayard, though, may have been frank in conversations with his superiors. General Frémont quotes Bayard's reaction to the rout: "It was reported almost in remonstrance by General Bayard, in regard to both men and animals, that the cavalry should never have been sent forward as they were at Harrisonburg—'the horses staggering in the ranks from exhaustion, and the men having been without rations, other than fresh beef, for two or three days.'" [41]

The press had at least one eyewitness at the rout of the First New Jersey Cavalry. Charles H. Webb of the *New York Times* learned from a civilian of the presence of some one hundred Confederate cavalry and several companies of infantry at a crossroads two miles from the New Jersey position. Webb passed the information to Wyndham, who replied that he waited for orders and was "loth to make any demonstrations until he received them." Soon a scout rode up to tell the colonel he could easily capture some tired rebel cavalry and infantry about two miles away. The scout's tempting report apparently aroused Wyndham's adventurous soul. Turning to Webb, he said: "We'll have a little fun, then; would you like to see it?" Ordering the bugler to sound "To Horse," Wyndham got the regiment underway.

Webb rode with the colonel at the head of the column until they reached the crossroads. No enemy were present, but the road entered a deep woods. Webb sensed danger and decided he would be safer at the center or at the rear of the column. He realized also that his tired horse could not be depended on for a rapid withdrawal in case of trouble. Webb suspected a trap and wondered how Wyndham did not. The colonel ordered Shelmire's company to the front. He did not deploy them as dismounted skirmishers but had the company ride boldly into the woods. Nor did he take the precaution to hold back a reserve for an emergency. Evidently he assumed that the scouts had reconnoitered the woods and that only the reported small rebel force awaited them. The New Jersey regiment rode on "with sabre at shoulder and carbines ready."

Shortly Webb heard some scattered firing ahead and galloped up to find out its cause. On the way an orderly dashed by, shouting: "There's trouble ahead, and I'm going for reinforcements." Webb dismissed the few shots as not indicative of much danger. The situation changed drastically, however. "I was jogging leisurely along in the centre of the cavalcade," Webb related, "when the head came charging down upon us. 'Fall back! Fall back! Ashby's cavalry and Jackson's whole army are coming.'" Not wishing to be ridden down by the routed horsemen,

Webb drew his mare into a side path in the woods and began to pick his way as best he could. In the meantime the stampede continued at a mad pace. Describing the conduct of demoralized men, Webb said: "Our long cavalcade, those in the rear and even in the centre, [were] utterly ignorant of what the exact danger was that threatened, galloping wildly as for their lives, and hurling in their precipitate flight sabres, carbines, blankets and everything else to the earth that could possible add an ounce to their weight." Kargé and the officers finally rallied the troopers—some at the initial starting position, others nearer Harrisonburg. Webb said with candor: "The cavalry charge of Col. Wyndham was a terrible piece of imprudence, and though he has paid the penalty, perhaps with his life, I can scarcely forbear commenting on it." [42] For a journalist, Webb displayed a keener understanding of the military situation than a man considered to be an experienced soldier.

The First New Jersey cavalrymen would soon get over the humiliation of their defeat and redeem themselves. As for Kargé, the overall pursuit of Jackson had a positive side, for the campaign brought General Bayard and Kargé together in combat operations. While Bayard did not abuse the chain of command, he treated Kargé as one of his commanders, often assigning him missions in person. [43] Kargé was twelve years older than his brigade commander, but notwithstanding the difference in their ages, he respected and admired the younger man's leadership and warm human qualities. This first campaign sparked a relationship that developed into empathy and friendship.

4

Bayard's Cavalry Holds Off Jackson

Bold Actions along the Rapidan River

The defeat of the First New Jersey Cavalry Regiment near Harrison-burg on 6 June reflected the misfortunes of Union forces in Virginia in the spring of 1862. President Lincoln's strategy to trap Stonewall Jackson in the Shenandoah Valley failed. Jackson marched too fast and fought rear guard actions too stubbornly to be caught. And then in two quick strokes he lashed back at his pursuers at Cross Keys and Port Republic.

At Richmond, General Lee stopped McClellan's Army of the Potomac on the outskirts of the Confederate capital. In the Seven Days' Battles in late June, Lee drove McClellan away. Meanwhile, the President brought General John Pope from out West to command the scattered forces south of Washington. Pope had commanded the Army of the Mississippi, which had captured two Confederate strong points on the Mississippi: New Madrid and Island No. 10. His success brought him some prominence, and Lincoln selected this forty-year-old general to command the newly constituted Army of Virginia. General George Bayard's Cavalry Brigade became part of Pope's army.[1]

By the third week of June 1862 the First New Jersey Cavalry occupied a campsite about three miles from Manassas Junction. The regiment spent several weeks refitting its depleted ranks before being ordered south of the Rappahannock.[2] Bayard wrote: "My brigade has been so completely broken down by my long and rapid journey to and with the 'Pathfinder' that I need two weeks' rest at least for my horses." He sent a requisition to Washington for six hundred horses to replace those lost and broken down.[3] Bayard also needed fresh troopers to fill vacancies. The mobilization system, which called for replacements by units rather than by individuals, tended to cause battle-tested regiments to dissipate to mere shells and even disbandment.[4]

The First New Jersey Cavalry pursued an aggressive recruiting policy. Following the hard campaign in the Shenandoah Valley, Lieutenant P. Jones Yorke, the adjutant, returned to New Jersey to gain new members. At the same time, he attempted to bring back deserters. The *Newark Daily Mercury* published the names of 120 deserters from the regiment, calling attention to Yorke's promise of pardon to all who turned themselves in at Trenton without delay. Otherwise, the newspaper article warned, "they will be apprehended and severely punished." The New Jersey press performed a recruiting service in another way. They published the battle actions of state units, and the First New Jersey got its share of publicity. Isaac Newning, the regimental communications sergeant, appeared to be the correspondent of the regiment. On occasion he made direct appeals for volunteers.[5] During the whole period of the war, the regiment recruited three times its authorized strength, or more than thirty-three hundred men, replacing losses due to combat, desertion, and other reasons.[6]

As the early part of the summer turned hot and dry, Kargé's regiment sought the inner coolness of the woods, where the work of rebuilding the regiment went on. Stragglers returned to duty. Kargé procured new clothing and supplies, and filled the vacancies in the officer ranks and among the noncommissioned officers. After a few weeks he could show a force of more than six hundred men, ready for action with the Army of Virginia.[7]

General Pope had the threefold mission of protecting both the nation's capital and the Shenandoah Valley, while posing a threat to Lee, who faced McClellan at Richmond. By mid-July Pope ordered the cavalry brigade of General John P. Hatch to move on the strategic town of Gordonsville, where the railroads from the west, south, and east converged, and to destroy those railroads. Hatch marched slowly while Lee reacted swiftly. The Confederate general met the threat by occupying that town with Jackson's two divisions.[8] The First New Jersey Cavalry took part in Hatch's exhaustive and fruitless maneuvering. Kargé received orders to cross the Rappahannock, after McDowell placed Bayard's brigade in temporary support of Hatch. Reaching the county seat of Culpeper, the brigade marched to join Hatch at Madison Court House. Hatch seemed over-cautious and too ready to believe rumors of enemy movements and strengths. Hence he gave up his mission of seizing Gordonsville and rode back to the safety of General Franz Sigel's troops at Sperryville. Bayard covered the withdrawal by reconnoitering toward Gordonsville, and all troops returned to Culpeper.[9]

The First New Jersey cavalrymen were outspokenly indignant of

General Hatch's fears of the enemy. They believed he had retreated from an imaginary foe. Organizing a stronger cavalry force twenty-four hours later, Hatch again rode south to Madison Court House. While Bayard feinted toward Gordonsville, Hatch moved on Charlottesville. Reaching the vicinity of Stannardsville, Hatch received a report of a Confederate presence in Charlottesville. This was enough to cause him to turn back again, and the whole command returned to Culpeper. The cautious performance of Hatch was enough for General Pope, too. He reassigned Hatch to King's division at Fredericksburg and replaced him with Brigadier General John Buford, Jr. At the key post of Culpeper, Brigadier General Samuel W. Crawford took charge, commanding a brigade in Banks's Second Corps. He had been a Regular Army medical officer, but at the beginning of the war had obtained a commission in the infantry.[10]

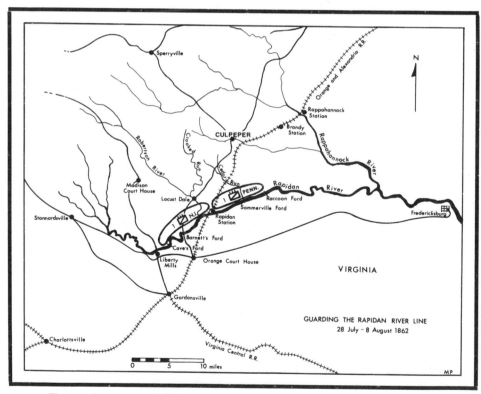

GUARDING THE RAPIDAN RIVER LINE
28 July - 8 August 1862

Toward the end of July 1862, Bayard received orders to advance his brigade to the Rapidan river. His mission: Hold the line of the river from

Raccoon Ford west to Cave's Ford, and there connect with Buford's pickets deployed from Madison Court House. Bayard defended some fourteen miles of the river with two understrength regiments, the First New Jersey and the First Pennsylvania. Along the entire line the regiments skirmished daily and alone, because their nearest infantry support was some twelve miles behind them.[11] As the days passed, the number of Confederates along the Rapidan increased noticeably. In response to General Banks's urging to maintain close contact with the enemy, General Crawford made a reconnaissance in force to Orange Court House on 2 August with the First Vermont and Fifth New York Cavalry Regiments. He set up a diversion at Barnett's Ford by ordering a battalion of the First New Jersey to engage the enemy there. Beaumont, commanding the battalion, found the rebels at the ford occupying a mill. He drove them away in a brisk fight, suffering only two men wounded. The enemy, though, continued to dispute the area for several hours by harassing the federal cavalrymen with long-range carbine fire. Suddenly

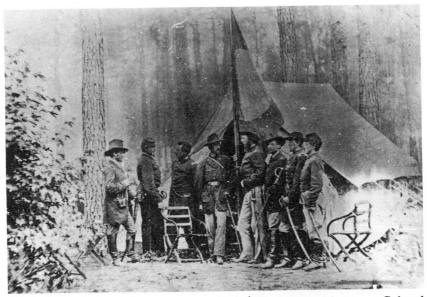

The officer in battle dress (*left of flag staff*) is believed to be Lieutenant Colonel Joseph Kargé, commanding officer of First New Jersey Cavalry Regiment. Brigadier General Samuel W. Crawford (*holding flag*) commanded the Post of Culpeper, Virginia, in early August 1862. COURTESY OF NATIONAL ARCHIVES.

the rebels galloped away when word reached them that Crawford had captured Orange Court House in their rear. Crawford had engaged the Seventh Virginia Cavalry in a lively firefight. Having accomplished his mission, he withdrew across the Rapidan at Raccoon Ford.[12]

During the two weeks of continual reconnaissance along the Rapidan, detachments of other cavalry regiments performed temporary duty. Some units resorted to plunder and wanton destruction. Their rowdy conduct seemed to follow the harsh orders Pope had issued to the civilians of Virginia. Either take an oath of allegiance or leave the country, he warned, or be treated as spies. Pope told his troops to live off the land. He also warned the citizens that he would make them repair damages caused by Confederate guerrillas. The consequence was that Pope seized harmless civilians, took hostages, and placed iron restrictions on the Virginians within his area of control. Pyne said that men of the First New Jersey Cavalry tried to engage in pillaging once or twice on an early march, but that Kargé cracked down immediately. He insisted that all requisitioning be regulated by proper authority.[13]

On the night of 7 August 1862 the Confederates made a strong attack against the First Pennsylvania Cavalry at Cave's Ford and Walker's private ford. They forced the Pennsylvanians back and seized a bridgehead on the north bank of the Rapidan. The rebels were Stonewall Jackson's men. Jackson had decided to attack Pope's scattered forces before the federal commander could reunite them. He pointed his thrust at General Banks's exposed Second Corps near Culpeper Court House. Jackson's command numbered twenty-four thousand to Banks's force of nine thousand. As soon as the Confederates made the lodgement, Bayard called Kargé into consultation to outline a plan for driving them back. Doubting reports that the enemy had crossed in force, Bayard directed Kargé to execute a sweep around the enemy's west flank with a part of his regiment and cut off their escape at the river. Bayard, meanwhile, would lead the remainder of Kargé's regiment and the First Pennsylvania in a frontal attack to drive the rebels back upon Kargé. One New Jersey squadron, Companies D and F, was left on picket duty at Rapidan Station. Kargé took the First Battalion and Company L, commanded by Captain Hugh H. Janeway. Only twenty years old and a natural-born cavalryman, Janeway possessed the audacity and the alertness called for by this dangerous mission. The remaining five companies, under the command of Beaumont, passed to Bayard's immediate control.[14]

At 3:00 A.M. on 8 August, Kargé set the maneuver into motion. As his companies moved out, Bayard rode up to him and whispered some fresh information. "No matter," Kargé was overheard to say; "I will go on. It may do good." Riding to the head of the column, he led his small force of 160 troopers on their daring mission. Pyne believed that Bayard had confidentially passed on to Kargé the information that they faced overwhelming numbers of Confederates—as high as 15,000. Kargé's and Bayard's actions do not support Pyne's estimate. As a seasoned officer, Bayard understood the advantages of surprise and bold effort in overcoming mere numbers, but he was not foolhardy. Bayard undoubtedly knew he faced a superior force of rebel cavalry. Yet he willingly took a calculated risk to achieve decisive results.[15]

Kargé's force rode confidently over ground made familiar by the constant reconnaissance of the past two weeks. Pushing on, Kargé sent Captain Janeway's company ahead as the advance guard. While cutting through heavy woods, Janeway's company became separated from the main body. A short distance from Cave's Ford, Company L rode up to the home of Colonel James Walker, where several Confederate soldiers lounged about the veranda, seemingly unconcerned by the approach of the horsemen. They did not expect Union cavalry to be operating in the midst of the Confederate army. Quickly the New Jersey troopers closed in and surrounded the house, taking twenty-two prisoners. These rebels, whose camp lay behind an adjacent hill, had come to the house for breakfast. The Union troopers surprised them just as the hostess placed the hot food on the table. Janeway's men took what food they could stuff in their haversacks, complimented the hostess on her cooking, and set off immediately with the prisoners in the direction of their own force. Kargé, meanwhile, kept discovering hoofprints only several hours old. The tracks extended along several avenues of approach, indicating the presence of strong forces of Confederate cavalry. He decided to withdraw at once to avoid capture. Dispatching a messenger to find Janeway, he rode to the top of a nearby hill to try to catch a glimpse of his missing company. Just then the captain's orderly galloped up, saluted, and announced: "Captain Janeway has the honor to report that he has ridden into the enemy and taken twenty-two prisoners, together with a rebel lieutenant and a colonel of militia. He is bringing off the prisoners, but would like support, if possible, as he took them in sight of their encampment." As soon as Janeway joined him, Kargé began to withdraw along the route of his advance, approximately four miles deep into enemy-held territory. He was slowed down by the presence of the prisoners, who boasted of the certainty of their own release and the capture of the brash Yankees.[16]

Some miles away Bayard carried out his part of the plan. With the First Pennsylvania Regiment and the five companies of the First New Jersey, Bayard advanced all the way to the Rapidan. Scouts of Beaumont's force sighted a large enemy supply train, encamped and protected by strong cavalry units. About the same time, a Negro came into Bayard's lines to warn the Federals that General Ewell's division had crossed the river and continued to advance. Bayard became convinced that the rebels were too strong to attack. He ordered Beaumont to withdraw and dispatched a messenger with instructions to Kargé to return at once. Bayard and Kargé had reached the same conclusion.[17]

Beaumont's companies kept falling back slowly and in good order, although the rebels now had them under attack. About three miles from the ford, Bayard relieved the New Jersey battalion with the First Pennsylvania. He was anxious to insure Kargé's escape, and he fell back to the road on which he believed Kargé would return. There he halted the command and held his position for thirty minutes against heavy Confederate fire. During this holding engagement the rebels severely wounded two Pennsylvania men. Soon Kargé's force approached the ground defended by Bayard's troopers, who greeted their comrades with cheers of welcome and relief. Even before the shouting had subsided Bayard ordered a resumption of the withdrawal. Kargé's rear guard, following a few minutes behind and under enemy fire, made a wide sweep to throw off their pursuers before reaching the safety of their regiment. The Confederates threw artillery fire into the pursuit, and while crossing Robertson's river the Union cavalry was under heavy fire from both artillery and musketry. Once all units had crossed, Bayard ordered Jones of the First Pennsylvania to destroy the bridge, thus stopping the further movement of the enemy's artillery. Earlier Bayard had alerted the brigade supply train to displace north to Culpeper. The contingent of the First New Jersey, under Quartermaster William M. Hazen, broke camp hastily and failed to take the regiment's portable forge and a considerable amount of baggage.[18]

Leaving Robertson's river, the Union cavalry continued to give ground slowly for some five miles to Cedar Run. Bayard employed every terrain obstacle and clump of woods to delay the pursuers. The rear guard fought off the enemy's advance, forcing them to stay within supporting distance of their reserves. Thus Bayard consumed the entire day in a grudging withdrawal. Taking up a defensive position behind Cedar Run, he posted the First Pennsylvania on picket duty and bivouacked the New Jersey regiment one mile farther north. Exhausted by the arduous fighting and lack of sleep, the New Jersey men dropped to the ground for some much-needed rest.

At Rapidan Station, Captain Boyd's squadron never received Bayard's order to retire. The men remained at their post throughout the day of 8 August, while their regiment withdrew to Cedar Run. In the evening Boyd left the post briefly and got cut off by enemy cavalry. He evaded capture all that night and the following day, finally making it on foot to friendly lines just when the Battle of Cedar Mountain began. The chaplain of the First Rhode Island Cavalry met the greatly relieved captain, who had recognized the federal cavalry by their colors. "Early in the forenoon, while with our skirmish line," the Reverend Frederic Denison said, "I had the surprise and pleasure of receiving from the base of Cedar Mountain one of General Bayard's officers who had been cut off two days before." [19]

In Boyd's absence Captain John H. Lucas commanded the squadron and continued to maintain the outpost. Lucas dismissed the protests of his lieutenant that the squadron defended an untenable position. Three times that night the Confederates drove in the New Jersey pickets, and each time Lucas forced the enemy back beyond his line. When Boyd did not show up by morning, Lucas ordered Sergeant John Kinsley and a Private Gourlay to ride to the regimental command post for instructions. The two reached the campsite without detection, only to find it swarming with Confederates. Gourlay galloped back at once to warn the outpost. Lucas, quietly rounding up his men, started to weave his way to Union territory. They had gone some distance when three enemy regiments of cavalry appeared. The commanders of these troops, having been repelled by Lucas's obstinate defense, decided to encircle the outpost and attack it from the rear. Lucas evaded the Confederates by turning off the road and disappearing into dense woods. He continued on a bearing that brought the squadron to the Culpeper road and to the safety of their own forces. [20] Companies D and F acquitted themselves well. They had guarded the east flank of General Pope's army at a most critical time, when only the cavalry and Crawford's infantry brigade opposed Jackson.

Kargé's bold movements several miles behind Confederate lines and his squadron's stubborn defense of Rapidan Station undoubtedly caused Jackson to overestimate the actual federal strength at his front. These actions contributed to Jackson's delay in his march on Culpeper by one full day. Historian Douglas Southall Freeman gave a word picture of Jackson's performance when he said "Jackson fumbles at Cedar Mountain," referring to the confusion among Jackson's divisions on the march to the battle area. Nonetheless, Bayard's and Kargé's aggressive operations helped to unbalance Jackson's drive, and, in contrast to the exploits of the federal cavalry, Jackson grew furious with the inept performance of his own cavalry chief, General Beverly H. Robertson. The delay gave General Pope time to gather some scattered forces to block Jackson's advance, but not before Banks and Jackson engaged in a spirited battle at Cedar Mountain on 9 August.[21]

The night before the battle Bayard received cavalry reinforcements: the First Maine under Colonel Samuel H. Allen and the First Rhode Island, commanded by Colonel Alfred N. Duffié. Bayard immediately relieved the First Pennsylvania along Cedar Run with Duffié's regiment. The following morning, as a bright sun began to show in the sky, Bayard moved the First New Jersey and the other two cavalry regiments to augment Duffié's forward position. He explained his deployment thus: "I drew up the cavalry to the right and left of the roads, taking down fences, so that they would have an unimpeded field of action." General Benjamin S. Roberts, chief of cavalry on General Pope's staff, modified Bayard's dispositions somewhat. Concerned about Banks's left flank, he directed Bayard to pull the Maine regiment out of line and deploy it more to the rear and left, in order to guard and patrol all roads on that eastern flank. Two battalions of the Pennsylvania regiment performed the same mission on the right flank. Thus Bayard's Cavalry Brigade, supported by deployed artillery batteries, formed the first line of defense.[22]

Located in a cornfield, Kargé's First New Jersey Cavalry held the center of the defensive line. Pyne said: "The tops of the well-grown maize waved all around us, save where a battery, drawn up in sections on the rising hill, had trampled it down in passing to its position on our left." The road from Culpeper to Barnett's Ford lay on the New Jersey right. Across the road the Pennsylvania cavalry faced the enemy. On the New Jersey left, the Rhode Island Cavalry occupied a position near a battery and well in front of it so that the regimental line was almost at right angles. Cedar Mountain stood out clearly from the battle area,

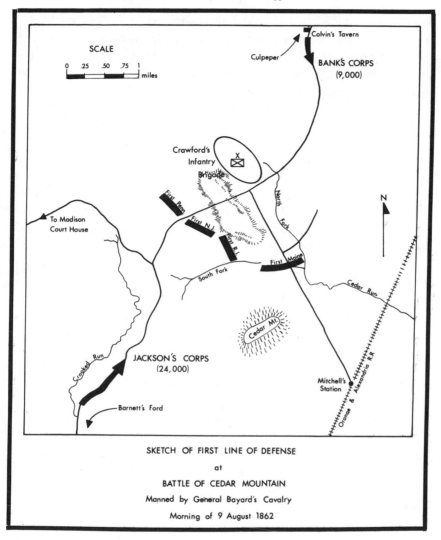

SKETCH OF FIRST LINE OF DEFENSE

at

BATTLE OF CEDAR MOUNTAIN

Manned by General Bayard's Cavalry

Morning of 9 August 1862

which "was much wooded, with intervening strips of cultivated land." The New Jersey troopers observed Confederate infantry filing steadily toward their left near the foot of the mountain. They also saw a Confederate battery, emplaced on a rising piece of ground and poised to fire against them. Except for sporadic artillery fire, conducted for determining the range to probable targets, the battlefield remained relatively quiet, and the men settled down to a wait of several hours.[23]

Opposing Banks's Second Corps were two, and later three, of Jackson's divisions. Jackson placed General C. S. Winder's division to the left of the Culpeper road. General Richard S. Ewell held the right side of the road, and General A. P. Hill's large division, earmarked for reserve duty, approached the battle area. Jackson outnumbered Banks three to one in total strength. Banks had Crawford's brigade in immediate support of Bayard's cavalry. He later placed the second brigade of General Alpheus S. Williams's division on the right of the Culpeper road, opposite Winder. And General Christopher C. Augur's division faced Ewell's Confederates.[24]

Kargé was ill on the day of the battle. He had been wracked with a burning fever for two days. Trying to stay in the saddle became nearly impossible for him, as the hot sun sapped his strength. Reluctantly he turned over the command of the regiment to Beaumont and retired to a regimental ambulance under the care of Assistant Surgeon Ferdinand V. Dayton. Not wanting to miss any action, though, Kargé emerged on the field whenever the tempo of artillery fire picked up. After the alarm subsided, he again returned to his ambulance.[25]

The battle lines of the First New Jersey had remained inactive for several weary hours when suddenly the enemy artillery opened up in earnest. The rounds hit short. Kargé, on his feet immediately, took advantage of the smoke screen from the exploding shells to move the regiment forward about one hundred yards, out of the area of bombardment. Physically unable to resume command and to lead in person, he quietly left the regimental position and joined Bayard at his command post, where he could see the action and still respond to an emergency. There he sat in the saddle, limp and feverish. Only after Bayard had withdrawn the cavalry to the second defensive position would Kargé bow to the general's order to leave the field of battle.[26]

Confederate artillery and skirmishers, meanwhile, continued to engage the New Jersey troopers, who maintained their position with the mobility of cavalrymen and the firepower of breech-loading carbines.

They had some casualties, too, but the artillery battery they protected kept up a destructive shelling of the enemy. The Confederates hesitated to charge Bayard's men, for fear that the cavalry acted as a screen for strong infantry forces in reserve. The deception worked well, but the defensive line of the First New Jersey soon became difficult to hold, for the enemy committed additional artillery. The ordeal was brief. About this time a group of New Jersey men heard the voice of General Banks behind them. "It has been bravely done," Banks said. "They stand like veterans." Having boldly faced the enemy all day with a light cavalry force, Banks now withdrew his exposed troopers. He personally directed Bayard to move the brigade to a position in rear of the infantry. While pulling back, the First New Jersey passed through a field of exploding rounds that severely wounded two platoon leaders. Lieutenant Garrett Beekman absorbed some two pounds of iron in the shoulders, and Lieutenant Alanson Austin's thigh was almost severed from his body. Surgeons amputated Austin's leg on the battlefield, but he did not survive. These and other casualties in the regiment totaled sixteen, including two killed and fourteen wounded.[27]

The First New Jersey Cavalry took up a position on the left flank of the line selected by General Banks. Although the regiment remained in battle-ready condition, it did no more fighting. The First Pennsylvania, though, performed one more act. They rescued an artillery battery threatened by Jackson's infantry. Bayard ordered Major Richard I. Falls's battalion to charge the rebels. Riding up to a point where he faced his target, Falls formed two squadrons and moved out promptly, for the enemy already had him under fire. The squadrons rode at a rapid gait to within fifty yards of the Confederate lines. On Falls's command "Charge," the 164 troopers shouted and cheered and galloped for the enemy. The attack exploded into a spectacle of fierce emotions. The Pennsylvanians ploughed into the rebel infantrymen, cutting them down with sabers and scattering them in all directions. In the thick of the fight, Falls drove his saber through the neck of a Confederate soldier. But notwithstanding the fury of the Pennsylvanians, they could not overcome a murderous fire from two regiments, which decimated the squadrons. The brief, savage encounter cost the cavalrymen ninety-three casualties in dead, wounded, and missing. But they saved the battery.[28]

General Pope's plan for Cedar Mountain called for Banks to be on the defensive. Banks maintained that he had received orders to attack Jackson as soon as his corps came up, and Banks seemed anxious to give battle. About 5:30 P.M., after shelling the rebels for two hours, Banks struck Winder with the troops of Williams's division. Crawford's brigade in the lead delivered the smashing blow, supported vigorously by General George H. Gordon's brigade. Crawford's soldiers braved heavy fire to charge the rebels and engage them in hand-to-hand fighting. The perfectly executed attack demolished the Confederate left flank.

Becoming alarmed over the disintegration of his flank, Jackson rode into the chaos to try to stabilize the front by his presence and exhortations. When he had attained some semblance of organization, he moved to the rear, much to the relief of his officers. Now A. P. Hill's reserve division counterattacked and forced Banks to retreat, although the fighting continued until 11:00 P.M. The fierce battle cost Banks 2,381 casualties and Jackson 1,365 casualties in killed, wounded, and missing.[29]

General Williams wondered what had become of Ricketts's division and a part of Franz Sigel's First Corps, some twelve thousand to fifteen thousand troops, which Williams had passed that morning on the way to the battle zone. "If they had arrived an hour before sundown," Williams said, "we should have thrashed Jackson badly and taken a host of his artillery. As it was, they came up sometime after dark and took up a position that greatly relieved us." The next day, 10 August, Jackson did not renew the fighting; meanwhile, Pope brought up strong reinforcements. The two armies held their ground. On the night of 11 August, Jackson withdrew to Gordonsville and Pope followed him to the Rapidan river.[30]

The county seat of Culpeper overflowed with wounded men from the battlefield five miles to the south. The August weather, unbearably hot, added to the distress of the wounded in the makeshift hospitals, which had little, if any, ventilation. Also, owing to a scarcity of medical supplies and attendants, the suffering of the wounded and the dying became greatly aggravated. Pyne said that the field hospital of the First New Jersey Cavalry, run by Assistant Surgeon Dayton, was, on the other hand, a model of efficiency. A sanitary and well-ventilated building served as the hospital. The wounded lay on beds made up of dry and clean straw, and the attendants brought them wholesome food. As each of the more than one hundred patients was evacuated to Washington, he received a draught of light wine to sustain him during the journey. The wounded from Dayton's hospital arrived in markedly better condition than those from other field hospitals, and surgeons in Washington noted the difference.[31] The accomplished manner in which Dayton cared for the battle casualties reflected Kargé's professional standards. The commander thought highly of him, and in the summer of 1863 Dayton would become the regimental surgeon of Kargé's Second New Jersey Cavalry Regiment.

Following the Battle of Cedar Mountain, Kargé found his regiment utterly exhausted. Nearly all the horses were unshod and suffered from sore backs. The men were worn out by the constant riding, lack of sleep, and irregular nourishment. They had totally committed themselves. At a time when Union horse soldiers had yet to learn to operate effectively, the New Jersey troopers made giant strides toward the levels of performance achieved by the cavalry in the latter part of the war. "For once the Federal cavalry was being fought with skill and daring," Burke Davis wrote, "and Pope had flung the shifting screen of blue riders for as much as twenty miles before him—it was a handicap to which Jackson was not accustomed."[32] To be sure, the New Jerseymen did not form the only federal cavalry to oppose Jackson, but they had defended the most critical area—around Barnett's Ford, where Stonewall's divisions crossed.

General Bayard relied heavily on Kargé, assigning him the most demanding and responsible missions. Immediately following the two tedious marches and countermarches with General Hatch to Madison Court House, Bayard on 28 July ordered Kargé's regiment to the Rapidan, in advance of the brigade, to seize and hold the key crossings at Barnett's Ford and Rapidan Station. At this time Kargé commanded nearly 600 well-equipped and mounted troopers. Reaching the river, he drove the Confederate cavalry away and set up strong pickets to his front along the roads emanating from Orange Court House. Tactically as important, he also placed pickets north of the Rapidan, behind him, along the roads from Culpeper. Alone and with his flanks exposed, Kargé guarded against surprise, for the Rapidan could easily be forded all along the line in this dry season. The right flank, from the direction of Liberty Mills and Cave's Ford, seemed especially vulnerable. The enemy cavalry had gathered there in force. To repel surprise attacks, Kargé kept a reserve force of 160 men in camp, constantly saddled and under arms.

The First New Jersey patrolled the river line and skirmished with the rebels almost incessantly for three days, forcing Kargé to seek help from

General Crawford at Culpeper. Crawford promptly sent him 125 troopers from the First Michigan Cavalry. This small augmentation proved inadequate, since Kargé assessed that the Confederates had the capability of mounting a surprise attack in force, leading to the possible annihilation of his command. "To avoid this catastrophe," Kargé said, "I had to tax both my men and horses with an extraordinary amount of labor." Finally, some relief came with the arrival of Bayard and the First Pennsylvania Cavalry. Bayard divided the mission between the two regiments. Still, the defensive screen extended fourteen miles along the Rapidan, and the rebel cavalry became increasingly aggressive as Jackson prepared to march north. "The consequence was," Kargé said, "that from the 28th of July till the 9th of August neither man nor beast had any rest—few horses ever had their saddles removed from their backs and the men themselves seldom experienced any sleep." Kargé told Bayard that his officers did their work bravely and without complaining, even though some regiments remained uncommitted and did little. "Whenever any work had to be done," Kargé said, "we were sent to perform it—when other Cavalry Regts were laying by nursing their men and horses and reaping laurels for their fine appearance." [33] Bayard appreciated the performance of the First New Jersey and continued to rely on Kargé. Nevertheless, in the psychological aftermath of the grueling campaign, the regiment appeared to be emotionally spent and badly in need of a few days of rest to regain its equilibrium.

Charges against the Commander

Political Intrigues and Petty Jealousies

Immediately following the Battle of Cedar Mountain, Major Myron H. Beaumont challenged the fitness of Lieutenant Colonel Kargé to command the regiment. With the support of about a third of the officers, the executive officer preferred court-martial charges against the commander. Beaumont forwarded the charges and specifications, dealing with "cowardice" and "conduct unbecoming an officer and a gentleman," to Kargé on 13 August 1862. In the forwarding letter, Beaumont said that he and the other officers "honestly believe you to be a coward and desire your removal from the regiment." [1]

Beaumont's action undoubtedly caused a great deal of anxiety for Kargé, a proud and sensitive individual. Beaumont not only made the charges, as he had the right to do, but also provided a copy to General Bayard at the same time. The procedure violated army regulations. Only if Kargé balked or refused to pass the charges to the court-martial authority would Beaumont gain the right to bypass the commander. [2] Furthermore, he went outside the army to transmit a copy to New Jersey Governor, Charles S. Olden. Beaumont thus attempted to embarrass Kargé and impugn his reputation back home. This was political demagoguery, since the charges had not been substantiated. In effect, the second-in-command marshaled the available physical and psychological factors to unseat his commanding officer.

The motivation for Beaumont and his fellow accusers appears to have been rooted in the emotions, jealousies, and differences that had developed months before during the organization of the regiment. Kargé's fight with Colonel Halsted over the question of discipline and methods of training had split the officers into two factions. During the periodic absences of Halsted, Kargé commanded the regiment with an iron hand, which many of the citizen-soldiers found unbearable. Feelings ran high in those early days, and the strain of combat since then did little to remove the friction. Kargé's foreign birth was also a cause for resentment. The prejudice of some officers toward Kargé reflected the attitudes held by segments of the civilian population. Recall that the appointment of the Englishman Sir Percy Wyndham to the command of the regiment in February 1862 prompted the *New Brunswick Times* to question the need to appoint foreigners to command positions. The *Times*, however, conceded that Sir Wyndham came highly recommended and was "an accomplished Italian [*sic*] officer." [3]

Beaumont based his allegations on incidents in combat. Specifically, he charged his commander with cowardice on 6 June 1862, when General Turner Ashby ambushed the regiment near Harrisonburg. He alleged that Kargé made no strenuous effort to rally the regiment during its rout and was among the first to flee from the field. Available accounts of the ambuscade do not support the allegation. It is known that enemy rifle fire incapacitated Kargé's horse about the time Ashby's cavalrymen charged the milling New Jerseymen, and several of Kargé's men rescued him from imminent capture. Whether he managed to escape on another horse or ride double with a fellow soldier is not known. Nevertheless, for someone alleged to have been "among the first to flee from the field," Kargé had personal knowledge of the bravery of Captains John Kester, Robert Boyd, and Virgil Broderick, who were among the last in the retreat.

Another specification read that on or about 30 July 1862 Kargé deported himself in an "excited and frantic manner" upon receiving news of the approach of the enemy. Beaumont accused Kargé of waving his arms and shouting for his orderly and bugler, thereby causing "numerous doubts and suspicions to be loudly expressed as to his courage." With regard to his mannerisms, Kargé behaved somewhat flamboyantly, and could be demonstrative on suitable occasions such as the one that occurred in early training, when he brandished his saber and threatened to run it through the brawlers and trouble-makers of the regiment.

The final specification dealt with the events of 9 August 1862, the day of the Battle of Cedar Mountain. Beaumont alleged that Kargé left "the field of battle while his Regiment was being engaged with the enemy and nobly standing firm, pretending to be sick and unable to ride, but returning to the Regiment after they had retired to a place of safety, and again disappearing on the approach of the enemy, and again joining the Regiment after the danger was over." [4]

In response to these charges, Kargé remained firm and outwardly composed. He forwarded the papers to Bayard and also issued Regimental Order No. 171, 14 August 1862, in which he praised the regiment for its gallant performance in the recently concluded battle. "The commanding officer of this regiment," Kargé said, "takes the first opportunity of expressing his high gratification of the cool and brave behavior of both the men and officers during the last action. Although himself severely indisposed, he was watching the movements of the regiment, and its intrepidity while under a galling fire, with unlimited pride." Kargé also singled out Beaumont's handling of the regiment, praising him for his coolnes and steady conduct under heavy artillery fire.[5]

At brigade headquarters the youthful Bayard reacted to the charges with indignation. He felt as if his own brother were accused of crime. In passing the charges to the court-martial authority, Brigadier General Benjamin S. Roberts, the Chief of Cavalry, Bayard emphasized: "I cannot and do not believe any such thing regarding Col. Kargé—I know Col. Kargé to have been sick on the 8th of August, and he left the field by my order twice repeated." Bayard added an unusual reminder when he stressed: "Col. Kargé is a *Pole* and has been wounded in European service and had his horse killed in the Shenandoah Valley—and I would trust him before any officer in my command—and I therefore merely forward these charges, but they are utterly and totally *disapproved*." Bayard's reference to Kargé's nationality acknowledged the fighting reputation of the Polish soldier worldwide. The brigade commander probably believed that his statement "Kargé is a *Pole*" sufficed to demolish the charges. Concluding his letter to Roberts, Bayard said: "I think Col. Kargé too old a soldier to be proved none at all by such new beginners."[6]

Bayard's strong defense of Kargé sprang from more than a sense of loyalty. Bayard had come to value the courage and leadership of Joseph Kargé and to rely on his professional judgment. Writing his mother on 3 September 1862, Bayard said: "I trust Wyndham and love Kargé, no one can hurt them in my estimation." Bayard referred to political intrigues and petty jealousies that plagued the service and even infected his own brigade. Samuel J. Bayard, the general's father, explained this point some years after his son's untimely death. He wrote: "Considerable efforts had been made by certain parties, principally from New Jersey, to prejudice General Bayard against Lt. Col. Kargé and Col. Wyndham. But knowing them to be good officers, he gave no ear to their disparagement."[7]

General Roberts, a mature officer of fifty-two years and a West

Pointer of the Class of 1835, disposed of the charges on 17 August, four days after Beaumont made them. Roberts took the time to probe the matter, notwithstanding the fact the Federal Army of Virginia was highly preoccupied with Generals Lee and Jackson at that critical period—the Second Bull Run Campaign. Roberts questioned the available witnesses and discussed the matter with Beaumont. Recording his findings on the charge papers, Roberts wrote:

> I find nothing to justify these charges. After an examination of the officers whose names are noted as witnesses, I was convinced that many of them had mistaken the manner of Major Kargé, which is empressé, for excitement from fear. Major Beaumont confessed that he is now convinced that the charges were hastily made and are in fact without foundation.[8]

Roberts's language on the formal charge papers is careful and judicial. Yet his personal reactions were more like Bayard's. The cavalry chief expressed astonishment "at the conduct of the officers who so hastily made the grave charges against their commanding officer and as hastily withdrew them." Colonel Edmund Schriver, the chief of staff of the Third Corps, labeled Beaumont's ill-considered action as slander. "An officer failing to make good charges of such character," Schriver said, "should be the subject of a court martial himself." Kargé, however, did not press charges against Beaumont or any of the other officers. By demonstrating restraint and tolerance, he emerged from the affair with his reputation enhanced. Schriver commented on this point to Bayard: "Lt. Col. Kargé in abstaining from such a course showed great magnanimity, and the officers who combined against him should show their appreciation of his forgiveness by making the fullest apology to him."[9]

Chaplain Pyne, who knew of these charges, did not include this episode in his account of the regimental history. He had refused Beaumont the satisfaction of being named a coaccuser. Kargé's subsequent behavior toward Beaumont remained evenhanded. As a man of high principle, Joseph Kargé continued to work with his senior subordinate for the good of the regiment and the Union cause. During the course of this regrettable incident, it was Kargé who demonstrated the character of an officer and a gentleman.

6

Clash of Cavalry

Skirmishes and Engagements:
Brandy Station to Fredericksburg

Following the Battle of Cedar Mountain, General John Pope's Army of Virginia reoccupied the Rapidan river line. The federal cavalry fanned out on picket duty along the river. Bayard's brigade guarded the center of the federal army, aligned on Rapidan Station. His pickets extended from the Robertson River on the west to Somerville Ford on the east.[1] Pope expected some major action by General Lee, who did not disappoint him. Deciding to strike Pope before General McClellan could augment him with troops from the abandoned Peninsula Campaign, Lee conceived an excellent plan to catch Pope's army in the area between the Rapidan and the Rappahannock rivers. In a preliminary move, Lee massed his forces behind Clark's Mountain, located some ten miles southeast of Cedar Mountain. The plan called for Jeb Stuart's cavalry to dash across the Rapidan to the Rappahannock river, where they would destroy the bridge at Rappahannock Station and cut off Pope's route of withdrawal. Lee then would cross the Rapidan at Somerville Ford to attack Pope's left and rear in an attempt to destroy him.[2]

Pope gained an unexpected advantage when he discovered Lee's plan through a chance capture of Confederate orders. During a scouting mission in the vicinity of Louisa Court House, the First Michigan Cavalry Regiment seized Major Norman Fitzhugh, carrying Lee's letter of instructions.[3] Aware of Lee's plans, the Union general decided to withdraw immediately to the more secure position of the Rappahannock river line. On 18 August 1862 Bayard received orders to cover the withdrawal of the Army of Virginia from the vicinity of Cedar Mountain. At this time he commanded five regiments of cavalry: the First New Jersey, First Pennsylvania, First Rhode Island, First Maine, and the Second New York. The cavalry maintained a protective screen while General Sigel's trains rumbled off for Sulphur Springs, some twenty-five miles to the northwest. The wagons moved all through the night of

18 August and the next day, followed by the corps troops. Bayard's cavalrymen brought up the very rear of the corps rear guard. They reached Culpeper just after dark on the nineteenth and continued to Brandy Station but halted there for the night.[4]

The hour was midnight. The weary troopers of the First New Jersey waited patiently in place while the brigade staff made arrangements for the night's bivouac. Finally, they received word to halt along the fence that bordered the road. Too tired to prepare any food, "the troopers threw themselves down and slept on their arms beside their accoutred horses." A few men were ordered out as pickets and had to postpone their sleep a little longer. At dawn's first light the regiment rose quickly. The men managed to prepare a hasty breakfast of coffee, broken biscuits, and fresh corn from an adjacent field, before Bayard ordered reconnoitering parties on all the roads. In the First New Jersey, Kargé dispatched Captain Broderick's Third Battalion to scout in the direction of Culpeper.[5]

A squadron of the First Maine, moving south on the Raccoon Ford road, were the first to make contact with the enemy cavalry. Since the Confederates displayed considerable strength, the Maine troopers fell back slowly to the support of Lieutenant Colonel Judson Kilpatrick with his Second New York Cavalry. He disputed the rebel advance and allowed the various reconnaissance parties to return. Bayard ordered the First Pennsylvania to augment Kilpatrick. At the same time the brigade commander instructed Kargé to place his regiment on the enemy's flank. Once in position, Kargé dismounted his troops and, as the enemy rode into range, he surprised them with flanking fire. "There was a rapid exchange of shots," Pyne said; "several horses rushed riderless across the front of our dismounted men, and then the whole body of rebels hurried back from the scene of action . . . ."[6] Kargé's use of dismounted skirmishers followed sound, professional tactics. He employed the mobility of cavalry to reach a threatened point or an assigned area quickly, but, once on the scene, he dismounted his men to capitalize on the greater and more accurate firepower of foot soldiers. In the brief skirmish the First Maine and the Second New York each lost several men wounded. The latter regiment was called the "Harris Light Cavalry" in honor of Senator Ira Harris, who had helped to organize it.[7]

The brigade resumed its slow withdrawal to the Rappahannock. The Maine and Rhode Island regiments led the way, having departed earlier. The remaining three regiments moved in beautiful precision across gently undulating terrain. The battalions of each regiment alternated in "halt, wheel, and retirement while the skirmishers, covering the rear of all, conformed their maneuvers to the movement of the whole body. Nothing but an attack in force could have hurried the regulated movement." The countryside around Brandy Station and south of the ford near Rappahannock Station is open terrain and offers an ideal area for cavalry operations. Bayard noted the tactical importance of this ground as he rode across it, and he stopped to deploy his regiments to repel the expected enemy attack. He drew up the Second New York beyond a strip of timber that separated the river from the open ground to the south. He placed Kargé's regiment to the right of Kilpatrick's and some six-hundred yards in rear. Kargé's mission: support Kilpatrick. As a reserve, Bayard formed the First Pennsylvania just behind the timbers, to be committed should the Confederates penetrate that deeply. In preparing for the first real cavalry engagement of the war, Bayard made excellent dispositions of his three regiments. General Jeb Stuart, Lee's cavalry chief, enjoyed a numerical advantage of four regiments, since two of Bayard's units, the First Maine and the First Rhode Island, had already crossed the Rappahannock. The two regiments would miss the clash of Confederate and Union cavalry at Brandy Station, the forerunner of the large-scale battle the following June.[8]

Clouds of dust first marked the approach of the Confederates. Shortly, sharp echoes of carbine fire indicated the initial contact between the enemy and Union skirmishers. They stopped the rebel advance elements, which belonged to the command of Brigadier General Beverly H. Robertson, with whom Jeb Stuart rode.[9] Because of Pope's restraining order to avoid a general engagement, Bayard kept from attacking the rebels. On the part of the Confederates the delay was temporary. As soon as the leading regiment closed up, it formed and charged with wild yells. The attack caught Kilpatrick's unit in the execution of a maneuver, General Bayard said, and his men had their backs to the enemy at the time. The ferocious charge and the screaming seem to have panicked Kilpatrick's inexperienced men, and they ran. While Kikpatrick rallied his regiment, the rebel cavalry galloped on. Kargé, in position on the flank to hit the enemy, gave the order to charge, but for some unknown reason the regiment held back. He galloped off, followed only by his adjutant, Lieutenant Penn Gaskell, and the General's aide-de-camp, Lieutenant William Bayard. The trio charged into the enemy horsemen. In the ensuing hand-to-hand fighting,

Kargé was shot through the leg and incapacitated with a painful and serious wound. The enemy now attacked the First New Jersey regiment and, as General Bayard explained:

> I regret to say that, contrary to their previous history, they too began running. I, as soon as I saw this, ordered Captain Broderick, commanding the rear battalion of the Jersey cavalry, to place his men in the timber just in his rear and let his men use their carbines, from which position he repulsed the enemy. Seeing the enemy going around the timber, I quickly rode through it, and hastened the forma-

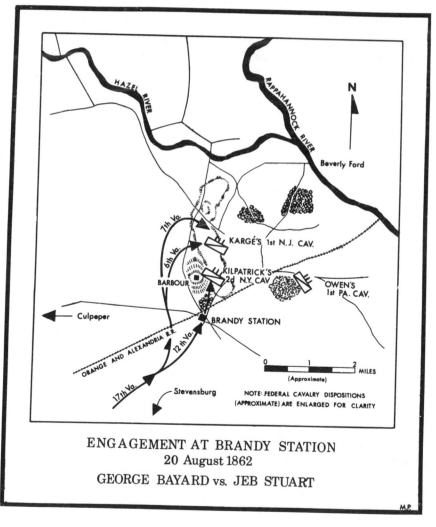

ENGAGEMENT AT BRANDY STATION
20 August 1862
GEORGE BAYARD vs. JEB STUART

tion of the Pennsylvania cavalry. As soon as the enemy appeared, I ordered Maj. R. I. Falls to charge them with his battalion, and he quickly cleared the enemy from sight. The enemy now withdrew, and the fight closed.[10]

Henry Pyne's account of Brandy Station differs considerably from Bayard's report. "Down came the enemy, charging along the road," Pyne relates, "and Kilpatrick was ordered to meet them." The Second New York swept over the low hill where they first had assembled. The New Yorkers moved at a steady gallop in column of platoons toward their first formidable encounter. Kilpatrick drew back initially and rode alongside the regiment to check on the movement and to lend encouragement to his inexperienced troopers. The two forces came in sight of one another. As Kilpatrick spurred his horse to get to the front and order the buglers to sound "Charge," the lieutenant of the leading platoon sharply drew rein and backed his horse right through the ranks behind him. Instinctively, the nervous troopers followed the lieutenant's example, and the whole front of Kilpatrick's column halted in great confusion. At the same time the Confererate cavalry hit the New Yorkers, scattered them over the field, and continued charging through the broken center. The victorious rebels swept around the flank of the First New Jersey. Part of the charging horde who attacked frontally were repulsed by Captain Sawyer's forward line of skirmishers. Sawyer held fire until the rebel cavalry closed in almost on top of his position. Then, on command, his men poured in three volleys of deadly carbine fire, which stopped that attack, and the enemy remnants broke away.[11]

The unexpected rout of the Second New York forced Kargé to change front with his line, in order to bring the main New Jersey body into action. The tired horses responded slowly to the command and, before the half wheel had been made and the line once more put in motion, the rebels swooped down on his front and flanks. The infighting was fierce and hectic. Firing and emptying his revolver at close range, Kargé flung his weapon at the heads of the nearest rebels and dashed among them with his saber. The New Jersey men around Kargé drew their sabers too, and the ferocity of their attack cleared the enemy in their immediate vicinity. The New Jersey battle position, however, had become indefensible when the encircling charge of the rebels broke both flanks of Kargé's line. This condition forced him to employ his fall-back tactic—to get to the position of his reserve battalion and rally under cover of its countercharge. "Skirmishers and main body, with one accord," Pyne said, "spurred as rapidly as possible to the rear, fighting hand to hand as they did so, with the foremost of their pursuers." Sweeping past the position of the reserve battalion, Kargé's men were surprised to find it deserted. They were compelled to continue the retreat along the railroad track to the woods—the position of the First Pennsylvania, the brigade reserve.[12]

Earlier, Kargé's reserve battalion under Captain Broderick had been pulled out by General Bayard and moved to positions along the edge of the timbers. They witnessed the hot race between their fellow troopers and the enemy. At the very moment the rear elements were about to fall into enemy hands, Broderick's men rushed out from the underbrush and fell on the flank of the pursuing rebels. Simultaneously, Captain Lucas wheeled his company on them from the opposite side. This double charge, which Kargé had confidently expected to occur at the first regimental reserve position, cut the rebels in two and drove the mass of them back with loss. Meanwhile, Major Falls's Pennsylvanians attacked those rebels who had penetrated the woods, cutting them down and dispersing the remnants. Not to be outdone, Kargé with Adjutant Penn Gaskell charged on a party of fifteen rebels and drove them back. Kargé gave up the fight when a shot from a rebel's pistol wounded him severely in the leg.[13]

A comparison of the battle accounts of Bayard and Pyne brings up two questions. Why did Kilpatrick execute a maneuver at the very moment the rebel cavalry charged him? Kilpatrick's regiment stood ready on the highest available ground, which gave him a clear view of the approaching enemy cavalry. In fact, he was able to see, and was warned by, the dust cloud much before the actual troopers could be distinguished. For his men to have had their backs to the line of attack just as the rebels hit them seems incredible. According to Pyne, the rout of Kilpatrick's regiment forced Kargé to order a maneuver, so as to face the enemy who had swept to his flanks. It appears that Kargé was the one caught executing a maneuver.

The second question concerns Kargé's charge on the rebels. Why did only Gaskell and Bayard, the two aides, follow Kargé? Either the regiment did not hear or understand Kargé's command, or it decided to mutiny en masse at that moment. Neither of these reasons seems logical. Pyne explains that the charge of Kargé and his adjutant, in which Kargé suffered a severe wound, took place against a band of some fifteen rebels at the very end of the battle, and not against an entire regiment at an earlier point in the engagement. The charge of the two men by themselves against fifteen Confederates seems a reasonable action, considering that the rebels had engulfed the First New Jersey regiment in a fierce attack.

Henry Pyne's *History of the First New Jersey Cavalry Regiment* is replete with eyewitness detail that indicates a conscientious recording on a periodic, if not daily, basis. Bayard, on the other hand, wrote his report 13 October 1862, almost two months after the engagement. In the interval he was fully occupied with continuous cavalry operations, involving the Second Bull Run Campaign and the defense of the capital, when General Lee invaded Maryland and fought the Battle of Antietam. Some particulars of Brandy Station may have escaped Bayard by mid-October. He admits this possibility in the opening paragraph of his report: "At this late day I must depend much upon my memory, as many of my papers have been misplaced, and it is impossible at present to find them."[14]

Confederate General Robertson's report of Brandy Station shows that he attacked the First New Jersey with two and possibly three regiments, a far superior force than indicated in other historical accounts. Robertson said he found General Bayard's brigade beyond Brandy Station, drawn up in line of battle on a commanding hill and "evidently determined to dispute our progress." His report continues: "As soon as practicable I ordered a charge and led the Twelfth Virginia Regiment (Colonel A. W. Harman's) directly against the center of their line, while the Sixth and the Seventh were directed against their flank [Kargé's regiment]." Robertson said that his men charged gallantly, and after a brief hand-to-hand contest he routed the federals with the loss of several killed and a number wounded, capturing sixty-four prisoners, including several commissioned officers.[15]

The First New Jersey Cavalry suffered severe losses. Forty men were missing, presumably captured, from a total of 250 troopers who engaged in the fighting. Others had also been captured but were rescued by the final charge of Captains Broderick and Lucas. Seriously disabled, Kargé was evacuated from the regiment. Notwithstanding the losses, the mission of protecting the withdrawal of the Army of Virginia had been accomplished. "Pope had moved his Army and its trains over twenty miles of open country and through many awkward defiles," Pyne concluded, "without leaving them a wagon, a horse or a gun, as trophies of their pursuit."[16]

Joseph Kargé's injury kept him out of action for five weeks. Almost by coincidence, the Confederates released Colonel Wyndham from captivity through a prisoner-of-war exchange. He immediately resumed command of the First New Jersey Regiment, which became occupied with extensive reconnaissance during the Second Bull Run Campaign. The officers and men of the regiment, meanwhile, hoped for Kargé's rapid recovery, and they eagerly awaited his return. In response to urgent pleas from Bayard, Kargé rejoined the regiment before his wound had fully healed.[17] On the evening of 23 September 1862, while the regiment was encamped near Bailey's Cross Roads, Virginia, the men learned that Kargé had come back. They quickly gathered in front of his field quarters and sounded off with cheers ''three times three that made the welkin ring.'' Emerging from his tent, Kargé told them how pleased he was to be with the regiment again. The men again responded with ''three times three.'' The following morning, troopers of Company A brought out a beautiful set of horse equipment that they had purchased. One of the sergeants presented the gift to Kargé as a token of their esteem. At ten o'clock the same day, the regiment held a dress parade in Kargé's honor, and, at the close, the adjutant read a letter from Governor Charles S. Olden. The New Jersey executive thanked the regiment for the honor they had brought their state. He expressed his admiration for the valor of the officers and men in covering the withdrawal of the Army of Virginia from the Rapidan to the Rappahannock. Kargé then concluded the ceremony with a brief speech to the assembled regiment.[18]

The feeling of welcome and camaraderie that prevailed on Kargé's return to duty contrasted sharply with the atmosphere of suspicion and recrimination of just six weeks ago, when Beaumont preferred court-martial charges against his commander. Kargé probably had this in mind when he said: ''The hearty welcome you have tendered me on my return amongst you has sufficiently demonstrated to me that I am in full possession of your confidence—the greatest pride and glory of a soldier.'' He added that he wished to share with them the hardships and the achievements on the battlefield. The only favor he asked for was ''implicit obedience to orders, good will and true fellowship.''[19]

General Bayard had experienced a sudden need for able cavalry commanders, and this was what had prompted him to ask Kargé to report back from convalescence early. On 10 September 1862 General George McClellan thrust great responsibility and authority on Bayard when he gave the young general the sole command of all cavalry forces in the

Defenses of Washington, south of the Potomac. McClellan charged Bayard with the mission of scouting the movements of the Confederates and reporting them to Headquarters, Army of the Potomac. General Banks, commanding the Defenses of Washington, reconfirmed Bayard's mission in Special Orders No. 18, dated 27 September 1862.[20] In accomplishing his new duties Bayard assigned the available cavalry units to the several corps and independent commands. He gave Wyndham the command of General Sigel's cavalry. Kargé not only took charge of the First New Jersey but also received the command of a light brigade, organized for quick thrusts into enemy-held areas. On one of his first assignments Kargé led a force of detachments from several regiments on a reconnaissance of the Leesburg area and westward to the base of the Blue Ridge Mountains. General McClellan wished a close watch kept on the Confederate army, which was camped along Opequon Creek, west of Harper's Ferry. Lee had moved his army there to recuperate from the hard fighting at the Battle of Antietam, 16-17 September 1862. In coordination with Kargé, Wyndham took Sigel's cavalry on a quick march through Thoroughfare Gap to harass Lee's lines of communication.[21]

Kargé followed the reconnaissance to Leesburg with a dash to Warrenton—a successful action that demonstrated his careful planning and bold execution. Receiving orders 28 September to attack Warrenton, Kargé commenced the operation at six the following morning. His command consisted of 200 troopers of the First New Jersey under Major Ivin D. Jones, 150 of the Second New York under Major Otto Harhaus, and 150 of the First Pennsylvania under Major Richard I. Falls. Kargé led them from Centreville on the Warrenton turnpike through Gainesville and New Baltimore. To secure his flanks, he sent out patrols to a distance of two miles, but he found no trace of the enemy. Planning to seize Warrenton by surprise, Kargé ordered skirmishers out on the several roads leading from Warrenton—south, east, and west. At precisely 2:30 P.M. his advance guard of New Jerseymen charged into the town. Kargé followed immediately with two squadrons, leaving two squadrons as a reserve one-half mile north of the town. He met no opposition. Approximately thirty Confederate cavalrymen dashed out of Warrenton when Kargé's advance guard entered, and escaped in the direction of Culpeper.[22] Isaac Newning reported that "when the Jersey boys charged through the town with a yell, the rebel cavalry skedaddled in panic; but we captured many of them. We also captured 200 or 300

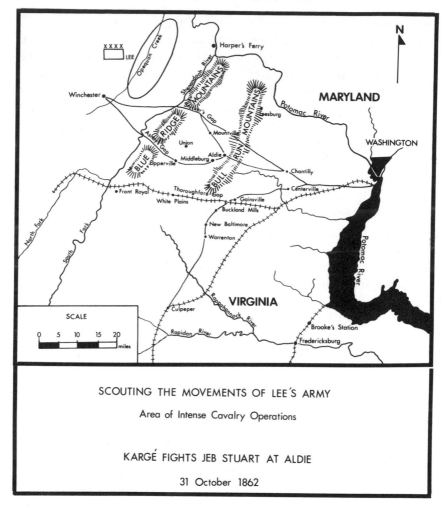

SCOUTING THE MOVEMENTS OF LEE'S ARMY

Area of Intense Cavalry Operations

KARGÉ FIGHTS JEB STUART AT ALDIE

31 October 1862

conscripts and Major Payne, chief quartermaster of General Long-street's division." Kargé had anticipated a sizable force of Confederate cavalry and had every reason to believe he would meet with strong resistance. Newning said: "There was an irresistible determination in the charge."[23]

Kargé found Warrenton filled with some fourteen-hundred Confederate sick, wounded, and stragglers. The latter crowded around his men and engaged them in conversation. The civilians also came out into the streets and appeared friendly. Newning commented on the behavior of the Confederates: "While in Warrenton, I was perfectly astonished at the reception we met. The conscripts and many of the prisoners cheered us, and did not hesitate to say that, had they an opportunity to get home, they would never be found in the rebel army again.'' Relative to the morale of the civilians, Newning said: ''I also expected to find among the citizens the same exultant spirit that is found in their army. On the contrary, everyone was talking about overtures of peace, deploring their heavy losses in Maryland and cursing the folly of their leaders in venturing over the Potomac.''[24]

Every house in Warrenton seemed filled with severely wounded Confederate soldiers. Despite the presence of some forty surgeons, deaths occurred at the rate of fifty a day. The surgeons performed amputation of legs and arms with sickening frequency. Conditions in the crowded hospitals were unsatisfactory, aggravated by a shortage of food and medical supplies. Patients lay on the bare floors, wrapped in old blankets; and in some of the houses the sick and wounded literally decayed in their own filth. A delegation of ladies asked Kargé to request help from United States authorities to alleviate the suffering of the military patients and of the inhabitants. The continual fighting around Warrenton caused the two belligerents to strip the countryside of provisions, and the inhabitants feared starvation.[25]

Kargé paroled all the Confederates, and they were eager to get their papers. ''My officers had their hands full to issue them,'' Kargé said. He assured the Southerners that the scrap of paper would free them from military service. The Union troopers observed impeccable discipline. Not one unkind word was said on either side during the three-hour-long occupation of Warrenton. ''My troops behaved in a splendid manner and made a very favorable impression among the inhabitants of the town and prisoners,'' Kargé said. Precisely at 5:30 P.M. Kargé's force left the town and proceeded eight miles on the Warrenton Pike to Buckland Mills, where it encamped for the night. The next morning at six, the troopers returned to Centreville.

In his report to General Heintzelman, commanding the Defenses of Washington south of the Potomac, Kargé recommended a fifty percent increase in the size of the cavalry force employed in this defensive sector. He pointed out that of the available one-thousand cavalrymen, two hundred were habitually not present for duty because of sickness or the unfit condition of their horses. With a force increased to fifteen-hundred mounted men, Kargé suggested that six hundred of this number be used for large reconnaissance missions, four hundred to perform outpost duty and close-in scouting, and the remaining five hundred to constitute a reserve. Endorsing Kargé's report to General Sigel, Heintzelman said: "I expect to increase the cavalry force in the advance."[26] Meanwhile, Kargé continued to lead reconnaissance forces on sweeping missions, thus gaining information on the dispositions and movements of Confederate units.

In mid-October 1862 General Julius Stahel recommended Kargé for promotion to the rank of brigadier general. Stahel, who commanded the First Division in Franz Sigel's newly redesignated Eleventh Corps, began the administrative process with a letter to the corps commander. Like Kargé, a revolutionary, Stahel had fought with Louis Kossuth in the unsuccessful Hungarian uprising of 1849. It appears that Kargé and Stahel met for the first time in America as soldiers in the Civil War, and they became friends. In his letter of 12 October 1862, Stahel said that Kargé's "thorough military knowledge and accomplishments have secured the confidence and respect of both officers and men." He told Sigel that Kargé had been "ordered some time since to your Armée Corps." Acting favorably on the recommendation, Sigel forwarded not only Stahel's letter but also a copy of Governor Olden's letter, which lauded Kargé's ability. Sigel, writing from his command post at Fairfax Court House on 14 October, called Kargé a "gentleman and an accomplished officer" and one who deserved the favorable consideration of the administration. He said to Major General Heintzelman: "I recommend him to you as an officer qualified to take the command of a Cavalry Brigade, and respectfully ask you to forward the enclosed letters to the General in command of the Cavalry for his action."[27]

Heintzelman knew Kargé as the tough professional who had whipped the raw New Jersey regiment into an effective unit. He concurred fully in the recommendation and sent it one step higher to General Nathaniel Banks, the commander of the overall Defenses of Washington. As part of Bayard's brigade, Kargé had fought under Banks at Cedar Mountain. Banks, too, recommended favorable consideration, and now the paperwork reached the War Department, where the Adjutant General referred the recommendation to Brigadier General John Buford, chief of cavalry, Army of the Potomac. Buford reacted negatively and killed the promotion. Submitting his comments to the Adjutant General on 1 November 1862, Buford stated: "I have had no acquaintance with Lt. Col. Kargé—neither have I heard mention of his services." Buford may have been technically correct in this statement, but he undoubtedly knew of the First New Jersey Cavalry Regiment, for Buford's and Bayard's brigades operated side by side along the Rapidan and Rappahannock rivers during the summer of 1862. Union cavalry regiments were not so numerous then as to escape the attention of an old dragoon like Buford. He made a vague reference to this possibility when he added: "My impression is that he served in Virginia under Gen. Bayard." With a ring of finality Buford concluded: "Col. Kargé is not with this Army."[28] The recommendation died in the War Department, and Kargé's reaction is not known. Nonetheless, his performance of duty continued to be motivated by unswerving devotion to his adopted country.

The promotion episode with the negative response of Buford illustrates the undercurrent of resentment between Regular Army and volunteer officers during the Civil War. For obvious reasons the General-in-Chief and the Adjutant General, in particular, surrounded themselves with regular officers, who were knowledgeable in army administration. These officers became appalled by the large number of political appointments of civilians to general officer rank by the Lincoln administration. Consequently, the regulars tended to view all promotions of nonregulars with a jaundiced eye and usually impeded them with administrative tactics. As late as February 1865 Major James A. Connolly complained of the interminable delay of his expected promotion. Connolly, a divisional staff officer in Major General William T. Sherman's army, had been recommended for promotion to lieutenant colonel by brevet, following the capture of Atlanta, Georgia, 2 September 1864. Again, when Sherman took Savannah in December 1864, Connolly's division commander, General Absalom Baird, resubmitted the recommendation for promotion. By now Connolly had become disillusioned. He mailed home an official copy of Baird's promotion letter for safekeeping as a memento. On 6 February 1865, near Robertsville, South Carolina, he wrote his wife, with evident sarcasm: "If I were a 'regular officer,' I would feel very sure of the brevet, but being only an 'irregular,' the 'regular' gentlemen about the adjutant general's office at Washington will stick the recommendation into a pigeon hole and leave it there 'three years, or during the war.'"[29]

At the end of October 1862 a humorous camp incident occurred that portrays Kargé as the serious-minded officer he was and yet possessing a sense of humor. The First New Jersey, along with the entire brigade, bivouacked one night near Fairfax, inside the line of pickets of the

Defenses of Washington. In the dead of night Kargé was awakened by the sharp crack of a rifle from the direction of the picket line. In a moment a half dozen more shots were fired, and they seemed to be dangerously close. Kargé leaped to his feet and shouted for the bugler to sound "To Arms." The roused cavalrymen threw off their warm blankets and grabbed their carbines. Spreading out through the woods, they looked for the enemy but found none, except a trembling corporal from the picket line. He begged to see the commanding officer. Facing the stern-faced Kargé, the corporal explained that he told his men to shoot a litter of young pigs that passed near their outpost. He thought the pigs would make a succulent addition to their rations. The apologetic soldier belonged to a fresh regiment of "nine-month" troops, all of whom, from the colonel down to the corporal, were ignorant of military duties. Therefore he did not perceive the significance of his action to disciplined troops, who interpret such firing as an indication of the presence of the enemy. He realized that the firing may have been improper only after the bugles had sounded and noticed the commotion in the regiment's bivouac area.

The New Jersey troopers were upset to have had their sleep interrupted by a handful of New York militiamen bent on improving their army menu, but Kargé was furious. As Pyne described the scene: "All the rich stores of a vocabulary acquired in the Prussian Life Guards were exhausted without apparent relief to his feelings." Expecting to get the impact of the colonel's boot, the unhappy corporal fled into the darkness, as the amused officers broke out into hearty laughter. The infuriated commander relaxed and said quietly, "The scoundrel did not even bring the pigs as an atonement."[30]

In the morning the brigade marched to Chantilly, where Bayard set up a regular camp from which to conduct reconnaissance sweeps. His mission: Scout the movements of General Lee's army, then in process of changing its base from Maryland to the Rappahannock River. Bayard immediately set out on a reconnaissance toward Winchester, and before daylight 30 October the brigade marched on the road to Aldie Gap. Reaching this point, Bayard held the First Pennsylvania and the Tenth New York Cavalry regiments to guard the pass and directed Kargé to continue west to Ashby's Gap with the First New Jersey and the Second New York, and two pieces of artillery. Kargé's command passed through Middleburg without opposition and continued toward Upperville, eight miles away, where General Longstreet's corps was thought to be. Encountering rebel pickets, Kargé charged them, taking several prisoners and dispersing the rest. In Upperville he met a force of enemy cavalry, which he drove out of town and pursued for about a mile and a half. With the approach of darkness, however, he fell back to Aldie for the night.[31]

The following day, 31 October, Kargé reconnoitered through Thoroughfare Gap via Middleburg and back again without seeing the enemy. On the Snickersville pike, three miles from Aldie, he made contact with Union pickets from the Army of the Potomac. Kargé instructed Captain Kester to patrol the Snickersville road with his company, and Captain Lucas to patrol the Middleburg road. These roads join at Aldie. With his security established, Kargé encamped the remainder of his brigade about a quarter of a mile east of the Gap. He took advantage of the lull to order up the brigade forges and put the farriers to work, tightening or replacing the horses' shoes. It was an automatic response, because Kargé understood the need to maintain his horses in the best possible condition. As the saying goes: "An army marches on its stomach but cavalry marches on its horses' feet."[32]

The peaceful camp scene changed abruptly when a party of First Rhode Island cavalrymen came galloping through the pass, yelling to the New Jersey troopers to mount and follow. The riders did not stop but shouted out that an overwhelming force of Jeb Stuart's cavalry had charged down the Snickersville turnpike and captured all of General George Stoneman's pickets but themselves. While the fleeing Rhode Islanders dashed on, the New Jersey troopers mounted their horses and galloped to engage Stuart's cavalry, for Kargé knew that the crossroads at Aldie had to be held to prevent Captain Lucas's company on the Middleburg road from being cut off. Meanwhile, Captain Kester's pickets were the first to challenge the charging rebels. Assembling his men in the Aldie village street, Kester waited for the Confederates. When the approaching rebels saw the determined band of Union cavalry, they slowed down somewhat but continued to advance. When they reached carbine range, Kester's men fired a telling volley; then, with drawn sabers and loud cheers, they charged the startled Southerners, who about-faced and galloped away.

Close behind Kester's company came the rest of the First New Jersey, eagerly joining the pursuit. Suddenly, the drama of the situation became heightened when a fresh rebel column emerged from around a bend in the road and charged to meet the New Jersey attack. The two columns of galloping horsemen approached each other on a collision course. But just when the shock seemed inevitable, the head of the enemy regiment broke and turned. Again it was a pursuit of the rebels, but not for long. An enemy squadron unexpectedly appeared on the flank and brought down New Jersey men and horses with deadly fire. Now the New Jersey regiment turned to escape the fire and deploy for a fight. The last man in the retreat, Captain Henry Sawyer, was hit by a bullet in the loins but managed to stay on his horse. Two or three other troopers had their horses shot from under them, and they were captured.

Kargé stabilized the situation when he galloped up with the Second New York Regiment. At the sight of the reinforcements, the rebels broke off the fight and pulled back. Kargé occupied a hill beyond the town with two regiments and two pieces of artillery. The rebels, also in possession of artillery, opened up to start a duel. The rebel units were the Third, Fourth, and Ninth Virginia Cavalry Regiments, supported by a battery of four guns, all under the command of Jeb Stuart.[33]

Thus far the engagement remained a stand-off between Stuart and Bayard. Pyne said that there was "a fair opportunity of testing the ability of the famous rebel under circumstances favorable to him." However, each time the Confederates formed to charge the New Jersey skirmish line, the Yankees dissuaded them with heavy carbine fire. Kargé, meanwhile, sought to attack Stuart. Placing Captain Lucas's company in position to threaten the rebel right flank, Kargé ordered a squadron of the Second New York to approach the enemy from the left flank along a screened road. The New York unit reached its position, but for some unknown reason the squadron commander failed to press the attack. In the meantime the artillery duel continued harmlessly all afternoon. "The first signs of approaching night," Pyne said, "were gladly welcomed by both parties as an excuse for a dignified retirement.[34]

General Bayard said that he withdrew deliberately to get behind the roads that led from the direction of Haymarket, Gainesville, Centreville, and White Plains. These roads exposed his left flank to attack and he had been compelled to picket them in force. General Stuart, on the other hand, explained that information of the advance of federal troops from the direction of Mountville deterred him from further action. He feared an attack from Mountville, since it lay to his rear. Stuart retired just at dark to a bivouac area a few miles west of Middleburg, learning subsequently that the reported federal advance from Mountville was false. Stuart had planned to make a reconnaissance in force of the entire

Piedmont region of Virginia, to interfere with any advance of the Army of the Potomac. At the same time he sought to cover General Lee's lines of withdrawal to the Rappahannock area. The engagement at Aldie, however, thwarted him and endangered his own retreat. On Sunday, 2 November 1862, General Alfred Pleasonton caught Stuart at a disadvantage at Union and forced him to retreat through Ashby's Gap to the protection of his own infantry.[35]

Kargé's continual scouting and skirmishing in the area of the Blue Ridge Mountains during the month of October 1862 was part of the cavalry operations that preceded the movement of the Union and Confederate armies to the Rappahannock River line. The Union cavalry scored most of the successes.[36] On 3 November 1862 Bayard's Cavalry Brigade joined the Army of the Potomac near Upperville, as the Army moved south to Warrenton.[37] The First New Jersey, assigned the task of protecting the long line of supply wagons, was attached temporarily to Army headquarters. Kargé, however, displaced with Bayard to the Rappahannock and took command of a force of six-hundred cavalry near Freeman's Ford.[38] Meanwhile, Beaumont commanded the First New Jersey in carrying out the mission of guarding the wagon trains. The men rode constantly, and, although they performed their duties well, they felt let down with a rear-area mission. As one of them complained: "It seems strange for our Regiment to be in the rear, for hitherto we have always occupied the extreme advance." He said the rebels call them the "Jersey Cut-throats" and "Jersey Dare Devils," and he took pride in the hard-won reputation. "Our regiment is spoken of by them," he wrote, "just as the famous Ashby's Cavalry was spoken of by us." Even though the Confederate opposition usually outnumbered the regiment, it gallantly carried out its missions. "At this moment, 400 rebel Cavalry are close at hand," he wrote, "and we are compelled to keep constantly saddled, for our nearest support is several miles distant, and we number but 250."[39]

General Pleasonton reinforced the New Jersey trooper's feelings when he defended the gallantry of Union cavalry in his official report of 17 November 1862. The general admitted that no one was more painfully conscious than he of the prevalent opinion that Union cavalry has been deficient in its duty. Wherever there existed a foundation for such an opinion, Pleasonton stressed that the fault did not rest with the cavalry. He wrote that the "rebels have always had more cavalry in the field than we, and whenever we have fought them their numbers were two to three to one of ours.'' Such a difference showed up in the hard riding the horses had to perform. Good horses were broken down by it; inferior ones were literally thrown away in such service. ''The rebel cavalry are mounted on the best horses in the South,'' Pleasonton continued, ''while our cavalry are furnished a very inferior animal, bought by contract, and which is totally unfit for efficient service.''[40]

The assignment of Bayard's brigade to the Army of the Potomac pleased the young general. On 4 November 1862 he issued a letter-order to his command, opening with an exuberant salutation: ''Soldiers! Our aspirations are now gratified. We are in the Army of the Potomac!'' He told his men: ''I will lead you to the front where I hope you will do no less than the other Brigades of Cavalry.'' He warned them that anyone failing to perform his duty would be ''*marked*,'' for Bayard said that he would frankly state the failure ''to the General.'' Attempting to inspire them, he said: ''Those who honor themselves and the Cause they serve shall be mentioned in orders to the Head Quarters of the Army.'' The letter-order was issued ''by order Brig. Gen'l Bayard, Commanding Brigade'' and signed by the general's aide-de-camp, Captain W. Leski.[41]

If Bayard expected to serve under McClellan, he would be disappointed. Four days after his brigade joined the Army of the Potomac, President Lincoln replaced McClellan with Major General Ambrose E. Burnside. The new commander, who did not relish such vast responsibility, nevertheless developed a plan to march on Richmond from the vicinity of Fredericksburg. In preparation for this campaign, Burnside reorganized the army into three ''Grand Divisions,'' each consisting of two corps and a cavalry division or brigade. Bayard's brigade became the cavalry force of the Left Grand Division, commanded by Major General William B. Franklin.[42]

Military operations now shifted eastward to the lower Potomac. The First New Jersey, relieved of its security detail, moved to Falmouth and encamped at Brooke's Station on the Acquia Railroad, where it engaged in picket duty from Stafford Court House to the Potomac river. Bayard interrupted the routine picket duty on 20 November 1862, when he ordered the First New Jersey Cavalry, augmented by the Second New York Cavalry, on a raid into King George County. The Confederate government had accumulated supplies of corn and wheat in that county and kept transporting these provisions across the Rappahannock river below Fredericksburg. Kargé's troopers were told to stop this movement. Penetrating the county quickly, Kargé placed security details at Leedstown and Port Royal ferry and encamped the main body near the King George court house. He took some prisoners, but the real booty consisted of fifteen-hundred bushels of corn and wheat, collected on the east bank of the Rappahannock near Port Conway. On the opposite shore at Port Royal long lines of wagon teams, guarded by some 150 rebel cavalrymen, waited to transport the grain to Richmond. Kargé immediately took them under fire with his ten pieces of "flying artillery." He dropped two shells among the rebels before they knew of the attack. A correspondent reported that "such a skedaddling on a small scale has not been witnessed during the war . . . to the infinite amusement of our men." The federal cavalrymen found the planters friendly, and they noted a feeling of war weariness among the citizens.[43]

Just as the First New Jersey had penetrated Confederate-held territory so, too, the enemy conducted operations behind Federal lines. At Dumfries on 2 December 1862 a New Jersey outpost suffered a humiliating surprise, resulting in the loss of several men and the temporary abandonment of the outpost. The Confederate attack involved Second Lieutenant Jacob H. Hoffman and a party of fourteen troopers of Company F. Captain Lucas had placed them on the outpost that formed part of the rear security for the Army of the Potomac. Hoffman quit his post, and during his absence the rebels attacked the mounted sentries from the front and rear. Completely taken by surprise, the New Jersey troopers were unable to fire a shot in defense.

Kargé's anger over the incident brought out some down-to-earth language in his report. He said that Hoffman had posted his sentries indifferently and allowed them to lay aside their arms. Then the lieutenant left his post about 6 P.M. "according to the custom of many of our patriotic officers, to provide for his belly in a neighboring house, leaving his command to the care of Providence." The housekeeper was a young and attractive female whose husband served as captain in the Confederate army. One of the Jersey outpost sentries saw her return to her house on horseback about 4 P.M., the time Lucas posted the reliefs. It was clear to Kargé that the attack resulted from a premeditated plan, coupled with the negligence of Hoffman. The attackers captured six men, but eight managed to escape. "Among the former," Kargé wrote, "is the worthy lieutenant, who certainly has not neglected his duty as a gallant man, so far as the fair sex is concerned."

Kargé's sarcasm revealed his dismay and embarrassment over the incompetence of an element of his command. In addition to the six prisoners, the losses included sixteen horses, fifteen sabers, fourteen pistols, and thirteen carbines. Because his orders and instructions for pickets were strict and explicit, Kargé charged the troopers the cost of the lost equipment. Bayard approved this action and, in addition, asked that Lieutenant Hoffman be dismissed from the service. General Franklin concurred and forwarded the reports to Army headquarters, with the recommendation that Hoffman be dishonorably discharged from the service of the United States. Kargé's frank report, however, had irritated the prim Franklin enough to comment in his endorsement that "the style and matter of this report show that Colonel Kargé himself is entirely unacquainted with his duty, so far as the duty of making reports of criminal neglect on the part of his subordinate officers is concerned . . . ."[44]

The period of late fall of 1862 seems to have been a difficult time for Kargé. The weather had turned damp and cold, and his leg wound caused him a great deal of pain. He had returned to the regiment on 23 September, when the battle wound was not fully healed. And then the following two months were filled with day upon day of hard riding and skirmishing with the enemy. As a consequence, the aggravated injury caused him sleepless nights. During the day he could barely stay in the saddle. He experienced not only physical pain but also the frustration of not being able to perform his duties completely as commander. To obtain proper medical treatment, he asked Bayard for a leave of absence of twenty days. Regimental Surgeon William Phillips, having examined Kargé, certified his disability and the need to treat the wound in a more suitable environment. Kargé felt so strongly about the urgency for a leave of absence that he offered his immediate and unconditional resignation in the event his request were denied. Bayard recommended approval, noting that "Col. Kargé joined his Regiment on my earnest prayers that he would do so, but as it appears too soon for his own health, I sincerely trust that this leave will be granted." General Franklin approved the request on 2 December but stated that he could not grant the leave because of the "informality" of the surgeon's certificate! He forwarded the paperwork to the War Department.[45] Meanwhile, Kargé prepared the regiment for the upcoming battle.

General Burnside waited anxiously as his engineers brought up pontoons for the bridging of the Rappahannock. Finally, on the night of 10 December, the advance began and the battle of Fredericksburg commenced.[46] General Franklin crossed his Left Grand Division below the town on December 12, leading with William F. Smith's corps, followed by Bayard's cavalry, with John Reynold's corps last. Bayard marched the brigade to the front immediately for a reconnaissance of the enemy's positions and strength, passing on this information to Franklin. The next morning Bayard held his regiments in readiness for any mission he might be called on to perform, but finding little to do he left about 2 P.M. for Franklin's headquarters. He met Franklin with staff officers and a few generals near the river in a grove of trees behind the Bernard Mansion.[47] Dismounting, he sat down to rest at the base of a tree. Since rebel artillery had the grove under intermittent attack, a fellow officer cautioned him about his needless exposure. Bayard politely declined to move and conversed with those around him. In a little while he stood up, and at that moment a shell struck him below the hip and shattered his thigh near the joint. Several officers carried him to the Bernard house, serving as a temporary hospital, where doctors administered morphine to ease the pain. When he regained consciousness, he asked about his chances of recovery. "There is a chance, General," a surgeon said, "if you survive the shock of amputation." Bayard replied that he could not live with his leg gone and declined the operation. He dictated his last will and several letters, including one to his fiancée; and he personally signed the correspondence. Gradually losing strength, he died some twenty-four hours after being struck by the shell.

Bayard's unexpected death occurred four days short of his twenty-seventh birthday, 18 December, the date arranged for his marriage. Bayard had set the wedding date before he knew of General Burnside's plans for Fredericksburg, and he had obtained a leave of absence for this purpose. But, on learning of the coming battle, he decided to remain with his brigade and lead it in the fighting. Ironically, he was buried on the day of his planned marriage.[48]

The First New Jersey Cavalry, as well as the entire cavalry brigade, received the news of Bayard's death with shock and disbelief. "Every officer and man in the brigade felt that he had lost a personal friend, and the mourning of the troopers was sincere and enduring," Pyne said.[49] To Kargé, the untimely death of George D. Bayard was a great personal loss. From months of rugged campaigning, Kargé had developed a strong affection and respect for his commander. The two had also established a smooth operational relationship. Bayard understood Kargé, trusted him, and valued his dedication and professional ability.

He frequently singled out Kargé for praise in official reports. His long report of 13 October 1862, covering the summer operations along the Rapidan and Rappahannock rivers, is especially noteworthy. Bayard wrote his corps commander, Major General Irvin McDowell:

> It is natural in closing a report of this character, covering the length of time that this does and including the number of actions and skirmishes it does, that I should have many men to point out as distinguished for their gallantry and good behavior. Lieutenant Colonel Kargé I would particularly name as always ready and valiant, and I would particularly ask that the general would notice him.[50]

Bayard's death created an immense void in Kargé's life, adding uncertainty to his future. He was disabled by his old wound, which had reopened and threatened the loss of his leg. Having received no response to his request for leave,* he resigned his commission on 22 December 1862 and returned to his family in Belleville, New Jersey. Thus the first part of Joseph Kargé's Civil War service ended on a note of personal disappointment. Yet he carried away the hard-won respect and affection of the First New Jersey Cavalry Regiment. Beaumont, who assumed command of the unit, issued Regimental Order No. 305 on 27 December 1862, renaming the encampment for a period of seven days from Camp Bayard to "Camp Kargé."[51]

*The War Department granted the leave 5 January 1863.

Return to Action

Colonel Joseph Kargé Organizes the Second New Jersey Cavalry
Regiment

The year 1863 turned decisive in the Civil War. The twin Union
victories at Gettysburg and Vicksburg signaled the eventual defeat of
the Confederacy. The year also became one of decision for Kargé,
although hometown activities in the opening month seemed likely to
confirm his retirement from combat. On 15 January a number of prominent citizens of Belleville held a dinner "to testify their appreciation
for the gallant services of their fellow citizen, Colonel Kargé." The
testimonial took place at the Mansion House, with a round of toasts
and the reading of letters of congratulations. The brief speech by the
guest of honor reveals a man dedicated to the overthrow of slavery.[1]

Although Kargé appreciated the friendly gesture of his townsmen,
he was too restless to stay away from the fighting while the war
continued to inflame the nation. By March of 1863 Kargé's leg wound
had healed, and he felt ready for the field again. This time he wanted to
return to action with his own unit of cavalry, and he got the backing of
many distinguished citizens of the state. In addition, he received letters
of support from Generals Heintzelman, McDowell, and Sigel. "I have
always found you untiring in organizing and disciplining your Regiment," Heintzelman wrote, "energetic and faithful, and possessed of
those true qualities of an officer, which both our Army and Country
may justly feel proud to engage."[2]

The *Newark Daily Advertiser* reported 10 March 1863 that Colonel
Joseph Kargé "has tendered his services again to the government. He
will probably be appointed a Brigadier General." Kargé asked New
Jersey Governor Joel Parker for authority to recruit and train a cavalry
regiment, and the governor gave his approval. In May former Governor Charles S. Olden and several state officials petitioned the War
Department that it authorize the raising of a regiment of New Jersey
cavalry to be called "2d Regiment" and to be commanded by Joseph

Kargé. President Lincoln personally signed and endorsed this petition on 12 June 1863, with a request that the General-in-Chief and the Secretary of War consider it at once.[3]

Suddenly the Confederate invasion of the North propelled Kargé into the center of hectic defense preparations. By 17 June 1863, the Confederate Cavalry Brigade of Brigadier General Micah Jenkins occupied Chambersburg, Pennsylvania. The main Confederate forces, still in Maryland, marched rapidly for Pennsylvania, and the greatest possible excitement now seized the North.[4] Pennsylvania Governor Andrew G. Curtin called upon New Jersey and other states to rush militia units to the defense of the invaded state. Governor Parker responded immediately with a proclamation on 17 June calling upon all citizens to act "with unprecedented zeal . . . to meet and organize into companies, and report to the Adjutant General of the State, as soon as possible, to be organized into Regiments as the Militia of New Jersey . . . ." Simultaneously, the Adjutant General's office issued General Orders No. 2 in support of the proclamation and calling for a sufficient number of volunteers to form ten regiments of infantry and two of cavalry.[5]

The next day, 18 June, Parker appointed Joseph Kargé the Chief of Cavalry, New Jersey Militia, with the rank of colonel. Newspapers published Kargé's military notice that he was "authorized to recruit and organize two Regiments of Cavalry, to serve for thirty days, unless sooner discharged, to aid in repelling an invasion of the State of Pennsylvania." Companies wishing to offer their services were instructed to report to Kargé's headquarters* at the Adjutant General's office in Trenton. Notwithstanding the preparations to repel General Lee's invasion, Kargé also moved ahead with plans to organize a cavalry regiment for federal service. He placed notices in New Jersey newspapers to promote recruiting of individuals for a "Regiment of Cavalry for the United States service, to serve for the term of three years, unless sooner discharged."[6]

By the end of June the situation in Pennsylvania became somewhat stabilized. The Army of the Potomac, under its newly appointed commander, George Gordon Meade, marched rapidly to oppose the rebels. Lee now gathered his scattered forces to Cashtown, recalling also Jenkins's cavalry brigade from near the capital city of Harrisburg.[7] The

---

*Historically, Kargé's headquarters, built in 1757, had served for a time in the American Revolution as the headquarters of General Casimir Pulaski's Cavalry.

[MILITARY NOTICE.]

——

TRENTON, N. J., June 18, 1863.

By order of his Excellency the Governor of this State, I am authorized to recruit and organize two Regiments of Cavalry, to be mustered into the service of the State of New Jersey, to serve for thirty days, unless sooner discharged, to aid in repelling an invasion of the State of Pennsylvania.

Companies wishing to offer their services will report at my headquarters at the Adjutant General's Office in Trenton.　　　JOSEPH KARGE,
je 19 d1w　　　　　Chief of Cavalry, N. J. M.

The *Daily State Gazette and Republican* of Trenton published Colonel Joseph Kargé's Military Notice on 23 June 1863, following Kargé's appointment as Chief of Cavalry, New Jersey Militia. This same notice appeared in the *Newark Daily Advertiser* on 19 June 1863. COURTESY OF LIBRARY OF CONGRESS.

CAVALRY,

TRENTON, N. J., June 23, 1863.

His Excellency, the Governor of this State, has issued authority to me to raise one Regiment of Cavalry for the United States service, to serve for the term of three years, unless sooner discharged

Persons wishing authority to recruit for said regiment, will apply to me forthwith, in person, at the Adjutant General's Office, in Trenton.
　　　　　JOSEPH KARGE,
jn24d&wtf　　　　　Colonel.

The *Daily State Gazette and Republican* of Trenton first published Colonel Kargé's Cavalry notice on 24 June 1863. The newspaper continued to print this notice almost daily during the recruiting period of 24 June–3 September 1863. COURTESY OF LIBRARY OF CONGRESS.

unopposed movements of the Confederates through the Pennsylvania countryside had greatly alarmed the citizens. However, the near panic that had gripped the Middle Atlantic area began to subside. The danger was by no means over, but a calmer resolve set in. Although Parker had ordered some New Jersey militia to Pennsylvania, he now recalled them. The *Daily State Gazette and Republican* took issue with the publicly stated reason that "their services are no longer needed." The paper gave credence to a rumor of some disagreement between the governors.[8]

By 3 July the Trenton newspaper dropped Kargé's "Military Notice" for two short-term cavalry regiments but published the "Cavalry Notice" for the three-year regiment on the front page. The need for militia to repel the rebel invasion evaporated when Lee met defeat at Gettysburg 1-3 July. Resuming normal recruiting activities, the New Jersey Adjutant General on 11 July issued General Order No. 4, calling for volunteers into the federal service for a term of three years. The order announced the formation of only five regiments of infantry and one of cavalry. The Adjutant General assigned Colonel Kargé the responsibility for recruiting the cavalry regiment.[9]

With Kargé's headquarters in Trenton, the capital city became the focal point of his recruiting and training efforts. Kargé opened a recruiting office over Barwis's Clothing Store on State Street above Greene and appointed Alexander A. Yard second lieutenant and recruiting officer. Yard advertised for "able bodied men, returned volunteers, and patriots generally" for Company I, declaring it "the best way honestly to avoid the draft." Kargé expanded the organizing effort over the state and established twelve stations, each under a regimental officer enlisting for a designated company. These local offices were set up in Jersey City, Newark, Morristown, New Brunswick, Asbury, Princeton, Trenton, Bordentown, Burlington, Camden, Salem, and Burrsville.[10]

Kargé looked for qualified men with military experience for his company commanders. Thus, in Jersey City, Captain Michael Gallagher signed up volunteers for his company. He had earned a reputation as a fighter with the Eighty-eighth New York Volunteers. In the Battle of Chancellorsville 1-4 May 1863, Gallagher survived with only four men in his unit.[11] This brave officer would give his life in the gallant action of the Second New Jersey Cavalry Regiment at Egypt Station, Mississippi, in December 1864. The *Newark Daily Adver-*

tiser, commenting on Kargé's search for none but qualified officers, said: "Colonel Kargé is too careful of his reputation to surround himself in such an undertaking by any but officers of the highest standing." Continuing, the newspaper said: "The names of those already on its rolls are an assurance that the new regiment will be one to which it will be an honor to belong." [12]

Approximately one hundred men were needed for each company, and twelve companies made up a cavalry regiment. The organization of each company consisted of a captain, first lieutenant, second lieutenant, first sergeant, quartermaster sergeant, commissary sergeant, five sergeants, eight corporals, two trumpeters, two blacksmiths, one saddler, one wagoner, and between a minimum of sixty privates and a maximum of seventy-eight privates. To fill these units with volunteers, the federal and state governments offered substantial bounties. The federal government gave one hundred dollars to new enlistees and four hundred dollars to veterans. The State paid an extra two dollars a month to a single man, while the families of married men and widowed mothers of single men dependent on them for support received six dollars a month, in addition to the monthly pay from the federal government. Privates got the lowest pay, thirteen dollars per month. [13]

Horses had to be procured early so that cavalry training could begin without delay. The horse has been called a "cavalryman's companion and friend, upon whom his life may depend—his second self." [14] Lewis Perrine, the State's Quartermaster General, advertised for 1,000 horses for the Second New Jersey Cavalry. "They must be sound in all particulars," Perrine specified, "from 15 to 16 hands high, not less than 4 nor more than 11 years old, color to be bays, browns, blacks, or sorrels, good square trotters, bridlewise, and of size and strength sufficient for the purpose above named." The *State Gazette* reported a week later that some 150 horses already were on hand. Purchasing agents bought horses on contract, paying from $119 to $150 per horse. [15]

The men of the Second New Jersey were quartered first at Camp Perrine, located in the city. Kargé found the site unsatisfactory from a military viewpoint. The soldiers had little opportunity to perform camp duties or to become accustomed to field conditions. Officers found it difficult to maintain order and discipline. Consequently, Kargé looked for and found a better location for a training area, approximately two miles north of Trenton, between the Canal and Assunpink Creek, and on 8 August the troopers marched to the new site. In short order Kargé established the camp and named it Camp Parker in honor of the governor. The men lived in A-tents, which were laid out with regularity. The construction of stables began almost immediately. The adjoining drill ground contained a sizable forty acres. The water supply was abundant for both culinary and bathing purposes, thereby contributing to the comfort and health of the men. Camp Parker became a model of order and neatness. Meanwhile volunteers arrived daily in Trenton, prompting the *State Gazette* to say: "Too much praise cannot be bestowed upon Col. Kargé for the untiring zeal and energetic manner in which he has pushed forward recruiting for the regiment, and the discipline to which he has already brought his men . . . ." This newspaper continued to report the progress of recruitment. On 26 August it said the regiment now numbered about seven hundred men. Three days later it said: "Three companies for Col. Kargé's Cavalry Regiment are being recruited in this county [Mercer]." And in Trenton, Captain H. C. Paxson, recruiting with Lieutenant Yard, reported that his company exceeded the minimum number and continued to gain. Captains William V. Scudder and Edward P. Mount each had approximately sixty men in their companies.[16]

The regiment gained volunteers steadily, notwithstanding the growing opposition to the draft, particularly in the East, which surfaced in a number of draft riots in the summer of 1863. Nonetheless Kargé experienced his share of problems, especially with bounty jumpers. These were unscrupulous men who enlisted, collected the bounty, deserted, and then repeated the cycle until caught. Kargé used stern measures against deserters when they were apprehended; more important, he tried to discourage bounty jumpers from enlisting in his regiment. On one occasion he ordered a deserter paraded under mounted guard through the principal streets of Trenton. The culprit carried a placard on his back that read in large letters, "Perjurer, Thief and Deserter." This individual, however, walked along unconcerned, as if disgraceful punishment were not unusual. Kargé habitually punished attempted desertion by court martial.[17]

On another occasion two of Kargé's sergeants were confronted by civilians over the apprehension of a deserter. Kargé had instructed the sergeants to pick up the man at the town arsenal and to escort him to camp. Taking the soldier into custody, the sergeants marched him some distance when a crowd of men tried to free the prisoner. They rushed the guards, pulled one from his horse, disarmed and beat him. The other sergeant, meanwhile, put spurs to his horse and rode quickly to headquarters for Kargé. The colonel galloped to the scene. He retook the deserter and obtained the release of the sergeant and his arms. He then ordered a full squadron of cavalry to march the deserter along Broad Street. No one tried to interfere.[18]

Kargé also took other measures to discourage desertion. He posted a strong guard and a patrol of the most reliable men around the camp. The officers, too, looked for signs and information indicative of potential desertion. Several times they were able to frustrate attempted desertions, but some scoundrels got away. One evening nine men who had collected their bounties dashed past a sentry and disappeared into the bushes. Although the guard fired on them, the deserters made good their escape in the darkness. The next day two of the bounty jumpers were caught in Trenton. In reporting on the desertion problem of the regiment, the *State Gazette* noted that the "great body of soldiers are true men, and it is only the worthless portion of them who cause any trouble."[19]

One trooper complained that quite a few New York City rowdies deserted after they had been paid their enlistment money by officials of Hoboken and Jersey City. He said a number of them were captured and "mercy shown them by shaving their heads, eyebrows, whiskers and mustaches." He said he wished he had the authority to shoot "the cowardly, thieving poltroons."[20] Some unscrupulous individuals ran a business of helping soldiers to desert. One Sunday Kargé caught such a rascal in Camp Parker. The man carried a substantial amount of civilian clothing for would-be deserters. Kargé's action against the individual is not known, but the *State Gazette* declared that such men "will be made an example of."[21]

Another problem arose when Kargé discovered that some civilians supplied soldiers with liquor. The whiskey peddlers came up in boats along Assunpink Creek to the vicinity of the camp; by prearrangement, a recruit would make an excuse to go to the creek for the alcohol. Determined to stop this practice at the source, Kargé laid a trap for the peddlers and soon caught one of them in the act. He seized the man and confiscated his liquor and the money obtained from the soldiers. He had the individual tied to the flagpole in full view of the troopers. After an hour or two, Kargé ordered the man's head shaved and beard cut off, and then ran the scoundrel out of camp. He threatened to deal even more severely with the next offender.[22]

Kargé's brand of instant punishment probably reflected the mood of the nation in 1863. There was no time to engage in formalities. The war to preserve the Union had taken on a new meaning, becoming a war of survival. General Lee's invasion of Pennsylvania had demonstrated this change. Therefore Kargé devoted himself to the task of organizing and training a cavalry regiment in the shortest time.

With the strength of the regiment increasing daily, the number of visitors to Camp Parker rose also. Kargé welcomed the visits of family members, friends, and patriotic citizens. But, wishing to exclude the shady characters and troublemakers, he set up a system of entry by pass. Citing Kargé's desire to eliminate unwelcome prowlers, newspaper editors cooperated by repeatedly publishing his notice. Kargé asked all visitors to report first to the camp commander, Captain Marcus L. W. Kitchen, who was assisted by the Adjutant, J. Lacey Pierson. Those individuals with legitimate reasons were allowed to enter.[23]

By 11 September the regiment exceeded eight hundred men. Approximately four hundred more would bring the strength up to complement. In a report to General Robert F. Stockton, Jr., the State Adjutant General, Kargé said that ten companies were now mustered in, and he expected the remaining two companies to reach recruiting goals in a few days. The build-up took place by company units so that training could begin for a complete unit. Kargé advised Stockton against moving the regiment piecemeal to Washington, as being disruptive of good discipline and training. He said he also wished to complete the mounting of the regiment in New Jersey, where horses of a superior quality could be procured.[24] Almost six hundred horses had been purchased thus far, and Quartermaster General Perrine closely inspected the animals for fitness. All horses were judged to be suitable for active service of any character, and Perrine continued the procurement for an additional six hundred horses.[25] Meanwhile, two more weeks of recruiting brought the regiment up to strength. Finally, on 25 September 1863, the Field and Staff of the regiment stood a muster ceremony, conducted by First Lieutenant Joseph P. Asch, Fifth United States Cavalry. The total regimental strength was 44 officers and 1,105 noncommissioned officers and privates.[26]

In the process of recruiting and organizing his regiment, Kargé became the unexpected recipient of an action of Secretary of State,

Department of State
Washington, July 6ᵗʰ 1863

To His Excellency
    Richard Yates,
        Governor of Illinois —

Governor,
        Two Prussian Officers Messrs Von Parmentz
And Von Rudolphe, who were recommended by
the American Legation at Berlin to the United
States Government and to the Prussian Legation here, by the Secretary of State in Berlin
Are desirous to offer their services to the Army
in the West
                At the request of the Baron Von
Gerolt, the Prussian Minister, I beg leave to
present them to Your Excellency and to recommend their applications to your favorable
Consideration
                                Wm H. Seward —

Letter of Secretary of State to Governor of Illinois, 6 July 1863. COURTESY OF
STATE LIBRARY OF NEW JERSEY, TRENTON.

William H. Seward. This diplomatic touch involved two Prussian officers, Erich von Pannwitz and Julius von Rudolphi, who wished to serve in the Union army. The American Legation at Berlin and the Prussian Minister in Washington, Baron Von Gerolt, recommended Von Pannwitz and Von Rudolphi to the United States government. The two Prussians had expressed a desire for combat action in the Western theater. Accordingly, Seward wrote Illinois Governor Richard Yates on 6 July 1863, recommending favorable consideration of their applications. The fortunes of war intervened, and the two volunteers found themselves in Kargé's regiment the following month. They were mustered into the Second New Jersey Cavalry on 26 August 1863, for a period of three years.[27]

The assignment of Von Pannwitz and Von Rudolphi to the Second New Jersey Cavalry was logical. Kargé spoke fluent German and, as a former Prussian officer, knew the military philosophy of that army. Then, too, the War Department had earmarked the Second New Jersey for the Western theater of operations, thus meeting the two officers' choice of combat zones. Kargé gave Von Pannwitz the command of Company L and recommended him for a captaincy. Von Rudolphi became First Lieutenant and second-in-command of the same company. Kargé thoughtfully assigned Second Lieutenant Sigismund von Braida to Company L. When Von Braida resigned in March 1865, Kargé filled the vacancy with Mortimer von Strautz. Company L could indeed be styled Kargé's "Prussian unit."[28]

The key officers of the regiment were veterans. Kargé selected Captain Marcus L. W. Kitchen to be the regimental executive officer and second-in-command. Kitchen was promoted to the rank of lieutenant colonel. Kargé and Kitchen had served together in the First New Jersey Cavalry, where Kitchen was the adjutant initially and then the commanding officer of Company A. The next senior officers were the three majors who commanded the three battalions composed of four companies each. The ranking major was Frederick B. Revere, formerly with the Fourth New York Cavalry Regiment, in which he commanded Company E. The second ranking major, P. Jones Yorke, had earned a fighting reputation in the First New Jersey Cavalry. This young officer would enhance his gallant name in the service of the Second New Jersey. Peter D. Vroom, Jr., the junior major, had served as adjutant of the First Regiment of New Jersey Infantry. Both Yorke and Vroom would do well on the battlefield and become brevet colonels at the end of the war.[29]

The regiment gained a highly qualified surgeon in the person of Ferdinand V. Dayton, former assistant surgeon of the First New Jersey Cavalry. He would watch over the health of the men throughout the active life of the regiment and, for this dedicated service, be brevetted lieutenant colonel prior to his discharge on 24 October 1865.[30] For the position of quartermaster officer, Kargé selected his brother-in-law, James M. Baldwin, who joined the staff on 25 September 1863, the day the Field and Staff were mustered in at Camp Parker. Baldwin would serve the regiment with devotion, being among the very last to be mustered out of the service, 1 November 1865.[31] The chaplain, Edwin N. Andrews, joined the regiment at Eastport, Mississippi, on 6 December 1863. While on duty at Memphis, Tennessee, he wrote a memorable "Chaplain's Address," set to rhyme and dedicated to the soldiers of the First Brigade, Second Division, Cavalry Corps. At the time, July 1864, Kargé commanded the First Brigade, composed of the Second New Jersey, Nineteenth Pennsylvania, Fourth Missouri, Seventh Indiana, and First Mississippi (Union) Cavalry Regiments. Unfortunately, sickness plagued the thirty-two-year-old chaplain, and he remained with the unit for only fourteen months. Taking the advice of the surgeon, Andrews resigned his appointment on 21 January 1865.[32]

One more member of the Second New Jersey should be mentioned: Jacob H. Hoffman, the lieutenant who had outraged Kargé for dereliction of duty in the First New Jersey Cavalry and then been dismissed from the army. Hoffman enlisted in the Second New Jersey Cavalry on 1 September 1863. Undoubtedly surprised to see Hoffman again, Kargé gave him a chance to make good, and the repentant soldier did not disappoint the colonel. After serving as sergeant in Company M for almost a year, in July 1864 Hoffman received a commission of second lieutenant to fill a vacancy in Company B. By the end of the year, he was promoted to first lieutenant and returned to Company M.[33]

Prior to the regiment's departure for the war zone, Kargé held a review for the governor. A newspaper reported that on 28 September Camp Parker presented a brilliant scene as guests arrived in carriages and by horse. Among the distinguished individuals were Commodore Robert F. Stockton, Quartermaster General Lewis Perrine, Adjutant General Robert F. Stockton, Jr., and General George M. Robeson. The presence of many ladies "gave additional pleasure and animation to the occasion." By 10 A.M. the entire regiment had assembled under arms on the parade ground. The troopers and horses put on a creditable appearance for the visitors. Prior to the review the companies performed various movements with a degree of precision that evoked favorable comments despite the short time the regiment had been trained.

Governor Joel Parker and his party arrived at 11:00 A.M. They made a quick circuit of the parade ground, observing the appearance and condition of the men and horses. The regiment then passed in review in the order of its squadrons, two companies per squadron. As each company rode past the governor, he gracefully saluted their colors. By 11:45 the review ended, and Kargé invited the governor and guests to inspect his little city of tents and stables. Everything looked neat and clean, and Camp Parker appeared to be a pleasant military home. Following the inspection the officers of the regiment held a reception for the governor, his staff, and the guests. "The occasion, altogether, was a very pleasant one, long to be remembered by the guests as well as by their gallant hosts," the Trenton newspaper said.[34]

The next morning the Second New Jersey Cavalry marched along Warren and West State streets. The *Daily State Gazette* gave a brief description of the regiment's appearance and general capability. The privates seemed to be a healthy and robust group of men, the account read, and with additional training would undoubtedly make fine soldiers. A number of them appeared to be awkward horsemen, requiring perhaps a few more weeks in the riding school. "The horses—[*] purchased by Mr. George McKelway—are all stout, serviceable animals, and although they gave evidence of imperfect care, they looked as if they could carry their riders through a campaign with credit." Most important, the regiment was thought to be carefully officered, and the men could be expected to become well drilled.[35]

The Second New Jersey Cavalry departed Trenton for Washington on 5 October 1863, making a brief stop in Philadelphia. A reporter for the *Philadelphia Inquirer* noticed that a group of forty soldiers had had their heads shaved. He learned that they were apprehended deserters of the regiment, and he also noted how closely they were guarded.[36] The regiment arrived in the District of Columbia the next day and immediately crossed the Potomac into Virginia, where it occupied a campsite midway between the Long Bridge and Alexandria. The War Department assigned the regiment temporarily to Major General George Stoneman's Cavalry Bureau. The campsite, located on attractive ground, extended to the banks of the river, and it lay alongside an excellent drill ground. Kargé named it Camp Stockton. Without any delay the commander began intensive training in horsemanship and in the use of the saber, two capabilities of a true cavalryman. The one month spent at Camp Stockton was the "advance training phase" for the regiment.[37]

Kargé continued to stress discipline. He established a provost guard of forty-eight of the most reliable and disciplined soldiers, under the command of First Lieutenant Clarence Linden. The duties of the provost guard were to maintain discipline in camp and on the march, to apprehend deserters, and to otherwise maintain good order. Kargé formed a special unit of men caught in the act of desertion, placing them for a time in the "Squad of the Chameleon." Members of this squad were denied the wearing of the United States uniform and were employed for all fatigue details and other hard labor from reveille to retreat. Soldiers were warned not to associate with anyone on the chameleon squad until he had redeemed himself and was removed from the squad.[38]

Regimental activities occasionally extended beyond the boundaries of Camp Stockton, for General Stoneman assigned Kargé scouting and escort missions. Thus Stoneman introduced an element of danger into the cavalryman's training. Company A experienced combat action first when it skirmished with Colonel John Mosby's Confederate guerrillas on 18 October 1863. Under command of Captain Gallagher the company escorted some one thousand horses to the cavalry camp of the Army of the Potomac at Fairfax Court House, about fifteen miles west of Alexandria. At this time the troopers were armed only with sabers, since the regiment had not yet received its carbines.[39] The company delivered the horses without incident, but on the return Gallagher had traveled about three miles along the Fairfax-Alexandria turnpike, to the vicinity of Annan Dale bridge, when he saw a band of guerrillas making off with a sutler's wagon. The partisans disappeared into a nearby woods. Halting the company on the road, Gallagher instructed his lieutenant to wait with the company while he pursued the partisans with six troopers. Seeing Gallagher's small party approach, the rebels fired on them, killing the captain's horse and wounding one corporal. Pressing the attack, Mosby's men captured Gallagher and two men. At the sound of the firing the lieutenant quickly led the main column to the scene of the action, where he found some thirty armed rebels lined up on the edge of a woods. The guerrillas, perceiving they were outnumbered, fled the area. The lieutenant, however, decided wisely that pursuit without fire arms was impractical, and he resumed the march to the regimental camp. Before reaching Alexandria, the New Jersey troopers met a small train

of wagons on their way to Fairfax Court House. One wagon carried a
United States paymaster with $130,000 in cash. The cavalrymen turned
the train around and escorted it back to Alexandria.[40] The captured
Gallagher served confinement in a Richmond prison for about four
months, when he managed to escape with a party of fellow prisoners in
February 1864. They had tunneled their way for fifty-one days along a
distance of sixty feet, using knives, chisels, and files, finally emerging
into an old tobacco shed. Gallagher then rejoined the regiment.[41]

The day following Gallagher's capture, Kargé ordered Majors Yorke
and Vroom on a reconnaissance sweep to Annadale, some ten miles
from Camp Stockton. Yorke led Companies B and C by way of Bailey's
Cross Roads, while Vroom with Companies G and L reached Annandale
by another route. They encountered no enemy, and the two squadrons
returned to camp safely. Again the troopers were armed only with the
saber. Kargé reported the execution of the reconnaissance to General
Stoneman, who had ordered the sweeps.[42]

Although the regiment still awaited the delivery of carbines, the men
had been equipped with various items of field gear. James Baldwin got
the credit. Writing to the *Newark Daily Advertiser*, a trooper praised
Baldwin as "our very efficient and energetic Quartermaster, who has
furnished officers and men with everything pertaining to his department." This unofficial correspondent also had some reflective comments. He said that, while the regiment trained at Camp Parker, some
found fault with Kargé's treatment of certain members of his command .
These critics, though, were not aware of the class of people with whom
Kargé had to contend. The writer identified this group as "murderers,
robbers, pickpockets and villains of all descriptions, hailing from the
cities of New York, Philadelphia and Baltimore, who enlisted for the
sole purpose of robbing the State of New Jersey of her generous bounties." He called Kargé "a brave officer, an excellent disciplinarian and
everything that constitutes a good commander."[43]

By 9 November 1863 the Second New Jersey Cavalry was en route to
the Western theater. The War Department ordered the regiment to
proceed to Eastport, Mississippi, to join General William T. Sherman's
Army of the Tennessee. Shortly before the regiment's departure,
Brigadier General Henry E. Davies attempted to have the Second New
Jersey assigned to his brigade, a unit of the Third Division of the Cavalry
Corps commanded by Major General Alfred Pleasonton. In his letter of
31 October 1863, Davies asked for the Second New Jersey in order to
build up his brigade, which, he said, was "the smallest and reduced by

severe campaigns." Brigadier General Judson Kilpatrick, the division commander, recommended approval. In his endorsement he wrote that the Second New Jersey "is now commanded by Col. Kargie—one of the best Cav officers I have ever known." [44] The attempt of Generals Davies and Kilpatrick to divert Kargé's regiment came too late, since the War Department had firmly committed the Second New Jersey to the Western theater. The regiment traveled the first leg of its journey on the Baltimore & Ohio Railroad.

The transport of cavalry by rail and water during the Civil War proved to be grossly inadequate. Personnel of the United States Military Railroads packed the horses of the Second New Jersey Cavalry into freight cars that had no facilities for watering and feeding the animals. At Bellaire, on the Ohio river, the cavalrymen led their horses off the train and allowed them to swim the river. They brought the animals again into the confined space of the cars for the remainder of the movement to Cincinnati, where the regiment arrived 15 November. After waiting two days, the men and the horses boarded eight transports, of which the *Monsoon* served as Kargé's headquarters. Once again the facilities for feeding, grooming, and watering the animals were little improved over those found aboard rail transport. The regiment steamed down the Ohio river to Paducah, Kentucky, and then up the Tennessee river to the Union supply base of Eastport in northeastern Mississippi, where the regiment disembarked on 29 November 1863. [45]

General Sherman's army, meanwhile, had departed Eastport for the Chattanooga battle area, rushed there by General Grant's order. Consequently, the Second New Jersey missed the planned juncture. As Kargé explained: "I was ordered to report . . . to General Sherman at Eastport; but owing to the inadequacy of transportation, the Regiment reached the latter place too late to make a junction with Sherman's Army in a move then from Memphis, Tenn. to Chattanooga." [46] The Second New Jersey Cavalry nevertheless remained assigned to Sherman's Department of the Tennessee. While awaiting fresh instructions, Kargé employed his troopers in reconnaissance sweeps of the Eastport region. Confederate horsemen, under the command of Brigadier General Phillip D. Roddey, disputed the federal control of northeastern Mississippi. Thus on 4 December 1863 a New Jersey squadron clashed with Roddey's troopers and drove them out of Iuka. Although it was a satisfying little victory, the regiment suffered its first combat death—Private Charles E. Reed of Company I. [47]

Receiving additional assignment orders, Kargé embarked the regiment on transports December 6 and moved down the Tennessee River to the Ohio. The troops landed at Columbus, Kentucky, where Kargé reported to Brigadier General Andrew J. Smith, commanding the district. No sooner had the regiment disembarked than a fierce storm lashed the area for three days and subjected man and beast to heavy rains, snow, and hail. The perverse weather caused widespread sickness, forcing more than one hundred New Jersey troopers to be hospitalized.

General Smith ordered Kargé to join the cavalry brigade of Colonel George E. Waring, Jr., at Union City, Tennessee, some twenty-five miles south of Columbus. Wading, swimming, and fording overflowing rivers, creeks, and swamplands, the regiment consumed a total of three days to reach its destination. The Tennessee bottoms were so insufferably bad that Kargé exclaimed that comparatively the meadows between Newark and Jersey City were "a splendid racing ground."[48] Although named Union City, the locality was not a city, nor could it be called a village. It lay in the woods at the crossing of two railroads. Colonel Waring described the area thus: "For many a mile around, the forests and swamps were wellnigh impenetrable, and the occasional clearings were but desolate oases in the waste of marsh and fallen timber." He called the roads "wood trails leading nowhere in particular, and all marked a region of the most scanty and unfulfilled promise."[49] The New Jersey troopers probably felt disappointed with the location of the brigade headquarters, but at least they now belonged to a parent organization.

Kargé gave immediate attention to the condition of the horses. After six weeks of almost constant movement aboard transports under very difficult conditions, the animals had grown weak, gaunt-looking, and sickly. Many of them were found to have their tails and manes half eaten off. Their appearance prompted some banter from the other brigade cavalrymen, and Kargé's regiment soon became known as the "New Jersey Bobtails."[50]

Sherman's Meridian Expedition

A Lost Opportunity

Colonel Joseph Kargé's area of operations in the Department of the Tennessee became northern Mississippi and western Tennessee. His prime antagonist turned out to be General Nathan Bedford Forrest, one of the most aggressive of all cavalry commanders. The fortunes of war brought the two into the same combat zone, for on 14 November 1863 the Confederate high command assigned Forrest the mission of fighting the federal forces in West Tennessee, and later expanded his area of responsibility to include northern Mississippi.[1]

Just two days after Kargé's regiment had joined Colonel Waring's cavalry brigade at Union City, Tennessee, the Second New Jersey marched in the first of several attempts to destroy Forrest. This elusive general entered federally controlled West Tennessee from Mississippi in early December 1863. Establishing himself at Jackson, he recruited one regiment within ten days and promptly ordered it to Mississippi. Meanwhile he continued to recruit at a rate of from fifty to one hundred men a day, including some Kentucky deserters from Union forces.[2] Major General Stephen A. Hurlbut, commanding at Memphis, decided to put a stop to Forrest's impudent activity. He planned a three-pronged drive to corner him in the vicinity of Jackson. Hurlbut ordered General A. J. Smith's infantry at Columbus and Waring's cavalry at Union City to move south. Brigadier General Joseph A. Mower's infantry at Corinth, Mississippi would advance north, and Brigadier General Benjamin H. Grierson's cavalry at Memphis would march east toward Bolivar, in coordination with Mower.[3] Although each of the three forces exceeded Forrest's little army, the Federal commanders lacked a sense of urgency. Smith delayed for several days to complete his preparations, and Grierson accordingly postponed his march. Hurlbut's plan was an open secret in hotels from Memphis to Nashville. The precise hour of the march remained the only unknown element. An officer of the Second New Jersey Cavalry said, with evident sarcasm: "Doubtless, this publicity

Lieutenant General Nathan Bedford Forrest. COURTESY OF NATIONAL ARC-
HIVES.

was permitted from a desire to prevent the effusion of blood unnecessar-
ily by giving Forrest time to get out of the way."[4]

Waring's brigade, with the Second New Jersey Cavalry, departed
Union City on 23 December 1863 for the twenty-five-mile march to
Dresden. The cavalry stayed in Dresden on Christmas Day but moved
southeast the next day to New Caledonia and Huntington. Waring
waited here for Smith's infantry to close up, while his troopers scoured
the countryside for forage. Receiving information on 28 December that

Forrest had evacuated Jackson, Waring made a forced march of thirty-eight miles to reach the town. "On we went that day," a New Jersey officer said, "regardless of the bad roads, the wretched state of our horses and everything else, and got into Jackson about nine o'clock, pretty well used up." Fortunately, the weather had remained mild, but dead horses and stragglers lined the route of advance.[5]

Forrest quit Jackson on Christmas Eve and put himself beyond the reach of General Smith's column. It was now up to Mower and Grierson to catch Forrest, but they failed. Marching and fighting, feinting and bluffing, and with a measure of luck, Forrest eluded his pursuers and escaped to Mississippi with his livestock, supply wagons, and some thirty-three hundred men, mostly unarmed.[6] The basic objective of

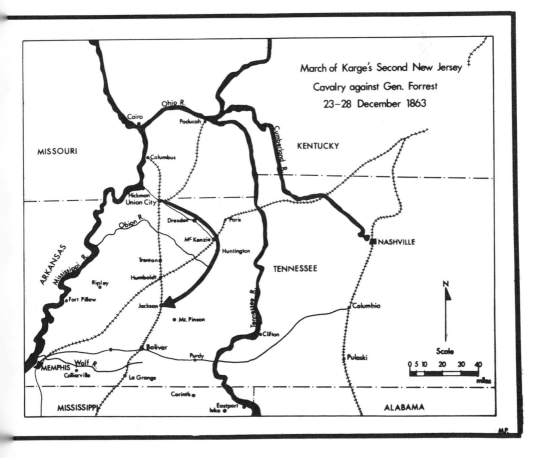

capturing Forrest or destroying his command did not succeed. The broader purpose of dislodging Forrest from Tennessee, though, had been accomplished. The result looked more political than military, for Washington was relieved of the embarrassment of watching Forrest recruit successfully in a federally controlled state. Kargé's regiment had done some hard marching without ever getting close to Forrest.

For several days Waring's cavalrymen made themselves comfortable in Jackson—the horses in livery stables, the men quartered in stores, and the officers in the homes. The return trip to Union City became exceedingly difficult, for the weather turned intensely cold in the wake of a snow and sleet storm. Departing Jackson on 2 January 1864, the Second New Jersey Cavalry marched over roads covered with ice and snow. That first morning the temperature dipped to fourteen degrees below zero, Fahrenheit. The icy roads were particularly rough on the animals. Soon the bodies of horses, felled by fatigue and the intense cold, marked the route of advance. The march continued in the severe cold to near Huntington, where the regiment found its baggage train.[7] On reaching Paris Kargé received orders to remain there for reconnaissance missions. He preferred to go on with the brigade to Union City to rehabilitate his regiment; he pointed to the jaded condition of his horses, but to no avail. To make matters worse, the assignment placed him under a colonel of a Missouri infantry regiment, whom General Smith had left there to command the post. "As a general thing," Kargé said, "I exceedingly dislike to be under the orders of a volunteer Infantry officer, who seldom knows more about cavalry than a goose of Astronomy."[8]

Kargé's fears of the misuse of his cavalry proved accurate. He pursued a few horse thieves and guerrillas. Although the work could have been done by a sergeant with twelve men, the infantry colonel ordered Kargé out with five-hundred cavalry. Fortunately, the ordeal lasted only two weeks, because Kargé received orders to report at once to Dresden. At the moment he rode some seventy miles to the south, near Jackson, on a mission to intercept a raid by a reported one thousand rebel cavalry from Forrest's command (the actual number turned out to be about twenty-five). Kargé marched the regiment in bitterly cold weather to Dresden, where he got additional instructions to proceed immediately to Union City. The Second New Jersey arrived at Brigade headquarters on 20 January, with scarcely a man who did not have some part of his body frostbitten. A total of seventy-eight men were hospitalized with sickness and frostbite. Earlier, on the march from Jackson to Paris, Private James H. Norcross of Company H had both feet severely frozen,

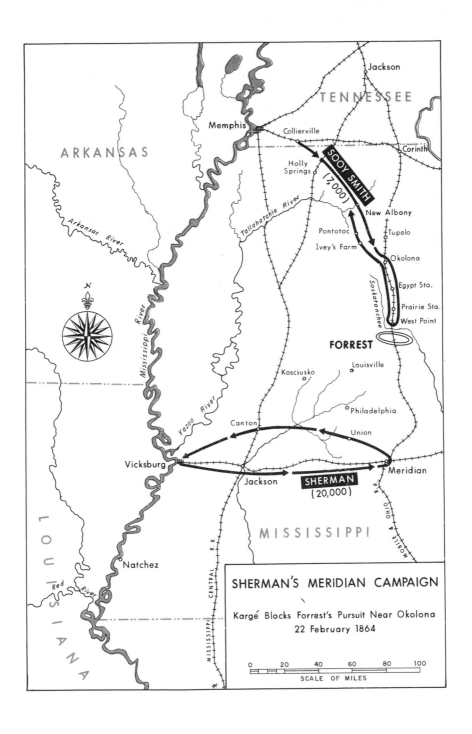

SHERMAN'S MERIDIAN CAMPAIGN

Kargé Blocks Forrest's Pursuit Near Okolona
22 February 1864

SCALE OF MILES

and surgeons found it necessary to amputate them. The intense cold had almost leveled the regiment. Publishing the men's appeal for mittens, the *Daily State Gazette* disclosed: "In one company, out of sixty men only thirty are reported for duty."[9]

With scant chance to refit, the New Jersey Bobtails were thrust into their first major campaign—the Meridian Expedition of General William T. Sherman. He aimed to break up the Confederate railroads in and around Meridian, Mississippi, and to inflict as much damage as possible during February 1864, in order to be prepared by the first of March to assist General Nathaniel Banks in a similar campaign in the Red River country around Shreveport, Louisiana. The overall objective of the coordinated campaigns called for an enlargement of federal control along the Mississippi river, in an attempt to release troops now guarding the river for the upcoming Georgia campaign. "At the same time," Sherman explained, "I wanted to destroy General Forrest, who, with an irregular force of cavalry, was constantly threatening Memphis and the river above, as well as our routes of supply in Middle Tennessee."[10]

Sherman planned to lead twenty thousand infantry troops from Vicksburg east to Meridian, a distance of 150 miles. He ordered a cooperating column under the command of Brigadier General William Sooy Smith, General Grant's chief of cavalry, to move from Memphis by 1 February with seven thousand lightly equipped cavalry troops. Sherman expected Smith to march a distance of 250 miles and join him at Meridian approximately 10 February. As a diversion Sherman planned yet a third expedition, up the Yazoo river by gunboat and transport. He hoped to divide the defending forces and to divert some Confederate strength to the Yazoo from his two main movements.[11]

Colonel Waring received orders on 21 January 1864 to join Sooy Smith's expeditionary force. The immediate problem centered on the separation of the brigade at Union City from Smith, some 150 miles away in Memphis. Waring's command of twenty-five hundred mounted men consisted of the Fourth Missouri with a battery of artillery, the Second New Jersey, the Seventh Indiana, the Nineteenth Pennsylvania, and a battalion of the Second Illinois Cavalry Regiments. Waring planned to cross the brigade over the Obion river at Sharp's Ferry, twenty-three miles southwest of Union City, and ride for Trenton. Although the ground had been frozen hard and was covered with snow, a thaw set in on the first day of the movement. The roads grew deep with mud and slush, and every creek overflowed its banks.[12]

The Second New Jersey Cavalry took up the march at 7:30 A.M. on 22 January. Kargé was six miles from the Obion when Waring called on him to superintend the crossing of the brigade. Leaving his regiment in bivouac, Kargé immediately rode to the ferry site to begin operations. He had available a rope ferry that transported eight horses at a time, but the work proceeded at high risk. The flat boat carrying Lieutenant Colonel J. C. Hess of the Nineteenth Pennsylvania capsized, causing the loss of seven horses. In passing through an adjoining swamp Hess lost an additional twenty-three horses. The Seventh Indiana Cavalry swam their horses, losing several animals and some weapons but no men. After innumerable and almost insurmountable difficulties Kargé succeeded in getting nearly three regiments to the southern bank safely.[13]

Waring and his escort crossed the Obion at 9:00 P.M. on the second day, under a full moon and with the temperature at a summer level. The river had overflowed its banks in places, so that Waring landed in two feet of water. For a distance of three miles from the ferry he found the road through the river bottoms almost impassable for wagons and difficult even for cavalry. In one place, the water stood two to four feet deep and filled with large cakes of broken ice, which caused the horses and men to stumble every few steps. Waring sent word to the Nineteenth Pennsylvania not to try the bottoms until daylight. Unable to see the water-covered road in the darkness, Waring rode a distance of fourteen miles instead of the actual five to reach camp at the late hour of 4:00 A.M.

As the Obion continued to rise, Kargé changed the ferry site six times in eight hours to take advantage of every inch of dry ground on either shore. Meanwhile the swamp on the far side began to approach an impassable level. Kargé asked Colonel John Shanks, Seventh Indiana Cavalry, to go down river for a distance of twelve miles to find boats and other likely crossing points. The search proved fruitless, and Shanks noted that the river grew wider and the banks were in a worse condition than at Sharp's Ferry.[14] Finally, the swift current swept away cable and boat, leaving Kargé stranded with his own regiment, part of the Fourth Missouri with three mountain howitzers, and the entire brigade supply train and regimental baggage trains. He had no choice but to lead the brigade element on a long detour to the east as far as Huntington, and then swing southwestward below Jackson to the Hatchie river. Kargé informed Waring of his decision through Shanks, who was the last man to cross at Sharp's Ferry. Waring had confidence in Kargé. In a report to

General Andrew J. Smith on 27 January, Waring said: "He has taken the best course, and has the energy to get through if any man can."[15]

Waring slowed down his rate of march to allow Kargé time to join him some days later. The going was tough. Kargé found the roads so bad that at times it took several hours to move the wagons one mile. While he kept fighting the mud, parties of guerrillas also harassed his movement. Nevertheless, he brought the column out safely, assisted by Waring, who had secured the river crossing sites at Mount Pinson and Bolivar for Kargé. The divided elements met at Bolivar, and the brigade continued to its destination, Collierville, where it arrived on 8 February 1864. Because of the encumbrance of the supply and baggage trains, which traveled a distance of 220 miles, the march consumed eighteen days. "Had it not been for the sudden thaw which rendered the Obion River impassable," Waring explained, "we could have come by way of Ripley, only 120 miles, and would have made the march in eight days, as the road was comparatively good and the river crossings in tolerable condition."[16]

Besides the abominable terrain, Waring must be held mainly responsible for delaying the expedition. Why he insisted on waiting for his wagons is not clear. If an early joining with Sooy Smith was mandatory, he could have ordered the wagons to return to Union City from the Obion river. The unencumbered cavalry of the Second New Jersey and Fourth Missouri could then have ridden fairly rapidly around the Obion. Waring admitted that the "supply train was a heavy encumbrance during the whole march and caused at least a week's delay." He also said that the train "was of very little use to the main column, which lived off the country nearly all the time and could have done so entirely." In addition to Waring, General A. J. Smith must take part of the blame. From his headquarters at Columbus, Kentucky, Smith issued the movement order to Waring, instructing him to "proceed with all possible dispatch" and to reach his destination of Moscow, Tennessee, "as soon as practicable." But Smith did not state any target date that might have been critical to the operation. Available accounts indicate that no superior informed Waring of the 1 February date of departure set by Sherman.[17]

The tardy arrival of Waring's brigade held up General Sooy Smith's expedition by ten days. The delay was appreciable but not decisive to the campaign. Nonetheless the late start provoked a controversy between Sooy Smith and Sherman, who saw no need for Smith to wait for Waring's brigade. Sherman maintained that the two brigades on hand gave Smith a sufficient force of some five thousand cavalrymen. Smith rebutted that Sherman told him to wait for Waring's brigade so as to be strong enough to go anywhere.[18] As Grant's cavalry chief explained in a letter to General Sherman on 2 February 1864: "I feel eager to pitch into them, but I know that it is not your desire to 'send a boy to mill' . . . ." Once having gained Waring's brigade, General Sooy Smith's command became indeed the most formidable cavalry force ever assembled in the Western theater.[19]

On the eve of its first major campaign the Second New Jersey Cavalry Regiment had been marched and countermarched for eight weeks, including the arduous move to Collierville. This excessive marching in extreme weather conditions had taken its toll. An officer's letter read: "You may judge how greatly our command has suffered from sickness, death and capture when I tell you that our company alone, which left Washington 94 strong, does not number now more than 32 present." Kargé reported his regiment as 494 enlisted men strong on 11 February 1864, the day Sooy Smith's cavalry force moved out. This number represented a loss of approximately fifty percent from full strength.[20]

At Vicksburg, General Sherman began the march to Meridian on 3 February, late by two days. He led two corps of infantry under the commands of Major Generals Stephen A. Hurlbut and James B. McPherson, and a cavalry brigade commanded by Colonel Edward F. Winslow. Sherman encountered negligible opposition in reaching Meridian on 14 February. Meanwhile General Sooy Smith started south from Collierville with a division of three cavalry brigades under the command of Brigadier General Benjamin H. Grierson, some light artillery, and the Fourth United States Cavalry Regiment.[21]

William Sooy Smith, called "Sookie" Smith, was a young-looking thirty-three years, handsome in appearance but somewhat anxious in demeanor.[22] A West Pointer of the class of 1856, Smith resigned his commission the year following graduation to become an engineer and bridge builder. In June 1861 he reentered the service as colonel of the Thirteenth Ohio Infantry Regiment. Promoted to brigadier general in 1862, he later became the chief of cavalry of General Grant's Western command, the Military Division of the Mississippi. As a commander, Smith tended to vacillate when he gave orders. Nevertheless he had displayed coolness and clear thinking under fire, and he seemed determined to destroy Forrest and his troublesome army once and for all.[23]

Benjamin H. Grierson, the second-in-command, came from a non-

Brigadier General William Sooy Smith. COURTESY OF NATIONAL ARCHIVES.

military background. He had been a music teacher in Jacksonville, Illinois, before entering the army as a volunteer general's aide in May 1861. He soon received a major's commission in the Sixth Illinois Cavalry. From the beginning he demonstrated organizing ability and imagination. His promotions came quickly, as he established a reputation of a bold cavalry leader in operations in western Tennessee and northern Mississippi. His most famous exploit was the cavalry raid through Mississippi for sixteen days in April 1863. Grierson's normal command was the cavalry division of the Sixteenth Army Corps, headquartered at Memphis.[24]

Although Sherman saw an advantage in having Grierson on the expedition because of his familiarity with the Mississippi area, the operation had one too many generals. Grierson commanded the cavalry division of three brigades, and Smith commanded the expeditionary force, which consisted of the same cavalry division and the Fourth U.S. Cavalry Regiment. The two generals often, and unknowingly, countermanded each other, to the confusion and harassment of the troops.

Benjamin H. Grierson as Colonel. COURTESY OF LIBRARY OF CONGRESS.

Sooy Smith's command marched in three columns over different roads as nearly parallel as the roads would allow.[25] It appeared to Waring that the brigades marched by themselves without any apparent coordination by Smith. Waring learned later that the details of the order of march had been passed to the other two brigade commanders, but that he had been overlooked. This annoyed him, but, more important, the lack of coordination caused misunderstanding and unnecessary delays.[26] Waring's brigade marched without incident for three days. On 13 February, the Second New Jersey pitched camp at Walker's Mills, eight miles beyond Holly Springs, Mississippi. Kargé found the civilians hostile and forage scarce. A guerrilla killed a New Jersey trooper in the act of foraging. The woods and swamps of this region made it easy for small bands of irregulars to spring from ambush and disappear just as quickly.[27]

The brigade remained in camp all of the next day, 14 February, since the commanding general had issued no orders. Resuming the march the next morning in a heavy rainstorm, it reached Tippah Creek, where it spent the remainder of the day and the entire night in crossing the swollen stream.[28] From Tippah Creek, Smith began a sustained march to reach the Tallahatchie river at New Albany. Accordingly, Kargé put his regiment in motion at 5:00 A.M. Barely had the last trooper of Smith's command crossed than the rising waters made the river impassable.[29]

Having come together for the first time at New Albany, the expeditionary force continued south in a column of brigades. Smith pressed them onward through rough, rocky, and wooded country. At day's end on 18 February, the brigades reached Okolona, where the nature of the terrain changed. "An interminable fertile, rolling prairie lay before us in every direction," Waring said. The region was the granary of the rebel army, since the Confederate government compelled the planters to cultivate large amounts of corn as well as cotton. The destruction of subsistence for the Confederate armed forces was a secondary mission of the expedition, and Smith's troopers executed this task with enthusiasm. For the next two days, as the column moved south to West Point, the flames of burning corn and cotton lit up the sky with a continuous red glow.

Sooy Smith, under firm orders to respect the rights of the civilians, made no attempt to destroy dwellings or to seize bare necessities; the slaves, however, became infected with a passion for destruction. They deserted the plantations and joined the soldiers in burning the government corn stacked in cribs along the railroad. Unfortunately, their aroused emotions also led them to burn down whole plantations. "As we marched, the negroes came *en masse* from every plantation to join our column," Waring said, "leaving only fire and absolute destruction behind them." He called the incidents of this desolation sickening and heartrending.[30]

In just two days, Smith's column grew by two thousand slaves and one thousand mules.[31] Although their loss would have some crippling effect on the Mississippi economy, the large numbers of Negroes had a more immediate influence on Smith. They interfered with his ability to march rapidly and to fight. For a commander already late for a rendezvous, Smith's raiding activities indicated a subtle change in plans, and Sergeant James Larson of the Fourth U.S. Cavalry perceived this shift. Larson observed: "He did not push forward as he had been doing, and we made long stops every day on the march, while large detachments were sent out in all directions to destroy everything that could be of use to the enemy, and gather all the horses and mules they could find."[32]

On 19 February, the Second New Jersey Cavalry reached Egypt Station with Waring's First Brigade and Colonel La Fayette McCrillis's Third Brigade. Smith now ordered Kargé to march some five miles south to Prairie Station and there to engage the enemy, reported to be two regiments strong. Kargé thought it strange that Smith should select the Second New Jersey from among the eleven available regiments of the two brigades. His regiment had not been tested in battle, whereas the Western regiments were composed of three-year veterans. Then, too, some regiments had enjoyed a long rest at Collierville and were in better physical condition. Nonetheless Kargé promptly accepted the assignment as an opportunity to lead his regiment in combat. "I ordered at once the Captains of the different Squadrons to inspect their arms anew," Kargé said, "and started with my boys to look for Mr. Secesh."[33]

Kargé reached Prairie Station at sundown. When his advance guard reported the enemy to be in sight, he galloped to the front to check the enemy strength and to look over the ground. Across a wide, sweeping plain, Kargé saw a line of troopers drawn up near the depot, but numbering far less than one regiment. Perhaps the remainder kept out of sight, Kargé thought. He led his regiment forward in anticipation of a rousing clash. As the distance narrowed, the vigilant Kargé recognized the "enemy" as Union cavalry—the advance of Lieutenant Colonel William P. Hepburn's Second Brigade. General Smith had ordered Hepburn that morning to march on another road via Aberdeen. The setting sun gave just enough light for Kargé to identify Hepburn's troopers. "Had I delayed ten minutes longer," Kargé said, "I might have engaged my own friends, not being able to tell them from foes on account of the darkness." The incident gave Kargé some doubts about Smith's generalship. It seemed that Smith did not know what disposition he had made of his forces.[34]

The next morning at eight, 20 February, the Second New Jersey marched for West Point. It occupied the center of the column, for Smith had assigned Hepburn the advance. About 2 P.M. Kargé heard some firing up front, but despite frequent delays the march continued to West Point, where the regiment camped for the night. Kargé got a warning to exercise the utmost caution, since the enemy held both flanks and the rear. At West Point Smith stood less than one hundred miles from Meridian, but, for the first time, Forrest opposed his advance. The night passed quietly with occasional firing by pickets; at dawn, the firing became brisk. Although Kargé strained to engage "the so-long-sought-for enemy," he learned to his surprise and dismay that Colonel Waring had received orders to retire to Okolona.[35]

General Sooy Smith made an astonishing decision. He stopped his advance and ordered a withdrawal. He explained that he did not want to enter a trap prepared by Forrest. Smith received and apparently believed rumors of Forrest's growing strength.[36] But a more rational explanation is that Sookie Smith lost his nerve. Highly critical of Smith, Waring said: "Our commander had evidently no stomach for a close approach to the enemy, and his injunctions at Colliersville that we were to try to 'Fight at close quarters!'—'Go at them as soon as possible with the saber!'—and other valorous ejaculations were in singular contrast to the impressions he evinced as the prospect of an actual engagement drew near."[37] Before the start of the expedition Smith had boasted to Sherman: "I will pitch into him wherever I find him." And to General Grant he had said: "I have been anxious to attack him at once, but General Sherman thinks I had better await his movement."[38] The decisive moment had come, but the commander was found wanting.

Kargé got a preview of Smith's change in resolve in the early morning hours of 21 February. Promptly at midnight he was roused from his sleep as he lay "under a glorious Mississippi oak tree" by a summons to report to General Smith in person. "I found him propt up with pillows in an armchair," Kargé said, "ghastly pale and evidently under great physical suffering." Smith asked Kargé the condition of his regiment. "Always ready if any work is to be done, General," Kargé replied. The general mumbled something incoherent and dismissed Kargé with the parting remark that "we will march tonight." Kargé left convinced that "the good General was entirely bewildered and that he had given full play to his imagination which was wrought up [to] the highest pitch by silly reports, either of his scouts or by secesh sympathizers, of the enormous strength of the enemy." Smith evidently had forgotten Sherman's letter of instructions, in which he said the rebel cavalry in the entire state did not exceed Smith's seven thousand.[39]

Waring estimated that Forrest had "about our own number of cavalry, but without artillery, of which we had twenty good pieces." Forrest said his command did not exceed twenty-five hundred men. Waring believed that the open country offered good fighting terrain and gave the better drilled and more organized Union cavalry a decided advantage. Smith now had the opportunity of defeating the best cavalry force in the Confederate army.[40] Had he broken through for a junction with Sherman near Meridian, the combined Union army could have raided and destroyed Selma, Alabama, with its war production facilities, one full year before General James H. Wilson's capture of that vital center.

At West Point, meanwhile, Forrest assessed Smith's retrograde action correctly as a full retreat, and he began a relentless pursuit. The federal retreat began in an orderly manner. The Second New Jersey Cavalry, as part of the First Brigade, occupied the center of the column, where it guarded the mule train and the Negroes. Hepburn's Second Brigade held the rear. Kargé could tell from the intensity of fire that heavy skirmishing took place. The fighting occurred along the Saskatonchee River, three miles south of West Point. Smith had ordered Hepburn to stage a demonstration at Ellis's bridge as a deceptive maneuver. Hepburn's Second Iowa Cavalry, under Major Datus E. Coon, engaged the rebels with rifles and occasional artillery rounds from two twelve-pounders. The enemy employed no artillery of their own. Although Coon had firm control of the situation, he withdrew after two hours in compliance with orders. He left convinced that the federal strength exceeded the enemy's at least four times.[41]

The center of Smith's column had marched unmolested some twenty miles toward Okolona when Kargé caught his first glimpse of the enemy—a body of about six hundred troops in an open field to his right. Responding to Waring's order, Kargé moved his regiment to engage the enemy. He headed for a wooded area where he planned to position his troopers along the edge. There, hidden from the enemy's view, he would hit them with flanking fire as they came into range. Before the Second New Jersey had reached the woods, though, the enemy withdrew. Kargé returned to his place in the column, and the regiment continued to march until 2 A.M. to a point three miles south of Okolona.[42] Four hours later the Second New Jersey rode again. Passing Okolona, the cavalrymen turned into the old Pontotoc road. Suddenly the routine of the march changed. Waring ordered Kargé to return to a strong defensive position a short distance to the rear, and to deploy the regiment. Kargé had barely completed his dispositions when troopers of the Fourth U.S. Cavalry passed by, "exhibiting the marks of pretty severe handling."

The Fourth Regulars had gallantly fought the rebels in Okolona that morning, 22 February, losing ninety-five men while holding the town until the main force had marched off. They then acted as rear guard, without help, against a superior force of hard-charging rebels. McCrillis rushed two regiments from his Third Brigade to the aid of the Regulars; but when the relief force came to within nine hundred yards of them, McCrillis's troopers suddenly stopped, looked, and panicked. "Although they were not within reach of the bullets at all," Sergeant Larson related, "their ranks broke, and they went to the rear as fast as, or perhaps faster than, they had come to the front." Larson called it "a most disgraceful cavalry stampede, the only one I witnessed during the whole war." By disciplined maneuver, the Fourth Cavalry continued to withdraw in the face of superior enemy forces until they were relieved by other units.[43]

As the Fourth Cavalry passed by Kargé's position, he saw evidence of hard fighting in the appearance of the men and horses. Concluding that a general engagement was close at hand, Kargé decided to establish himself more firmly. The position he held "was in every way a superior one for effective defense." He dismounted a part of his command and so positioned the troopers that they could sweep with carbine fire not only the front but also the entire left flank. The ground afforded ample protection for both the men and horses. To the left of the road stood a large house surrounded by a half-dozen solid Negro log cabins. He gathered fifty volunteers to occupy the buildings, but just then Waring ordered him to resume his place in the column of march. "I did it with great reluctance," Kargé said, "for I knew by frequent discharges of fire-arms that General Grierson was still engaging the enemy in the rear with the Third Brigade."[44]

The New Jersey Regiment had marched not more than a mile and a half when Waring again deployed the brigade to face the enemy. He ordered Kargé to take a position on the left side of the road. Kargé quickly occupied a gully with part of the regiment and placed Major Yorke in charge. Next he positioned twenty-five dismounted men on an elevated piece of ground, facing a bend in the road, and entrusted this group to Adjutant Pierson. A small force under Captain Von Pannwitz occupied several buildings on the right of the road. Kargé put his reserve behind Pierson's carbineers. While he was still disposing his regiment the routed cavalrymen came rushing by, victims of the stampede and failure to support the Fourth Cavalry in Okolona. As General Smith explained it, a portion of the Third Brigade "stampeded at the yells of our own men charging, and galloped back through and over everything, spreading confusion wherever they went . . . ."[45] Kargé feared that the fleeing troopers might also stampede his men, but they held steady. Manning a key blocking position, he was entrusted with a vital role: Break the Confederate pursuit, or at least delay it to prevent the panic from infecting the whole command. Kargé met the test. On the heels of the dogged Federals came the charging Confederates. "Fire low and sure was my only command," Kargé said, "and fire they did." Surprising the rebels, the New Jerseymen poured volley upon volley of carbine fire into the midst of the attacking horsemen. Yorke stood firm, Pierson kept the road cleared, and Von Pannwitz maintained a galling fire. Armed with the Spencer carbine, the Second New Jersey men delivered a heavy and concentrated amount of fire.[46]

Kargé's fight was a holding action for Smith, who prepared a defensive position on suitable ground at Ivey's Farm, some ten miles to the northwest, near Pontotoc. Here a ridge spread out into a wide, open field, and Smith deployed a line of dismounted men from four regiments. He directed that an artillery battery be emplaced near the road, from which it could enfilade any enemy column on the road. To the right of the battery he readied the Fourth Missouri Cavalry and six companies of the Seventh Indiana for a saber charge. He placed the Third Tennessee Cavalry on the extreme right, with orders to charge the enemy in the flank should they make their expected frontal attack on the dismounted skirmishers. Smith seemed to have regained some semblance of leadership. This was his first appearance on the battlefield; he had been leading the retreat.[47]

While Smith laid out his defense at Ivey's Farm, Kargé continued to block the rebel advance for a full hour, despite Forrest's strong pressure on his men. The New Jersey regiment had the support of a squadron of the Fourth Missouri under Captain Oscar P. Howe and a part of the Second Illinois under Captain Franklin Moore. When Waring pulled out the Second Illinois, Kargé paid closer attention to the weakened right flank. He concluded that Yorke's group of skirmishers in front of the

regimental center was too exposed, and he ordered Yorke to fall back
slowly to the main regimental defense line. The rebels now attacked the
right flank and threatened to cut the regiment's lines of communication
to the rear. Kargé ordered a deliberate withdrawal. "I am proud to say,"
he reported, "that neither an officer nor a man of my command showed
any unbecoming haste to withdraw himself from the enemy fire."[48]
Lieutenant Charles H. Dod gave an overview of their behavior under
fire. He stressed that the Second New Jersey turned to face the dreaded
Forrest in the midst of disgraceful and disorderly conduct on the part of
other troops. Despite a brisk fire of musketry from the enemy, Dod said
that the New Jersey squadrons "stood unflinching until they were
ordered to fall back and then left the ground as quietly and cooly as they
ever marched from Dress Parade."[49]

In the fight near Okolona on 22 February 1864 the Second New Jersey
suffered twelve casualties. Captain Erich von Pannwitz and Lieutenant
Ebenezer Montgomery were severely wounded. Lieutenants C. Stever
Schwartz and Carnot B. Meeker were also wounded. In addition six men
were wounded and two were missing or captured. The horses of several
officers, including Kargé's, were shot dead by enemy fire. Montgomery
was left disabled on the battlefield, helpless for lack of an ambulance. At
first Kargé believed that he had been captured, but a newspaper later
reported Montgomery to be recovering in a Memphis hospital.[50]

Relieved of his blocking mission, Kargé marched to a position a
quarter of a mile beyond Ivey's Farm; Forrest promptly moved up to
attack Smith. The battery of the Fourth Missouri Cavalry and the entire
federal line of skirmishers opened fire on the advancing rebels with
destructive effect. Colonel Jeffrey Forrest, whose brigade led the attack,
fell dead in the onslaught, and General Forrest was emotionally overcome by the personal tragedy. He dropped all thoughts of fighting as he
grieved over the loss of his brother. But, recovering himself, he then
attacked with even greater ferocity. Smith, in turn, ordered the saber
charge by the Fourth Missouri cavalrymen, who courageously executed
the charge against withering fire. When the cavalrymen were unable to
make physical contact with the rebels, who were protected by a high rail
fence, they broke and retreated at great speed. Their officers, however,
rallied the men on the line of their original formation without the loss of a
single straggler.[51] The charge impressed Forrest. It had a psychological
effect on the Confederates, for the saber attack diminished the rebels'
eagerness to continue the pursuit. As Waring said: "Forrest's whole
advance had been stopped and ended by six hundred Fourth Missouri

Dutchmen, galloping, yelling, and swinging their sabres at several thousand men well secured behind a rail fence."[52]

To be sure, some sharp fighting still remained. One flanking enemy column jeopardized the safety of the battery of the Fourth Missouri. A brilliant charge by a portion of the Seventh Indiana and two detachments of the Fourth Missouri saved it.[53] By this time, however, Forrest's troopers had become so fatigued by the dogged pursuit that the fighting fell off noticeably.[54] Yet Smith kept up an almost continuous march to reach the safety of Tennessee. Notwithstanding the hard fighting during the day at Okolona and at Ivey's Farm, Smith pressed his tired troops on into the night. The Second New Jersey halted in the vicinity of Pontotoc at 2:00 A.M., 23 February but the men got little rest. At 4:30 A.M. the regiment marched again when Smith ordered Kargé to push forward to New Albany to save the bridge and seize the ford for the crossing of the Tallahatchie river. Kargé found a party of some seventy-five Confederates preparing to destroy the bridge, but he foiled their plans and drove them off. He guarded the passage of the entire force and then, bringing up the rear, rejoined Waring's brigade three miles to the northwest, on the road to Holly Springs. The column marched seven more miles that night.[55]

The Second New Jersey reached Collierville on 25 February 1864. Kargé's first concern was forage for the horses and food for his men. He satisfied this need the next day. Two days later a sudden cold snap and heavy snowstorm lasting forty-eight hours struck the horses with deadly effect and the regiment lost almost all its mounts. The animals had become exhausted by the long journey from Washington and then by the constant riding of the past two months. Kargé was left with only 161 horses, of which 55 could be called serviceable.[56]

General Sooy Smith reported a total of 388 casualties, a relatively small number for the fifteen-day expedition. Fifty-four were killed, 179 wounded, and 155 captured or missing.[57] More damaging than the physical loss was the demoralizing effect on the cavalry regiments. Waring said that the men of his brigade were "worn and weary, sadly demoralized and almost dismounted." He reported losing fifteen hundred horses. He saved his most telling remark for the commander. In Memphis, the morning following the return of the expedition, a surprised Waring saw "the spectacle of General Sooy Smith, no longer ill, and with no trace of shame or annoyance on his face." Waring noted: "He had shed his modest and prudent attire, and shone out with all the brass radiance of a full-fledged major-general."[58]

Smith tried to give his expedition the look of success. In his report he played up the destruction of cotton, corn, and railroads, the capture of horses and mules, and the rescue of many Negroes. The *New York Times* blasted Smith's self-styled achievements. "The public has been told of Smith's great success," the *Times* rebutted, " . . . but to assign this as the object of this expedition is an insult to common sense. Smith failed." Looking for scapegoats, Smith cast doubt on the fighting abilities of two of his three brigades. "There was but one of my brigades," he said, "that I could rely upon with full confidence." Smith explained that the conduct of the other two on the march indicated such a lack of discipline as to create in his mind the most serious apprehension as to their probable conduct in battle. He concluded that any reverse to his command, as it was situated at West Point, would have been fatal.[59]

Since Smith singled out Hepburn's brigade for praise in his official report, it is evident that he had reference to Waring's and McCrillis's brigades as the two in which he lacked confidence. Nevertheless he praised the brilliant charges made by Waring's two regiments, the Fourth Missouri and the Seventh Indiana. Despite the fact that the few instances of real fighting in that discouraging retreat were unique, Smith overlooked the successful blocking action that Kargé's regiment interposed at Okolona between the Federals and the hard-charging rebels. Kargé's stubborn fight gave Smith the time to steady the stampeding Third Brigade and to set up the defensive position at Ivey's Farm. Smith did not mention Kargé by name but nonetheless gave him indirect praise when he said of the stampede: "Organized forces were immediately thrown to the rear and the enemy handsomely repulsed." The rank and file, on the other hand, recognized the performance of Kargé's regiment, and New Jersey newspapers reported: "It was acknowledged that the 1st Brigade was the best behaved; and of that brigade the 2nd N.J. won first laurels, Col. Kargé distinguishing himself above all the officers in the field." Waring's report also singled out Kargé's holding action during the rout of the Third Brigade. "This position was gallantly held," Waring said, "by the Second New Jersey and Second Illinois Cavalry against a sharp attack."[60]

Kargé made a frank remark about the conduct of the expedition, and this indiscretion may have had something to do with General Smith's coldness toward him. Shortly before reaching Memphis, Kargé openly vented his frustration. "This whole movement," he exclaimed, "has been characterized from beginning to end by imbecility." For this "compliment," Smith placed Kargé in confinement for three days.[61] Kargé also reacted angrily when newspaper articles implied that the tardy arrival at Collierville of two Eastern regiments, the Second New Jersey and the Nineteenth Pennsylvania, delayed the expedition and thereby contributed to its failure. The *New York Times* repeated this story in an editorial, which went on to place the blame where it belonged. The *Times* said: "The charge that delay on the start was caused by the slow movements of Pennsylvania and New Jersey regiments may have some truth in it, but as there were but two of these regiments, and they new and raw at that, they ought not to have been considered essential to the expedition, or of consequence enough to have caused an hour's delay. The failure is more likely attributable to want of pluck and dash in its Commander."[62]

Something can also be said in support of McCrillis's regiments, which stampeded at Okolona on 22 February. General Grierson admitted that he did not know the cause of the rout, but he said that these regiments later redeemed themselves and proved worthy of confidence.[63] Grierson at this time was in the rear with McCrillis's troopers, while General Smith at the head of the column led the retreat. Smith should have been at the position the most critical to the command—in the rear, facing Forrest. Had Smith been around to show a little fight, some of it might have rubbed off on McCrillis's men. Waring said that the Third Brigade had taken part in the hurried retreat of the day before and, having seen no reason for it, imagined itself surrounded by an overwhelming enemy. "It had lost all confidence in the commanding general," Waring declared, "and its discipline dissolved."[64]

General Sherman differed with Smith on the effectiveness of his cavalry. Although he was not intimately familiar with each regiment, Sherman possessed an understanding of their general quality. In his letter of instruction he told Smith: " . . . you have the best and most experienced troops in the service, and they will do anything that is possible." Furthermore, Sherman expressed confidence that Smith's troops were "superior and better in all respects than the combined cavalry which the enemy has in all the State of Mississippi." In response Smith said on the eve of his departure: "My command is in splendid condition." When it was all over Sherman called Smith's performance unsatisfactory and the ten-day delay of his expedition unpardonable. Sherman added that "the mode and manner of his return to Memphis was not what I expected from an intended bold cavalry movement."[65]

Smith's really unpardonable act was his decision at West Point to retreat. His action denied the troops the opportunity to fight Forrest. They were ready and eager. Waring said that the Union cavalry could have faced Forrest and fought him successfully a hundred times, but the commanding general turned down every recommendation to fight.[66]

Sooy Smith's late start from Collierville did not nullify the Meridian Expedition. Once underway, Smith made good progress to West Point, and Sherman took Smith's tardiness into account. Sherman arrived in Meridian on 14 February 1864, four days off his own target date, and remained there for one week. His army destroyed the city and the railroads for a distance of twelve miles in every direction from the city. While at Meridian, Sherman kept watch for Sooy Smith, or for any news of his whereabouts. He had instructed him to try to communicate by scouts and spies from the time he reached Pontotoc, where Smith arrived on 17 February. Apparently he never tried.[67]

On 20 February Sherman ordered a slow withdrawal from Meridian. Still hopeful of joining with Smith's cavalry, he swung northward on the return to Vicksburg. Sherman took Hurlbut's Corps and Winslow's cavalry brigade and moved "to the north to feel for General Smith." Arriving at Union, some twenty-five miles northwest of Meridian, Sherman made another determined effort to locate Smith. He sent Winslow with three cavalry regiments to Philadelphia and on to Louisville, almost fifty miles due north, over the very roads by which Grierson had marched during his famous raid in April 1863 and over which Sherman assumed that Smith would now come. Carrying instructions for Smith to join Sherman at Canton, Winslow executed his search mission. He reached a crossroads ten miles south of Louisville without finding any elements of Smith's command, which at this time was in full retreat to Memphis. At the crossroads Winslow sent out two messengers to the east to join Smith, if possible. Then, following orders, Winslow turned west through Kosciusko to Canton, arriving at this rendezvous at 2 P.M. on 25 February.[68]

Sherman continued to believe that Sooy Smith, somewhere and somehow, was moving south through Mississippi to join him. On 28 February Sherman issued orders to his army at Canton to remain there until "about March 3 to hear from and assist, if necessary, the cavalry expedition under the command of Brigadier General William Sooy Smith . . . ." Hurlbut's corps could not delay beyond 3 March because it had to be back in Vicksburg and ready by 7 March to embark for the Red River campaign.[69]

Sherman had every reason to be dissatisfied with Smith's performance. His censure of Sooy Smith started a controversy between the two men that lasted more than a decade.[70] A matter of immediate concern to Smith was the appointment of Sherman to the command of the Military Division of the Mississippi on 12 March 1864. Sherman succeeded Ulysses S. Grant, who became the general-in-chief of the armies of the United States. The chief of cavalry, in disfavor with the new commander, resigned his commission 15 July 1864 to return to his civilian occupation of engineer and bridge builder.[71]

For the first time in three months the Second New Jersey Cavalry had a chance to recuperate. A much-needed reorganization and reequipping of the regiment occurred. Assessing the performance of his command, Kargé congratulated the officers and men on their exemplary conduct during the expedition into Mississippi. In Regimental Orders No. 115, issued 8 March 1864, he said, "I am proud of you." Kargé told the regiment that they had shown, under the most difficult circumstances, that Jerseymen know how to face the enemy. "You have endured patiently and without murmur, heat, cold, hunger, and thirst." He could say with conviction that his men followed readily and cheerfully wherever danger threatened the most. "And for all that," he said, "God bless you."[72]

Despite the lack of aggressiveness of the expeditionary force commander, the Second New Jersey Cavalry performed well in the Mississippi campaign. The regiment, however, had not been sufficiently challenged, and its potential had yet to be demonstrated to senior commanders. Nonetheless, Kargé could be proud of his regiment. It was tough and disciplined, and the hard campaigning had imbued the men with a feeling of confidence in his leadership. As Lieutenant Dod said: "His example of personal daring is beyond all praise—and it is only the truth to say that his soldiers have a thorough confidence in his military capacity and the strongest affection for his person."[73]

There was a time in training when some of Kargé's soldiers had threatened to shoot him the first chance they got in battle. The experience of the Meridian campaign, however, caused a change in attitude. With obvious pride Kargé wrote the New Jersey Adjutant General: "I always told them that it would come to that, but the fools did not believe me."[74]

Toughened by three months of hard campaigning, the Second New Jersey Cavlary felt ready to take on Forrest again. That indefatigable fighter planned to return to West Tennessee to go "after those 3,000 men whom he had to come away without at Christmastime."[75]

Kargé Beats Forrest

The Raider Meets "a Foe Who Doesn't Plead Weakness"

General Nathan Bedford Forrest marched his entire command for West Tennessee on 16 March 1864. Within a few days the Confederates occupied Jackson and reached for Paducah, Kentucky, where the federal garrison withdrew to the safety of nearby Fort Anderson. Forrest meanwhile dispatched the Seventh Tennessee Cavalry to capture Union City. Colonel William L. Duckworth, the regimental commander, outwitted the federal officer into surrendering his garrison without firing a shot. The rebel colonel created the impression of overpowering strength, and even faked the presence of the dreaded Forrest. While Forrest may have enjoyed attacking Yankee garrisons, he made the foray primarily to recruit men and procure horses and supplies. The Union cavalry at Memphis did not contest the raid, since Grierson's division had dropped to a low of two thousand troopers. In early March eight veteran regiments were furloughed, leaving only five small ones. The cavalry remaining was sufficient for garrison duty alone, and the Second New Jersey found itself on patrols or manning pickets for the protection of Memphis.[1]

Forrest moved about freely in the area between the Tennessee and Mississippi rivers. The region had become an empty shell. Except for a few posts along the rivers, General Sherman abandoned the patrolling of interior areas and stripped his geographical command of troops to build up his field army for the invasion of Georgia. From his own movements and that of scouts, Forrest noted the marked absence of federal troops. He deduced Sherman's grand design and tried to alert General Joseph E. Johnston, commanding the main Confederate army in the West. "I am of the opinion," Forrest wrote on 6 April, "that everything available is being concentrated against General Lee and yourself." Forrest proposed the countermove that had a good chance of stopping Sherman's campaign to capture Atlanta. He called for an attack on Sherman's lines of communication through Tennessee, on which the federal commander totally depended for his flow of supplies and reinforcements. In the letter to Johnston, Forrest said: " . . . if all the cavalry of this and your own department could be moved against Nashville . . . the enemy's communication could be utterly broken up." [2]

A short time later Forrest again suggested his counterattack plan, this time to President Jefferson Davis. He urged that his cavalry be combined with General Stephen D. Lee's for a march into Middle Tennessee and Kentucky, in order to divert the Federal armies and nullify Sherman's grand strategy. The Confederate government gave Forrest's letter perfunctory treatment.[3] But Sherman understood the kind of Confederate counterstrategy that Forrest advocated. Sherman was also keenly aware of the damage that Forrest's cavalry alone could inflict on the federal rear area, while his invasion army battled the Confederates in Georgia. Accordingly, Sherman ordered that Forrest be attacked and destroyed, or at least pinned down by aggressive operations somewhere along the Mississippi river.[4] Forrest must be kept away from "his lifeline to the rear—the railroad back through Chattanooga and Nashville to the Ohio river." Sherman stressed the importance of this lifeline when he wrote: "That single line of railroad, four hundred seventy-three miles long, supplied an army of 100,000 men and 35,000 animals."[5]

The Confederate raider's widespread movements also worried General Grant, who ordered Sherman and Hurlbut to bag Forrest. From his headquarters at Culpeper, Virginia, Grant instructed them: "Send Grierson with all your cavalry with orders to find and destroy him where found." Anticipating Grant's order, Sherman diverted the division of Brigadier General James Veatch for an attack on Forrest. Veatch, in motion with his infantry to join Sherman's army near Chattanooga, now traveled from Paducah, Kentucky, along the Tennessee River to Purdy, Tennessee, where he could cut off Forrest's escape into Mississippi.[6] Veatch arrived at Purdy on 30 March and entered an apparent vacuum. He saw not the slightest sign of military activity, and no one told him to remain there. From information obtained locally, Veatch concluded that Forrest would not show up for days, if at all. He decided to leave Purdy and continue to Prospect, Tennessee, in line with his original movement orders. Actually, Sherman had not been specific in his initial instructions, and on 2 April he issued follow-up orders for Veatch to remain at Purdy. Unfortunately, Veatch did not receive them until he had arrived at Prospect, some one hundred miles to the east. The exasperated Sherman declared that Veatch committed a blunder in quitting Purdy.[7]

At Memphis, meanwhile, Grierson carried out his part of the plan in a half-hearted manner. On 3 April he ordered Colonel George Waring's brigade to march on the Somerville road, in an attempt to push Forrest eastward against Veatch. The Nineteenth Pennsylvania Cavalry, leading the advance, came upon an enemy picket some fifteen miles from Memphis, and fighting broke out. Waring ordered up the Seventh Indiana Cavalry to the support of the Pennsylvanians. Although Waring estimated the rebel force to be larger than his, the enemy withdrew "in such a manner as to seem to invite us to follow into the swamp, which lay immediately in front of our position." At this time too Waring's scouts reported discovering a very large supporting enemy force on the flanks. Overestimating the rebel strength at two thousand men, Waring decided to call off the fight. He had instructions "not to bring on a general engagement with a superior force." Consequently, Waring did not commit the Second New Jersey Cavalry, and he retired the brigade to Raleigh, near Memphis. In actuality Waring had been bluffed by a Confederate force of some two hundred men, commanded by Lieutenant Colonel J. M. Crews.[8]

The inept performance of his subordinates again upset Sherman. He tried hard "to drive Forrest to the wall," but all measures had failed. Sherman placed the blame on "the timidity of our officers at Memphis."[9] But Hurlbut believed that his forces were nothing more than adequate for defense. Two of his veteran cavalry regiments, the Third Michigan, thirteen hundred strong, and the Seventh Kansas of eleven hundred troopers, awaited fresh horses in St. Louis. "It is the absence of veterans and the lack of horses that has caused the Forrest raid," Hurlbut told General McPherson, Sherman's subordinate. But the testy Sherman began to suspect that Forrest could not be prevented from marching his raiders out of Kentucky and West Tennessee. Grant too gained this impression, and he asked Sherman whether "a bolder commander than General Hurlbut will be required for holding the Mississippi firmly."[10]

On 12 April Forrest attacked Fort Pillow on the Mississippi, some forty miles above Memphis. Both white and black troops manned the fort, and an officer of limited experience commanded them. The Confederates overpowered the garrison. In the confusion of the fighting many Negro soldiers were killed when further resistance appeared useless. Some of them allegedly resumed fighting after they had once surrendered. The "Fort Pillow Massacre" created a storm of protest throughout the North and prompted a congressional investigation. The massacre became the atrocity story of the Civil War.[11]

Sherman grew furious with Hurlbut over the Fort Pillow affair. He could not understand why federal troops occupied the fort when he had ordered the site abandoned before the start of the Meridian Expedition in February. He told Grant: "General Hurlbut must have sent this garrison up recently from Memphis." Thoroughly exasperated, he exclaimed: "I don't know what to do with Hurlbut." Grant replied by wire the same day, 15 April, to relieve Hurlbut and replace him with Cadwallader C. Washburn. Acting promptly, Sherman transferred Hurlbut to Cairo, Illinois, as Washburn arrived at Memphis on 23 April. The new West Tennessee District commander said he found matters in a deplorable state and the troops in wretched condition. He

Major General C. C. Washburn. COURTESY OF LIBRARY OF CONGRESS.

complained to his Tennessee Department commander, General McPherson: "The cavalry was all broken down, and less than 2,000 could be mounted." Nevertheless he set to work at once to improve the condition of the regiments, so that he could move against Forrest.[12]

Washburn came from a distinguished political family. His brother Israel was the War Governor of Maine, while brother Elihu represented Illinois in the Congress and also chaired the House Military Affairs Committee. The three brothers had served in the Congress together before the war. After representing Wisconsin in the Congress for three terms, C. C. Washburn resigned his office to join the army. Following the war, he reentered politics, served a term in the Congress, and then was elected governor of Wisconsin, 1872-73.

The day after Washburn took command at Memphis, Brigadier General Samuel D. Sturgis arrived, ordered by Sherman to take charge of the cavalry and to whip Forrest. Sherman explained that he wanted "to give life to that command." Sturgis had been chief of cavalry of the Department of the Ohio for nine months. Earlier he had commanded a division in the Army of the Potomac and had fought at South Mountain, Antietam, and Fredericksburg.[13]

With the arrival of Sturgis, Grierson asked to be relieved, since he saw no need for two cavalry generals in the same command. He had chafed under the weak leadership of Sooy Smith in the debacle of the Meridian Expedition, and Smith left Grierson a worn-out and demoralized command. The assignment of Sturgis indicated a possible replay of the same distasteful episode. Grierson asked Sherman "to be relieved from duty with the cavalry at this point, and ordered to Illinois and Iowa for the purpose of reorganizing, arming, mounting, and equipping the regiments of my old division, now absent on furlough." Sherman kept Grierson at Memphis.[14]

Washburn took immediate and vigorous measures to build up his combat strength. He seized all the serviceable horses in Memphis, as Sherman had urged him to do. Washburn also called on Brigadier General J. McArthur, commanding at Vicksburg, to reinforce Memphis with his available cavalry. Thus, only five days after taking command, Washburn could tell McPherson that he would mount an expedition against Forrest on 30 April and that Sturgis would command the force. In the temporary absence of Grierson, Waring took charge of the cavalry division and Kargé assumed command of the First Brigade. The Second Brigade was commanded by Colonel Edward F. Winslow, who had

Brigadier General Samuel D. Sturgis. COURTESY OF NATIONAL ARCHIVES.

performed so well for Sherman in the Meridian Expedition. Winslow had just come up from Vicksburg with 550 men and 800 horses.[15]

On the morning of 30 April 1864 Sturgis left Memphis with a force of three thousand cavalry and thirty-four hundred infantry. He marched east toward the Hatchie river, in a coordinated move with a large infantry unit that he believed steamed up the Tennessee river to the vicinity of Purdy. The two-pronged drive was Sherman's old plan, which Veatch had bungled and which Sherman's subordinate commanders still tried to execute. The cavalry found the going rough, making only seventeen miles the first day. The heavy rains had ruined the roads and raised the level of all creeks so that crossings could be made only at bridge sites. In some instances this meant repairing the old bridges or building new ones. The second day out Kargé marched his brigade twenty-two miles to Oakland. Meanwhile the infantry under Colonel William L. McMillen traveled by rail to the Wolf River near Moscow. Detraining, McMillen's soldiers encountered a most difficult and time-consuming crossing.

Marching with the cavalry, Sturgis reached Somerville. He paused here to wait for McMillen to pass over the Wolf River, in order to keep the infantry within supporting distance of the cavalry. The commander wanted to avoid the possibility of Forrest's coming between the two elements of his command. Sturgis marched in the general direction of the enemy, but he needed specific information on the enemy's movements. He also wanted to seize the bridge at the Hatchie river to permit his uninterrupted advance. He turned to Kargé to lead a light force on a rapid march to Bolivar. The special command consisted of the Second New Jersey Cavalry, four hundred strong, under Major P. Jones Yorke, the Tenth Missouri Cavalry, two hundred strong, and two pieces of artillery. In all, Kargé commanded a select group of seven hundred men. Sturgis placed the remainder of Waring's cavalry division five miles east of Somerville, where he could support Kargé or oppose an enemy advance from the north until McMillen was heard from. Kargé led his small brigade out of Somerville at 1:30 P.M. and marched rapidly toward Bolivar, twenty-three miles away. Within seven miles of the Hatchie river, he ran into Confederate pickets whom he pursued to a defensive position one mile west of Bolivar. Here Kargé found a rebel force that he estimated to be eight hundred strong, blocking his advance from behind formidable entrenchments. These were old earthworks constructed by General Grant's army two years before, and the rebels were taking full advantage of this protection.,[16]

Kargé had two options. Having found the enemy, the principal part of his mission, he could send word to Sturgis and wait for Waring's cavalry division to reinforce him for the attack. This was the safe course of action, especially if Forrest should have additional elements of his command immediately beyond the Hatchie. The late hour of 6:00 P.M. offered another sound reason for delaying the attack until morning. But apparently Kargé had had his fill of simply marching and countermarching. Motivated by a fighting instinct, he decided on the second option— to attack Forrest—and this notwithstanding the Confederate general's great reputation. It was formidable indeed, and Forrest's subordinates were justly proud of their invincible commander. But his string of victories had also made them very cocky. A short time before the engagement at Bolivar, Brigadier General James R. Chalmers congratulated the soldiers of his First Division on their recent operations. He boasted:

> The once arrogant Grierson, who has never recovered his equanimity since his flight from Okolona, ventured out with two brigades to look after us, when Lieutenant Colonel Crews, with his dashing battalion, defeated his advance guard, and sent him hurriedly back to Memphis, where he remained trembling behind his fortifications and frightened at every mention of the name of Forrest.[17]

While Kargé undoubtedly respected the reputation of Forrest, he did not fear him. Nor was he impressed with Forrest's aura of "invincibility which most certainly affected the resolution of commanders sent against him."[18] Although eager to launch his attack, Kargé would not order his mounted troopers in a frontal assault on dismounted and entrenched skirmishers. Instead, he brought up the two pieces of artillery to give him some bombardment effect. Then, engaging the rebels in a sharp fire fight, Kargé deployed Captain Michael Gallagher's squadron to the flank, to charge the left of the enemy line. However, a deep ravine blocked Gallagher's advance, and Kargé had to forgo that maneuver.[19]

The rebels at Bolivar were Company E of the Seventh Tennessee Cavalry Regiment and McDonald's Battalion, commanded by Lieutenant Colonel J. M. Crews, the same man who had cowed Waring near Memphis a month earlier. The men of Company E had been recruited from Bolivar and the surrounding farms of Hardeman County. They found themselves defending their home town.

Crews communicated the approach of Union cavalry to Forrest, who ordered the Bolivar contingent "to check the Federal advance in order that everything on wheels moving south might have a better chance to escape." Once the battle had begun, however, Forrest with his select one hundred-man escort unexpectedly galloped up to the battle area and took charge.[20] The fighting seemed too close for Forrest to miss, and he made this engagement his fight. Furthermore, he was not content merely to defend his position. His combative nature impelled him to attack Kargé, apparently to teach the brash Union colonel a lesson. In characteristic fashion Forrest carried out a furious charge against Kargé's men.

"That Devil" Forrest usually routed the Yankees with such tactics, but Kargé did not run. Forrest, his attack blunted, quickly withdrew to the safety of the entrenchments.[21] The Confederates estimated Kargé's strength at two thousand and believed they inflicted a heavy loss of forty or fifty killed and wounded. The rebels knew that the Union calvarymen fought at a disadvantage against their own protected positions, for "one man in a trench was worth three in an assault."[22] Kargé's estimate of eight hundred rebels, on the other hand, was a realistic figure. According to Forrest the number became three hundred, when he ordered several hundred unarmed men, whom Crews escorted, to leave Bolivar for Ripley, Mississippi.[23]

Combining firepower with maneuver, Kargé began to squeeze the Confederates out of their trenches. He sensed victory and now ordered the Second New Jersey to charge the fortifications boldly. Unable or unwilling to withstand the Union charge, the defenders abandoned their positions and retreated in confusion toward the town. Maintaining the momentum of the attack, Kargé directed his cannoneers to fire several rounds into Bolivar. As a rebel cavalryman told of the shelling: "One struck the residence of Mrs. Brooks, another went through the roof of the stable on the Harkins place, and I saw one cut off the top of a cedar in front of the Dr. Peters place . . . ." Chagrined to think that Company E was being chased through its home town, he said: "It threw a damper over every tender sentiment, and all thoughts of love vanished into thin air, for we were thanking our stars that we had escaped death at the hands of the Federals."[24] Although the rebels retreated to the safety of the far bank of the swollen Hatchie, Forrest made sure to block further pursuit by destroying the bridge. The hour was past 8:00 P.M., and darkness began to settle over the battlefield. With the bridge out and being unfamiliar with the terrain, Kargé halted operations for the night. The engagement, which General Forrest called a "sharp affair," cost Kargé two men killed and five wounded. The Confederates lost seven killed and twenty wounded, including four officers, one of whom was Forrest's adjutant general, Major J. P. Strange, whose right arm was shattered by a minié ball.[25]

The *New York Times* reported 9 May that "Forrest has at last found a foe who doesn't plead weakness." The day before, the *Times* headlined the column on the war in Tennessee: "Forrest's Cut-throats Defeated by Gen. Sturgis." The brief article described the engagement in which "the advance of Gen. Sturgis' cavalry, 700 strong," beat Forrest. The news item concluded that "Gen. Sturgis is in hot pursuit." [26] Sturgis's pursuit, however, was anything but hot. Receiving Kargé's battle report during the night of 2-3 May, Sturgis ordered the cavalry division to Bolivar at daylight. Rather than pursue Forrest with his horsemen alone, Sturgis also ordered the infantry to Bolivar and delayed the pursuit.

Sturgis still believed that he acted in coordination with an infantry force near Purdy. His scouts soon brought back information that convinced him that there was neither a cooperating force at Purdy nor one on the way. He also learned that the rear of Forrest's command cleared Purdy the night of 2 May and moved on to Tupelo. Notwithstanding Forrest's two-day marching advantage, Sturgis finally ordered the cavalry division to ride to Ripley, where he thought that Forrest might make a stand. But the elusive raider had gone farther south to Okolona.

The Union commander felt unprepared for an extended expedition into Mississippi. He found the countryside destitute of forage, and his food supply was low. Waring and the two brigade commanders agreed with him that pursuit of Forrest deep into Mississippi, without food and forage, would only invite disaster. From the vicinity of Ripley the expedition marched back to Memphis, arriving 11 May. Sturgis reported to Sherman: "I regret very much that I could not have the pleasure of bringing you his hair, but he is too great a plunderer to fight anything like an equal force, and we have to be satisfied with driving him from the State." As for Washburn, the disappointed general experienced the first of several frustrations in his attempts to destroy Forrest. Washburn explained to McPherson: "I have done all that it was possible for any man to do since I came here." Could he have had the cooperating force from the direction of the Tennessee River, Washburn believed that he would surely have destroyed Forrest. He consoled himself with the thought that West Tennessee and Kentucky were now clear of any organized rebel forces. [27]

In the engagement at Bolivar the main effort fell on the Second New Jersey Cavalry. Company E, under the command of Lieutenant Lewis Rainear, opened the fight and took the brunt of the action. The regiment lost two men killed—Orderly Sergeant E. E. Cooper of Company F and Private George Schweitzer of Company H. In addition five troopers were wounded and twenty horses were killed or wounded. Yorke wrote the New Jersey Adjutant General that the regiment behaved nobly. "I am happy to say," he added, "that the Second New Jersey Cavalry enjoys the best reputation, and the esteem not only of the commanding general but all the troops in this department."[28]

Joseph Kargé witnessed a convincing battle test of his regiment. As the commander of the advance force of the Sturgis expedition, he gave the regiment the chance to fight, and against the dreaded Forrest, at that. Kargé beat Forrest. The "Invincible Raider" would later meet defeat again at Tupelo on 14 July 1864 at the hands of Major General Andrew J. Smith, and at Selma, Alabama, on 2 April 1865, against Major General James H. Wilson. Smith and Wilson were the only Union generals to defeat Forrest.[29] Kargé, the colonel, beat Forrest first at Bolivar, Tennessee, on 2 May 1864.[30]

Battle of Brice's Cross-Roads

Kargé Makes Daring Raid behind Enemy Lines

To Sherman, Forrest loomed a greater threat than the Confederate Army in North Georgia. Determined to destroy Forrest at all costs, Sherman explored unusual sources of help. On 23 May 1864 he asked the Governors of Indiana, Illinois, Iowa, and Wisconsin for twenty thousand militia "to cover my communications." He told them his march into Georgia had added another one hundred miles to his railroad lifeline. He wanted General Washburn to employ part of this militia, with a cooperating force from Memphis, in a raid against Columbus, Mississippi. The purpose again was to "prevent Forrest and Lee from swinging over against my communications.[1]

No sooner had Sturgis returned to Memphis from the fruitless pursuit of Forrest in early May than Washburn began preparations for another expedition into Mississippi. Evidently not wanting Sturgis for his field commander, Washburn ordered his return to Sherman's headquarters. Sherman, however, immediately sent Sturgis back to Memphis, and the itinerant general arrived as Washburn neared the final stage of readiness. Since Sturgis was the ranking general among the brigadiers, Washburn believed that he had no choice but to give him the command. The expeditionary force consisted of a cavalry division of three thousand under General Grierson, three infantry brigades of some five thousand soldiers, and twenty-two pieces of towed artillery. Sherman had telegraphed Washburn that a force of six thousand would be required, but Washburn increased it to nearly eight thousand. Washburn also provisioned the command amply, since the area of northern Mississippi had been fought over and devastated repeatedly. The supply trains carried rations for eighteen days in some 250 wagons. "I saw to it personally," Washburn said, "that they lacked nothing to insure a successful campaign.[2]

On 1 June Grierson took up an advance position at LaFayette (Rossville), thirty-three miles east of Memphis. His First Cavalry

Brigade under Waring, fifteen hundred strong, consisted of the Fourth Missouri, Seventh Indiana, Nineteenth Pennsylvania, and the Second New Jersey. When General Sturgis detailed the Pennsylvanians as his personal escort, he temporarily assigned to Waring's brigade a detachment of two hundred troopers from the Third and Ninth Illinois Cavalry. Winslow led the Second Cavalry Brigade, composed of the Third Iowa, Fourth Iowa, Tenth Missouri, and Seventh Illinois. Winslow reported his strength as 1,489, some 300 troopers less than credited him by Sturgis. The strength of the Second New Jersey Cavalry Regiment had dropped to seventeen officers and 350 men; but, despite the frustrations of the Sooy Smith campaign, the spirit of the regiment remained high. Kargé looked forward to engaging the rebels again.[3]

General Washburn formally assigned Sturgis the command of the expeditionary force by orders of 31 May 1864, which Sturgis received the next day. Moving to an advance position, the infantry brigades traveled from Memphis by rail to a point just east of Collierville. Sturgis likewise rode a train with his staff to the vicinity of LaFayette and took personal command of the expedition on the morning of 2 June. He grouped the three separate brigades into a provisional division and gave the command to Colonel William McMillen. Colonel Alexander Wilkin then took charge of McMillen's First Brigade, two thousand strong. Colonel George B. Hoge commanded the Second Brigade, sixteen hundred strong, and Colonel Edward Bouton led the Third Brigade, twelve hundred strong, consisting of two regiments and one artillery battery of black soldiers.[4]

On 3 June 1864 the cavalry division led the march into Mississippi. The movement came not a day too soon. Washburn had received information that Forrest, with a fairly large mounted force at Tupelo, planned an expedition of some kind, most likely into Middle Tennessee. The information proved reliable, for General Stephen D. Lee granted Forrest permission to strike at Sherman's railroad from Nashville to Georgia. Forrest departed Tupelo with three thousand troops on June 1, the day the federal forces left Memphis to take up their advance positions. Reaching Russelville, Alabama, on 3 June, Forrest received orders to return at once to meet the challenge of the federal invasion. He raced back the seventy miles to Tupelo in two days.[5]

Washburn had ordered Sturgis to march directly for Corinth, via Salem and Ruckersville. Once Sturgis had captured Corinth and destroyed all supplies that his command could not carry, he would move south along the Mobile and Ohio Railroad to Tupelo, destroying the railroad along the way. Washburn expected Forrest to head north toward Corinth to save the railroad. In the event that Forrest did not react immediately, Sturgis would continue as far south as Okolona, where the infantry would rest for two days while Grierson's cavalry conducted raids to Macon and Columbus. Next the infantry would march west to Grenada, there to be joined by the cavalry, and the reunited command would return to Memphis.[6]

Bad weather plagued Sturgis from the start. Heavy rains drenched the countryside daily, causing the roads to become almost impassable. In spite of numerous delays the expedition made steady progress, but Sturgis had little information, if any, on the whereabouts of enemy concentrations. At the same time, his command was harassed from time to time by parties of Confederate scouts who were guided by information from the citizens. Sturgis noted this disadvantage in his reports: "Our movements and numbers are always known to the enemy because every woman and child is one of them, but we . . . can only learn the movements of the enemy and his numbers by actually fighting for the information."[7]

Having reached Salem, Sturgis decided to determine the enemy situation in the vicinity of Corinth. If there were Confederate forces there, he wished to isolate them by destroying the railroad track and cutting the telegraph line south of Corinth. He also wanted to seize the bridge on the Tuscumbia river, lying southwest of Corinth, to insure his rapid march on that town. Calling on his cavalry commander, Sturgis ordered Grierson to mount a reconnaissance force, composed of a select body of four hundred cavalrymen and "commanded by a competent officer." Sturgis and Grierson had one officer in mind for this daring raid and reconnaissance—Colonel Kargé. His force consisted of two hundred troopers of the Second New Jersey and two hundred from Winslow's brigade, two of whose units, the Tenth Missouri and the Seventh Illinois, each provided one hundred of their best men.

Kargé was assigned a specific mission: Ride via Ripley to Rienzi, on the Mobile and Ohio Railroad; there tap the telegraph line to gain Confederate information. Sturgis gave Kargé his only telegrapher for this purpose. Once he had obtained sufficient information, he was to destroy the telegraph line and any Confederate supplies, then, marching north along the railroad, was to destroy bridges and trestle work as far as the Tuscumbia River. Next he was to seize the bridge over the river on

TENNESSEE

Bolivar

June 3

Lafayette

MEMPHIS & CHARLESTON R.R.

Saulsbury

Grand
Junction

MISSISSIPPI

Tuscumbia R.

Corinth

STURGIS'   MARCH   June 5

K

Salem

Kossuth

Danville

Ruckersville

Holly Springs

KARGÉ'S ROUTE

Rienzi

Creek

Ripley
June 8

Boonville

Tippah

June 9

Tallahatchie R.

Stubbs'
Farm

New Albany

Brice's
Cross Roads
June 10

Baldwyn

Ellistown

Guntown

Oxford

Pontotoc

Tupelo

Okolona

MOBILE & OHIO R.R.

KARGÉ'S RAID TO RIENZI
AND RECONNAISSANCE TO CORINTH
(Battle of Brice's Cross Roads)
Kargé's Route, 5-8 June, 1864:
Kargé's Bivouac, Night of 7-8 June: ..... K
March of Sturgis to Brice's Cross Roads:
0   10   20   30
SCALE OF MILES

the road from Danville to Corinth, or, in case the river was fordable, to hold the ford on the road leading from Kossuth to Corinth. Finally, he was to gain all possible information on enemy forces at Corinth and communicate this intelligence to Grierson in the vicinity of Kossuth.

Sturgis asked a great deal of Kargé. The mission was not only ambitious but also very dangerous. Kargé's special force would march well beyond the protective arms of the command and risk being cut off and annihilated. Notwithstanding the danger, Kargé led his command from Salem at 6:00 P.M., 5 June, on an all-night march to Rienzi. His timetable called for arrival there as soon after daylight as possible.

It had rained every day for the past four days, and heavy showers fell again on the afternoon preceding Kargé's departure. Despite the muddy ground, Kargé set a fast pace for his troopers as a matter of utmost necessity. He had to insure that all reports to enemy commanders on his location at any particular time would lag behind his movements by a safe margin. Consequently, he drove his men hard. As Winslow later reported on the condition of the Tenth Missouri Cavalry: "This command had been nearly dismounted by the severe marching under Colonel Kargé toward Corinth." [8] Maintaining the fast pace, Kargé's troopers reached Ripley at midnight. "They remained only long enough to pass through, searching Dr. Whitlow's house," local citizens reported. Kargé departed Ripley on the Rienzi road. [9]

At Tupelo the next day Forrest received information that a Union cavalry force rode toward Rienzi. He determined to trap Kargé, and ordered Rucker's brigade, 700 strong, to ride north through Ripley in pursuit of him. Forrest also ordered Bell's brigade, 2,787 strong, to the same point. Forrest believed that Sturgis would follow Kargé. As the rebel commander explained: "The enemy had endeavored to cross the Hatchie River in the direction of Rienzi, but owing to high water had only succeeded in throwing forward about 500 cavalry, which entered Rienzi on the morning of the seventh and attempted the destruction of the railroad, but left hastily after burning the depot and destroying a few yards of the railroad track." [10]

Despite the swollen condition of the Hatchie, Kargé crossed his four hundred troopers without incident. He met with little opposition, but wherever he ran into parties of Confederates they were surprised to see Union cavalry. In Rienzi, Kargé moved quickly to gain information and to destroy Confederate government property. He employed part of the command as security along the avenues of approach to the village, for he knew that a surprise attack by one of Forrest's brigades would mean almost certain annihilation. The remainder of the command burned down the depot and destroyed a bridge of considerable length; also, to a limited extent, Kargé's troopers destroyed trestle work and tore up the rails. It was hoped that by destroying the railroad the Confederate trains would be bottled up in Corinth. But since Kargé's information indicated that the rebels had already gone to Tupelo, he saw no reason for extensive destruction of the track at the risk of prolonged delay.[11]

Notwithstanding the small size of his force, Kargé took a calculated risk and divided his command. He ordered Captain Amos P. Curry with his one hundred Missouri cavalrymen to seize the bridge on the Tuscumbia river, some ten miles to the north. Galloping to the crossing site, Curry found his way challenged by about one hundred rebel cavalry of Lieutenant Colonel John F. Newsom's regiment. The Missourians charged into the Confederates and a lively skirmish took place. Curry drove the rebels across the river, taking seven prisoners, but not before the Confederates succeeded in destroying the bridge and stopping further pursuit.

On 7 June, near the Tuscumbia River bottoms, Kargé sent a message to Grierson by courier. In anticipation of such contact, the general had ordered patrols to the Hatchie River and beyond. Kargé reported the absence of enemy forces at Corinth and placed the nearest concentration at Tupelo. He said that he had captured twenty-one rebels without the loss of a man or horse. "My command is in the best of spirits," Kargé wrote, "but my horses are very tired, owing to the heavy roads and forced march I have made the last twenty-four hours." Receiving Kargé's report, Sturgis changed his direction of march from Corinth to Ripley, on a southeasterly course for the Mobile and Ohio Railroad. He reminded Grierson to notify Kargé of the change in plans. Sturgis showed concern for the safety of Kargé's men, knowing that a Confederate cavalry brigade had followed them from the vicinity of Ripley to Rienzi. Nevertheless Kargé himself had the prime responsibility for the security of his command.[12]

Kargé did not know that Forrest had moved two brigades to surround his force of four hundred cavalrymen, although he was keenly aware of such a possibility. As he began his return march, he noted danger signals that indicated that the rebels virtually surrounded his small force. Kargé played the fox. Rather than travel along the well-defined roads, he led his men through the almost bottomless swamps. He impressed a local citizen to guide them and warned the man that he would forfeit his life if he betrayed them. The Mississippian led Kargé's command through the swamps to the Hatchie River. During this wretched movement several horses drowned, but Kargé had replacements, which he had seized along the way. That night of 7 June the men spent a miserable time on the banks of the river, thoroughly soaked, tired, and hungry. General Sturgis's telegrapher described Kargé's feelings: "I doubt if any swamp in the South was ever treated to more Dutch curses than he freely gave during the twelve hours we were forced by the situation of affairs to pass in that most dismal spot."[13]

At 4:00 A.M. the next morning Sturgis received word that Kargé had bivouacked his men for the night on an island in the Hatchie. Believing Kargé to be seriously threatened by the enemy, Sturgis directed Grierson to reinforce him with a regiment of cavalry, and promptly five hundred men with two howitzers from the Fourth Missouri and the Seventh Indiana regiments marched to Kargé's relief. Meanwhile, with the approach of daylight, Kargé's troopers felled trees across the turbulent river, which was very high from the heavy rains. The entire command then crossed on the trees, carrying their blankets and saddles and swimming the horses. Kargé quickened the march when rebel cavalry, having learned of his location, galloped in pursuit. Kargé escaped. The relief force joined him at about 8:00 A.M. just east of Ruckersville, and all arrived in Ripley that evening. Kargé had successfully accomplished his mision and eluded his pursuers over a distance of seventy-five miles. He brought back his raiding force not only intact but also augmented by twenty-one prisoners.[14]

Having modified his direction of march, Sturgis dispatched a message to Washburn on 9 June, informing him of the change. He also reported on Kargé's independent operation to Rienzi and Corinth. Highly complimentary of Kargé's performance, Sturgis said: "The colonel joined us last evening after a very severe march, which jaded his animals very much. I have as yet received no official report of his operations, but from what I learn of the telegraph operator with him, and others, the whole reconnaissance was conducted with the usual energy and intelligence of that fine officer." Sturgis told Washburn that Kargé crossed the Hatchie when the river surged high with flood waters. Further, Kargé had to fight off the pursuit of Bell's brigade from the vicinity of Ripley to Rienzi, and he lost no men but brought back prisoners and horses.[15]

At Ripley, Sturgis began to have doubts about the value of going on, and he called a meeting of his division commanders and one brigade commander, Colonel Hoge, who happened to be present. The commanding general stressed the exhausted and underfed condition of the animals, which had labored through the mud for several days. He mentioned the delays caused by the daily rains and the bad roads, which he believed had given the enemy time to concentrate their forces against him. He admitted his fear of a possible defeat and "the utter hopelessness of saving our train or artillery" in that event. Both division commanders agreed with him in the probable consequence of defeat, and Grierson also favored turning back. McMillen, however, urged the commander not to abandon the mission without a fight. McMillen reminded Sturgis that he had conducted a fruitless pursuit of Forrest only a few weeks ago and could not afford to return to Memphis empty-handed again. Sturgis made his decision: Continue the march. Although he still harbored considerable doubt, he reasoned that, even if the expedition should fail, his losses could be considered insignificant in comparison with the great benefits to Sherman in the protection of his lifeline.[16]

Sturgis was by nature a man of contradictions. He could be cool and warm, cautious and headlong, close and frank, prudent and reckless.[17] He wavered in his determinattion to carry out his mission, and this indecision had a negative influence on the command. He also faced a problem of recognition. Since he had played no part in organizing the expedition, he was unacquainted with his command. As he admitted: "I was an entire stranger to the troops and the organizations." To his credit, Sturgis improved his span of control by grouping the three separate infantry brigades into a division. Sturgis normally and habitually dealt with the two division commanders, and he had a speaking relationship with the brigade commanders. It is doubtful, though, whether he knew the regimental commanders, with the exception of Kargé.[18] If these problems did not suffice, Sturgis was also beset by a rumor that pictured him a drunkard. Some members of the command had seen the general intoxicated at the Gayoso Hotel in Memphis. An officer of the Second New Jersey Cavalry related: "I saw him with my own eyes the day before the troops started, so drunk that he could not tell a billiard ball from the cue he was trying to play with." The disastrous result of the upcoming Battle of Brice's Cross-Roads would bring the accusation that he was drunk on the day of the battle, an allegation that his division commanders categorically denied.[19]

Having made the decision to continue the march, Sturgis readied the command for imminent fighting. On the evening of 8 June he cautioned the brigade commanders to maintain strict discipline in camp and to act always as if the enemy were present. That night heavy rains drenched the camp. The following morning Sturgis ordered some four hundred sick and fatigued men and forty-one empty wagons to return to Memphis. He disposed of elements that would reduce his ability to fight. The day's march brought the command to Stubbs's Farm on the Ripley-Guntown road, some fifteen miles from Guntown. Again the rain poured down on the encampment for two hours.[20]

The fateful day of 10 June 1864 commenced by being very hot and humid. The cavalry division marched at 5:30 A.M., followed by the infantry at seven o'clock. Grierson led the cavalry, while Sturgis rode at the head of the infantry division. The wagon train followed last, protected by Bouton's black brigade. The animals labored to pull the wagons through the yellow, slippery clay. Waring's brigade had the lead that morning. Just before reaching the crossroads at Brice's house, six miles from Guntown, the advance struck a picket of the enemy, who attempted to destroy a bridge at Tishomingo Creek but fled. Arriving at the forks of the road at 9:45 A.M., Grierson sent out strong patrols on the different roads. Indications pointed to enemy concentrations at Baldwyn, six miles to the east, on the Mobile and Ohio Railroad.

At Brice's the roads led in three directions: northeast to Baldwyn, southeast to Guntown, and southwest to Ellistown and Pontotoc. Captain E. Hunn Hanson's squadron of the Fourth Missouri Cavalry had gone barely a mile on the Baldwyn Road when it met a heavy force of rebels and fighting erupted. Waring went to Hanson's support with the Second New Jersey, Third and Ninth Illinois, and a section of howitzers. He ordered a staff officer, meanwhile, to deploy the brigade along the edge of a thicket, one-half mile east of the crossroads. Finding the rebels too strong for him, Waring fell back to his line of battle and completed the deployment of his brigade. He manned the line with the Fourth Missouri, Seventh Indiana, and the Third and Ninth Illinois regiments. He held the Second New Jerssey in reserve, ready to reinforce the right wing should it be threatened. On this morning Lieutenant Colonel Marcus Kitchen, the executive officer, commanded the Second New Jersey, for Kargé had been assigned other duties. As Waring deployed his regiments on both sides of the

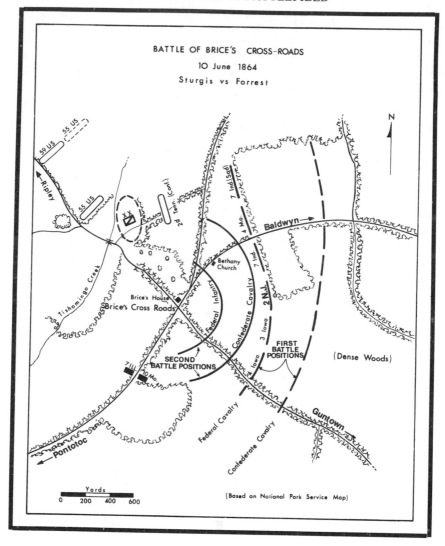

BATTLE OF BRICE'S CROSS-ROADS
10 June 1864
Sturgis vs Forrest

(Based on National Park Service Map)

Baldwyn Road, Grierson committed a portion of Winslow's brigade on the Guntown Road, extending the line to connect with Waring's right flank. Grierson retained approximately six hundred of Winslow's troopers in reserve. Having established his line of skirmishers in a wide arc, with the crossroads about a mile to the rear, Grierson sent a message to Sturgis, informing him that he had met the enemy and that he could hold his position if the infantry came up promptly.[21]

The battlefield was heavily timbered and further choked with an undergrowth of blackjack and scrub oak. Some cleared land lay around the Brice's house, and an open belt about a quarter-mile wide cut across the Baldwyn Road. Overall, however, the heavy vegetation of the battlefield permitted skirmishers to approach to within a few yards of each other without being observed. Forrest used the screening effect to advantage, since the federal troops could not see that he had attacked with an inferior force.[22] Grierson described the first four hours of fighting: "The enemy advanced upon us in large numbers, with double line of skirmishers and line of battle, with heavy supports; we succeeded, however, in holding our own and in repulsing with great slaughter three distinct and desperate charges." In Waring's sector the brigade repulsed the first two assaults. The third one, involving hand-to-hand fighting, forced back the brigade's right flank, although Waring committed the Second New Jersey and the reserve of the Seventh Indiana. Falling back a short distance, Waring formed a second line, which he held until the infantry relieved him.[23]

With a force of thirty-five hundred troopers, Forrest had launched a fierce attack against Grierson's cavalry on a battleground of his own choosing. The night before, General Stephen D. Lee, the department commander, met with Forrest at Booneville to outline his general plan. Lee intended to battle Sturgis somewhere near Tupelo, but he gave Forrest a free hand. Accordingly, Forrest decided to attack the invasion army with his own command, despite the Union superiority of two to one. His scouts brought back accurate information of the concentration of the Federal cavalry and infantry at Stubbs's Farm. In his own mind Forrest was quite certain how Sturgis would conduct operations the next day. Like a prophet, he predicted the action to his subordinate commanders. He said that Sturgis would send out the cavalry ahead of the infantry, and the mounted troops would reach the crossroads three hours in advance. In that time he planned to defeat Grierson's cavalry. When the fighting began, he went on, Sturgis would hurry up the infantry. "It is going to be hot as hell," he added, "and coming on a run for five or six miles, their infantry will be so tired out we will ride right over them."[24] Despite his confidence, Forrest did not defeat Grierson during the four hours of savage fighting. He pounded the Union cavalry severely and forced them back from the initial point of contact. Both sides fought as dismounted infantry because the heavy vegetation prevented the employment of mounted troops, and Grierson considered his defense a holding action for the infantry.

Grierson's courier reached Sturgis about mid-way between Stubbs's Farm and Brice's. The infantrymen were then struggling through the swampy bottoms of the Hatchie River, made the more difficult by the heavy rains of the past several days. No sooner had Sturgis received Grierson's first message than a second one arrived. Grierson informed him that the enemy was about six-hundred strong and that he would hold his position, but he still called for the infantry. Sturgis, having directed McMillen "to move up his advanced brigade as rapidly as possible without distressing the troops," rode to the crossroads, which he reached at noon. He found nearly all of the cavalry engaged and "the battle growing warm." As Forrest stepped up the tempo of the attack, Sturgis ordered a section of artillery, which had not as yet been employed, to fire on the enemy's reserves. The Confederate artillery replied at once with great accuracy, bursting every shell over or near the Union guns.

Sturgis received frequent calls for reinforcements, but he had none to offer as yet. He said that Winslow, whose brigade held the right of the line across the Guntown road, "was especially clamorous to be relieved and permitted to carry his brigade to the rear." Sturgis feared that Winslow might abandon his position without authority. This feeling sprang from his discovery that Waring, through some misunderstanding, had prematurely withdrawn his brigade and exposed the left of the battle line. Sturgis at once filled the gap with his escort, some one-hundred troopers of the Nineteenth Pennsylvania Cavalry.[25]

While marching to the battle area with the lead infantry brigade, McMillen kept receiving orders to hurry, and, despite the mud and oppressive heat, he accelerated the march. Ordering Hoge to move in quick time without any halts, McMillen rode ahead with his staff to the crossroads, "where everything was going to the devil as fast as it possibly could." He said the cavalry kept falling back rapidly in disorder, and the roads at the fork were crowded with retreating cavalry, led horses, ambulances, wagons, and artillery. Already the rebels poured artillery rounds on the crossroads and continued the shelling during the arrival of the infantry. Hoge's brigade, exhausted by the rapid march and sultry air, reached the battlefield at about 1:30 P.M. Some twenty percent of the brigade had dropped out from heat exhaustion, for the temperature approached one hundred seven degrees and not a ripple stirred the air. McMillen rushed the regiments to the position held by Waring's cavalry on the Baldwyn Road. He then began the relief of Winslow's cavalry and completed the turnover with Colonel Alexander Wilkin's brigade. The cavalry withdrew to the Ripley Road, about a quarter of a mile west of the crossroads.

Sturgis and McMillen had deployed the infantry regiments in the face of heavy enemy fire. In fact, before the federal infantrymen were firmly in position, the rebels launched a very strong attack along the entire line and on both flanks. On the right, where McMillen then happened to be, the Federals gave way and lost some ground. McMillen brought up reinforcements to charge the enemy and regain the ground, driving back a portion of General Abraham Buford's Confederate division on the west of the Guntown Road. Although McMillen achieved some success on his right, the regiments to the left of the Guntown Road were thrown back to the crossroads in confusion. Neither positive orders nor entreaties would move them to fight back. The soldiers had become too exhausted to respond, and some were so fatigued they were unable to load their weapons.[26]

McMillen needed help. But of the troops not engaged, Bouton's brigade guarded the supply train, and Grierson's cavalry, still an organized body, became immobilized by Colonel C. R. Barteau's attack on the extreme left flank, well to the rear of the crossroads. Barteau's one regiment, the Second Tennessee Cavalry, deliberately made so much noise in the brush as to fool Grierson into believing that the Confederates were there in great numbers. Meanwhile the rebels continued to force the federal infantry back to the crossroads. Unable to hold the forks, McMillen decided to retire across Tishomingo Creek to the west bank, about one-quarter mile to the rear. He set up a temporary defense line on the east bank to protect the withdrawal. Across the creek he found the two regiments of Bouton's brigade. Ordering Bouton to hold his position as long as possible, he looked for another battle line on the first piece of suitable ground.[27]

About two miles from the crossroads, McMillen found Sturgis and Grierson. The commander had withdrawn most of the supply wagons and artillery to this point. Sturgis told McMillen that he would continue the retreat to Stubbs's Farm, and he ordered Grierson to send cavalry ahead to halt the infantry at that point. The fact that Grierson assigned the task to Winslow and accompanied his brigade to Stubbs's appears to contradict Sturgis, who derogated Winslow's performance. Referring to the rout of his expeditionary force, Sturgis said: ''No power could now check or control the panic-stricken mass as it swept toward the rear, led off by Colonel Winslow, at the head of his brigade of cavalry, and who never halted until he had reached Stubbs', ten miles in rear.''[28]

At Stubbs's Farm Sturgis again decided not to make a stand but to continue the retreat another fifteen miles to Ripley. By this time, 9:00 or 10:00 P.M., the supply wagons and the artillery were lost, having become mired down in the swampy bottoms of the Hatchie and abandoned. Thus far Sturgis had failed to rally the troops, and the rout became worse with each hour. Sturgis now assigned Winslow's brigade the difficult task of protecting the rear of the column. All night long the defeated troops walked and stumbled along as fast as they could over the wretched road and in extreme darkness. To ease their load, many discarded various items of equipment; some even threw away their weapons and ammunition.[29]

Sturgis and McMillen arrived at Ripley about 5:00 A.M. on 11 June. The day happened to be the general's forty-second birthday. Under the circumstances it is doubtful whether Sturgis had the time to think of it. McMillen reorganized the infantry and by 7:30 A.M. reported that the division, although in fairly good order, was short of ammunition. This fact caused Sturgis to conclude that he could not make a stand at Ripley and would be forced to continue the retreat. He believed his only tactic was to stay ahead of the charging rebels. He gave the order to march on the Salem road, with Waring's brigade in the lead, the infantry following, and Winslow's cavalry forming the rear guard. The fast marching placed a great strain on the rear guard. Major Abial Pierce, Fourth Iowa Cavalry, explained the problem: " . . . the general in command was leading the retreat so rapidly that I was obliged to leave hundreds every mile who were unable to keep up." Finally, about 2:00 P.M. Pierce rode to the front of the column to complain to the general. In response, Sturgis called a halt to give the troops a short rest.[30]

Before resuming the march, Sturgis relieved Winslow of the rear guard duty, since his men and horses were nearly exhausted and the entire brigade was out of ammunition. Sturgis withdrew the Second New Jersey Cavalry from Waring's brigade and assigned Kargé the mission of protecting the rear. His regiment alone replaced Winslow's brigade. For all its fighting and marching, the Second New Jersey had maintained its integrity as a regiment. It was one of the few remaining organized units in possession of some ammunition. Kargé's regiment also was the only cavalry unit in the entire command armed with the Spencer carbine. Since they possessed the firepower of the Spencer, it would seem that the Second New Jersey ought to have been assigned the rear guard from the start. But, granted that Kargé's regiment was disciplined and well-armed, his troopers had also been through a hectic thirty-six hours without rest and sleep. Nonetheless, as a matter of duty, the regiment took up the most difficult and exposed position in the march. Darkness began to descend and the New Jersey troopers would endure that night, the following day, and another night before the nightmare of the retreat ended.[31]

Exhilarated by his victory, Forrest determined on nothing less than the destruction of the federal army. He planned to cut off the escape of the retreating column at Salem. While Buford's division attacked savagely in direct pursuit, Forrest drove Bell's brigade along another road to Salem. Reaching his attack position, Forrest found that his intended prey had eluded him; the federal rear had swept by. In addition, parts of the routed army had scattered on various by-roads leading to Memphis. Meanwhile, the fast pace made Kargé's task almost impossible to carry out. Stopping periodically to fight off the pursuing rebels, the New Jersey companies had to gallop hard to overtake the command or risk being cut off. The troopers taxed their horses severely, even though the animals had been constantly saddled and ridden for the past two days with scarcely any feed. And the riders, too, suffered from their cramped positions and the unceasing motion of their horses. During the night of 11 June, a group of from fifty to sixty New Jersey cavalrymen, including several officers, became separated from the regiment and were captured.[32]

Kargé conducted the rear guard fighting with grim determination for a distance of nearly fifty miles—from the vicinity of Ripley to Collierville. At one critical point two companies blocked the pursuit of a greatly superior force of rebels for three hours. Kargé's performance drew praise from Colonel DeWitt C. Thomas, who said that when "Colonel Kargé's Second New Jersey Cavalry took charge of the rear . . . we had no trouble to speak of, nor any danger of a stampede." Thomas commanded the largest part of the First Infantry Brigade, that portion which marched on the Salem Road.[33]

Earlier, on the morning of 11 June in Ripley, Sturgis called his military telegrapher aside. "You understand fully the situation of affairs," Sturgis told Fred W. Snell. "Forrest has not only whipped us, but has captured everything, and is following us up; he is not a mile in our rear now. He will follow us as long as he can pick up stragglers, even to Memphis." Closing one eye, as was his habit in conversation, Sturgis continued: "You must start at once and go to the point you left the telegraph wire and telegraph to General Washburn our situation, and ask him to send us out some troops as far as possible to help us, also to send all the rations and forage possible.''[34]

Escorted by twenty-five cavalrymen, Snell rode off at 5:00 A.M. for the point, within three miles of Collierville, where ten days ago he had left the telegraph line tied to a gatepost. Although guerrillas infested the countryside, Snell maintained a bold and fast pace. He rode a magnificent thoroughbred captured from a Confederate colonel. The escort commander insisted on going slower, but Snell believed the hapless condition of the army required him to speed on ''at a rattling rate.'' By noon six troopers had fallen behind. That evening the cavalry escort wanted to stop for the night ten miles short of its destination. Snell, however, persuaded the remaining eleven cavalrymen to continue after a brief rest, and at 11:00 P.M. they reached the gatepost. Groping in the darkness for about ten minutes, Snell was overjoyed to find the wire still there and live. He attached his pocket instrument to the wire and raised the operator in Memphis. While waiting for General Washburn to come to the telegraph office, he fought to stay awake. He passed on to Washburn the key facts of the debacle and of Sturgis's call for help. Completing the transmission, Snell covered himself with a rubber blanket and fell into deep sleep.[35]

The head of the retreating column reached Collierville at 8 A.M. on Sunday, 12 June. The men were utterly exhausted. They had fought and marched, without rest and food, for two days and two nights. Three miles away Snell still slept when Captain S. L. Woodward of Grierson's staff found him and shook him roughly. ''For God's sake, wake up,'' Woodward cried, ''there's no time to lose. Send this message as quick as God will let you, and then skip out of this; I'll saddle your horse for you.'' The gravity of the situation came back to Snell as he regained consciousness. Sounds of firing on the flank also prompted him to hasten. He telegraphed Grierson's request for cavalry ammunition and then galloped to Collierville. From the morning of 10 June until midnight of the eleventh, he had traveled 110 miles.[36]

At noon, 12 June, the relief train from Memphis arrived with two-thousand fresh infantry soldiers and supplies. Sturgis intended to remain in place until the morning of 13 June, to rest the troops and await the appearance of any groups that might have become separated from the main column. Toward evening he learned from the commander at White's Station of a large enemy force approaching from the southeast. His beaten army was in no condition to fight. Not wishing to be intercepted, Sturgis ordered the troops to march that night to White's Station, some seventeen miles closer to Memphis. The sick and feeble had already been evacuated to Memphis by rail. Sturgis now moved the remaining infantry and dismounted cavalry by rail also, but he ordered all men with horses to march. The weary and muscle-sore cavalrymen endured great physical pain from those last seventeen miles. One Iowan exclaimed: "No experience in that terrible campaign is recalled by the cavalry with a keener memory of suffering than the dreadful march of that night." The column limped into White's Station at daylight the next morning.[37]

The casualty statistics alone proclaimed the Sturgis expedition a disaster. A total of 2,240 officers and men were killed, wounded, or missing. Nearly three-quarters of this total were prisoners. As Colonel Hoge reported: "The retreat had been through a hilly country, hard to travel, and the roads being muddy and the men being without provisions, and keeping up with the cavalry reduced them to an exceedingly exhausted condition, and many fell unavoidably into the hands of the enemy."[38] Lieutenant Colonel Charles G. Eaton, commanding the Seventy-second Ohio Volunteer Infantry Regiment, said that many of his soldiers could not keep pace with the lead cavalry brigade, and they left the road to seek safety in the woods. A band of 143 determined soldiers, though, stayed with the cavalry to Collierville. They marched a distance of almost ninety miles in forty-eight hours. After resting part of the day, these soldiers were so sore and stiff that they needed help to walk. "Some of them," Eaton said, "too footsore to stand upon their feet, crawled upon their hands and knees to the cars."[39]

In the retreat from Ripley, Wilkin's infantry brigade left the main column on the Salem road and proceeded north toward Saulsbury, Tennessee. Captain William W. Woods, who had been cut off at Ripley, joined Wilkin with six companies of the Fourth Iowa Cavalry. Wilkin brought in his force of sixteen-hundred infantry and the cavalry element safely to Collierville. Describing his soldiers' condition, he said: "Nearly all were barefooted, their feet badly blistered and swollen, and in some cases poisoned. Most of them had eaten nothing for three days, and all had suffered for want of food."[40]

Grierson's cavalry division of nine regiments suffered a total of 333 casualties. Kargé's Second New Jersey Cavalry alone took 25 percent of this number. Its losses were six killed, nine wounded, and sixty-five missing, for a total of eighty casualties. Captain Charles C. Reiley, commanding Company A and killed in action at Brice's Crossroads, was the lone officer to die in the cavalry division. Five men were killed, one of whom was Sergeant Jesse L. Harrison, the standard bearer. He fell instantly when a rifle ball passed through the staff of the regimental standard and entered his head. The other troopers to die in battle were Frederick Droga, Donald Frazer, John Hoff, and Thomas Riley. Seven officers were listed as missing: Lieutenants Stever C. Schwartz, Adrian S. Appleget, Lewis Rainear, L. Henry Smith, Julius von Rudolphi, Sigismund von Braida, and Assistant Surgeon John L. Krauter.[41]

Having begun the expedition with seventeen officers, Kargé lost one-half, most of them during the rear guard operation. This severe loss of officers indicated the quality of command, for the officers stayed with their troopers and led them in the most dangerous periods of the battle and during the rear guard action. Sturgis acknowledged the gallant performance of the regiment in his official report, which singled out only two commanders: McMillen and Kargé. Sturgis said: "I cannot refrain from expressing my high appreciation of the valuable services rendered by that excellent and dashing officer, Col. Joseph Kargé of the Second New Jersey Volunteers, in his reconnaissance to Corinth, and his subsequent management of the rear guard, during a part of the retreat, fighting and defending the rear during one whole afternoon and throughout the entire night following."[42] Grierson likewise gave praise, if grudging. He said mildly that he was indebted to his two brigade commanders, Waring and Winslow, and to his aides for their invaluable support. With respect to Kargé, Grierson said: "Col. Joseph Kargé, of the Second New Jersey Cavalry, is also deserving of especial praise for the gallant manner in which he conducted the expedition to Rienzi."[43] The future would bring Grierson and Kargé together as a highly effective team.

The debacle of the Sturgis expedition aroused a controversy that lasted well beyond the war. The issue became prominent again in the newspapers and in the Congress in 1882, when Sturgis was appointed governor of the Soldiers' Home in Washington, D.C.[44] But the present was of immediate concern to Sturgis. He asked Washburn to relieve him from duty temporarily, while a board of officers investigated the causes and failure of the expedition. Granting his request, Washburn directed Sturgis to report by telegraph to the Secretary of War, Edwin Stanton.[45]

While awaiting the secretary's response, Sturgis felt compelled by the derogatory stories in the newspapers to send his aide, Captain W. C.

Rawolle, to visit Sherman "in order that you may receive a true version of the circumstances which led to the failure of my expedition." Sturgis may have had reference to an account by a member of an Illinois regiment in the *Illinois State Journal*. The *Chicago Tribune* and Trenton's *State Gazette and Republican* also carried the same story. The three newspapers added caustic comments, based on the bitter words of the soldier who said, in part: "The fight at Guntown was the worst managed affair of the war. Our men were never formed in line of battle, but sent in by regiments, to be cut to pieces; and we were whipped in detail!" Speaking of the retreat, he said:

> Some of our cavalry were ahead and we fell in with them. We passed Gen. Sturgis and staff two miles out of town. *He was trying to get away as fast as he could, leaving every one to take care of himself* .... Gen. Sturgis told the men to "Look out for themselves." What think you of such a miserable General as this! No death he could suffer would be sufficient punishment for him!

The writer described the pitiful condition of his regiment. He said that some men came in on Tuesday, 14 June, two days after the main column had reached Collierville. Few came out of the retreat with their shoes. As an expedient the soldiers used coats and drawers, which they tore into strips and wrapped them around their bare feet. The writer said that every man who fell behind the rear guard was shot if he did not surrender at once. "They followed us eighty miles like wolves," he added.[46]

The traumatic experience of the retreat undoubtedly influenced the Illinois soldier to make his harsh judgment. According to the military philosophy of Carl von Clausewitz, it is in the retreat that "the feeling of being conquered," which first seized the commander and his senior officers on the battlefield, now spreads through the ranks. This feeling becomes intensified by the thought of being forced to leave many brave comrades in the enemy's hands, and further aggravated "by a rising distrust of the chief Commander, to whom, more or less, every subordinate attributes as a fault the fruitless efforts he has made...."[47]

In Georgia an aroused Sherman received preliminary reports of the ill-fated expedition and wired Secretary Stanton 15 June: "I will have the matter of Sturgis critically examined, and, if he be at fault, he shall have no mercy at my hands."[48] At Memphis, Washburn convened a Board of Investigation, which met 27 June and deliberated daily until 30 July 1864. The disaster at Brices's Cross-Roads, according to the testimony of General Sturgis, resulted from undertaking "an altogether impractical expedition."[49] Grierson attributed the defeat to the inflexible orders he had received from Sturgis: to fight and push on. Had he been able to exercise his judgment, Grierson said, he would have fallen back on the infantry. More basic, he would have marched the cavalry on the flanks of the infantry, and they would have gone into action together.[50] McMillen said the piecemeal commitment of his infantry regiments, exhausted by the rapid march and depleted by cases of heat exhaustion, was the immediate cause of defeat. He also believed that withdrawing the cavalry from the battlefield, especially Winslow's brigade where he happened to be at the time, contributed to the defeat. He said that Winslow volunteered to remain with the infantry but withdrew after being ordered away for the second time.[51]

In the sector held by Waring's brigade, the Second New Jersey Cavalry was fully capable of continuing the fighting. Major Peter D. Vroom, commanding a portion of the line, was ordered to fall back. He objected to yielding a position that he believed he could hold. Vroom twice sent the acting regimental adjutant, Lieutenant Lambert L. Mulford, to General Sturgis to protest the order to retire. The general responded peremptorily to fall back at once. Reluctantly, Vroom did.[52]

The failure of General Sturgis to make a stand after crossing Tishomingo Creek contributed heavily to the defeat. Colonel Thomas testified at the Board of Investigation that the hill across the creek gave a splendid position for a defensive stand.[53] Bouton's two regiments and an artillery battery were already in position there. Having been scarcely engaged, they were fresh troops and eager to fight. The ammunition train and supply wagons with ten days of rations were there; only a few wagons had been lost thus far. McMillen moved to organize a defensive position along that line when Sturgis countermanded him and ordered a rally at Stubbs's Farm, some ten miles to the north. Sturgis made a bad decision. The retreat to Stubbs lay across the Hatchie River bottoms, where the ammunition and supply wagons and the artillery got bogged down in the mud, and all towed loads were abandoned. The resultant shortage of ammunition prevented Sturgis from making a stand anywhere else on the line of retreat.

The disastrous defeat of his command at Brice's Cross-Roads on 10 June, 1864 marked the low point in the Civil War service of Brigadier General Samuel D. Sturgis. Sherman did not again entrust him with a command assignment, and Sturgis finished the war "awaiting orders."[54] His opponent Forrest gained a brilliant tactical victory at a cost of 492 casualties, only about one-fifth the number of federal losses.[55] Yet, by drawing Forrest back to Mississippi, Sturgis achieved the strategic purpose of his campaign, for Sherman's lines of communication through Middle Tennessee remained secure.

Higher Command and More Frustration

Kargé Commands Cavalry Division in "Pursuit" of General Forrest

Despite the disastrous results of the Sturgis expedition, Colonel Joseph Kargé enhanced his reputation as a bold cavalry leader. General Grierson, in a reorganization of the cavalry division, promoted Kargé to the command of the First Cavalry Brigade. At the regimental level, the Second New Jersey Cavalry also underwent reorganization, following its heavy casualties in the same campaign. The regiment now lost its executive officer, Lieutenant Colonel Marcus Kitchen, who resigned 30 June 1864, for reasons of poor health.[1] Kargé replaced Kitchen with the young and vigorous P. Jones Yorke. Promoted to lieutenant colonel, Yorke took charge of the regiment when Kargé moved up to command the First Brigade. Captain Philip L. Van Rensselaer, commanding Company F, filled Yorke's vacated position of battalion commander and received the promotion to major.[2]

On the West Tennessee District level, General Washburn began to prepare for yet another campaign against Forrest. At Sherman's direction, Washburn placed the expedition in the hands of Major General Andrew J. Smith, who recently returned with six-thousand infantry soldiers from the Red River campaign in Louisiana. These veterans were part of a larger force being assembled for an attack on Mobile, Alabama. Sherman, however, changed priorities; Forrest had to be kept pinned down in Mississippi and away from the federal lines of communication in Middle Tennessee. Sherman believed that the Confederate Raider had become more vulnerable. "I don't see what Forrest can have except his cavalry, and the militia under Gholson," Sherman said. "They should be met and defeated at any and all cost."[3]

Smith organized a small army of about fourteen thousand troops, composed of two infantry divisions and a cavalry division of three-thousand troopers. He set up headquarters at La Grange, while Grierson's cavalry bivouacked at Saulsbury, some fifty miles east of Memphis. Washburn, meanwhile, sought to insure the success of Smith's expedition by staging a diversion. He conceived a bold march across the middle of Mississippi to sow confusion and destruction in the rear of Forrest. Washburn's plan called for a cavalry brigade of one-thousand troopers to move by ship to Vicksburg and from there to make a lateral dash across the state to the Mobile and Ohio Railroad. Washburn gave Kargé the command of this raiding force, assigning him the mission of breaking up some sixty miles of railroad from Macon to Meridian. His brigade would also destroy part of the Mississippi Central Railroad, running through Jackson and Canton. Because the proposed operation would take place in the district commanded by Major General Henry W. Slocum, Washburn asked Slocum by message to reinforce Kargé's cavalry brigade with troops from the Vicksburg garrison and to direct the overall effort.[4]

On Independence Day, Kargé's cavalry marched from White's Station to Memphis, and the next day the command sailed down river aboard eight steamers. Confederate spies, no doubt, reported the departure and followed the ships to their destination. Such movements could not be kept secret from foe or friend. The *Newark Daily Advertiser* reported on 9 July: "Col. Kargé of the Second New Jersey Cavalry has started out on an expedition, but to what point is not known." On the day Kargé's brigade left Memphis, General Smith's soldiers marched into Mississippi.[5]

At Vicksburg, General Slocum ignored Washburn's plan to strike the Mobile and Ohio Railroad, and he apparently was not aware of Kargé's movement. Slocum failed to cooperate because he considered Washburn's message "an imperious command." Washburn, the politician turned general, was junior in rank to Slocum, although both were independent district commanders under General James B. McPherson.[6] With no attempt to coordinate operations against the enemy, Slocum led an expedition of his own to Jackson. He marched a force of twenty-two hundred infantry and six-hundred cavalry to destroy the railroad bridge over the Pearl River, some fifty miles from Vicksburg. Slocum had responded to a stinging message from Sherman for allowing the Confederates in the Jackson area to repair the railroad. "If you permit the enemy to regain the use of that bridge and of the Mississippi Central Railroad," Sherman admonished, "you need not expect military favors from General Grant or myself.'' Sherman urged Slocum to conduct a weekly raid against the railroad and especially that bridge. In earlier fighting in Mississippi, Sherman had personally directed the destruction of the enemy's communications, and he wanted to continue to deny their use.[7]

Slocum led his force of twenty-eight hundred men to Jackson, although he smarted at Sherman's reference to favors. He answered his superior that ''without any particular desire to secure favors from yourself or any other person, I shall continue faithful in the discharge of my duty.''[8] Slocum explained that he often received conflicting orders from Sherman and from Major General Edward R. S. Canby, who on 7 May 1864 assumed command of the newly established Military Division of West Mississippi. Canby's geographical command comprised the Departments of the Gulf and of Arkansas. President Lincoln also charged him with the responsibility of keeping the Mississippi River open. Lincoln logically placed the troops on both banks of the river under Canby. But the distinction between garrison and field units stationed along the river was imprecise. With Sherman in Georgia and Canby in New Orleans, the two commanders had difficulty maintaining close coordination, and both Slocum and Washburn found themselves at times in awkward situations. Still, no major problems arose.[9]

Reaching the Pearl River, Slocum destroyed the bridge and a portion of the Mississippi Central Railroad, but not without a fight. Confederate forces under General Stephen D. Lee tried to cut off Slocum's withdrawal. In the severe two-hour engagement that followed, each side suffered some two-hundred casualties.[10] On the day Slocum fought, Kargé's brigade arrived at Vicksburg. The two-and-a-half-day trip was uneventful, except for an exchange of gunfire near Bolivar, Mississippi, on 6 July, when the enemy fired from land into several transports and slightly wounded a trooper of the Nineteenth Pennsylvania Cavalry. The Federals promptly returned the fire and dispersed the enemy. Kargé's flotilla docked at 5:30 P.M. on 7 July. Disembarking his brigade immediately, Kargé marched it eight miles to Clear Creek on the Jackson road. The troopers broke camp the next morning at six for the journey to the Big Black River. Here Kargé met Slocum on his return from Jackson. Kargé explained the proposed cavalry operation, but Slocum disapproved. He considered it impracticable and ordered Kargé to return to Vicksburg. The brigade marched back twenty-four miles to the Four-Mile Bridge on the Vicksburg, Jackson and Brandon Railroad.

Pitching camp for the night, the one-thousand troopers probably felt that they had made a useless trip, for they could have marched with the A. J. Smith expedition.[11]

Admittedly, it is difficult to fault a commander on the ground. Nonetheless, did Slocum view the operation from his own tactical capability, or did he try to look at the broader, strategic requirement? His force of twenty-eight hundred infantry and cavalry was sufficient for the opposition he had encountered at Jackson. Kargé now augmented him with a select brigade of one-thousand cavalrymen. Washburn indeed proposed bold strategy, but Slocum favored caution. Nevertheless Slocum undertook a limited diversion. In identical messages to his superiors, Generals McPherson and Canby, Slocum informed them that

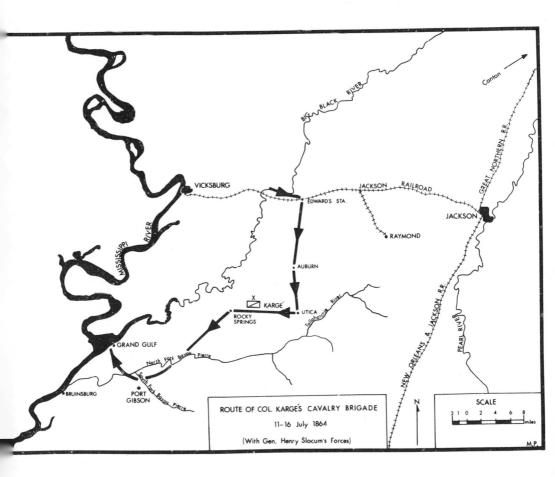

ROUTE OF COL. KARGÉ'S CAVALRY BRIGADE

11–16 July 1864

(With Gen. Henry Slocum's Forces)

he would march on Canton, located some twenty-five miles north of Jackson, on the Mississippi Central Railroad. This movement would directly help A. J. Smith, since it would pin down Confederate forces that otherwise would reinforce Lee and Forrest.[12]

On the evening of 9 July 1864 Kargé received Slocum's order to return to the Big Black River. He broke camp early, marching at 4 A.M. and reporting on arrival to Slocum's cavalry chief, Brigadier General Alfred W. Ellet. Slocum's combined force crossed the Big Black at dawn on 11 July. The first day, Kargé's brigade marched twenty-four miles via Edward's Station to Auburn, where it camped for the night. The infantry, some two-thousand strong under Brigadier General Elias S. Dennis, camped near Raymond. The *New York Herald* reported: "The expedition under General Slocum, reinforced by the cavalry sent by General Washburn, was marching again for the interior of Mississippi."[13]

Abruptly, Slocum changed his operational plan. He swung south-westward to the Mississippi River, in the opposite direction of Canton. He gave no reason for abandoning the advance on Canton, and Kargé, now operating in the area between the Big Black and Bayou Pierre, reached Utica the second day out. His brigade traveled twelve miles, skirmishing all day long with light enemy forces. The following morning, before the brigade broke camp, Major Samuel O. Shorey led a party of the First Mississippi (Union) Cavalry on an assigned task. A superior enemy force attacked Shorey's men, wounded Shorey severely, and forced his troopers to the security of the brigade encampment. At noon the brigade moved out on Slocum's time schedule. Skirmishing again along the route of march, it traveled a distance of twenty miles to Rocky Springs.

As the force marched for Port Gibson, Slocum's own cavalry led the advance, followed by the infantry, and protected from the rear by Kargé's command. Growing bolder, the rebels charged Kargé's troopers repeatedly for an hour. Although they were driven off each time, the enemy continued to follow. Sporadically, they made stabs at some part of the column, but Kargé's men repulsed them, all the while protecting the infantry and maintaining the pace of the march. While in the vicinity of Port Gibson on 14 July, a strong enemy group surprised a foraging party of the Second New Jersey Cavalry and captured twenty-six of them. That evening the brigade camped one mile south of Port Gibson, the site of a fierce battle between Generals Grant and John C. Pemberton on 1 May 1863. Slocum's force continued the march to Grand Gulf on the Mississippi river, where the Confederates made a final, determined attack. Promptly at dawn on 16 July the rebels struck both the cavalry and the infantry and drove the pickets in to the main body. Slocum counterattacked the eager enemy with shattering effect on their fighting spirit, and Kargé's report explained the action: ''the enemy attacked at daybreak, but were badly whipped and driven demoralized from the field, leaving their dead in our hands.''[14]

While Slocum was marching to the Mississippi, his transports sailed to Grand Gulf to meet him. The infantry boarded the vessels late on the night of 16 July, following the hard engagement of that day. Kargé's cavalry embarked at noon the next day on steamers of General Ellet's Mississippi Marine Brigade. The trip up river was short for Kargé's troopers. He disembarked them twenty miles south of Vicksburg and continued on land to within three miles of the town. After an overnight bivouac, Kargé marched his cavalry to Four-Mile Bridge to await the arrival of transports, and 20 July the brigade sailed for Memphis. Kargé's losses for the six-day action were three killed, five wounded, and twenty-seven missing.[15]

Slocum's campaign through contested Mississippi terrain was a model of strict discipline and efficient execution. His force held the attention of a sizable group of Confederates. As a diversion for A. J. Smith's expedition against Forrest, however, Slocum's march had little influence. It turned out to be a vastly different expedition from what Washburn had visualized and what Kargé had planned for. Meanwhile, in northern Mississippi, Smith's column met elements of Forrest's cavalry in the vicinity of Ripley. Grierson kept driving them away. Smith continued on a southerly course until he reached Pontotoc, where he turned east toward Tupelo to come astride the Mobile and Ohio Railroad. To block him, General Stephen D. Lee concentrated a force of nine-thousand infantry and cavalry.[16]

Lee, the commander of the Department of Alabama, Mississippi, and East Louisiana, found himself in a predicament. The enemy threatened him from three directions: from the north by Smith; from the west at Vicksburg by Slocum; and from the south at Mobile by the anticipated Canby-Farragut attack. Lee seemed anxious to dispose of Smith, so as to give his attention to Mobile.[17] The Confederate commander, though, had the advantage of interior lines, and he controlled the Mobile and Ohio Railroad, in service from the Gulf Coast to the Tennessee border.

Since Lee opposed Smith with troops he would need at Mobile, the railroad was key to his capability to make strategic dispositions. In this context, Wasburn's strategy to strike that railroad with Kargé's cavalry brigade makes Slocum's disapproval seem like a bad decision.

On 14 July 1864 Lee attacked Smith in a strong position at Harrisburg, two miles west of Tupelo. Misinterpreting Smith's caution for fear, Lee pressed the attack vigorously. The federal artillery fire and the counterattacks by the infantry threw back the rebels with very heavy losses. Although the battle had turned decidedly against the enemy, Smith concluded the next day that he would have to be satisfied with his victory at Harrisburg as the total accomplishment of his campaign. He explained that his troops were short of rations and ammunition, and he retreated to Tennessee.[18]

Lee called Harrisburg a drawn battle, while Washburn hailed it a victory. Washburn claimed that the Sturgis disaster had been redeemed and the "invincible" Forrest rendered more vulnerable. Sherman and Grant were not convinced. They had expected Smith to pursue Forrest. While Sherman thought well of "Old A. J.," he was enthusiastic about Smith's infantry division commander, Brigadier General Joseph A. Mower. Sherman called Mower "one of the gamest men in our service," and promised him a promotion to major general if he would "pursue and kill Forrest."[19] The Smith expedition fell far short of that expectation.

In answer to Washburn's report that Smith's expedition "has been a complete success," Sherman fired back: "Order Smith to pursue and keep after Forrest all the time." Sherman emphasized that Forrest would continue to be Smith's target until either he or Grant recalled him from this mission. "It is of vital importance," Sherman stressed, "that Forrest does not go to Tennessee."[20]

Smith got the word on his return to Memphis, and he immediately instructed the division commanders to prepare their units as rapidly as possible for another campaign into Mississippi. Washburn again placed Grierson's cavalry under Smith, a larger force than before. Having gained several regiments for a total of fourteen, Washburn expanded the cavalry division and reorganized it as the Cavalry Corps, District of West Tennessee. Washburn also obtained the services of Brigadier General Edward Hatch, an experienced cavalry officer who had participated in Grierson's famous raid through Mississippi in April 1863.[21]

Grierson organized the Cavalry Corps of some five-thousand troopers into two divisions of two brigades each. He gave the command of the First Division to Hatch and of the Second Division to Winslow. Taking charge of the First Brigade in Winslow's division, Kargé commanded the Second New Jersey, Nineteenth Pennsylvania, Seventh Indiana, and the First Mississippi, for a total of fifty-two officers and 1,383 men. The strength of the Second New Jersey at this time had dropped to a low of thirteen officers and 290 men.[22]

Washburn exuded optimism on the probable success of the coming expedition. He wired Sherman that he had "sent forward a force that can whip the combined force of the enemy this side of Georgia and east of the Mississippi." Indeed, Washburn had assembled a small army of ten-thousand infantry and five-thousand cavalry. He pushed Smith's base of operations from La Grange south to Holly Springs, when his advance cavalry units seized that Mississippi town. He also ordered the repair of the Mississippi Central Railroad to Holly Springs and on to the Tallahatchie river, some fifteen miles deeper into the state. Signal personnel established telegraph communications from Memphis to the Tallahatchie. Supplied for a march of twenty days, Smith planned to start out after Forrest as soon as his units reached that river. Washburn ordered Smith "to push after Forrest wherever he may be and to go as far as Columbus, Mississippi, in pursuit of him, if necessary," and to destroy all railroads north of there. While overseeing the preparations for the expedition, Washburn kept Sherman informed of all plans, and Sherman evidently believed the objectives of the expedition to be reasonable. In fact, he instructed Washburn on 7 August to have Smith march for Decatur, Alabama, once Smith reached Columbus, for the purpose of joining his field army. The federal commander in the West had planned for some time to acquire Smith's troops for the Georgia campaign.[23]

On 1 August 1864 General Hatch marched his division from Memphis to Holly Springs, which he occupied unopposed. The major part of the infantry traveled by rail to Holly Springs; some went farther south to Waterford. Other units detrained at La Grange and marched to Holly Springs. Kargé's cavalry brigade escorted and protected the artillery and supply wagons. His regiments departed White's Station 6 August on a direct route for Holly Spring and arrived there two days later.[24]

Forrest did not rush to interfere with the federal build-up at the Tallahatchie. He felt obliged to conserve his strength while awaiting the development of Smith's objectives. Forrest's victory over Sturgis at

Brice's Cross-Roads and the fierce attacks on Smith at Harrisburg had taken their toll. His effective force dropped to some five-thousand troops, and he lost an unusually large number of experienced field officers and brigade commanders. Despite his weaknesses, Forrest attempted to protect northern Mississippi with forces at Grenada and Pontotoc, and he opposed Smith directly at Abbeville with his strongest brigade under Chalmers. He ordered Chalmers "to blockade fords, fortify positions, and repair the works on the Tallahatchie and Yalobusha Rivers."[25]

Reacting to Chalmers' presence along the Tallahatchie, Smith decided to seize the crossing site. On 8 August, Hatch's division and Colonel John W. Noble's brigade of the second division attacked the enemy. General Mower supported the cavalrymen with two infantry brigades. Striking hard with overpowering force, Hatch quickly drove Chalmers away, and Mower's engineers bridged the river by nightfall. In the morning Hatch again attacked the rebels on the high ground beyond the river and drove Chalmers back in a running fight of eight miles to Hurricane Creek. Here Chalmers put up a stand from a strong position on the south bank, but a charge by Noble's brigade dislodged the rebels. Maintaining the momentum, Hatch pursued the enemy to Oxford. Again the rebels made a stand, but another determined attack expelled them from the town. Hatch pursued Chalmers south of Oxford until night brought an end to the fighting.[26]

Hatch showed aggressive leadership. Employing his superior numbers to advantage, he did a great deal more than seize a bridgehead on the Tallahatchie, but he gave up his gains. On the morning of 10 August, "hearing nothing of the enemy . . . I moved back to Abbeville." Why he abandoned Oxford is not known, unless the withdrawal reflected Smith's caution, for the field commander was not prepared to advance. Heavy rains had washed out sections of the railroad and caused some delay in getting supplies through to Holly Springs. Smith also seemed to be overly concerned with the security of his wagon trains. He ordered Noble's brigade at Abbeville to countermarch twenty miles north to Holly Springs, where Kargé's brigade performed guard duty. Smith told Winslow to keep his division at Holly Springs until all trains and the infantry had departed that point. The movement of Noble's brigade appears to have been a useless march, but Smith apparently was not ready to "plunge" deeply into Mississippi.

From 10 August to the 18th, Smith kept his command in place for no apparent reason. Columbus lay some 150 miles away, but he seemed in no hurry to get there. Meanwhile Forrest reinforced Chalmers and kept up a daily routine of skirmishing. On 13 August, Hatch's cavalry, in cooperation with Mower's infantry, attacked the rebels at Hurricane Creek and drove them to Oxford. Having accomplished this task, Hatch once again withdrew to the Tallahatchie on Smith's orders.[27]

On 17 August Kargé took command of the Second Cavalry Division—his first opportunity to lead a division. Grierson had relieved Winslow, who suffered great pain from an old wound. Winslow left by train for Memphis, and Kargé stepped up to take charge of the division. Lieutenant Colonel Joseph C. Hess, Nineteenth Pennsylvania Cavalry, assumed command of Kargé's brigade for the duration of the expedition. The next day Grierson ordered Kargé to march his division to Abbeville, since all government property and supplies at Holly Springs had been removed.

Kargé's shift to the Tallahatchie River line indicated that the long-awaited march might take place after all. Indeed, General Smith began to stir a bit. He inched Grierson's cavalry corps toward Oxford. The First Division in the lead ran into some rebels and drove them off easily. Kargé's Second Division joined General Hatch on the south side of Hurricane Creek. Finally, the methodical Smith set the date of 22 August for the capture of Oxford and then enveloped the town with unusual precision. Promptly at 6:00 A.M. Grierson started Hatch's division on the right flank of the infantry and Kargé's division, less one regiment, on the left flank. "With this regiment I moved in advance of the center column," Grierson said, "entering Oxford about 8:00 A.M. simultaneously from the north, east, and west." He found Oxford empty of rebels. Two hours later Smith received the astounding news that Forrest had raided Memphis the day before in a daring pre-dawn attack.[28]

The desperate situation facing Forrest more than likely forced him to make the raid on Memphis. The Confederate leader knew that Smith's force greatly outnumbered his, and he believed that he could not defeat the Federals in battle. Yet, determined to stop Smith, Forrest resorted to a dramatic gamble. On 18 August, he assembled a special force of two-thousand troopers in the public square of Oxford. Just ten miles to the north, Smith's army dallied at the Tallahatchie, oblivious to the nearness of Forrest. The Raider left Chalmers some two-thousand soldiers to put up a front against Smith. All that Forrest asked of Chalmers was to deceive and delay Smith for two days. At dusk on 18 August, Forrest marched off for Panola (Batesville). It rained hard, and the mud was knee deep. The same bad weather that affected Smith also plagued Forrest, but that indefatigable general drove his men to new heights of human endurance. The Confederate troops crossed the swollen Tallahatchie on the morning of the nineteenth; the following day, a mile above Senatobia, they crossed the flooded Hickahala Creek by means of a suspension bridge woven of grapevines. Six miles farther north the rebels again built a bridge to get over the booming Coldwater River. On Saturday evening, 20 August, Forrest reached his hometown of Hernando, where he rested. He still had twenty-five miles to go, but by 3:00 A.M. Sunday the raiding force, now dwindled to fifteen hundred troops by the hard marching, reached the outskirts of Memphis.

Forrest set himself three objectives. First, he aimed to capture three federal generals: Washburn, Brigadier General R. P. Buckland, commanding the garrison, and Hurlbut, the former West Tennessee District commander, who was on a visit to Memphis. Second, he proposed to storm the Irving Block military prison; and third, he planned to attack the Union garrison, take prisoners, horses, and whatever supplies he could carry off. Approximately half of the rebel force entered the city; the remainder Forrest held in reserve. Although the rebels hoped to penetrate in silence, a federal picket recognized the intruders and opened fire. The Confederates now charged yelling and cheering, and the alarm spread throughout the city. Washburn escaped in his nightclothes to the safety of Fort Pickering, one-half mile from his residence. Buckland left his quarters to mobilize the garrison; Hurlbut was not at the Gayoso Hotel as expected. Guards at the Irving prison repulsed the attack. Buckland called the militia of loyal citizens into action, and Forrest soon found the resistance formidable. By 9:00 A.M. he withdrew from the city, escaping easily from the hastily organized pursuit.[29]

Beyond its dramatic effect and Washburn's embarrassment, the attack accomplished little. Washburn reported that "they obtained no plunder, but about 250, 100-days' men were captured." The raid did not impress Sherman. "If you get a chance, send word to Forrest I admire his dash but not his judgment," Sherman told Washburn. "The oftener he runs his head against Memphis the better."[30]

Some historians maintain that Forrest's raid on Memphis caused the recall of Smith's expedition.[31] This view cannot be justified. Washburn did not recall Smith's troops to protect Memphis; neither did his superior, General Oliver O. Howard, commanding the Department of the Tennessee. The man above Howard, General Sherman, did not take such action. On the contrary, Sherman constantly stressed the need to pursue and destroy Forrest. At the War Department, the next higher and final authority, neither General Grant nor the Secretary of War attempted to override their field commanders with a recall order. It is a fact, though, that Smith never got beyond Oxford and that his expedition degenerated into a useless exercise. But the reason is not Forrest's daring but rather Smith's incompetence. Following three weeks of effort, Smith "captured" Oxford on 22 August, after Hatch had seized it once before and then abandoned the town. Furthermore, Smith failed to employ his strong cavalry corps for aggressive reconnaissance missions. He misused his cavalry to guard the supply wagons and two divisions of experienced infantry soldiers. Washburn complained justifiably that Smith, with forty-eight hundred cavalry only ten miles from Oxford, knew nothing of Forrest's presence there or of his march on Memphis. It is doubtful whether Smith intended to penetrate far into Mississippi, let alone march the 150 miles to Columbus. As for destroying Forrest, Smith would very shortly have the chance to demonstrate his commitment to this mission.

At Memphis, Washburn organized an immediate pursuit of Forrest with the available cavalry, some 650 strong. He believed this force could do no more than harass Forrest for a short distance. His powerful Cavalry Corps was with Smith at Oxford, and Washburn now planned to spring Grierson's troopers into a hard-charging pursuit. Washburn dispatched three messages to Smith, ordering him to send one division west to Panola and the other north to Abbeville. Washburn concluded that Forrest could follow only two avenues of escape: through Panola or east of Abbeville via Holly Springs, since between these two points the Tallahatchie surged high and impassable from heavy rains. Washburn visualized that, with one division to dispute the Panola crossing and the other riding through Abbeville toward Holly Springs, the two forces would close in on Forrest until they struck his trail. Then, with a strong effort to overtake him, Forrest could be captured. Washburn counted on the exhausted condition of the retreating rebels to slow them down. "Their horses must be much jaded," Washburn said in his message to Smith, "and they can be caught." From captured rebels Washburn learned that Forrest planned to retreat eastward via Holly Springs, and in his third message he modified his orders. Washburn instructed Smith to

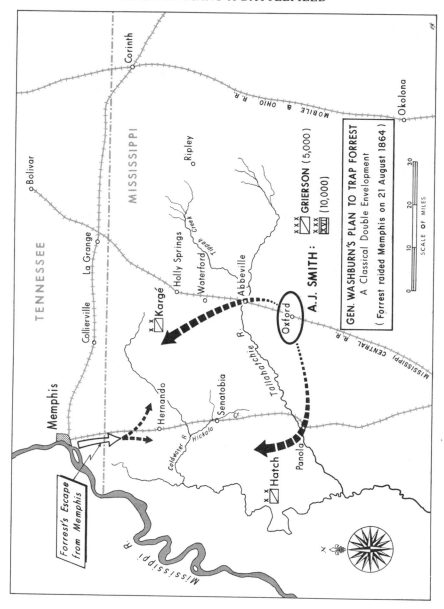

reduce the Panola force to fifteen hundred cavalry and to send the rest north through Abbeville.[32]

About noon of the day of the raid, 21 August, Washburn got his three dispatches transmitted as far as La Grange but no farther, because the telegraph line south of that point had been cut. He ordered the commander of the La Grange garrison to rush the dispatches by messenger, and Major John M. Graham, Seventh Illinois Cavalry, galloped off at 1:00 P.M. with a mounted escort of one-hundred men. He rode hard that day and night, arriving in Oxford between ten and eleven o' clock the next morning, 22 August. He delivered the orders to Smith in the presence of Generals Grierson, Mower, and Hatch. The expeditionary force commander responded promptly, passing the orders to Grierson, who directed Kargé to march his division to Abbeville and Hatch to ride for Panola. Cautious as ever, Smith told Grierson to hold Kargé's division at Abbeville for further orders.

Smith controlled his cavalry as rigidly as plays on a chessboard. What Grierson needed in this situation was a mission type of order, that is, a general directive that would give him essentially a free hand to pursue Forrest. As an experienced cavalry commander, Grierson did not have to be instructed each step of the way. Hatch's division, meanwhile, had marched only a few miles on the Panola road when Smith, for reasons unknown, countermanded Grierson and ordered Hatch to return to Abbeville.[33] Smith's behavior raises the serious question of whether he intended to go after Forrest.

At Memphis, Washburn continued to get reports of Forrest's movements. He learned that Forrest passed through Hernando with his entire force and continued south on the Panola road. Becoming convinced that Forrest would cross the river at Panola, Washburn sent a fourth message to Smith, who received it at Abbeville early Tuesday morning, 23 August. "If not intercepted at Panola," Washburn ordered, "he should be caught between Yocona and Tallahatchie." Washburn also instructed Smith to have the cavalry that might have gone to Holly Springs to come south of the Tallahatchie again.

In explaining his cavalry dispositions, Smith said that the first three messages inclined him to believe that Forrest would retreat through Holly Springs, and so he ordered Kargé's division to march there. Smith said he ordered Hatch to Panola prior to the receipt of the dispatches. Following the occupation of Oxford, Smith detailed Hatch "to proceed to Panola and destroy the railroad from that point south along the line."

On the arrival of Graham with Washburn's messages, Smith then recalled Hatch to Abbeville.

Grierson's report of the expedition contradicts Smith's. The cavalry commander states that he ordered Hatch to Panola *after* the receipt of the news of Forrest's attack on Memphis. Even though Washburn at first believed that Forrest's route of escape via Holly Springs seemed the more probable, he still specified that Smith send a force of fifteen hundred cavalry to Panola. But Smith ignored the Panola route. He said that he ordered Hatch to return to Abbeville to join Kargé and then to ride at once to intercept Forrest. Neither Kargé nor Hatch received any such orders, and there was no pursuit. Instead, both cavalry divisions crossed the Tallahatchie river on Smith's orders and by controlled stages moved to Holly Springs, where the expedition came to a quiet end.[34]

Grierson saw Forrest's raid on Memphis as a rare opportunity to cut loose with the cavalry for a dash into Alabama and Georgia. Forrest, having removed himself from the Oxford area, would be powerless to stop the federal horsemen from inflicting "what mischief they could." Although Grierson urged this course on Smith, the commander refused. Grierson then proposed to pursue Forrest. Smith consented, but soon recalled Hatch to join the command on the north side of the Tallahatchie.[35]

General Smith's failure to pursue Forrest can only be described as gross negligence and insubordination. He apparently feared for the safety of the infantry too much to let the cavalry go. Washburn said outright to Sherman: "Major General Smith disobeyed my orders." Had Washburn's orders been obeyed, Forrest might have been trapped between the Coldwater and Tallahatchie rivers, for his escape would have been nearly impossible.[36]

Smith demonstrated incredible caution and lethargy. His force outnumbered the rebels' four to one, yet Smith behaved as if he had the inferior number. He showed little enthusiasm for this second expedition to bag Forrest. Perhaps he had become discouraged by the number of times he was diverted from joining Sherman's army in Georgia. Nevertheless, Forrest's raid on Memphis, however much it embarrassed Washburn, offered an excellent chance to catch the Confederate raider. Smith made no effort to intercept him, and the expedition simply fell apart from his fear and indecision.

Smith's insubordinate conduct also denied Kargé the opportunity to lead his division in a drive to destroy Forrest. Colonel John W. Noble, commanding the Second Brigade of Kargé's division, summed up the cavalrymen's expectations: "The bridge being down over the Tallahatchie, it was repaired by this brigade by 12 o'clock at night, the men and officers working with great zeal, in the hope that the [cavalry] corps would aid at least in punishing the enemy, then reported to have made a daring raid upon Memphis." The cavalry's hopes fell quickly. Having crossed the river early on the morning of 23 August, the horsemen advanced a mere two miles. The following day Smith held them in camp. On 25 August, they marched eleven miles to Holly Springs, where Smith kept them bivouacked for several days. Meanwhile Forrest made good his escape.[37]

Washburn probably grew frustrated over the inaction of his field commander. Coincidentally, he received General Henry Halleck's message to rush all forces that could be spared to Sherman. On 1 September, Washburn ordered Smith's infantry division shipped to Nashville.[38] But once again the fortunes of war intervened. Smith's flotilla of steamers got no farther than Cairo, Illinois, when the War Department diverted him to Missouri to help defend that state against the invasion army of Confederate Major General Sterling Price. Arriving at St. Louis about 10 September, Smith refused to march into Arkansas to engage Price. The cautious Smith, with sixty-five hundred infantry, remained in place to await developments. In contrast, Brigadier General Thomas Ewing, commanding the District of St. Louis, sought to fight the enemy at the first opportunity.[39]

Price entered Missouri on 19 September 1864, marching on a line for St. Louis. Ewing disputed his advance at Pilot Knob, some seventy miles to the southwest. Although a strong fort stood at Pilot Knob, its garrison numbered less than one-thousand soldiers. Still, Ewing held up the march of twelve thousand rebels for three days before he was forced to retreat.[40] Smith meanwhile stayed near St. Louis with a veteran division, apparently content to let Ewing do the fighting.

At Memphis, Washburn reacted swiftly to the threat of Price's army. Cooperating with Major Generals Frederick Steele and William S. Rosecrans, the department commanders in Arkansas and Missouri, Washburn rushed Mower's division of seven-thousand troops, including nineteen hundred cavalry, to Little Rock. Washburn believed in stopping Price in Arkansas. Eager to expedite the movement of his reinforcements, Washburn did not allow time for the shoeing of horses on the return of the cavalry from Oxford. He sent Winslow's Second

Division, with Kargé commanding the First Brigade and Lieutenant Colonel George Duffield, Third Iowa Cavalry, leading the Second Brigade. Both units were at reduced strength, since only the better-mounted men left for Arkansas.[41]

Crossing the Mississippi, Winslow's cavalry on 2 September marched on the military road to Clarendon, some one-hundred miles away. The route led almost entirely through swamps and bayous, and the men labored in foul waters to repair the road and to bridge four bayous. While crossing Blackfish Lake, seven men of the Fourth Missouri Cavalry sank in an old flatboat and drowned. The division forded the St. Francis and L'Anguille rivers without difficulty and reached Clarendon on the morning of 6 September. Winslow noted that it would be "quite impracticable to move a column by this route during the wet season." The unwholesome air and water of the marsh country, along with the sultry weather, caused considerable illness among the troops. At Clarendon, Winslow evacuated some one hundred sick men on hospital ships to Memphis. But, Clarendon was not the cavalry's destination, for General Steele allowed only a one-day pause before ordering Winslow to advance thirty-nine miles to Brownsville, located near Little Rock. While the cavalry moved overland, Mower's infantry traveled by ship on the Mississippi and the Arkansas rivers to arrive at Brownsville on 12 September. The Second New Jersey Cavalry, which had accompanied Mower, rejoined Kargé's brigade. At Brownsville, Kargé became sick and was evacuated to Memphis.[42]

Steele did little to stop Price, who bypassed Little Rock. Mower grew irritated with Steele's indecision, and on 18 September he set off in pursuit of Price. Marching vigorously, Mower insisted that the infantry keep up with the cavalry.[43] Once in Missouri, Winslow's small division became the Fourth Brigade of Major General Alfred Pleasonton's Provisional Cavalry Division. Pleasonton pursued the rebel army aggressively into the western part of the state. He attacked Price at Westport and Big Blue on 23 October and at Marais des Cygnes, or Osage River, on 25 October, soundly whipping him and driving his shattered invasion force back to Confederate territory. Earlier Pleasonton had detached the Second New Jersey and the Nineteenth Pennsylvania regiments from Winslow's brigade and assigned them "other duties." This diversion did not keep the Second New Jersey from the decisive battles. It fought at the Big Blue and at Osage River. In the absence of field grade officers, Captain Michael Gallagher commanded the regimental element of 225 troopers. The New Jersey Bobtails finally returned to Memphis on 20 November 1864. Having been gone for eighty-one days, they still wore the summer uniform.[44]

Ferdinand V. Dayton, surgeon of the Second New Jersey Cavalry, served Pleasonton as surgeon-in-chief of the division. The assignment suddenly and vastly expanded his responsibilities. Accepting the challenge, he demonstrated organizational skill and leadership in directing his doctors and supervising the medical activities over long distances and in rapidly changing situations. Pleasonton recognized Dayton's achievement when he included him among the staff officers cited for conspicuous "gallantry and fidelity throughout the campaign."[45]

The *Newark Daily Advertiser* reported the action of the Second New Jersey in the victories of General Pleasonton. The paper said that the regimental adjutant, Lieutenant J. Lacey Pierson of Newark, was among the wounded in a hospital at Fort Scott, Kansas. The *Advertiser* also reported erroneously that Kargé commanded a brigade in the gallant fighting at the Big Blue and Osage.[46]

Although sickness kept Joseph Kargé from campaigning against Sterling Price, the colonel had distinguished himself as a brigade and division commander during summer operations in Mississippi. Time and again General Grierson had called on Kargé for high-level command duty. General Washburn, too, showed confidence in Kargé's leadership and had named the colonel to command the raiding force in the proposed attack on the Mobile and Ohio Railroad. Kargé's earlier performance in the reconnaissance to Rienzi and Corinth had impressed Washburn. The success of this independent action in the Sturgis expedition revealed Kargé as an astute, daring, and determined leader—the very qualities called for in a commander to lead the bold dash across the middle of Mississippi. However, General Slocum's failure to cooperate with General Washburn, and his undue caution, denied Kargé the opportunity to execute the proposed diversion in support of the first A. J. Smith expedition in July 1864. The next month Smith failed to obey the orders of his superior for an aggressive pursuit of General Forrest, thereby stripping Kargé of his good fortune of commanding the Second Cavalry Division in the planned pursuit.

Gallant Victory at Egypt Station

Kargé's Brigade Charges Rebel Stockade on Horseback

By early October 1864, Colonel Joseph Kargé returned to duty at Memphis, commanding the First Brigade of the Second Division, Cavalry Corps.[1] He did not go back to Missouri to rejoin Winslow's division, reduced to a brigade in General Pleasonton's Cavalry Division, since no appropriate command was available there. In Memphis he witnessed a sudden buildup of the Second New Jersey Cavalry, which had steadily lost strength during its year in service. The regiment now gained hundreds of one-year draftees from New Jersey and soon exceeded its authorized strength.[2] The Consolidated Morning Report for 31 October 1864 shows the regiment stationed at Camp Howard, near Memphis, under the command of Lieutenant Colonel P. Jones Yorke. All twelve companies were at maximum strength of 100 enlisted men and an additional 242 were listed as "Unassigned." The "Present for Duty and Absent" stood at 39 officers and 1,446 enlisted men. Nine officers and 222 enlisted men in Missouri were carried as "On Expedition." Although the personnel level stood at maximum, the regiment lacked a sufficient number of horses. The report shows a total of 867 horses, of which 771 were serviceable.[3]

In late October 1864, Grierson's Cavalry Corps was broken up by a sweeping reorganization of the cavalry forces in the Military Division of the Mississippi. Dissatisfied with the manner in which his subordinate commanders employed their cavalry, Sherman sought to centralize operations. To aid him General Grant transferred Brevet Major General James H. Wilson to the West. "I believe Wilson will add 50 percent to the effectiveness of your cavalry," Grant said. Sherman abolished the office of chief of cavalry at his own headquarters and at the several departments of his geographical command. He consolidated the cavalry into one large Cavalry Corps with Wilson at the head, charging him to reorganize the forces under his command and to bring into the field the greatest number of mounted troops possible.[4]

The twenty-seven-year-old Wilson, West Point class of 1860, rose rapidly in rank to become one of the "boy wonders" of the war. He first served as a topographical engineer in the Western theater. In January 1864 Wilson came to Washington to head the recently established Cavalry Bureau. The Secretary of War had selected Wilson to run the bureau in order to vitalize that arm. Wilson had directed the bureau for two months when Grant gave him the command of the Third Cavalry Division, Army of the Potomac, and in October Grant chose him to be Sherman's cavalry chief.[5] Wilson acted immediately. On the day he became chief, 24 October, he wrote General Howard to telegraph to Grierson, "directing him to send Hatch's division at once . . . to join me in the field." He also asked Howard, successor to McPherson, to instruct Grierson to keep his remaining division in a ready condition, prepared to join the Cavalry Corps for a movement through Mississippi, Alabama, and Georgia. He advised Grierson to do all in his power to bring back Winslow's cavalry in Missouri, in order to mount the largest possible force, and on 2 November Grierson left for St. Louis. During his absence of several weeks, Kargé commanded the cavalry forces at Memphis.[6] General Wilson, meanwhile, proceeded with his reorganization plans. On 6 November 1864, he designated Grierson's division the "Fourth Division, Cavalry Corps, Military Division of the Mississippi." But Grierson's assignment turned out to be a mere paper exercise. A clarification of General Canby's command placed the Mississippi area more firmly under his control, with the result that Grierson's division remained at Memphis.[7]

Although no major expeditions took place in the fall of 1864, the commander employed the available cavalry at Memphis on wide-ranging patrols and combat reconnaissance missions. There were occasional forays across the Mississippi River into Arkansas. On 30 November Kargé raided a Confederate supply train and captured fifty rebels, seven wagons, mules, and provisions. The prize, though, was a Confederate adjutant general with fifty thousand dollars in cash.[8] Yorke also conducted a raid into Arkansas with a force numbering some 350 men. The group consisted of several companies of the Second New Jersey Cavalry, one company of the Fourth Iowa Cavalry, and 50 soldiers of the Eighth Iowa Infantry. Yorke's party departed Memphis by steamboat on 29 November and landed up river at Osceola, where it picked up the trail of a rebel wagon train carrying arms. Yorke marched his men through a swamp for eighteen miles before he overtook the train of twenty wagons at Big Lake. Surprised by the Yankee fire, the outnumbered enemy abandoned the train and escaped into the swamp. Yorke destroyed the wagons and nine hundred stand of arms in perfectly serviceable condition. On the return march, his men picked up mules and cattle, skirmished with guerrillas, and took some prisoners. Yorke's losses were nine horses.[9]

While little fighting occurred along the Mississippi in the fall of 1864, the area of dramatic action centered in Middle Tennessee. Washburn had alerted General Howard that Forrest planned to strike at Sherman's communications. A much greater threat than Forrest developed when General John Bell Hood decided to abandon Georgia and march his Confederate army into Tennessee. Hood believed his army to be too weak to stop Sherman's drive to the sea, and he gambled that his invasion of the North would pull Sherman out of Georgia. Hood concluded that the time had come for exceptionally bold strategy. It was a desperate move, but perhaps the rebel general thought he needed only a little luck to turn the tables.[10]

Sherman reacted to the Confederate threat, although he refused to give in to Hood's strategy. The confident Sherman sent General George Thomas back to defend Tennessee, reinforcing the "Rock of Chickamauga" with two infantry corps but keeping his own army strong at sixty thousand veterans. Hood's impending march into Tennessee highlighted the importance of Southern railroads. The Mobile and Ohio and the Memphis and Charleston lines served as resupply channels to his base on the Tennessee river at Tuscumbia, Alabama. Hood reached Tuscumbia on 31 October and waited for Forrest, whose cavalry he needed to lead the march. While Hood waited and Forrest tarried at Jackson for three weeks, Thomas pulled his scattered forces together. His strength rested on the reinforcements from Sherman—the corps of David S. Stanley and John M. Schofield, with the latter's corps positioned at Pulaski, Tennessee, to oppose Hood.[11]

The Confederate commander moved north on 19 November, the day after Forrest joined the Army of Tennessee. Delayed briefly along the Duck River at Columbia, Hood fought the Federals at Spring Hill on 29 November and followed them to Franklin. The next day he made a savage frontal attack against Schofield's entrenched soldiers and suffered heavy losses—6,252 casualties against the federal loss of 2,326. During the night Schofield retired to Nashville, where the army of George Thomas occupied fortified positions around the city. Hood with

31,000 troops faced Thomas with 49,000. General Grant urged Thomas to attack at once. "The country was alarmed, the administration was alarmed, and I was alarmed lest . . . Hood would get north," the general-in-chief declared. Although the War Department tried to goad him into immediate action, the imperturbable Thomas waited until his forces became thoroughly prepared.[12]

As Hood's army stood menacing Nashville, the War Department ordered the commanding officer at Memphis to "immediately endeavor to cut the Mobile and Ohio Railroad so that Hood's army cannot be supplied by that route."[13] An aroused Washington was by no means certain of General Hood's ultimate defeat. In the past, Confederate commanders had often achieved striking successes with inferior forces, and Hood's audacity, perhaps recklessness, might succeed. Hood also entertained the possibility of gaining troops from Texas, and the fastest route for such reinforcements was the Mobile and Ohio Railroad.[14] Major General Napoleon J. T. Dana, the commander at Memphis, received General Halleck's order to destroy Hood's communications. Dana had only recently arrived in Memphis, as the commander of the newly organized Department of the Mississippi. As department head, Dana reported to Canby. Washburn, who had served at Memphis for nearly eight months, remained a district chief but was assigned the post and District of Vicksburg.

Dana replied as follows to Halleck's order on 8 December: "I can operate successfully against the enemy's communications if I have the cavalry." At the time Dana could muster only one thousand cavalrymen at Memphis, but he had ordered up four regiments from Vicksburg, totaling some fifteen hundred troopers, which he expected to see in five or six days. He also asked for Winslow's cavalry, en route from Missouri to General Thomas at Nashville. Conflicting orders had caused Winslow to halt at Cairo, Illinois, to await Halleck's decision whether he should proceed to Nashville or Memphis. Halleck ruled in favor of Thomas, but nonetheless, when Grierson's division marched into Mississippi, Winslow's brigade formed part of the division.[15]

The day Grierson's cavalry departed Memphis, 21 December, Dana informed Canby of his actions. He said that to have moved early against the Mobile and Ohio with the small infantry force available to him would have produced nothing but disaster. "I have complied with General Halleck's orders," he said, "by what I consider a hazardous undertaking." He said the heavy rains of the past ten days overflowed the rivers and streams and placed the roads knee-deep in mud. He emphasized that "nothing but the peremptory order received and the appreciation of the vital importance of the undertaking would have induced me to venture such a risk." To carry out Halleck's order, Dana felt compelled to assume authority he did not possess. First, he ignored the chief of staff's decision with regard to Winslow and directed his cavalry to Memphis instead. Second, he seized horses in transit for the Department of the Gulf to mount his own cavalry. Third, he asserted authority over nine infantry regiments and two artillery batteries, commanded by Brigadier General M. K. Lawler and belonging to General Canby's Reserve Corps. Admitting that he had placed himself in a delicate situation by these actions, Dana said: "If I can accomplish the end at which I aim, I shall be content with suffering any personal mortification."

Dana assigned Grierson the mission of striking the Mobile and Ohio Railroad above Tupelo and destroying it as far south as Meridian; next, if safe, to dash one hundred miles east to Cahawba, Alabama, to release Union soldiers imprisoned there; and finally, to return to Memphis or, if necessary, to march to Vicksburg, Natchez, or even Pensacola. Grierson faced as much danger as perhaps on his raid through Mississippi in April 1863. He could muster a total of only thirty-five hundred cavalrymen, the smallest force of any expedition undertaken in 1864. Although he would not have Forrest to contend with, Grierson faced a numerically superior enemy. Dana told Canby that the rebels had between five thousand and six thousand men at Corinth, two thousand at Holly Springs under General Wirt Adams, three thousand at Oxford, and strong guards along the Mobile and Ohio Railroad.

Dana appreciated the great danger in which he had placed Grierson. He ordered Lawler to support the cavalry with a feint toward Corinth, so as to immobilize its strong garrison. Lawler employed his nine infantry regiments, aided by three Memphis regiments under Brigadier General Elias S. Dennis. Dana's plan also placed great responsibility on Kargé. The general ordered Kargé's First Brigade to move out in advance of the main body and operate alone for twenty-four hours. The plan called first for Kargé to demonstrate toward Bolivar and reinforce Lawler's feint; next, to cut the telegraph line between Grand Junction and Jackson to the north and Corinth to the east; and then to overtake Grierson at Ripley, Mississippi, where the general would arrive with the brigades of Winslow and Colonel Embury D. Osband.[16]

On 19 December 1864 Kargé marched his force of 1,101 officers and

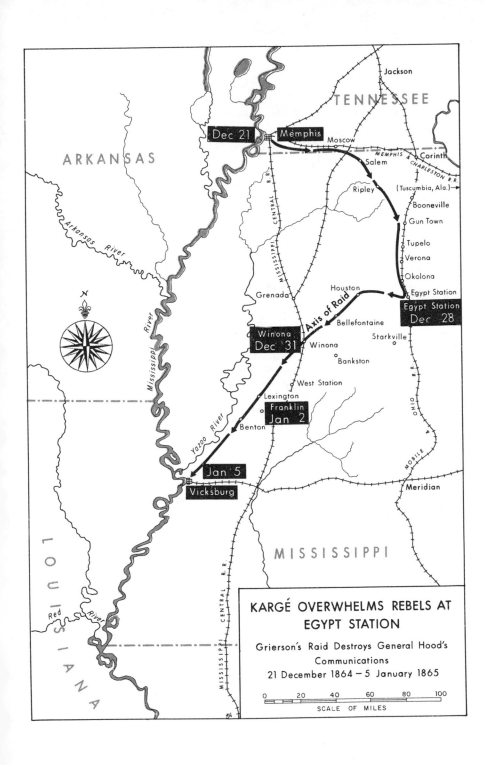

KARGÉ OVERWHELMS REBELS AT
EGYPT STATION

Grierson's Raid Destroys General Hood's
Communications
21 December 1864 – 5 January 1865

men into a driving rainstorm. The Second New Jersey Cavalry under Yorke, 742 strong, made up two-thirds of the command. Along with the New Jersey Bobtails, Kargé had detachments of his old team: the Fourth Missouri, Seventh Indiana, and the First Mississippi Mounted Rifles. He lacked the Nineteenth Pennsylvania Cavalry, which had been transferred to General Wilson's command.[17] Reaching the Raleigh crossing site on the Wolf River, Kargé found the river overflowing its banks for a considerable distance. The raging waters frustrated several attempts to reach the opposite side and spoiled some ammunition as well. Unable to make the crossing, Kargé turned back to Memphis. Two days later Grierson put Dana's plan into execution again; but, in the interest of time, the command moved as a unit. The men rode without artillery and without wagons and, Dana added, "without a wheel to cumber their difficult and dangerous march." The division carried a twenty-day supply of light rations on pack mules. Dana exhorted Grierson to let nothing but an evident impossibility prevent the accomplishment of the mission. Expressing confidence in Grierson, Dana said: "You have some fine officers and a good body of men, and I confidently rely on your triumphant success."[18]

Grierson's command moved east along the Memphis and Charleston Railroad to convey the impression of an attack against Corinth. Reaching a point three miles beyond Moscow, Grierson changed to a southeast direction, marching through Early Grove, Tennessee, and heading toward Ripley via Lamar and Salem. At Early Grove, Grierson ordered the Tenth Missouri Cavalry to ride for La Grange and Grand Junction, where the unit destroyed the telegraph line and two stations. Captain Frederick R. Neet and his Missourians caught up with the column at Salem.

On 24 December Kargé sent Major Van Rensselaer's battalion of the Second New Jersey on an independent mission of destruction. Van Rensselaer's 150 troopers galloped from Ripley to Booneville on the Mobile and Ohio, and before dawn on Christmas Day they destroyed the telegraph line and tore up a mile of railroad track. They also wrecked the bridge across Twenty-Mile Swamp, burned down two large houses filled with quartermaster and commissary stores, and a caboose on the railroad containing arms, ammunition, and railroad implements. Van Rensselaer's battalion rejoined Kargé's brigade on 26 December at Shannon Station, south of Tupelo, having traveled 113 miles. While Van Rensselaer carried on his destruction at Booneville, the Fourth

Illinois Cavalry, under Captain Anthony T. Search, destroyed the railroad and military supplies near Guntown with equally satisfying results.

On Christmas Day Kargé took the advance of the column, moving out at 6:00 A.M. for Old Town, some five miles north of Tupelo. The expeditionary force had marched rapidly thus far, and the sudden appearance of Union cavalry surprised Mississippians. In Old Town, Grierson learned that a contingent of Forrest's dismounted cavalry guarded a large supply of military stores at Verona. He ordered Kargé to make a forced night march to Verona but to attack the garrison only if, in Kargé's judgment, he could carry out the assault. Leaving his pack train behind, Kargé marched the brigade rapidly, crossing Old Town Creek in darkness. He halted briefly at Harrisburg, the site of General A. J. Smith's victory over the combined forces of Lee and Forrest. Deciding to make the attack, Kargé placed the Seventh Indiana Cavalry in the lead. The advance guard struck the enemy's pickets two miles outside the town; and the Seventh Indiana charged into Verona, dispersing some two hundred to three hundred rebels, who fled in the night. Kargé halted his main column on the outskirts of Verona to organize wrecking parties; working most of the night, his raiders destroyed two hundred wagons loaded with supplies for Hood's army. Most of these vehicles, marked "U.S.," had been captured by Forrest from General Sturgis the previous June at Brice's Cross-Roads. Kargé also destroyed two locomotives, thirty-two cars, and railroad track. His troopers set the torch to eight warehouses filled with ordnance, commissary, and quartermaster stores. The destroyed arms included 450 English carbines, 500 Austrian rifles, and two hundred boxes of ammunition for carbine and rifle. His raiders also set on fire a large number of fixed artillery ammunition, causing the rounds to erupt into continuing explosions from about 10:00 P.M. until 5:00 A.M. the following morning. Having destroyed the Confederate property and cut the telegraph line, Kargé marched his brigade back to Harrisburg, where he arrived at 6:30 A.M. His men had been on the move for twenty-four hours and had traveled fifty miles. After resting a few hours, Kargé's men were in the saddle at 11:00 A.M. They moved south rapidly, crossed the Tombigbee River, and marched until 9:00 P.M., when the brigade stopped for the night on the Okolona road. While Kargé attacked Verona, Grierson sent the Eleventh Illinois Cavalry, under Lieutenant Colonel Otto Funke, to destroy the nine hundred-foot-long railroad bridge across Old Town Creek and ten miles of track between the creek and Tupelo. With the help of pioneer troops,

Funke left the railroad a total wreck by morning, despite the darkness and the rain.[19]

As Grierson's raiders plunged deep into Mississippi, the Confederates gathered their scattered units to block his advance. They concentrated a considerable force at Okolona, but on the approach of the federal cavalry they fell back ten miles to Egypt Station. Reaching Okolona, Grierson tapped the telegraph line to intercept messages from Lieutenant General Richard Taylor, the commanding general of the Department of Alabama, Mississippi, and East Louisiana. Grierson learned that Taylor had ordered reinforcements from Mobile and other points to oppose him. During the night of 27 December a number of deserters informed Grierson that the promised help would not, in all probability, arrive before 11 A.M. the next day. Evaluating the information as reliable, he decided to attack the enemy at Egypt Station before they were reinforced. The opposition consisted of a mix of infantry and cavalry, estimated from twelve hundred to two thousand strong, and supported by a battery of four guns mounted on railroad flat cars. This artillery train had arrived from Mobile, transporting at the same time seven hundred infantry under the command of Lieutenant Colonel Ross E. Burke. His soldiers were armed with Springfield muskets of the latest design. For the first real battle of the expedition, Grierson called on Kargé to make the attack.[20]

Wednesday, 28 December 1864, dawned clear and pleasant. The Second New Jersey marched at 7:00 A.M. at the head of the First Brigade, and the brigade led the division. Kargé commanded Yorke: "Allow nothing to stop you." Within two miles of Egypt Station, the New Jerseymen met rebel cavalry, which they drove back upon a skirmish line just outside the village. Anchored on a stockade and protected by defensive works, the Confederate position stood almost invulnerable, and the stockade itself was screened from view of the attackers. Kargé ordered Yorke to charge the enemy's skirmish line, and he noted with satisfaction: "The impetuosity of the charge of the Second New Jersey Cavalry was so great that their skirmish line was at once driven in." Captain Gallagher's squadron broke through the center of the line along the main road that ran through the village and, as the troopers rode past the blockhouse, the defenders from within surprised the Yankees with heavy flanking fire. "The effect of this fire was very disastrous," Yorke said, "for it was here that I lost many men." Gallagher was shot down at the head of his squadron, pierced through the heart by an enemy bullet. Lieutenant John Burns, leading the other company of the squadron, was also killed in the same charge. Deprived of leadership, the squadron wavered, but Yorke seized control of the crucial situation. Riding to the head of Captain Charles F. Fernald's squadron, Yorke led the troopers at a gallop to nearby buildings and fodder stacks on the enemy's left center, which he believed to be the key to their position. From behind this protection Yorke's men poured a tremendous volume of fire at the rebel skirmish line. At the same time Captain Richard D. Mitchell's squadron threatened to outflank the enemy's left. The combined fire and movement forced the rebels to abandon their position and to retreat into the stockade. Yorke's bold thrust had placed the New Jersey troopers close to the stockade, in some cases within thirty yards of the portholes. The attackers lodged themselves under the shelter of the huts and houses of the village while preparing for the final assault.

Kargé formed his battle line with the Second New Jersey on the left and center. He manned the right with the two small regiments, the Fourth Missouri and the Seventh Indiana. The Confederate rail battery, which opened up on Kargé's troops during the attack, continued to shell his position. Although Kargé found the effect more harassing than damaging, he decided to capture the train with King's Battery. He pulled the Fourth Missouri and the Seventh Indiana out of line, but, before these troops had moved off, Grierson rode up and took personal charge of the detachment of 270 cavalrymen.

From tapping the telegraph line Grierson had learned that two rebel trains were rushing to deliver reinforcements to the garrison at Egypt Station. Taylor's subordinate, Major General Franklin Gardner, sought to stop the Yankee advance, and Grierson, in turn, tried to prevent the reinforcements from reaching the garrison. Actually, one of Gardner's relief trains had arrived, bringing Burke's 700 infantry and King's Battery. The second train approached the battle area with 500 infantry under the command of Colonel William W. Wier. A third train departed Corinth on 27 December with a force of 350 men, commanded by Colonel J. C. Cole, but, blocked by damage to the railroad, it did not get through.[21]

The immediate objective of Grierson's attack, the train with the battery, stood a half mile south of Egypt Station. On the approach of the federal horsemen, the Confederates tried to escape, but the engineer found that he did not have enough steam to move the entire train. With

Grierson's cavalrymen only three hundred yards away, the rebels abandoned all cars except those carrying the battery. The engineer now managed to start the locomotive rolling, and he soon outdistanced the troopers, who nevertheless kept up the race for some distance. The scene turned melodramatic. In pursuit, the Yankee cavalrymen charged down the track after the escaping train—horseflesh pitted against an iron machine. In retreat, the rebel artillerymen turned their guns on the horsemen and from their moving platforms fired repeatedly into the charging column, but with little, if any, effect.

Some five miles south of Egypt Station, General Gardner's second train approached the pursued train. The federal cavalry had meanwhile fallen more than a mile behind. Wier's infantry detrained, formed, and moved up the track toward the Yankees. Coming within range, Weir's men opened fire and forced the cavalry back to a position near Egypt Station. Here Grierson's entire force isolated Weir's soldiers from the village completely, taking up strong positions to the north, east, and south. Hearing no sounds of firing from the direction of Egypt Station, Weir concluded that Grierson had undisputed possession of the village. Soon the flames from burning railroad buildings convinced Weir that Gardner's attempt to stop Grierson had failed. Yet the Confederate garrison at Egypt Station had fought stubbornly against Kargé's onslaughts.[22]

With Grierson off to engage the rail battery, Kargé turned his attention to storming the stockade. He received unexpected reinforcement when Osband rode into the battle area with his brigade of three regiments. Assuming temporary command over the Third Brigade, Kargé ordered Osband to take up positions on the vacated right flank and to press the attack. The Third Brigade faced the dismounted cavalry of Brigadier General Samuel J. Gholson, who held a sheltered line from behind a railroad embankment. Getting the Fourth Illinois Cavalry into line, Osband ordered them to charge, and the attack routed Gholson's defenders from their position. The Illinois troopers pursued the fleeing rebels with pistol and saber for a distance of some five hundred yards to a timber line, where a deep ditch stopped further pursuit. Although the majority of rebels escaped, the Fourth Illinois captured fifteen and killed and wounded several more. Gholson received a very serious wound in the fight. Osband's successful charge cut off the escape route that had been open to the defenders in the stockade. He prepared to engage the fort from the rear. Moving into position, his men became exposed to heavy enemy fire, which quickly produced fifteen casualties. Before Osband could launch his attack, however, the Second New Jersey Cavalry overwhelmed the stockade in a furious charge.[23]

The initial assault against the skirmish line brought the New Jersey soldiers within shouting distance of the rebels in the stockade. For the final assault, two mounted squadrons attacked from the left and simultaneously three companies of dismounted skirmishers attacked from the right. Yorke controlled all movements with the regimental bugler, who sounded "Charge" and "Cease Firing" on Yorke's commands. Despite the uproar and confusion of the fighting, the disciplined cavalrymen responded to orders with precision. The *Newark Daily Advertiser* described the unusual action:

> All movements were ordered by bugle, and it is a remarkable fact that not a single instance of mistake or disobedience occurred during the whole affair. During the most rapid firing, while each man was wholly occupied in charging and discharging his piece, comrades falling around, horses rearing and plunging, amid general uproar and confusion, the bugle suddenly sounded *cease firing*. At once the order was obeyed, not a piece was discharged, not a soldier moved in his place until the bugler was again heard ordering the *charge*; then over shoulder was slung the carbine, out flashed the glittering steel, and on like an avalanche rushed the heroic Second.[24]

The New Jerseymen charged the blockhouse in the face of deadly fire. The two designated squadrons galloped through the village and swept to the rear of the fortification. Poking their carbines through the portholes, the men fired their seven-shot Spencers into the defending garrison. At the same blast of the bugle, the dismounted troopers burst from their cover, ran for the door of the stockade, smashed it down, and stormed into the enclosure. The savage attack overwhelmed the defenders and brought a quick surrender of some five hundred rebels, including Colonel Burke and fifteen line officers.[25]

Impressed with the fighting of the Second New Jersey, Grierson and Kargé congratulated Yorke and the regiment on their success. Grierson praised their bravery, calling the attack a "very rare thing for cavalry to charge and take an equal force, protected by stockade and artillery." Yet the victory was costly. The Second New Jersey alone suffered a total of ninety killed and wounded. Of this number three officers and sixteen men were killed, and two officers and sixty-nine men were wounded, many of them very seriously. The regiment lost more than eighty horses. The casualties in Kargé's First Brigade totaled 105 killed and wounded. Osband's Third Brigade had one killed and seventeen wounded. Winslow's Second Brigade did not engage in the fighting. The First Mississippi Mounted Rifles of Kargé's brigade also missed the action, since they guarded the pack train on this day.[26]

The *New York Times* published a correspondent's report of "Grierson's Last Raid," which read in part: "A fortification called Egypt, on the Mobile and Ohio Railroad, was carried by assault, and the garrison of 500 rebels captured, whilst Gen. Gardner was in sight with 2,000 infantry, which Gen. Grierson held at bay, while Col. Kargé's brigade charged the stockade on horseback." The *Times* said the whole country was in arms by this time, and forces were even brought from Macon, Georgia. Speaking of some of the damage, the paper said: "Forty miles of the Mobile and Ohio Railroad are so badly damaged that Hood's whole army cannot repair it in months. New pontoons, new wagons, and a large amount of supplies, en route to Hood, were damaged in the cars."[27]

Among the five hundred captured rebels, more than one hundred were so-called Galvanized Yankees, federal soldiers who had been captured or who had deserted and then took up arms with the Southerners to escape prison. They usually were untrustworthy and possibly hastened the surrender of the stockade, once the situation became hopeless. Notwithstanding the presence of these "Yankees," the soldiers under General Gholson made a gallant fight.[28] Colonel John W. Noble, commanding the Third Iowa Cavalry in Winslow's brigade explained that on the evening prior to the battle several of these men, having deserted and entered federal lines, gave the opinion that many of their number would not resist in battle. "In the engagement which ensued in the morning," Noble said, "this proved true in many instances, although the fight was a severe one and required great valor on the part of Colonel Kargé's cavalry to gain the victory."[29]

Southern newspapers defended the bravery of their men. On 5 January the *Meridian Clarion* reported the engagement at Egypt Station as very obstinate. The newspaper said: "Our men fought until the last round of ammunition was exhausted, before surrendering, though repeatedly ordered to cease firing," and continued that the fight occurred around the house of the section master of the road. "The inmates of the house, Mrs. Kellian and Mrs. Brown, remained indoors all the time, and, strange to say, received no injury, notwithstanding the house was perforated with balls.'' The *Clarion* added that General Gholson lost his arm at the shoulder joint and that his recovery was doubtful.[30]

Following the capture of the stockade, surgeons attended to the wounded of both armies, while General Grierson completed the destruction of all Confederate government property, including fifteen thousand rounds of ammunition and ten railroad cars loaded with clothing. Grierson abandoned the dash to the prison at Cahawba, Alabama, since the expedition had become encumbered with many prisoners and animals, and General Gardner opposed him with a large force. Changing direction, Grierson led his division rapidly due west to Houston. The Second New Jersey was forced to abandon one officer and thirty-nine men, who were left in the care of John L. Krauter, assistant regimental surgeon. These men were injured too seriously to be subjected to the rigors of the march. Nine badly wounded troopers of the Eleventh Illinois Cavalry were likewise left at Egypt Station. Doctor Krauter and the forty-nine wounded Federals became prisoners.[31]

The Confederates made no attempt to pursue. General Gardner impatiently waited for Colonel Thomas C. Lipscomb's (Mabry's) cavalry to come up from Macon, Georgia, before ordering a pursuit. Lipscomb arrived at Prairie Station, a few miles from Egypt, on the evening of 28 December. Early on the following morning, Lipscomb's cavalry pushed on after Grierson but could not overtake the fast-moving Yankees.[32]

While camped at Houston, Grierson tried some deception. He ordered demonstrations to be made to the north, toward Pontotoc, and to the southeast, toward West Point. Meanwhile the main column moved southwestward via Bellefontaine in the direction of the Mississippi Central Railroad. At Bellefontaine, Grierson demonstrated toward Starkville, in an apparent threat to the Mobile and Ohio Railroad. At the same time he ordered Captain Warren Beckwith with a 120-man detachment of the Fourth Iowa to ride south to Bankston, the site of cloth and shoe factories. Beckwith carried out the destruction of these important plants, whose employees manufactured clothing and shoes for the Confederate army. Winslow reported that ''five hundred men were thus thrown out of employment.'' Beckwith's detachment endured in the saddle without rest for two days and one night.

On 31 December Kargé's brigade, leading the division, struck the Mississippi Central Railroad one mile north of Winona Station. Kargé ordered Yorke's cavalrymen to destroy all Confederate government property, and the New Jersey troopers wrecked two locomotives and some cars, tore up the railroad tracks, destroyed the depot, cut the telegraph line, and burned a large quantity of quartermaster and commissary stores. From the Second Brigade, Noble led a detachment of three hundred men north to Grenada, tearing up the railroad and destroying government property along the way. On the morning of 1 January Grierson assigned Osband the task of wrecking the railroad south of Winona "as far as practicable." Osband sent out strong dismounted parties from the Fourth Illinois and the Third U.S. Colored Cavalry for a distance of twenty-nine miles along the railroad, through Vaiden, and as far as five miles south of West Station. His men destroyed two and a half miles of track, nineteen bridges, and the intermittent station houses and water tanks.

Leaving Noble and Osband behind to carry out the assigned destruction, Grierson moved the column in a southwesterly direction through Lexington to Benton. Here Noble and Osband rejoined the division, but not without a fight from General Adams. The Confederates made a final attempt to intercept the Federals at Franklin on 2 January. Adams attacked two of Osband's regiments with troops led by Colonel Robert C. Wood, but Osband repulsed them. When Adams reinforced Wood with additional men, the fighting became a hotly contested engagement, and Adams believed he faced Grierson's entire command. Grierson, meanwhile, fifteen miles in the advance, kept sending urgent messages to Osband to break off the fighting and rejoin the column. This Osband did, and Adams's weary troops failed to pursue. Osband lost one officer killed and one wounded, three men killed, seven wounded, and two missing. He gave the Confederate losses as two officers and fifty men killed, and seven captured. "It was the hardest fought cavalry fight in which the brigade, as such, were ever engaged," Osband said. The seriously injured could not be moved, and Osband left two men at Franklin. Belatedly the next morning, Adams ordered Lieutenant Colonel George Moorman's battalion in pursuit, but to no avail. "The enemy made a forced march of twenty-seven miles from 2 o'clock on the afternoon of the 2d, making fifty miles that day," Adams explained, "and starting before daylight the next morning, hastened on to Vicksburg, outstripping all pursuit." [33]

Grierson's command reached Vicksburg on 5 January with some six hundred prisoners, eight hundred head of captured stock, and one thousand Negroes, who joined the column along the route of march. The troops arrived in good condition, having traveled a distance of 450 miles in sixteen days. The general's report summed up the extensive destruction of Confederate property, and he gave his losses as four officers and twenty-three men killed, four officers and eighty-nine men wounded, and seven men missing. He did not mention that more than fifty seriously wounded had to be abandoned and became prisoners. Grierson called the campaign "one of the most successful expeditions of the war," carried out at a time of the year when the roads and streams were almost impassable. He said that the raid "could not have met with such extraordinary success without the patient endurance and hearty cooperation which were evinced by my entire command, and all those who participated richly deserve the lasting gratitude of the Government and remembrance of their countrymen." [34]

Grierson immediately briefed General Washburn, and the Vicksburg commander telegraphed General Canby that same day, 5 January, to report the expedition "a complete success." Washburn listed the highlights and praised Grierson: "The whole affair has been most successful, and reflects great credit on Brigadier-General Grierson for the skill and dash with which it was executed." General Dana was likewise elated over the successful conclusion of his expedition. He now cast aside all misgivings about usurping authority; the end result sustained the extraordinary measures he took to comply with General Halleck's urgent appeal for action against General Hood's lines of communications. "I believe this expedition, in its damaging results to the enemy," Dana reported to Canby, "is second in importance to none during the war." [35] Dana even telegraphed the Secretary of War, telling Stanton: "Full particulars of this most brilliant raid will be sent by mail." To General Thomas, Dana declared: "All Hood's communications are now completely cut." Grierson's raiders not only wrecked the railroads and destroyed government property but also gutted vast quantities of food supplies collected for the Confederate army. A correspondent stressed this fact: "The fairest portion of Mississippi, from which the Rebels subsisted their army under Hood, has been penetrated and laid waste." Thus, when Hood's army, beaten at Nashville on 15-16 December, retreated to Mississippi, little, if any, food remained for the soldiers. Hood at Columbus and Forrest at Tupelo resorted to furloughing their men so that they could trade in cotton and procure their own supplies. [36]

The historian of the Fourth Iowa Cavalry Regiment commented that "Grierson had his usual good fortune in evading or misleading the enemy, so as to avoid conflict with any large force." [37] While General Grierson may have had his share of luck, the success of the campaign rested on solid factors. The first sprang from General Dana's strategy. He believed that the large Confederate force at Corinth had to be immobilized, and he accomplished this result with General Lawler's infantry demonstration. At the same time, General Grierson marched initially eastward for some fifty miles, along the Memphis and Charleston Railroad. The feint suceeded. General Gardner said he issued orders to his scattered elements on "the supposition that this move with cavalry, infantry, and artillery, and repairing the Memphis and Charleston Railroad, indicated an attack on Corinth, the base of supplies for General Hood's army." [38]

Organizing the expedition for rapid marching contributed to success. Grierson took no wagons or artillery; pack mules carried the ammunition and light rations. He moved so swiftly that the federal presence along the route of march caught civilians by surprise. Confederate commanders, too, conceded that General Grierson time and again evaded pursuit by rapid marching. Nonetheless, the weather and the condition of the roads were bad nearly all the time. Rain or snow fell on many days, and a hard freeze occurred on some nights. On occasion ice or a frozen crust covered the roads, but most of the time they lay in deep mud and neither loaded wagons nor towed artillery could have got through. The conditions on the march showed in the appearance of the column, when it reached Vicksburg on 5 January. A correspondent reported: "Both our own men and the Rebels [prisoners] were covered with mud, and as wet as a day's rain could make them." [39]

The high caliber of Grierson's brigade commanders favored success from the beginning. Kargé, Winslow, and Osband were experienced cavalry officers, and they demonstrated aggressive leadership throughout the campaign. At Egypt Station, where the Confederates made their strongest stand, Kargé attacked the fortified skirmish line and the stockade with grim determination. He had to subdue the rebels quickly or jeopardize the success of the expedition, and he carried out the assault with the ruthless efficiency demanded by the situation. At Lexington, Osband severely punished General Adams's troops and drained their spirit of pursuit.

An eagerness to fight and to carry out the assigned tasks marked the conduct of the regimental commanders. Most of them took part in the frustrating expeditions led by General W. Sooy Smith, Samuel D.

Sturgis, and Andrew J. Smith. Under Grierson's leadership they got the chance to fight and to act, and they responded with enthusiasm. Majors and captains led raiding parties on independent missions for periods of from twenty-four to forty-eight hours, risking capture or destruction and yet performing with skill and courage. All task forces executed their missions in an outstanding manner.

General Grierson, as well as his brigade commanders, clearly understood the critical importance of their mission to destroy the lines of communications of General Hood's Army of Tennessee. They executed this mission with great success, and the Confederates conceded as much. Colonel J. C. Cole, who commanded the relief force from Corinth, reported the damage to the Mobile and Ohio Railroad as very serious. He urged General Gardner to make immediate repairs. "In consideration of the importance of communication with General Hood's army, which is now at Iuka, being kept open," Cole said, "every effort should be made to push it through as rapidly as possible." On his own initiative, Cole ordered the impressment of Negroes to repair the railroad at once.[40]

Grierson's execution of the mission required constant reaffirmation. While military men understand the importance of an assigned mission, they are sometimes diverted by the exigencies of a situation. General Grierson always stressed the mission, and this priority caused some hard decisions. Abandoning the seriously wounded with the knowledge that they would become prisoners probably constituted the most difficult decision. Nonetheless, commanders took this hard course at two battlefields, Egypt Station and Lexington. The successful conclusion of the expedition, which General Dana called "second in importance to none during the war," thus resulted from sound planning and leadership.

Grierson gave high praise to "my entire command" for the "extraordinary success" of the campaign. Toward his brigade commanders he showed a more restrained manner, and in his report to General Dana he simply said that he wished "to express my thanks to Colonels Kargé, Winslow, and Osband for their cheerful support."[41] Privately, though, Grierson appeared ebullient. An officer who spoke with the general upon his return to Memphis declared: "He says Colonel Kargé's Brigade did splendidly, and that the Second New Jersey Cavalry is entitled to great praise."[42]

Officers of the Second New Jersey believed that the successful campaign against General Hood's lines of communication had produced a major generalcy for Grierson and the eventual star for Kargé.[43] Just one month after the expedition, Grierson received his promotion to Brevet Major General, U.S. Volunteers, and General Washburn at this time sought a promotion for Kargé. Although commanding the District of Vicksburg and no longer Kargé's superior, Washburn nonetheless asked for the promotion in a letter to President Lincoln on 22 January 1865. Grierson likewise recommended Kargé for one-star rank to the Secretary of War. In his letter of 15 January 1865 Grierson said: "He has particularly attracted my attention by his discipline in camp and in the field, and by his gallantry in action." Grierson stressed Kargé's outstanding performance in the recent expedition and concluded: "He is a hightoned, honorable gentleman, has served with distinction both in the Army of the Potomac and in the West, and I cheerfully and earnestly recommend him for promotion to the rank of Brigadier General."[44]

Kargé expressed great satisfaction with the results of the expedition and of the part played by his brigade. On 14 January 1865 he issued a congratulatory order that recognized the performance of the officers and men, underscoring the disciplined behavior of the troops under fire: "You exhibited such firmness and ready obedience to the orders of your superiors that victory crowned your efforts." To a strict disciplinarian like Kargé, discipline meant success in battle, and he now gave unstinting praise: "You have displayed a courage and discipline that cannot be surpassed." The discipline of the troops, in turn, reflected the high caliber of leadership. Significantly, the officers took the first fire of the enemy as they led their men, and Kargé's order highlighted this fact. He said: "Captain Gallagher fell shot through the heart, at the head of his men, while leading them." Kargé stressed that Lieutenant John Burns "fell mortally wounded at the head of his company, in the same charge." And likewise Lieutenant Stryker Burd was shot "while leading his men against a stockade."

Although Kargé admitted that the fruits of victory were sweet, he acknowledged that they were gained with the loss of brave and gallant men, and he expressed sorrow over the deaths of the three New Jersey officers and "many good and brave men." He recognized the performance of the entire brigade, even though the Second New Jersey numerically formed two-thirds of his command and took the brunt of the fighting. He singled out Captain Joel H. Elliott, commanding the Seventh Indiana, and Captain Theodore W. Hencke, commanding the

Fourth Missouri, as well as Lieutenant Colonel Yorke. Kargé said that he hoped the renown gained by the brigade "will be an incentive to both officers and men" to further exemplary performance. "By a continued display of such bravery, endurance and discipline," Kargé remarked "they will obtain an immortal name in the history of the war."[45]

13

Alabama Campaign

End of the War and Recognition

Upon his return from the successful expedition to destroy General Hood's lines of communications, Kargé asked for a leave of absence of twenty days to visit his family in Belleville, New Jersey. He had campaigned continuously for fourteen months, and the expected pause of several weeks before the next likely action seemed to offer the best time to see his wife and two sons again. The Second New Jersey Cavalry did not require his attention, since the regiment was in Yorke's capable hands. Kargé's superiors granted him the leave, and on 24 January the *Newark Daily Advertiser* reported that Kargé was "in the city for a short leave of absence." [1]

No sooner had the Second New Jersey reached Memphis from the grand raid than General Dana ordered the regiment relocated to Natchez. The commander of the District of Natchez, Brigadier General John W. Davidson, had asked Dana for additional cavalry to help maintain federal control in his area. Dana chose the Second New Jersey because it was his strongest unit and the only one in the department armed with the Spencer carbine. Dana told Davidson that he parted with the regiment with reluctance. The change in assignment, however, was relatively brief, since on 4 March General Canby ordered Dana to ship the regiment to New Orleans, in preparation for a campaign in Alabama. Kargé, who had assumed the command of the Provisional Brigade at Natchez on 3 March, was relieved three days later and ordered to move with his regiment at once. He did, arriving with the Second New Jersey in New Orleans on 8 March. This change resulted from General Grant's war plans. Earlier, in January 1865, the General-in-Chief had instructed Halleck to plan an independent campaign to capture Mobile, the last major seaport of the Confederacy, and then to seize Montgomery and Selma. Halleck assigned this mission to Canby. Halleck also ordered General Thomas to march a force from Tennessee against Selma and Montgomery concurrently with Canby's attack on Mobile. [2]

The Alabama campaign became a major undertaking, in which the cavalry assumed an important role. Acting on the recommendation of Grant, who praised Grierson as a "most successful cavalry commander," Canby gave the newly promoted brevet major general the command of the cavalry forces of the Military Division of West Mississippi. The General-in-Chief said that Grierson had set the first example in making long raids by going through from Memphis to Baton Rouge in 1863. Noting his more recent exploit, Grant wrote: "His raid this winter on to the Mobile and Ohio Railroad was most important in its results and most successfully executed. I do not think I could have sent you a better man than Grierson to command your cavalry on an expedition to the interior of Alabama." Grierson assumed the duties of his new command on 2 March 1865. Planning to field some twelve thousand cavalry for the campaign, he brought together most of the regiments of his old division and the cavalry at New Orleans, the brigade of Brigadier General Thomas J. Lucas. Grierson set out to organize a cavalry corps of three divisions, each with two brigades. General Thomas contributed the division of Brigadier General Joseph F. Knipe from Middle Tennessee. Grierson immediately assigned Kargé the command of the First Brigade of Knipe's division. The Second New Jersey, mustering an effective strength of 710 men, formed part of Kargé's brigade, as always.[3]

The federal expeditionary force grew to a strength of some fifty thousand troops. Along with Knipe's cavalry division, Thomas also provided sixteen thousand infantry of the Sixteenth Corps, commanded by General Andrew J. Smith. Canby had been reluctant to accept Smith into his command, telling Grant that Smith was somewhat deficient in the qualities of organization and preparation. Canby also felt that way about Major General Frederick Steele, another subordinate commander. What Canby wanted was a senior general, qualified to assume charge of the expedition in the event of an accident to himself. Nevertheless he told Grant that "anyone in whom you have sufficient confidence to place in that position would be acceptable to me." Thus Smith became one of the two senior generals under Canby.[4]

The commander's overall plan called for the reduction of the Confederate fortifications on the east shore of Mobile Bay and seizing control of the Tensas and Alabama rivers, which empty into the bay. Then, turning the strong works erected for the defense of Mobile, he would force the surrender or evacuation of the city. Canby began the mission from a position of strength, for Dauphin Island with Fort Gaines and the

companion Fort Morgan, both at the entrance to the bay, had been
captured in August 1864. For the current operation, Canby employed
two columns: one, 32,200 strong, which he commanded personally,
moved from the lower extremity of Mobile Bay along the east shore. The
second column, 13,200 strong, marched from Pensacola under the
command of General Steele. His column protected Canby's flank.[5]

The cavalry forces played a relatively minor role in the first phase, the
capture of Mobile. When the campaign began on 17 March 1865,
Grierson had been able to equip and mount only one division of twenty-
five hundred troopers, who marched with General Steele's column.
Grierson remained at New Orleans to prepare as large an additional force
of cavalry as possible. The Second New Jersey Cavalry, awaiting a
shipment of five hundred Spencer carbines, was one of the regiments
unable to depart in the initial movement. Along with shortages of arms,
horses, and transportation, Grierson experienced great difficulty in
obtaining the promised regiments. As of 22 March, none of the cavalry
from Memphis or Little Rock had arrived. The poor condition of
Knipe's division also contributed to Grierson's overall problem. It
seems that General James H. Wilson had simply cast off Knipe's unit
from his command, prompting Grierson to complain to General Halleck
that Knipe's eight regiments arrived at New Orleans "about half
mounted and very poorly armed." Grierson assigned four of the least
capable regiments to points on the Mississippi river to replace cavalry
already at the front.[6]

Relations between Wilson and Grierson appeared cool. When Wilson
became Sherman's cavalry chief, he assigned Grierson the command of
the Fourth Cavalry Division which, in actuality, was Grierson's division
at Memphis. The former music teacher seemed reluctant to serve under
the youthful West Pointer and appeared to take his time about assuming
the post. Irked by Grierson's delay, Wilson relieved him. He got part of
Grierson's cavalry, Winslow's brigade, but the Second New Jersey and
other regiments remained at Memphis. Wilson evidently could not
forget Grierson's "snub," even though their official relationship lasted
only a few weeks and involved nothing more than the publication of
orders that were quickly superseded. Despite their brief association,
Wilson brought up the Grierson episode eight months later in a lengthy
report on his raid into Alabama. Wilson wrote: "Brig. Gen. B.H.
Grierson had been originally assigned to the command of this division
[Fourth Cavalry], but failing to use due diligence in assembling and

preparing it for the field, he was replaced by Bvt. Maj. Gen. E. Upton, an officer of rare merit and experience."[7]

By early April 1865, Grierson had organized and equipped an additional forty-five hundred cavalry, including the Second New Jersey. The regiment sailed 5 April and was in the battle zone when the outer Confederate fortifications fell, Spanish Fort on 8 April and Fort Blakely on 10 April. Unable to defend Mobile, the rebel garrison abandoned the city to federal troops, who occupied it on 12 April. The conduct of the siege and the capture of Mobile demonstrated excellent planning and careful execution over some very difficult terrain and against well-developed fortifications. Nonetheless, Canby's powerful force simply overwhelmed the Confederate opposition.[8]

The day Mobile fell, Canby acted at once to execute the second phase of the campaign, the capture of Montgomery and Selma. He sent Smith's Sixteenth Corps straight for Montgomery along the axis of the Stockton and Montgomery stage roads. Steele's Thirteenth Corps moved on a parallel route to Smith's left. The Navy convoyed Steele's men on transports up the Alabama river toward Montgomery. One division marched along the Tombigbee river and together with the Navy closed an escape route for rebel gunboats. Grierson's cavalry protected the flanks of the two columns. Screening the left flank, the brigade of Brigadier General Joseph R. West marched west of the Tombigbee. Grierson, with two brigades of some four thousand troopers, departed Mobile on 17 April on the right flank of the federal advance. He had the added mission of securing the country between the Tallapoosa and Chattahoochee rivers, and as far north as Dadeville and West Point. Canby also targeted the town of Opelika for destruction. Notwithstanding this wide-ranging mission, Canby instructed Grierson to keep the best-mounted portion of his command ready for a thrust into Georgia, marching possibly to Macon.[9]

For the advance into the interior of Alabama, Grierson found himself with only six thousand instead of the twelve thousand cavalry he had planned on. Because of the reduced number of men, he could not justify divisional units for Generals Lucas and Knipe; and, in response to Canby's instructions, Grierson on 14 April organized one cavalry division of three brigades, assigning each of his three brigadiers—West, Lucas, and Knipe—to the command of a brigade. He placed the Second New Jersey in West's First Brigade. The reorganization forced Kargé to step down from the command of a brigade in Knipe's former division to that of his own regiment. Grierson at this time selected two New Jersey officers for his staff: Major Peter D. Vroom, Acting Assistant Inspector General, and Captain John N. Givens, Assistant Quartermaster.[10]

General Lucas accepted the lower brigade assignment, but Knipe objected and voiced his dissatisfaction "in a very decided manner." He went over Grierson's head to General Canby, threatening to resign rather than be demoted in command status. Knipe's recalcitrance caused turmoil on the eve of the march for Montgomery, and Grierson reacted swiftly. The protesting general commanded the Second Brigade for only two days, when Grierson relieved him of command and ordered him to report to General Canby for reassignment. In special field orders of 17 April 1865, Grierson gave Kargé the command of Knipe's brigade and also transferred the Second New Jersey Cavalry to him.[11] The change took place the day Grierson's division marched north to overtake Smith's column. Kargé's brigade comprised the Tenth Indiana, Major George R. Swallow; Twelfth Indiana, Major William H. Calkins; Thirteenth Indiana, Colonel Gilbert M. L. Johnson; Fourth Wisconsin, Lieutenant Colonel Webster P. Moore; Second New Jersey, Lieutenant Colonel P. Jones Yorke; and the Fourteenth Battery of the Ohio Light Artillery, Captain William C. Myers.[12]

Grierson caught up with Smith's infantry at Greenville on the morning of 22 April. Here he learned that General Wilson's cavalry had captured Columbus, Georgia, on 16 April, having previously taken Selma on 2 April and Montgomery on 12 April. Thus, with federal forces already in possession of the objectives of Canby's northern thrust, Grierson changed directions and moved rapidly eastward for Georgia. He wished to cooperate with Wilson in the capture, if necessary, of Macon and Augusta. Reaching Troy, Alabama, Grierson split the division, directing Lucas to march for Union Springs, while he rode east with Kargé's brigade toward the Chattahoochee River.[13]

It was on 29 April, at Eufala, Alabama, that the Second New Jersey Cavalry first heard the shocking news of President Lincoln's assassination. Having left Blakely on 17 April, before the word had reached Mobile, the regiment had marched through the interior of Alabama for the next twelve days. Not until the cavalry reached Georgia and the presence of other federal troops did they obtain information on recent events. It was at Eufala also that Grierson learned of the agreement to an armistice between Generals Sherman and Joseph E. Johnston. While awaiting developments, Grierson displaced Kargé's brigade across the

Chattahoochee to Georgetown and ordered Lucas to Eufala. The general wanted to have his assembled command in position for renewed fighting if necessary. Shortly, Grierson received notification of Johnston's surrender, 26 April, of all Confederate forces east of the Chattahoochee. With hostilities at an end in the East, Grierson marched the division to Montgomery, where he reported to General A. J. Smith. One company of the Second New Jersey, which had been held at Blakely, rejoined the regiment.[14]

During Grierson's march from Eufala to Montgomery, the war in Alabama, Mississippi, and East Louisiana ended. General Richard Taylor surrendered his command on 4 May at Citronelle, some forty miles north of Mobile. One major Confederate command remained in the war, the Trans-Mississippi Department of Lieutenant General Edmund Kirby Smith. Anxious to squelch any buildup of rebel capability in Texas, Grant ordered Canby to rush units there. Canby sent Steele's troops but retained the Sixteenth Corps and Grierson's cavalry to occupy Alabama and Mississippi.[15]

A flurry of excitement seized the federal cavalry units in early May 1865, when President Jefferson Davis attempted to escape to the West. Kargé and other cavalry commanders were alerted to cover the country between the Alabama and Chattahoochee rivers. Davis, however, never got beyond Georgia, for on 10 May the Fourth Michigan and the First Wisconsin Cavalry regiments in a joint effort captured him and his party near Irwinville.[16]

Although federal infantry almost exclusively occupied Alabama, General Smith directed Grierson to send one regiment of cavalry to occupy Talladega. Grierson ordered the Second New York Cavalry of Lucas's brigade to fulfill this mission. To keep the two brigades at equal strength, Grierson detached the Fourth Wisconsin and the Tenth Indiana regiments from Kargé's brigade and assigned them to Lucas. The next day, 11 May, Kargé and Lucas marched their brigades westward for Mississippi, passing through Kingston, Centerville, Marion, Greensborough, Eutaw, and Pickensville, arriving at Columbus on 20 May. Grierson placed Kargé in command of the Columbus area and sent Lucas's brigade to Vicksburg. With his staff, the general departed for New Orleans.[17]

Kargé's march from Montgomery to Columbus proved uneventful, except for an incident at the Black Warrior River on 17 May. Nightfall prevented Kargé from crossing his brigade, and two of the three regiments and the artillery battery were forced to spend the night in swampy bottomlands. An irritated Kargé complained to Grierson the next morning that the crossing had been delayed "by the innumerable halts of the brigade preceding me, for which I could see no necessity whatever, other than to pillage the houses on the road, which was done indiscriminately by that command." Kargé experienced discomfort and hardship countless times in combat, but he never tolerated the misconduct of troops, especially when their misbehavior affected the well-being and discipline of his command.[18]

Since departing Mobile on 17 April, Kargé's brigade had traveled a distance of some seven hundred miles. The route of march passed through country that had, for the most part, never been visited by federal troops since the beginning of the war. With the end of hostilities, the federal command displayed a conciliatory attitude toward Southerners. Thus Grierson forbade the taking of livestock and issued vouchers for all subsistence required by troops. He allowed local authorities to keep some three hundred thousand bales of cotton along the route of march. He captured but immediately paroled more than ten thousand Confederate officers and soldiers.[19]

On 26 May 1865 representatives of Generals Canby and Kirby Smith met at New Orleans to negotiate terms of surrender. Their agreement provided for the cessation of all resistance; the officers and men of the Trans-Mississippi Department received paroles and conditions similar to those granted General Robert E. Lee at Appomatox. On 2 June, at Galveston, Kirby Smith accepted the terms, and "thus the last significant army of the Confederacy surrendered."[20] On the same day, General Grant issued his congratulations to the "Soldiers of the Armies of the United States." Grant said in part:

> Your marches, sieges, and battles, in distance, duration, resolution, and brilliancy of result dim the luster of the world's past military achievements, and will be the patriot's precedent in defense of liberty and right in all time to come.[21]

The end of the war found Kargé still not promoted. His gallant and dedicated service had not been recognized, although the War Department at this time passed out promotions in great numbers. The majority of Kargé's contemporaries had already been promoted. His fellow brigade commanders on the Grierson raid into Mississippi, Winslow and Osband, were brevet brigadier generals.[22] Colonel John P. Shanks,

Seventh Indiana Cavalry, had been in the grade of brevet brigadier general for more than three months. Shanks and Kargé had served together in Colonel Waring's brigade in the Meridian Expedition of Brigadier General W. Sooy Smith. Colonel Datus E. Coon was a brevet brigadier general.[23] Kargé and Coon had served as colonels in command of brigades in Grierson's Cavalry Corps during August 1864.[24] In the recent Alabama campaign Colonel Morgan H. Chrysler commanded a brigade in Lucas's division, while Kargé commanded a brigade in Knipe's division. But by early May Chrysler received promotion to one-star rank by brevet.[25]

Grierson was conscious of the inequity of promotions. His letter to Secretary of War Stanton in January 1865 and that of General Washburn to President Lincoln had produced no apparent effect. Grierson now took the time in the midst of campaigning to enlist General Canby's help. Writing from Montgomery on 10 May 1865, Grierson frankly asked Canby to use his influence with the authorities in Washington for Kargé's promotion. "He has been bred a soldier," Grierson said, "and is one of the most valuable officers I have ever had under my command." He described Kargé as energetic, prompt, and *always* on duty. He told Canby that Kargé had participated in almost every expedition that he had undertaken for the past two years and that Kargé had performed in an outstanding manner. "The services which he has rendered," Grierson emphasized, "entitle him to the rank of full Brigadier General, and I respectfully and earnestly ask your influence to obtain it for him." Canby approved the recommendation on 2 June 1865 at New Orleans and forwarded the correspondence to the War Department.[26]

On 1 June Kargé received instructions from Grierson to march the Second New Jersey Cavalry to Vicksburg for the purpose of mustering out all soldiers whose terms of service would expire prior to 1 October. Grierson responded to General Orders No. 83, 8 May 1865, issued by the War Department, to reduce the volunteer cavalry forces of the army. The order affected principally the one-year draftees of the regiment. Kargé turned the command of his brigade to Colonel G. M. L. Johnston, Thirteenth Indiana Cavalry, and moved to Vicksburg. While the Second New Jersey encamped on the Big Black River, Grierson ordered all detachments on special missions reunited with the parent regiment. The Military Division of West Mississippi mustered out a total of 622 one-year men on 30 June and transported them to Trenton,

New Jersey, by way of New Orleans. The strength of the Second New Jersey now stood at approximately 450.[27]

In the summer of 1865 the War Department reorganized the various geographical commands to meet post-bellum requirements. General Philip H. Sheridan took charge of a new command at New Orleans, temporarily called the Military Division of the Southwest but soon renamed the Military Division of the Gulf. Sheridan brought in Major General Wesley Merritt as chief of cavalry and gave him the command of six cavalry regiments, including the Second New Jersey. Sheridan rushed to organize forces for service in Texas, where trouble brewed along the Mexican border. At Brownsville on the Rio Grande, American units faced the imperial troops of Emperor Maximilian in an atmosphere of hostility. Two contingents for service in Texas were cavalry forces: one under Merritt, four thousand strong, to proceed to San Antonio, and the second under Major General George Custer, four thousand strong, to move to Houston. Sheridan almost immediately revoked the assignment of the Second New Jersey Cavalry to Merritt's command. More than likely, the mustering out of the one-year men prevented the readiness of the regiment for prompt movement to Texas.[28]

Following the departure of the one-year men, the Second New Jersey remained on duty in Mississippi. The regiment was divided into sub-commands and stationed at three locations. Kargé, commanding the Post of Natchez from his headquarters at the corner of Franklin and Wall Streets, had six companies at his disposal. Yorke served at Port Gibson with four companies, and Colonel N. S. Gilson commanded the Post of Brookhaven with two companies. Kargé informed the editor of Trenton's *Daily State Gazette* on 5 August that "the health of the regiment is good, the principal sickness being 'home sickness.'"[29]

The Post of Natchez formed a part of the Department of Mississippi, commanded by Major General Henry W. Slocum. His department constituted one of three subordinate commands of General Sheridan's Military Division of the Gulf. Slocum, in turn, subdivided the Department of Mississippi into three districts. Kargé and the Second New Jersey Cavalry found themselves in the Southern District, which Brevet Major General John W. Davidson commanded from his headquarters at Natchez.[30]

Kargé's assignment to Slocum's Department of Mississippi ended an eighteen-month relationship with Brevet Major General Grierson. Fighting together in the many hard campaigns, the two had become fast friends. Grierson, who always seemed restrained in expressing appreciation to his officers, wrote Kargé a farewell letter of much feeling on 28 July. He particularly regretted the unexplainable lack of a promotion for Kargé, but he spoke like a prophet when he added: "I cannot believe, however, that your service will be allowed to pass unrewarded." [31] Four weeks later Joseph Kargé received notification of his promotion to brigadier general by brevet for gallant and meritorious service in the war, to date from 13 March 1865. His letter of acceptance reveals a few significant facts about him:

HEAD-QUARTERS POST OF NATCHEZ
Natchez, Miss., August 26th, 1865
To the Adjutant General
U.S. Army,
Sir,
I have the honor to acknowledge receipt of notice from the War Department, dated June 19th, 1865, informing me that the President has appointed me a Brigadier General of Volunteers by Brevet.
I accept the appointment—am forty years of age, a native of Poland, and my permanent residence is Belleville, Essex County, New Jersey.
I am, General, very Respectfully
Your Obedient Servant
/s/ Joseph Kargé
Colonel, 2d N.J. Vol-Cav'y

Kargé's promotion undoubtedly developed from the recommendations of Generals Washburn and Grierson in January 1865. Grierson's subsequent effort, the letter of 10 May 1865 to General Canby, was overtaken by events. General Grant forwarded the letter, favorably endorsed, to the Secretary of War on 18 July 1865. But by this date Kargé had been promoted. A final notation on the correspondence and addressed to Assistant Adjutant General, Colonel Samuel F. Chalfin, reads: "Already appointed." [32]

The *Natchez Courier*, reporting on Kargé's advancement, gave readers some biographical data about the new general in its issue of 2 September 1865. The newspaper praised his regiment as having won in the many engagements "an enviable reputation for valor and efficiency, and at the present time enjoys a reputation second to none in all this region." Complimenting Kargé's leadership in Natchez, the *Courier* added: "His prompt, intelligent and just manner of dispatching the business of his office as Post Commander has, as we understand, given entire satisfaction to those who have been brought in contact with him." [33]

When General Davidson took a leave of absence, Slocum placed Kargé in command of the Southern District of Mississippi; and Kargé, in one of his first orders as district commander, reunited the Second New Jersey Cavalry at Natchez under Yorke's command. At this time the army promoted Yorke to a brevet "eagle" colonel. Major Peter D. Vroom, a battalion commander in the Second New Jersey, likewise received a brevet colonelcy for war service. [34]

General Kargé, wishing to remain in the army, wrote General Slocum on 11 September asking for his "kind influence and recommendation to be retained in the service." Kargé also attempted to keep the Second New Jersey Cavalry on active duty. On 9 September 1865, the Department of Mississippi published Special Orders No. 47, which called for the immediate consolidation of the regiment into a battalion of six companies and the mustering out of excess commissioned and noncommissioned officers. Before the department's order could be carried out, the War Department moved to discharge the large force of civilian soldiers still on duty. General Grant issued orders to disband all cavalry regiments east of the Mississippi river. The Department of Mississippi proceeded to muster out the remaining personnel of the Second New Jersey Cavalry, discharging some at Natchez on 25 October but the majority on 1 November. Leaving the service at Natchez, Colonel Yorke and Captain Edward P. Mount leased a plantation of six hundred acres on the Mississippi below Vicksburg. They and several other officers remained in the South to engage in the cultivation of cotton. [35]

General Joseph Kargé was mustered out 1 November 1865, under the authority of Special Orders No. 76, Headquarters Department of Mississippi, dated 17 October 1865. He led the group of some four hundred proud veterans to Trenton, where they arrived on Sunday evening, 12 November, and marched immediately to the Trenton Barracks for processing. Among the returning officers were the Adjutant, Major J. Lacey Pierson; Kargé's brother-in-law, Captain James M. Baldwin; Assistant Surgeons, John L. Krauter and John R. Todd; and seven captains, seven first lieutenants, including Jacob H. Hoffman, and six second lieutenants. The day after their arrival, the ladies of Trenton entertained the troopers with a "splendid repast" in Bechtel Hall. Major James Haggerty, a witty Irish orator, welcomed the veterans with a speech "of much eloquence." To the citizens of Trenton, the cavalrymen looked to be in the very best of health. The *Daily State Gazette* said "the discipline of the regiment is excellent," and it also commented: "The men are perfect soldiers—neat and clean in their dress and equipments, and bearing every mark of the finest physical condition." Governor-elect Marcus L. Ward visited the Barracks to greet the men, who received him enthusiastically. "Every soldier appeared to regard Mr. Ward as a personal friend, and his reception must have been very gratifying to him," the *Gazette* reported.[36]

Major General Robert F. Stockton, Jr., the State Adjutant General, wrote General Kargé a letter of official farewell. He said in part:

> During your term of service from 1861 to 1865, whether in command of a regiment or brigade, all reports received by me have been most favorable to your character as a brave and daring cavalry officer, and serving in the army of the Potomac as also in the army of the south west, you had an opportunity of displaying qualities, which I understand, were gratifying to your superior officers and gave confidence in your judgment as an officer and your bravery as a soldier.
>
> Gen'l Bayard stated that you were a first class cavalry officer and should be a Brig. Gen'l.[37]

General Joseph Kargé had served his adopted country with great dedication for more than four years. He volunteered for active duty although he was thirty-eight years old at the time, married, and the father of two children. Motivated to help America in her time of crisis, the grateful citizen possessed the military experience that the volunteer armies needed. Although he began as the second in command of the First New Jersey Cavalry, he exercised command of the regiment for the greater part of 1862. Intrigue and prejudice plagued his efforts in the early days of "Halsted's Horse," but Kargé rose above this pettiness to lead the regiment gallantly in battle. Generals George D. Bayard and Franz Sigel recognized his leadership and entrusted him with the command of brigade-size forces, often operating on independent missions. He received a severe wound at Brandy Station on 20 August 1862. Although he returned to duty in a few weeks, the constant campaigning aggravated the injury and forced him to leave the service halfway through the conflict.

In 1863 Kargé could have sat out the remainder of the war. He had done his part. If he had wanted to make some slight effort, he could have served at home with the state militia. But Kargé sought combat action. With the support of prominent citizens of New Jersey, he recruited and trained the Second New Jersey Cavalry Regiment. He then led this regiment and cavalry brigades in hard campaigns for two years until victory was won. The four hundred seasoned soldiers he brought back to Trenton reflected their commander's sense of accomplishment in the war. Brevet Brigadier General Joseph Kargé had indeed earned a star on many a battlefield. And, when recognition finally did come, it brought deep satisfaction to the men of his regiment, to his fellow citizens of New Jersey, and to himself as the high point in an active military career.

Soldier Becomes Educator

Kargé Tries the Regular Army but Turns to Teaching

Joseph Kargé spent Christmas of 1865 with Maria and their sons, Ladislaus and Romuald. The year before, the general had attacked the rebels at Verona, Mississippi, in the campaign to destroy Confederate General John B. Hood's lines of communications. And the year before that campaign, he had marched in bitter cold weather in West Tennessee in a fruitless pursuit of General Forrest. Now, the country was at peace, although tension with France grew over the issue of the puppet Mexican empire of Archduke Maximilian. On the domestic front the nation faced serious problems of reconstruction.

The dismantling of the huge volunteer army raised the question of military requirements for the post-bellum period: What forces and how many for the pacification of the Southern states, for patrolling the Mexican border, and for the manning of Western frontier posts? By Act of 28 July 1866 the Congress increased the number of Regular Army infantry regiments from nineteen to forty-five, and cavalry regiments from six to ten. The expansion of the cavalry arm aroused Kargé's interest. On 15 August 1866 he wrote Secretary of War Edwin Stanton to ask for an appointment in the rank of major in one of the new cavalry regiments. The law provided that captains and field grade officers would be chosen in equal numbers from among the Regulars and volunteers. Lieutenants were to be selected from among wartime volunteers. To qualify, all officers must have served at least two years with good conduct during the war.[1] Kargé applied to the Office of the Adjutant General and personally gave Major General Edward D. Townsend letters of recommendation regarding his character, social position, and military record. The War Department had specified that such endorsements be submitted with the application.[2]

Because of his excellent relationship with New Jersey political figures, Kargé quickly obtained recommendations from a number of citizens. One joint statement to the Secretary of War bore the signatures of three members of Congress, three former governors, the attorney general for New Jersey, a United States judge, and a United States attorney. These individuals asked Stanton to appoint Kargé a colonel of one of the new regiments.[3] In addition to signing the joint statement, former Governor Cortlandt Parker personally urged Stanton: "He *ought not* to be put under any other person's command, but if you cannot make him Colonel, place him as near as possible to that rank." Parker also told Stanton: "It is within my knowledge that Gen. Bayard spoke of him openly as the best cavalry officer he knew."[4]

Former Governor Joel Parker wrote letters of recommendation to President Andrew Johnson and to Stanton. Parker, who had named Kargé the State's Chief of Cavalry during the crisis of General Lee's invasion of Pennsylvania, told the President that under Kargé's command the Second New Jersey Cavalry "became one of the most efficient in the Southwest." Parker added: "His military record will compare favorably with that of any officer in the Service." Governor Marcus Ward and the State's Quartermaster, General Lewis Perrine, also petitioned the Secretary of War. Perrine recommended Kargé for the position of field grade officer in the cavalry service.[5]

The War Department did not act on Kargé's application for almost a year. Finally, on 7 June 1867 Kargé wrote Townsend for the return of his documents, which he said were "the only evidences of an honorable career while in the military service of the country." The letter sparked some activity. General Grant recommended that the Secretary of War offer Kargé a first lieutenancy in the Eighth Regiment of Cavalry. Although Kargé had asked for a major's commission, he accepted the rank of first lieutenant and took the oath of office in Washington on 19 July 1867.[6]

Kargé's acceptance of a first lieutenancy was a mistake. He would come to realize this in time. In the summer of 1867, however, he wanted to make the army a career. Perhaps he believed that through dedicated service and hard work he would rise in rank as he had done in the war. But the conditions of frontier duty were vastly different from the campaigning of Civil War days. Indian fighting was an occupation "where officers learned all about commanding fifty dragoons on the western plains but nothing about anything else." It was unrealistic for Kargé to expect to receive the command of one of the new cavalry regiments, as his supporters had recommended. There were far too many former cavalry generals available for the ten regiments. Almost without exception these generals were reduced in rank in the small peacetime army. Weigley wrote: "Officers reverted to their permanent ranks, and some wartime generals found themselves once again captains."[7]

How did Joseph Kargé, a brevet brigadier general, United States Volunteers, compare in Regular Army rank with the field grade officers of the new Eighth Cavalry Regiment? The commanding officer and the second-in-command were Colonel John I. Gregg and Lieutenant Colonel Thomas C. Devin, respectively. Both had been major generals, U.S. Volunteers. The two majors in the regiment were William Gamble, former brigadier general, and William R. Price, former brevet brigadier general, the same rank as Kargé's. To compare wartime promotions, the army had advanced Price to major on 5 August 1864, when Kargé had been a full colonel for more than a year and at the time in command of a cavalry brigade. One could not expect General Grant and the War Department staff to make precise comparisons of this nature, but Grant's offer of a first lieutenancy clearly did not reflect Kargé's military capabilities nor his war service. Even within the Eighth Cavalry, E. V. Sumner, a former brevet brigadier general, commanded Troop L as a captain. Sumner was the son of Major General Edwin V. Sumner of Fredericksburg and Antietam fame.[8]

First Lieutenant Joseph Kargé joined the Eighth United States Cavalry Regiment for duty in October 1867.[9] He arrived with reinforcements at Camp Winfield Scott, Nevada, on 1 November and took command of the post and of Troop A, relieving Second Lieutenant John Lafferty. The camp, located at the north end of Paradise Valley in Humboldt County, had been established for less than a year. On 12 December 1866, Captain Murray Davis, then commanding Troop A, and his second-in-command, Lieutenant Lafferty, founded the post. Lafferty soon acquired the reputation of being a "terror to the Indians." In January 1867 he killed a number of them in the valley and drove others into the mountains. In March of the same year, when Indians ran off with a rancher's stock, Lafferty pursued them relentlessly in a snowstorm for nine days. He killed six and captured their arms.[10] Lafferty simply followed the practice of killing a few Indians every time they stepped out of line.[11]

Captain Davis departed at the end of February 1867, leaving Lafferty in command. Eight months later Kargé arrived and displaced Lafferty as commanding officer. Kargé disagreed with Lafferty at once over the manner of handling the Indians. Fighting Indians was new to Kargé, but he seemed to recognize the Indians' right to survive in a hostile environment. Kargé's background as a Polish revolutionary in behalf of his subjugated country made him more appreciative of the lot of the downtrodden Indian. He dealt fairly with them; and in time, winning their confidence, he brought peace to the area.[12]

The change in policy was not felt before additional rustling occurred. Shortly after Kargé took command of Camp Scott, Indians raided the eastern part of Paradise Valley and drove off nearly all the stock. In response to orders from the commanding officer of the District of Nevada, Kargé made a determined pursuit of the thieves. He left Camp Scott with twelve men and two Indian scouts on 22 November 1867, following the marauders' trail over rugged and desolate terrain into the southeastern corner of Oregon. As Kargé neared the Owyhee River, a sleet and snow storm obliterated the trail of the pursued so that even his scouts could no longer detect it. He abandoned the pursuit and returned to Camp Scott. Submitting a detailed report of his grueling ten-day march of 380 miles, Kargé closed it with a denunciation of the citizens of Paradise Valley. "I respectfully beg leave to add," he wrote, "that had they one tenth of the time which they spend in whiskey mills and gambling halls devoted in guarding their property, this never could have occurred."[13]

Striking again the following spring, some Indians stole all the horses of one rancher. The theft was attributed to a feared Indian named Big Foot, who had the help of twenty braves. Kargé ordered Second Lieutenant Pendleton Hunter to take three men to catch the responsible Indians and bring back the stolen property. When Lafferty volunteered to go in place of the inexperienced Hunter, Kargé refused, and the two officers engaged in a heated argument. Hunter left with his three-man party, joined by John Rogers, a local settler.

Shortly after Hunter departed, Kargé reconsidered his decision. He instructed Lafferty to reinforce Hunter with a small force of selected men. As Lafferty prepared to ride off, Rogers dashed in with the alarming news that Hunter had been attacked by Indians in a canyon eight miles away. They had killed the cavalrymen's horses, shot Hunter in the thigh and wrist, and mortally wounded two of the three soldiers. The third trooper, Private Thomas Reed, and Rogers managed to find protection behind a rock and hold the Indians at bay. Rogers then escaped to seek help. Kargé quickly marshaled his small garrison and, leaving Lafferty behind, galloped to the scene of the fight. With the

Site of Camp Winfield Scott, Nevada, in 1962. COURTESY OF NEVADA STATE
HISTORICAL SOCIETY.

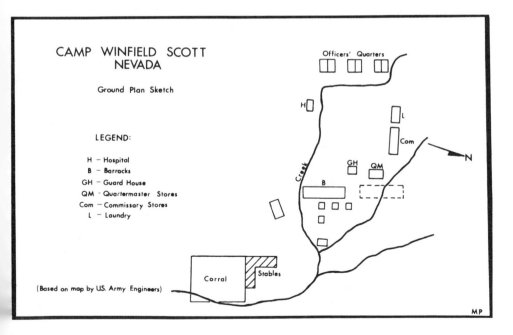

CAMP WINFIELD SCOTT
NEVADA

Ground Plan Sketch

Officers' Quarters

LEGEND:

H — Hospital
B — Barracks
GH — Guard House
QM — Quartermaster Stores
Com — Commissary Stores
L — Laundry

H

L

Com

Creek

GH   QM

B

N

Corral   Stables

(Based on map by U.S. Army Engineers)

MP

approach of the cavalry troop, the Indians hastily retreated and escaped. Reed had stubbornly held off some seventeen Indians, meanwhile protecting his wounded comrades and killing several of the attackers. For his gallant performance Kargé recommended Reed for a medal, which the army awarded the trooper.[14]

There was peace in the valley for the next eighteen months. Kargé carried out routine activities. Scouting and the furnishing of guards and escorts were almost continuous. Life was lonely and boring. Colonel Gregg's headquarters in early 1868 were located some two-hundred miles to the south at Churchill Barracks, Nevada. In May of the same year the headquarters were relocated to Camp Halleck, Nevada. The twelve companies, or troops, were scattered through California, Oregon, Washington Territory, Idaho, and Nevada. Having enlisted on the Pacific coast, the men were mostly "Forty-Niners," individuals who had worked in the mines for months and even years. They were a restless group, motivated by a spirit of adventure. They chafed under the restraints of military life and deserted with great frequency. At the end of 1867 nearly 42 percent of the Eight Cavalry Regiment had deserted. The officers, on the other hand, were experienced and selected veterans of the Civil War.[15] This professional talent was wasted. As Weigley explained: "For officers as well as enlisted men, the isolation and monotony of the frontier Army posed perils of stultification and worse." Moreover, service on the Indian frontier was harsh. The soldiers had to put up with dusty summers and bitter winters. At Camp Scott, a barracks for one-hundred men was constructed of adobe, with a shingle roof, and only one-half of the structure had a floor and ceiling. The officers' quarters consisted of two adobe buildings with four rooms each. As commanding officer, Kargé occupied a small stone hut. A rough stone building, with a ceiling only six and a half feet above the ground, served as the hospital and accommodated a maximum of six patients. The stables were built of cottonwood and willow sticks, and thatched with straw. These construction materials made the stables a constant fire hazard. Water for Troop A came from Cottonwood Creek, a mountain stream running through the camp. The army provided a minimum of sustenance. Exchanges, or cooperative stores to sell goods not issued to the troops, were not established until 1895. Post traders or sutlers as a group took advantage of the men, who in the lowest grade of private received only thirteen dollars a month.[16]

Perhaps the scenic environment of Paradise Valley soothed Kargé's days of isolation, for the valley reflects the beauty the name suggests. It lies within the encircling arms of tall mountains. The Santa Rosas form the western boundary and curve around the valley's north end to Spring Peak, 9,300 feet elevation, and to Thimble Mountain. On the south lie the Hot Spring Mountains. The Little Humboldt River flows through the valley, fed by Martin Creek and the streams from Thimble Mountain. In late spring the Santa Rosas are colored with blue, red, and yellow flowers. The valley itself comes alive with fields of brilliant wild-flowers—scarlet Indian paintbrush, purple lupines, and little, yellow, wild sunflowers. Early prospectors gave the valley its name, and the settlers who followed agreed.[17]

Kargé served in Nevada for two years. On 3 November 1869 he took an extended leave of absence. Back East again he met Dr. James

Professor Joseph Kargé, Ph.D. COURTESY OF NATIONAL ARCHIVES.

McCosh, the new president of the College of New Jersey, now Princeton University. McCosh offered Kargé the Chair of Continental Languages and Literature. Kargé promptly accepted and applied to the War Department for discharge.[18] Kargé's decision to change careers came at a most opportune time, for in 1869 the Congress reduced the number of infantry regiments by twenty. This drastic cut followed Congressional approval to restore the militias to the Southern states, in the expectation that local troops might assume much of the army's responsibilities there. The reduction forced the army to release some 750 officers with a year's pay.[19] The War Department transferred Kargé to the Ninth U.S. Infantry Regiment on 1 February 1870 and then placed him on the unassigned list on 4 May. He was honorably discharged from the service on 1 January 1871.[20]

Professor Kargé was happy at Princeton. The family lived in comfortable surroundings in the Borough of Princeton, and he dedicated himself to his role of educator. His twenty-two years at Princeton were quiet, unlike the dynamic and even hectic life he had experienced in the military, but they were characterized by the same outstanding qualities that marked his earlier years—"conscientious, punctilious, and vigorous discharge of duty, with no thought of sparing himself any labor or pains, and with a high ideal of his profession as a scholar and teacher." The demands on his time and energy were great, for he conducted all the practical instruction in French and German in the college. Toward the end of his professorial career, Kargé received some relief, when the college subdivided the departments and hired more instructors. Nevertheless, the many hours of daily classroom teaching left him too little time and opportunity for independent literary work.[21]

Kargé had been a well-informed student of European history, literature, and languages, having pursued these studies under eminent educators in his university courses as a youth. And now as a teacher he was ever conscious of the need to stay abreast of his profession and read learned journals relating to his department. He knew how to employ his knowledge and culture to illustrate and enliven his classroom work, interpreting and commenting on the literature read and adding more value to his formal lectures.

At times Kargé displayed certain eccentricities of manner and character. His students noted his deep and sometimes indignant tones. Occasionally he startled them with quick statements, springing from an impulsive and impetuous temperament, sensitive to inattention, carelessness, or unfitting conduct. With few exceptions, if any, his students valued his stimulating instruction, and they found him a kind, generous, and friendly individual. Outside the classroom the young men called on the professor in his comfortable study. It was lined with books and furnished with easy chairs much appreciated by the students. His callers usually found him behind a desk piled with manuscripts. If the visit was of more than a few minutes' duration, he would light up a cigar, a habit he had indulged in since manhood. Despite the years, he continued to present a soldierly figure.

To his colleagues, Kargé was a man of great integrity. His character was trustworthy, honorable, perfectly transparent, and devoid of intrigue or self-seeking motives.[22] Professor Kargé's fine scholarship, his amiable qualities, and his rare gifts as a teacher made him one of the best-known educators of his time.[23] In 1870, when Kargé joined the faculty, Princeton established the Woodhull Professorship in Modern Languages, and Joseph Kargé became the first incumbent. The following year Rutgers University awarded him the honorary degree of Doctor of Philosophy.[24]

The graduate school at Princeton became well organized under the presidency of Dr. McCosh. In the first venture of its kind, Kargé and Professor Cyrus F. Brackett led a group of young graduates on a geological expedition to the West. The success of this enterprise paved the way for many others that followed. Two graduates of the first "Kargé" expedition later gained distinction. Henry F. Osborn became president of the American Museum of Natural History and William B. Scott developed into an eminent geologist.[25]

Kargé always showed a high degree of adaptability to his environment. At Princeton he fitted himself not only into the academic life of the college but also into the social and religious activities of the town. As a conscientious citizen Kargé served a term on the Borough Council, where he was able to advance the interests of the community. He joined the First Presbyterian Church from religious conviction, but he deferred this action until the death of his mother, when he felt absolved from the obligation to respect her strong Catholic feelings in the matter.[26]

In 1874, at age fifty-one, Kargé's old combat wound began to give him trouble, and the government awarded him a pension of thirty dollars a month. That leg injury caused some incapacitation but not enough to prevent full-time attention to teaching.[27] Kargé's memories

of the Civil War may have been rekindled by the visit to Princeton of
General Ulysses S. Grant, who as president came for the commence-
ment exercises on 30 June 1875.[28] Undoubtedly, Dr. Kargé's full
academic life gave him little time for veterans' groups. Nonetheless in
1882 he joined the Military Order of the Loyal Legion of the United
States, Pennsylvania State Commandery. He also became a member of
the "Veteran Association of the 2d Regiment New Jersey Cavalry"
upon the founding of that organization in 1890.[29]

During the latter part of 1892 Professor Kargé occasionally experienced attacks of pain accompanied by weakness. His family and close
friends became concerned about his health. He himself minimized the
seriousness of these attacks. Nevertheless, he began to anticipate death
with calm fortitude, as the circumstances of his last hours show. During
the Christmas recess Kargé journeyed to visit his son Ladislaus, an
attorney in New York. On the afternoon of 27 December, he boarded a
ferry boat at Jersey City with a colleague who happened to accompany
him. Kargé, who had been reading Louis Bourdeau's book *Le Problème
de la mort*, told his companion: "I have but one desire concerning
it—that it come suddenly and without warning." The two travelers took
their seats on the upper deck and Kargé remarked on the sweeping view
of the harbor as well as the comfortable furnishings of the upper salon.
Gazing out over the water, the companion had his back toward Kargé
when he heard a gasp and a feeble attempt to speak. He quickly faced
about, only to find Kargé already unconscious, but still breathing.
Attempts to revive him failed, and shortly his breathing stopped. Before
the ferry reached the New York terminal, all signs of life had passed.
"Professor Kargé, in the same few moments, had crossed the river of
death."[30] An obituary in the *New York Times* disclosed that Kargé died
suddenly of heart disease. The newspaper said he was on the way to
New York from Princeton with Professors C. O. Huss and Henry Fine.
The obituary gave a resumé of his revolutionary activities in Europe and
his war service in America, including his being commissioned brigadier
general by brevet for gallant and meritorious service.[31]

In response to the desires of the family, President Francis L. Patton
and the Reverend Dr. James O. Murray, Dean of the College, conducted
a simple funeral service on 30 December at the Kargé residence. Among
those present from Trenton were General William S. Stryker, General
James F. Rusling, Charles E. Green, and Ira W. Wood.[32] When the
faculty and students reassembled after the holidays, Dr. Murray led the

regular Sunday service in the college chapel. He closed his sermon with a tribute to Professor Kargé, who had been present the previous Sunday. Dr. Murray said in part:

> Twenty generations of our students will recall "the General," as they were wont to call him, and will honor his memory as a faithful teacher, who had a high ideal of what education should be, and who to the measure of his abilities strove to maintain it.[33]

Epilogue

The Military Order of the Loyal Legion of the United States, Commandery of the State of Pennsylvania, published an *In Memoriam* circular to Brevet Brigadier General Joseph Kargé at Philadelphia, 20 March 1893. The tribute singled out the dramatic incidents of his life as a Polish revolutionary and as an American military commander. A three-man committee of his comrades, who prepared the circular, compared Kargé to such men as the Marquis de Lafayette and Thaddeus Kosciuszko. The Loyal Legion issued the *In Memoriam* by command of Brevet Major General David McMurtrie Gregg, who, like Kargé, had distinguished himself as a cavalry leader in the war.

One year later the Veteran Association of the Second Regiment, New Jersey Cavalry, adopted a resolution to honor the memory of Kargé at its fourth annual reunion held in Plainfield, New Jersey, on 1 March 1894. The veterans hailed Kargé's zeal in combat. They said he was "always the first to respond," and had carried the regimental colors over fifteen states and through the smoke of thirty-nine battlefields, returning the torn and stained colors to the State House as a perpetual memorial. "He has at last surrendered to the last great conqueror," his comrades noted.[1]

The imprint of Joseph Kargé on his times faded with the years. He left no direct descendants. Ladislaus had no children; Romuald had three, but they died before reaching maturity.[2] The memory of Kargé would have been more difficult to rekindle had it not been for the love and esteem of his Princeton University colleagues. In 1906 they erected a handsome monument over his grave. The inscription ends with these inspiring words: "A Gallant Soldier—Accomplished Teacher—A True Friend."

In 1938 Victor A. Wojciechowski of Trenton, New Jersey, began the first of what became annual visits to Kargé's gravesite by Polish American groups.[3] Wojciechowski gained the enthusiastic support of Albert Elsasser, chairman of the Cemetery Committee of the Trustees of the First (later Nassau) Presbyterian Church, which owns the cemet-

Military Order of the Loyal Legion of the United States.

COMMANDERY OF THE STATE OF PENNSYLVANIA.

In Memoriam

JOSEPH KARGÉ

Brevet Brigadier-General U.S. Vols.

DIED AT NEW YORK CITY DECEMBER 27, 1892

157

Military Order of the Loyal Legion of the United States.

HEADQUARTERS COMMANDERY OF THE STATE OF PENNSYLVANIA.

CIRCULAR NO. 9.
Series of 1893.
Whole No. 249.

Philadelphia, March 20, 1893.

Read at Stated Meeting of the Board of Officers.

JOSEPH KARGÉ.— Lieutenant Colonel 1st New Jersey Cavalry October 18, 1861; resigned and honorably discharged December 22, 1862.

Colonel 2d New Jersey Cavalry June 23, 1863; honorably mustered out November 1, 1865.

First Lieutenant 8th U.S. Cavalry June 12, 1867; transferred to 9th Infantry February 1, 1870; unassigned May 4, 1870; honorably mustered out January 1, 1871.

Brevetted Brigadier-General U.S. Volunteers March 13, 1865, "for gallant and meritorious services during the war."

Elected May 3, 1882. Class 1. Insignia 2436.

Born at Posen, in Prussian Poland, July 4, 1823.

Died at New York City, December 27, 1892.

Companion Kargé was son of a Polish Colonel of Cavalry who served under Napoleon, was graduated at the Universities of Breslau and Berlin, and was distinguished for attainments as well in languages as in history.

An enthusiastic republican, he in 1848 engaged in the movements having for their object the independence of his native land, was severely wounded in battle, taken prisoner, court-martialed and condemned to be shot, but escaping, he sought refuge in France and England, and in 1851, in the United States. On October 18, 1861, he was appointed Lieutenant-Colonel of the 1st New Jersey Cavalry, was wounded in battle near Rappahannock Bridge August 20, 1862, resigned December 22, 1862, and in the summer of 1863 raised the 2d Regiment New Jersey Cavalry, of which he was commissioned Colonel. The regiment was assigned to the 16th Corps, Army of the Tennessee, and was in constant service in the field until November 1, 1865, when it was mustered out. On March 13, 1865, he was commissioned by President Lincoln a Brigadier-General, by brevet, "for gallant and meritorious services during the war." He won and merited the confidence and esteem of his superior officers, by whom he was generally considered one of the most skilful and able cavalry leaders of the war.

After the close of the Civil War, he accepted a commission in the Regular Army and served some time on the Pacific Coast until 1870, when he was appointed Professor of Continental Languages and Literature in the College of New Jersey, where he remained until his death.

He took part in cavalry actions at Woodstock and Harrisonburg, Virginia, in June, 1862, Cedar Mountain and Rappahannock Station in August, 1862. Raided Warrenton, Virginia, in September, 1862, was in the cavalry action at Aldie, in October, 1862, and at the battle of Fredericksburg, December 11-13, 1862; also at Oko-

Iona, Mississippi, February 22, 1864; Bolivar, Tennessee, May 2, 1864; Guntown, Mississippi, June 10, 1864; Fort Gibson, Mississippi, July 15 and 16, 1864; Grand Gulf, Mississippi, July 17, 1864; Verona, Mississippi, December 25, 1864, Egypt Station, Mississippi, December 28, 1864, and many other minor affairs.

On his arrival in the United States he at once engaged in educational pursuits as an instructor. His advantages of manner and intellect soon won him the respec and warm regard of all with whom he came in contact, and the relations then formec continued with increasing interest and esteem as he advanced in life through the dis tinguished positions he afterwards held in army, educational and social circles.

Many influential men and women of to-day will recall with emotion how much they have been benefitted by his rare gift for imparting instruction, and hundreds of students will mourn his loss and be grateful for benefits bestowed.

In the army his position was conspicuous from the first. Having a thorough knowledge of the cavalry branch of the service, his rare intelligence, combined with unflinching bravery, his fire and dash, and wonderful energy, made him an ideal cav- alry leader. His services as regimental or brigade commander were constantly em- ployed in very responsible positions in raiding and reconnoitring, and were always satisfactory. He gave great attention to the wants of his command, looking carefully to their comfort and well being.

He was careful and skilful in manoeuvring troops, watchful and ever on the alert, and especially brilliant when under fire, where his personal skill and intrepidity were the pride of his command.

He was a strict disciplinarian, but as he at all times exhibited before his troops those sterling qualities of a true soldier, they learned to confide in, and respect and love him.

In the estimate of his character, as a knight "without fear and without reproach," is to be added the fact that he gave his adopted country his sword and services for the best years of his life.

He was of the same class of men as Lafayette and Kosciusko. His devotion to the country was not merely the result of a sense of duty, but rather of an all pervading sentiment, which rendered him insensible to any other thought, whether of comfort, home or family. He forgot everything but the glorious sentiment of liberty and the cause for which he fought. His death was sudden, of heart failure, while absent from his home in Princeton, on his way to visit friends in New York. He leaves a widow and two sons.

WILLIAM S. STRYKER,
Brevet Lieutenant-Colonel U.S. Vols.
WM. W. L. PHILLIPS,
Major and Surgeon 1st New Jersey Cavalry.
W. V. SCUDDER,
Captain 2d New Jersey Cavalry.
Committee.

By command of
Brevet Major-General D. McM. GREGG, U.S.V.,
Commander.

JOHN P. NICHOLSON,
Brevet Lieutenant-Colonel U.S.V.,
Recorder.

Official.
Recorder.

ery. Elsasser, professor of English at Princeton University at the time, recalled the visits of Wojciechowski and his fellow citizens. "He and his group," Elsasser said, "decorated the Kargé plot with Polish and American flags, and handsome wreaths with red and white ribbons." On each occasion the group "maintained watch the entire day!" Elsasser did more than merely cooperate with Polish American groups. He highlighted the Kargé monument in the conduct of public tours of the cemetery. Annually, on the Sunday nearest to Memorial Day, Elsasser personally led the visitors. He did not limit the tour to the gravesites of soldier dead but included the memorials to President Grover Cleveland, the presidents of Princeton University, to Paul Tulane, the benefactor of Tulane University, and other individuals who had distinguished themselves. "Kargé was always included," Elsasser said, "and his story [was] followed with interest."[4]

The initiative of Wojciechowski and Elsasser sparked renewed interest in Joseph Kargé's career. During the Centennial of the Civil War, many commemorative exercises were conducted in New Jersey and elsewhere to honor his contribution to the preservation of the Union and the freeing of all Americans. On 21 May 1962, the General Assembly of the State of New Jersey unanimously passed a Joint Resolution honoring General Joseph Kargé. A week later Governor Richard J. Hughes issued an "In Memoriam" Proclamation. Likewise, on 26 June 1962, Illinois Governor Otto Kerner issued an "In Memoriam" Proclamation. Chicago Mayor Richard J. Daley proclaimed 2 July through 7 July 1962 as "General Joseph Kargé Week in Chicago." Other officials who saluted Kargé were the governor of Ohio and the mayors of Cleveland, Ohio as well as of Newark, Elizabeth, and Sayreville, New Jersey.[5]

During the five-year period of the Civil War Centennial, the American-Polish War Centennial Committee, under the dynamic leadership of National Chairman Henry Archacki of New York, provided much of the effort to honor General Joseph Kargé. On Independence Day 1962 the Polish Legion of American Veterans, New Jersey State Department, conducted an impressive memorial. The exercise was cosponsored by the New Jersey Civil War Centennial Commission and the American-Polish Civil War Centennial Committee. Later, on 27 December 1962, the seventieth anniversary of Kargé's death became the occasion of another memorial service at the General's gravesite. The following year the centennial of the "Riding Out of the Second

New Jersey Cavalry'' took place at the headquarters of the New Jersey Historical Society in Newark, 21 September 1963. Mayor Hugh J. Addonizio stressed the event with a proclamation in which he set the period of 21-28 September as "General Joseph Kargé Week in Newark." Governor Hughes also proclaimed the same week as a statewide observance. His proclamation pointed out that Kargé was "one of the first of New Jersey's sons to fight for the Union."[6] The American-Polish Civil War Centennial Committee of Newark and the various Polish societies of that city cosponsored the event. On this occasion Miss Mignon Bouget Zulinski's portrait painting of Joseph Kargé—the first contemporary painting of the General—was presented to the New Jersey Historical Society.[7]

The American-Polish Civil War Centennial Committee held the closing Centennial tribute to Kargé on 9 November 1963 in Newark at the New Jersey Historical Society. The Federation of Polish Societies of Newark acted as cosponsor. This moving observance included the posthumous award to Kargé of the Gold Cross of Merit, with Crossed Sword and Citation, by the Polish Government-in-Exile (London). Colonel Benjamin T. Anuskiewicz, U.S. Army Retired, the Chairman of the Committee's Military Affairs Subcommittee, presented the Gold Cross to Executive Director Robert M. Lunny, who accepted the award on behalf of the New Jersey Historical Society. Officials of veteran organizations eulogized Kargé. They included National Commander John Dec, Polish American Veterans Association of America; Vice National Commander Matthew Misiur, Polish Legion of American Veterans; Captain James C. Coggill, Military Order of the Loyal Legion of the United States, Commandery of the State of New York; and the Reverend Galbraith Hall Todd, D.D., Chaplain-in-Chief, Military Order of the Loyal Legion of the United States. The guest of honor, Major General James F. Cantwell, made the concluding address. At the time, Cantwell served as Chief of Staff, New Jersey Department of Defense, and as President of the National Guard Association of the United States. Cantwell said, in part: "Joseph Kargé, immigrant, patriot, soldier and educator, exemplifies all the qualities that we should expect to find in a great American." And he concluded: "One hundred years ago, my predecessor, Brigadier General Robert F. Stockton, publicly and formally thanked General Kargé on behalf of the state of New Jersey. Today I renew that gratitude to the memory of General Joseph Kargé."[8]

The Civil War Centennial observances to honor the gallantry and self-sacrifice of General Joseph Kargé were led almost exclusively by Polish American organizations. State, municipal, and civic officials cooperated. Yet the initiative sprang mainly from the Polish side. It would be fitting that future commemorations be sponsored by groups representative of all America, uniting in tribute to a patriotic son of his native Poland and of his adopted America.

Appendixes

APPENDIX A: Kargé Congratulatory Order

(Expedition to destroy the lines of communications of Confederate General John Bell Hood, 21 December 1864-5 January 1865)

HEADQUARTERS FIRST BRIGADE CAVALRY DIVISION, M.D.M.
Memphis, Tennessee, January 14, 1865

(Circular No. 1)

The Colonel commanding takes this opportunity to congratulate the officers and men of the First Brigade for the brave and gallant manner in which they conducted themselves during the late expedition into Mississippi, under Brigadier-General B. H. Grierson.

In the heart of an enemy's country, and subject to circumstances having a demoralizing tendency, you have displayed a courage and discipline that cannot be surpassed.

In the face of the enemy, when deploying under a heavy and galling fire, or when charging his lines and intrenchments, you exhibited such firmness and ready obedience to the orders of your superiors, that victory crowned your efforts, and the foe, disheartened, appalled by such determination and bravery, was compelled to surrender.

But however sweet are the fruits of victory, they were not gained without the loss of brave and gallant soldiers; and it is with feelings of sorrow, that the Colonel commanding has to record the loss of three brave officers of the Second New Jersey Cavalry, and many good and brave men. Captain Gallagher fell shot through the heart, at the head of his men, while leading them. His Second Lieutenant, John Burns, fell mortally wounded at the head of his company, in the same charge. Lieutenant Stryker Burd was shot while leading his men against a stockade, in an endeavor to secure the enemy's colors.

It is a consolation to know, however, that the officers and men have fallen in a noble cause, and while bravely performing their duty.

The Colonel commanding trusts that the renown gained by the brigade during the expedition, will be an incentive to both officers and men to further efforts in the same direction. By a continued display of such bravery, endurance and discipline, they will obtain an immortal name in the history of the war.

Where (with but two exceptions) all have done well, it would seem invidious to designate particular persons as meriting special notice. The Colonel commanding, however, cannot refrain from mentioning, as worthy of special approbation, Lieutenant Colonel Yorke, commanding Second New Jersey Cavalry, Captain Elliott, Seventh Indiana, and Captain Hencke, Fourth Missouri Cavalry Volunteers.

/s/ Joseph Kargé
Colonel Commanding First Brigade

APPENDIX B: Letter of General Benjamin F. Grierson to Colonel Joseph Kargé

Headquarters Cavalry Forces
Dep't of Louisiana & Texas
New Orleans, La., July 28, 1865

Dear Colonel,

Our official intercourse having been broken by the removal of your regiment from my command, I desire to express to you my friendship, as well as my high appreciation of your valuable services as an officer.

I recall, with feelings of pleasure, our past intercourse and association in the field, during the numerous arduous campaigns in which we have participated and I feel it my duty to thank you most heartily for the earnest support and co-operation with which you have always favored me.

I regret exceedingly that the recommendations for your promotion which have been forwarded and which you have so nobly earned, have not received the desired consideration. I cannot believe, however, that your services will be allowed to pass unrewarded.

Accept my best wishes for the health and prosperity of you and yours and believe me

Truly your friend
/s/ B. H. Grierson
Bv't Maj. Gen'l

Notes

Preface

1. *New York Times*, 15 March 1863.
2. Joseph W. Wieczerzak. *A Polish Chapter in Civil War America: The Effect of the January Insurrection on American Opinion and Diplomacy* (New York: Twayne Publishers, Inc., 1967), p. 164.
3. George J. Lerski, "The United States and the January Insurrection," *Polish American Studies* 30 (Spring 1973): 48.

Prologue

1. *War of the Rebellion: A Compilation of the Official Records of the Union and Confederate Armies*, 128 vols. (Washington, D.C.: Government Printing Office, 1880-1901), 32, pt. 1: 693, 699, 702.

Chapter 1: Gallant Son of Liberty

1. E. M. Hopkins, "An Evening with Our Professor," *Nassau Literary Magazine* 43, nos. 4, 5, 6 (November 1887, December 1887, and January 1888), Princeton College, passim.
2. William A. Packard, *Joseph Kargé: A Memorial Sketch* (New York: Anson D. F. Randolph and Co., 1893), pp. 6-7; and Miecislaus Haiman, *Polish Past in America, 1608-1865* (Chicago: Archives and Museum of the Polish Roman Catholic Union, 1939), p. 123. Joseph Kargé was born at Potockie Oledry, a village near Poznan, according to baptismal records of St. Matthew's Church, Opalenica, Poland.
3. Packard, *Kargé*, pp. 8-10; and Mieczyslaw (Miecislaus) Haiman, *Historja Udzialu Polakow w Amerykanskiej Wojnie Domowej* [History of the Participation of Poles in the American Civil War] (Chicago: Drukiem Dziennika Zjednoczenia [Daily Union Press], 1928), p. 62.
4. Packard, *Kargé*, pp. 10-11.
5. Hopkins, *Nassau Literary Magazine,* passim.
6. Ibid. (January 1888), pp. 347-48.
7. Ladislas John Siekaniec, *The Polish Contribution to Early American Education, 1608–1865* (San Francisco, Calif.: R & E Research Associates, 1976), p. 33. The brother who accompanied Joseph to America was the Reverend Francis Kargé.

Chapter 2: New Citizen Turns Volunteer

1. Bruce Catton, *The Centennial History of the Civil War: The Coming Fury* (Garden City, N.Y.: Doubleday & Company, Inc., 1961), p. 313.

2. Ella Lonn, *Foreigners in the Confederacy* (Gloucester, Mass.: Peter Smith, 1965), pp. 146-47; and *Polish American Journal* (Scranton, Pa.), 26 June 1965.

3. Catton, *The Coming Fury*, p. 329.

4. Anne Sidwa, "Joseph Kargé," *Proceedings of the New Jersey Historical Society* 81, no. 4 (October 1963): 248.

5. Kargé's Pension Records; *Baldwin Genealogy, 1881*, National Archives; Local History Historian, New York Public Library. Maria Kargé's maiden name was Maria Theodosia Baldwin, daughter of David Johnson Caleb Baldwin, who was born in New Jersey in 1785 and settled in Orange. Maria's grandfather soldiered in the American Revolution. She was the widow of A. S. Williams, who died in February 1849.

6. Kargé's Pension Records, National Archives. Ladislaus, born 1 April, 1853; Romuald Francis, born 30 December, 1854.

7. John Y. Foster, *New Jersey and the Rebellion* (Newark, N.J.: Martin R. Dennis & Co., 1868), p. 408.

8. *Daily State Gazette and Republican* (Trenton, N.J.), 27 August 1861.

9. Henry R. Pyne, *The History of the First New Jersey Cavalry* (Trenton, N.J.: J. A. Beecher, Publisher, 1871), pp. 18-19; *Daily State Gazette and Republican*, 7 September 1861.

10. Pyne, *First New Jersey Cavalry*, pp. 19-20.

11. Private F. Rodgers to Major General George McClellan, 17 October 1861; Records of the First New Jersey Cavalry, National Archives.

12. Pyne, *First New Jersey Cavalry*, pp. 20-21; *Daily State Gazette and Republican*, 28 November 1861.

13. Pyne, *First New Jersey Cavalry*, p. 21.

14. "The Lesson and the Legacy," *Army Information Digest* 16 (August 1961): 51. (Official Magazine of the Department of the Army. A special issue commemorated the centennial of the United States Army in the Civil War, 1861-1865).

15. Col. G. F. R. Henderson, *Stonewall Jackson and the American Civil War* (London: Longmans, Green and Co., 1898; reprint ed., New York: Van Rees Press, 1946), pp. 616-17.

16. Lenoir Chambers, *Stonewall Jackson* (New York: William Morrow & Co., 1959), 2: 306; *Official Records*, 21: 641.

17. *Army Information Digest* 16: 51.

18. Kargé's Service Records, National Archives.

19. Pyne, *First New Jersey Cavalry*, pp. 21-22.

20. Ibid., p. 22.

21. Special Order No. 25, Office of the Chief of Cavalry, Headquarters, Army of the Potomac, Washington, D.C., 11 November 1861; Records of the First New Jersey Cavalry, Records Group 94, National Archives; Pyne, *First New Jersey Cavalry*, pp. 22-23.

22. Fairfax Downey, *Clash of Cavalry* (New York: David McKay, Company, Inc., 1959), p. 30.

23. *Daily State Gazette and Republican*, 4 December 1861.

24. *New York Times*, 5 December 1861, p. 3.

25. Ibid. The reporter's "Capt. Maas" is believed to have been Bogumil Mass.

26. Court martial papers in Kargé's Service Records. National Archives.

27. George Winston Smith and Charles Judah, *Life in the North during the Civil War* (Albuquerque: The University of New Mexico Press, 1966), p. 84.

28. Court martial papers in Kargé's Service Records, National Archives. British author General Colin R. Ballard wrote that regular officers of the European school (Kargé's case) would have been driven to fury and despair by the lack of discipline in both the Union and Confederate armies. *The Military Genius of Abraham Lincoln* (Cleveland, Ohio: World Publishing Co., 1952), p. 48.

29. Kargé's Service Records, National Archives.

30. Pyne, *First New Jersey Cavalry*, pp. 23-24.

31. Kargé's Service Records, National Archives.

32. Brigadier General George Stoneman to Brigadier General Seth Williams, (Assistant) Adjutant General of the Army of the Potomac, 22 January 1862. Records of the First New Jersey Cavalry Regiment, National Archives.

33. Henry R. Pyne, *The History of the First New Jersey Cavalry* (Trenton, N.J.: J. A. Beecher, Publisher, 1871; reprint ed., Earl Schenck Myers, ed., retitled *Ride to War*, New Brunswick, N.J.: Rutgers University Press, 1961), p. xxxii.

34. Ibid., pp. xiii, 9.

35. Pyne, *First New Jersey Cavalry*, pp. 24-25.

Chapter 3: In Pursuit of Stonewall Jackson

1. Pyne, *First New Jersey Cavalry*, pp. 38-39.

2. Ballard, *Military Genius of Lincoln*, pp. 75-76.

3. Pyne, *First New Jersey Cavalry*, p. 38.

4. Mark Mayo Boatner III, *The Civil War Dictionary* (New York: David McKay Company, Inc., 1959), p. 52; Samuel John Bayard, *The Life of George Dashiell Bayard* (New York: G. P. Putnam's Sons, 1874), p. 187.

5. J. R. Sypher, *History of the Pennsylvania Reserve Corps* (Lancaster, Pa.: Elias Barr & Co., 1865), pp. 182-83; Pyne, *First New Jersey Cavalry*, pp. 39-40; William Penn Lloyd, *History of the First Regiment Pennsylvania Reserve Cavalry* (Philadelphia: King & Baird, Printers, 1864), p. 19.

6. Colonel Vincent J. Esposito, chief ed., *The West Point Atlas of American Wars* (New York: Frederick A. Praeger, Inc., 1959), 1: 52; Ballard, *Military Genius of Lincoln*, p. 86; *Official Records*, 12, pt. 3: 219-220.

7. *Official Records*, 12, pt. 3: 219, 231-32; Robert G. Tanner, *Stonewall in the Valley* (Garden City, N.Y.: Doubleday & Company, Inc., 1976), pp. 208, 234-35, 246.

8. Pyne, *First New Jersey Cavalry*, pp. 40-41.

9. Ibid., pp. 42-43.

10. Pyne's account of the march of General Bayard's Cavalry Brigade to Front Royal contradicts the statement of Brigadier General Colin R. Ballard, *Military Genius of Lincoln*, p. 87, that it took McDowell eight days to march the seventy miles from Fredericksburg. *Official Records* also contradicts Ballard. Shields's division cleared Falmouth, opposite Fredericksburg, by noon of 25 May 1862 (*Official Records*, 12, pt. 3: 231) and arrived at Front Royal on 30 May. Reporting to McDowell, Shields wrote, "General: The First Brigade of this division, General Kimball commanding, preceded by four companies of Rhode Island cavalry, under Major Nelson, entered this place (Front Royal) at 11 o'clock this morning (May 30) and drove out the enemy, consisting of the Eighth Louisiana and four companies of the Twelfth Georgia and a body of cavalry.... We captured 6 officers and 150 men" (*Official Records*, 12, pt. 1: 682).

11. Esposito, *West Point Atlas*, 1: 52; *Official Records*, 12, pt. 1: 11, 708 and pt. 3: 322.

12. *Official Records*, 12, pt. 1: 283.

13. Ibid., p. 677; Pyne, *First New Jersey Cavalry*, p. 45.

14. *Official Records*, 12, pt. 1: 677-78. Four companies of Pennsylvania Bucktails were assigned to General Bayard's Cavalry Brigade for the pursuit of Stonewall Jackson. The remaining six companies continued to be assigned to Brigadier General George A. McCall's division located near Falmouth, Virginia, until 6 June 1862, when President Lincoln released McCall's troops to support McClellan on the Peninsula. *Civil War Times Illustrated* 4, no. 9 (January 1966): 20.

15. *Official Records*, 12, pt. 1: 678.

16. Bayard, *Life of George Bayard*, p. 214.

17. *Official Records*, 12, pt. 1: 681 and pt. 3: 347.

18. Ibid., pt. 1: 678; Sypher, *History of Pennsylvania Reserve Corps*, p. 184.

19. *Official Records*, 12, pt. 1: 678.

20. Pyne, *First New Jersey Cavalry*, p. 49; *Official Records*, 12, pt. 1: 679.

21. *New York Times*, 14 June 1862.

22. *Official Records*, 12, pt. 1: 651, 679.

23. Pyne, *First New Jersey Cavalry*, p. 50.

24. *New York Times*, 14 June 1862.

25. Pyne, *First New Jersey Cavalry*, p. 51.

26. Bayard, *Life of George Bayard*, p. 214.

27. *Official Records*, 12, pt. 1: 679.

28. *New York Times*, 14 June 1862.

29. *Official Records*, 12, pt. 1: 680.

30. The minié bullet possessed great smashing power. In 1848 Captain Claude Etienne Minié of the French Army developed the bullet, which revolutionized warfare. The U.S. Army adopted the minié principle in 1855, encasing the minié bullet and powder in a paper cover that was inserted into the barrel at one count. Soldiers employed the minié bullet extensively in the caliber .58 rifle musket. Francis A. Lord, *Civil War Collector's Encyclopedia* (Harrisburg, Pa.: The Stackpole Co., 1963), p. 15.

31. *Official Records*, 12, pt. 1: 680.

32, Pyne, *First New Jersey Cavalry*, pp. 54-55.

33. *Official Records*, 12, pt. 1: 18; Chambers, *Stonewall Jackson*, 1: 567.

34. *Official Records*, 12, pt. 1: 680; *Newark Daily Mercury*, 28 June 1862.

35. Esposito, *West Point Atlas*, 1: 53; *Official Records*, 12, pt. 1: 19.

36. Kenneth P. Williams, *Lincoln Finds a General* (New York: The Macmillan Company, 1949), 1: 203-4; and Esposito, *West Point Atlas*, 1: 53.

37. Burke Davis, *They Called Him Stonewall* (New York: Rinehart & Co., Inc., 1954), p. 192. *Official Records*, 12, pt. 3: 334, 340; Bayard, *Life of George Bayard*, p. 215.

38. Bayard, *Life of George Bayard*, p. 218.

39. *New York Times*, 18 June 1862.

40. Joseph Kargé to Governor Charles Olden, 1 July 1862, State Library of New Jersey, Trenton; *Official Records*, 12, pt. 1: 679.

41. *New York Tribune*, 12 June 1862; *Official Records*, 12, pt. 1: 25, 676-77.

42. *New York Times*, 14 June 1862.

43. *Official Records*, 12, pt. 1: 677, 679.

Chapter 4: Bayard's Cavalry Holds off Jackson

1. *Official Records*, 12, pt. 3: 435.

2. Foster, *New Jersey and the Rebellion*, p. 424; Pyne, *First New Jersey Cavalry*, p. 60.

3. Bayard, *Life of George Bayard*, p. 218.

4. Esposito, *West Point Atlas*, 1: 54.

5. *Newark Daily Mercury*, 17 July and 1 August 1862.

6. William S. Stryker, Adjutant General, *Record of Officers and Men of New Jersey in the Civil War, 1861-1865* (Trenton: John L. Murphy, Steam Book and Job Printer, 1876), p. 1254.

7. Pyne, *First New Jersey Cavalry*, p. 60.

8. Esposito, *West Point Atlas*, 1: 55; *Official Records*, 12, pt. 3: 435.

9. Pyne, *First New Jersey Cavalry*, pp. 64, 66; *Official Records*, 12, pt. 3: 474.

10. Pyne, *First New Jersey Cavalry*, pp. 68-69; *Official Records*, 12, pt. 3: 514; Boatner, *Civil War Dictionary*, p. 207.

11. Pyne, *First New Jersey Cavalry*, p. 70; Foster, *New Jersey and the Rebellion*, p. 425; *Official Records*, pt. 3: 525-26.

12. *Official Records*, 12, pt. 2: 88, 111-14, 178 and pt. 3: 521-22, 524.

13. John W. Thomason, Jr., *Jeb Stuart* (New York: Charles Scribner's Sons, 1930), p. 212; Pyne, *First New Jersey Cavalry*, p. 70; *Official Records*, 12, pt. 2: 50-52.

14. *Official Records*, 12, pt. 2: 88-89, 92; Esposito, *West Point Atlas*, 1: 56; Thomason, *Jeb Stuart*, pp. 217-18; Lloyd, *History of First Pennsylvania Cavalry*, p. 22.

15. Pyne, *First New Jersey Cavalry*, pp. 71-72; Foster, *New Jersey and the Rebellion*, p. 425.

16. *Official Records*, 12, pt. 2: 130; Pyne, *First New Jersey Cavalry*, pp. 72-75.

17. *Official Records*, 12, pt. 2: 92 and pt. 3: 550.

18. Ibid., pt. 2: 89, 92.

19. Ibid.; Rev. Frederic Denison, "The Battle of Cedar Mountain: A Personal View," no. 10, 2d series, *Personal Narratives of Events in the War of the Rebellion* (Providence: Soldiers and Sailors Historical Society of Rhode Island, 1881), p. 18; and Pyne, *First New Jersey Cavalry*, pp. 76-77.

20. Pyne, *First New Jersey Cavalry*, pp. 77-79.

21. Douglas Southall Freeman, *Lee's Lieutenants* (New York: Charles Scribner's Sons, 1943), 2: 15-16, 22; Chambers, *Stonewall Jackson*, 2: 106; *Official Records*, 12, pt. 2: 180; Lloyd, *History of First Pennsylvania Cavalry*, p. 23.

22. *Official Records*, 12, pt. 2: 93; Denison, *Personal Narratives*, pp. 14-16; Lloyd, *History of First Pennsylvania Cavalry*, p. 27.

23. Milo M. Quaife, ed., *From the Cannon's Mouth: The Civil War Letters of General Alpheus S. Williams* (Detroit, Mich.: Wayne State University Press, 1959), p. 100; Pyne, *First New Jersey Cavalry*, pp. 80-81.

24. Chambers, *Stonewall Jackson*, 2: 110; Williams, *Lincoln Finds a General*, 1: 265.

25. Pyne, *First New Jersey Cavalry*, p. 82.

26. Ibid., p. 83.

27. Ibid., pp. 86-88; *Official Records*, 12, pt. 2: 139.

28. *Official Records*, 12, pt. 2: 93, 140-41; Pyne, *First New Jersey Cavalry*, pp. 88-89; Lloyd, *History of First Pennsylvania Cavalry*, pp. 24-25.

29. *Official Records*, 12, pt. 2: 146-47, 151; Thomason, *Jeb Stuart*, p. 218; Esposito *West Point Atlas*, 1: 56.

30. Quaife, *From the Cannon's Mouth*, p. 101; Thomason, *Jeb Stuart*, p. 219.

31. Pyne, *First New Jersey Cavalry*, pp. 89-91.

32. Burke Davis, *They Called Him Stonewall* (New York: Rinehart & Company, Inc., 1954), p. 276.

33. Kargé to General George D. Bayard, 12 August 1862. Records of the First New Jersey Cavalry Regiment, National Archives.

Chapter 5: Charges against the Commander

1. Kargé's Military Records, National Archives.

2. Article 34, *Revised Regulations for the Army of the United States, 1861*. By authority of the War Department (Philadelphia: J. G. L. Brown, Printer, 1861; reprint ed., Gettysburg, Pa.: *Civil War Times Illustrated*, 1974), p. 505.

3. *New Brunswick* (New Jersey) *Times*, 27 February 1862.

4. Kargé's Military Records, National Archives.

5. Foster, *New Jersey and the Rebellion*, p. 429.

6. Kargé's Military Records, National Archives.

7. Bayard, *Life of George Bayard*, p. 241.

8. Kargé's Military Records, National Archives.

9. Colonel Edmund Schriver to General George D. Bayard, 18 August 1862. Records of the First New Jersey Cavalry Regiment, National Archives.

Chapter 6: Clash of Cavalry

1. *Official Records*, 12, pt. 3: 571.

2. Esposito, *West Point Atlas*, 1: 57.

3. Thomason, *Jeb Stuart*, p. 223.

4. *Official Records*, 12, pt. 2: 89.

5. Pyne, *First New Jersey Cavalry*, p. 93.

6. *Official Records*, 12, pt. 2: 89; Pyne, *First New Jersey Cavalry*, pp. 93-94.

7. Fairfax Downey, *Clash of Cavalry* (New York: David McKay Company, Inc., 1959), p. 57; Edward P. Tobie, *History of the First Maine Cavalry, 1861-1865 (Boston: Press of Emery & Hughes, 1887), p. 83; and Official Records*, 12, pt. 2: 89.

8. *Official Records*, 12, pt. 2: 88-90; Pyne, *First New Jersey Cavalry*, p. 94; Thomason, *Jeb Stuart*, p. 230. Thomason said that Jeb Stuart had four regiments to Bayard's five. Bayard, however, deployed only three regiments for battle, since the First Maine and the First Rhode Island had already crossed to the northern bank of the Rappahannock.

9. Thomason, *Jeb Stuart*, p. 228.

10. *Official Records*, 12, pt. 2: 90.

11. Pyne, *First New Jersey Cavalry*, pp. 95-96.

12. Ibid.; *Official Records*, 12, pt. 3: 617.

13. Pyne, *First New Jersey Cavalry*, pp. 96-97.

14. *Official Records*, 12, pt. 2: 88.

15. Ibid., pp. 726-27, 745-46.

16. Pyne, *First New Jersey Cavalry*, pp. 97-98.

17. Ibid., pp. 99, 122.

18. *Newark Daily Mercury*, 3 October 1862; Kargé's Military Records, National Archives. The Governor's letter reads as follows:

State of New Jersey
Executive Department
Trenton, September 1st, 1862

Lieut. Colonel
   Joseph Kargé
      Comd'g 1st N.J. Cavalry
   Sir

I have received and read with the most profound interest your graphic and spirited report of the part taken by your Regiment in covering the retreat of the Army of Va. from the Rapidan to the Rappahannock.

The discipline and bravery which enabled them to dispute so gallantly the advance of a vastly superior force, merits the highest encomiums, and I beg that you will express to the officers and men under your command my admiration of their valor, and my thanks for the honor they have done for their State.

I beg to tender you my sincere regrets that you have been wounded, whilst I congratulate both you and myself that the injury you have sustained, is no worse—your service on this and former occasions will ever be remembered by the people of this State and of the Country—for myself, I return you my profound thanks for your gallantry and skill, and shall be glad of an opportunity to testify at all times my high appreciation of your service.

I sincerely hope that your convalescence may be rapid, and that the Country may not long remain without your valuable aid in the field.

Your Obdt. Servt.

/s/ Ch. S. Olden

19. *Newark Daily Mercury*, 3 October 1862.

20. Bayard, *Life of George Bayard*, pp. 252-53; *Official Records*, 19, pt. 2: 377.

21. Pyne, *First New Jersey Cavalry*, p. 122.

22. *Official Records*, 19, pt. 2: 7-8; Lloyd, *History of First Pennsylvania Cavalry*, p. 33.

23. *Newark Daily Mercury*, 9 October 1862.

24. Ibid.; *Official Records*, 19, pt. 2: 8.

25. *Official Records*, 19, pt. 2: 8.

26. Ibid., p. 9.

27. Kargé's Military Records, National Archives.

28. Ibid.

29. Major James A. Connolly, "Diary and Letters," Illinois State Historical Society, *Transactions* (1928); p. 378. Connolly finally received his promotion to lieutenant colonel by brevet at the end of the war.

30. Pyne, *First New Jersey Cavalry*, pp. 123-25.

31. *Official Records*, 19, pt. 2: 141; *Newark Daily Mercury*, 6 November 1862.

32. *Francis Trevelyan Miller*, editor-in-chief, *The Photographic History of the Civil War* (New York: The Review of Reviews Co., 1911), 4: 45; Pyne, *First New Jersey Cavalry*, pp. 125-26.

33. *Official Records*, 19, pt. 2: 141; Pyne *First New Jersey Cavalry*, pp. 126-28; *New York Times*, 7 November 1862.

34. Pyne, *First New Jersey Cavalry*, pp. 128-29.

35. *Official Records*, 19, pt. 2: 125, 136, 141; Pyne, *First New Jersey Cavalry*, pp. 129-30. General Bayard refers to his cavalry command as a division on one occasion and as a brigade on another: *Official Records*, 19, pt. 2: 518, 524.

36. Esposito, *West Point Atlas*, I: 70.

37. Pyne, *First New Jersey Cavalry*, p. 130.

38. *Official Records*, 19, pt. 2: 138.

39. *Newark Daily Mercury*, 17 November 1862.

40. *Official Records*, 19, pt. 2: 128.

41. Letter-Order, Headquarters, Cavalry Brigade, Upperville, Virginia, 4 November 1862. General George D. Bayard's Military Records, National Archives.

42. Esposito, *West Point Atlas*, 1: 70; *Official Records*, 19, pt. 2: 557, 583 and 21: 57-61.

43. *New York Times*, 1 December 1862; *Newark Daily Mercury*, 4 December 1862; Pyne, *First New Jersey Cavalry*, p. 133.

44. *Official Records*, 21: 28-30.

45. Kargé's Military Records, National Archives.

46. Esposito, *West Point Atlas*, 1: 72.

47. Robert Underwood Johnson, ed., *Battles and Leaders of the Civil War* (New York: The Century Company, 1884-87), 3: 136-37.

48. Bayard, *Life of George Bayard*, pp. 273-74; Noble D. Preston, *History of the Tenth Regiment of Cavalry, New York State Volunteers* (New York: D. Appleton and Company, 1892), p. 56.

49. Pyne, *First New Jersey Cavalry*, p. 135.

50. *Official Records*, 12, pt. 2: 91.

51. Records of the First New Jersey Cavalry Regiment, National Archives. Kargé's resignation was accepted and confirmed by paragraph 5, Special Orders No. 29, Headquarters Left Grand Division [Army of the Potomac], 31 December 1862.

Chapter 7: Return to Action

1. *Newark Daily Advertiser*, 17 January 1863. Kargé said in part:

> I have already found my reward in the self-consciousness that God has granted me the privilege to arraign myself on the side of a cause which is the sublimest on record of human events, I mean the vindication of Republican principles with the annihilation of slavery. . . .
> "Our beloved country (God bless and speed her) has sounded the trumpet of war, and the descendants of the Pilgrims are fully aroused; they have outstripped Asia and Europe in the sacrifices of their blood and treasure to efface from their midst the dark blot which transfigured our otherwise benign institutions, and the task Europe has performed in 1800 years in vindicating the dignity of man, we will accomplish in less than five.

2. Major General Samuel P. Heintzelman to Colonel Joseph Kargé, 3 March 1863. Kargé's Military Records, National Archives.

3. Sidwa, "Joseph Kargé," *Proceedings of the New Jersey Historical Society*, p. 251.

4. Esposito, *The West Point Atlas*, 1: 93.

5. *Daily State Gazette and Republican* (Trenton), 20 June 1863.

6. Ibid., 23 and 24 June 1863; *Newark Daily Advertiser*, 19 and 25 June 1863.

7. Esposito, *The West Point Atlas*, 1: 95.

8. *Daily State Gazette and Republican*, 24 June 1863.

9. Ibid., 13 July 1863.

10. Ibid., 16 July 1863; Major General Robert F. Stockton, Jr., New Jersey Adjutant General, to Major Thomas M. Vincent, Assistant Adjutant General, Washington, D.C., 24 August 1863; Regimental Order Book, Second New Jersey Cavalry Regiment, National Archives.

11. *Daily State Gazette and Republican*, 8 August 1863.

12. *Newark Daily Advertiser*, 8 July 1863.

13. *Daily State Gazette and Republican*, 20 June and 29 July 1863; Albert G. Brackett, *History of the United States Cavalry* (New York: Harper & Brothers, 1865), p. 316.

14. Downey, *Clash of Cavalry*, p. 25.

15. *Daily State Gazette and Republican*, 4 August and 11 August 1863; Downey, *Clash of Cavalry*, p. 27.

16. *Daily State Gazette and Republican*, 11 and 29 August 1863. The official roster of the Second New Jersey Cavalry Regiment does not list a Captain H. C. Paxson. The New Jersey Adjutant General's report to the War Department (n. 10, above) shows Alexander A. Yard as the recruiter for Company I in Trenton.

17. *Daily State Gazette and Republican*, 25 August 1863.

18. Ibid.

19. Ibid., 25 August and 4 September 1863.

20. *Newark Daily Advertiser*, 21 August 1863.

21. *Daily State Gazette and Republican*, 18 August 1863.

22. Ibid.

23. Ibid., 8 September 1863.

24. Colonel Joseph Kargé to General Robert F. Stockton, Jr., 11 September 1863. Records of Second New Jersey Cavalry, State Library of New Jersey, Trenton.

25. *Daily State Gazette and Republican*, 3 September 1863.

26. William S. Stryker, Adjutant General of New Jersey, comp., *Record of Officers and Men of New Jersey in the Civil War, 1861–1865* (Trenton, N.J.: John L. Murphy, Steam Book and Job Printer 1876), p. 1320.

27. Secretary of State William H. Seward to Illinois Governor Richard Yates, 6 July 1863. Records of Second New Jersey Cavalry Regiment, State Library of New Jersey, Trenton; Stryker, *New Jersey Records*, p. 1309.

28. Erich von Pannwitz served with distinction for the life of the regiment. He was promoted to lieutenant colonel 24 October 1865. Along with Kargé, he was one of the last to be mustered out, 1

November 1865. His brother officer, Julius von Rudolphi, was promoted to captain on 12 October 1864 to fill the command vacancy of Company G (Stryker, *New Jersey Records*, p. 1309).

Sister Mary Patricia Jurczynska lists "Sigismund Braida" as a Pole in her master's thesis, "A Study of the Participation of the Poles in the American Civil War" (St. John College of Cleveland, 1949), p. 152. Mieczyslaw Haiman likewise identifies him as "Zygmunt Braida." Nonetheless, according to Von Braida's certificate of baptism, he was born on 3 September 1839 in Graz, Austria. On the same day, he was baptized "Sigmund Charles Eugene Louis" in the Catholic Church of the Holy Blood, Graz. His father was Eugene, Count Braida of Traubeck; mother: Caroline, Countess of Wagensperg (Pension Records of Sigismund von Braida, National Archives).

29. Stryker, *New Jersey Records*, p. 1255.

30. Ibid., p. 1256; *Daily State Gazette and Republican*, 8 August 1863.

31. Stryker, *New Jersey Records*, p. 1255.

32. Ibid., p. 1256; Andrews's Military Records, National Archives; Edwin N. Andrews, "The Chaplain's Address," Rutgers State University Library, New Brunswick, N.J.

33. Stryker, *New Jersey Records*, pp. 1262, 1314.

34. *Daily State Gazette and Republican*, 29 September 1863.

35. Ibid., 30 September 1863.

36. Ibid., 7 October 1863.

37. *Newark Daily Advertiser*, 28 October 1863.

38. Regimental Order Book Records of the Second New Jersey Cavalry Regiment, National Archives.

39. *Newark Daily Advertiser*, 28 October 1863.

40. Kargé's report to Major General George Stoneman, Chief of the Cavalry Bureau, War Department, 18 October 1863. Regimental Order Book, Second New Jersey Cavalry, National Archives.

41. *Newark Daily Advertiser*, 18 February 1864.

42. Foster, *New Jersey and the Rebellion*, p. 589; Kargé to General George Stoneman, Chief of the Cavalry Bureau, 18 October 1863. Regimental Order Book, Second New Jersey Cavalry Regiment, National Archives.

43. *Newark Daily Advertiser*, 28 October 1863.

44. Brigadier General Henry E. Davies to Captain C. C. Suydam, Assistant Adjutant General, Cavalry Corps [Major General Alfred Pleasonton, commanding], 31 October 1863. Records of the Second New Jersey Cavalry Regiment, National Archives.

45. *Newark Daily Advertiser*, 5 May 1864; Regimental Order Book, Second New Jersey Cavalry Regiment, National Archives.

46. Joseph Kargé to William S. Stryker, Adjutant General of New Jersey, 22 January 1875. State Library of New Jersey, Trenton.

47. *Newark Daily Advertiser*, 16 December 1863; Foster, *New Jersey and the Rebellion*, p. 591; Stryker, *New Jersey Records*, p. 1304.

48. Joseph Kargé to Robert F. Stockton, Jr., Adjutant General of New Jersey, 6 March 1864. State Library of New Jersey, Trenton.

49. George E. Waring, Jr., *Whip and Spur* (New York: Doubleday and McClure Company, 1897), pp. 93-94.

50. *Newark Daily Advertiser*, 5 May 1864.

Chapter 8: Sherman's Meridian Expedition

1. *Official Records*, 31, pt. 3: 694 and 32, pt. 2: 546.

2. Robert Self Henry, *"First with the Most" Forrest* (Jackson, Tenn.: McCowat-Mercer Press, Publishers, 1969), pp. 205-6.

3. *Official Records*, 31, pt. 1: 607.

4. *Newark Daily Advertiser*, 22 January 1864.

5. Ibid.

6. Henry, *"First with the Most" Forrest*, pp. 209-12.

7. *Newark Daily Advertiser*, 22 January and 5 May 1864; E. L. Wolcott, comp., *Record of Services Rendered the Government by Gen. B. H. Grierson during the War* (Fort Concho, Tex.: pvt. printed, 1882), pp. 130, 133.

8. Joseph Kargé to Robert F. Stockton, Jr., 6 March 1864, State Library of New Jersey, Trenton; *Newark Daily Advertiser*, 5 May 1864.

9. *Daily State Gazette and Republican* (Trenton), 27 January 1864; Joseph Kargé to Robert F. Stockton, Jr., 6 March 1864; Regimental Order Book (letter, 3 April 1865), Second New Jersey Cavalry, National Archives.

10. W. T. Sherman, *Memoirs of Gen. W. T. Sherman* (New York: Charles L. Webster & Co., 1891), 1: 422; *Official Records*, 32, pt. 1: 174.

11. *Official Records*, 32, pt. 1: 181-82; Henry, *"First with the Most" Forrest*, p. 219.

12. Waring, *Whip and Spur*, p. 105.

13. *Official Records*, 32, pt. 1: 272, 281, 286.

14. Waring, *Whip and Spur*, p. 105; *Official Records*, 32, pt. 1: 262-63, 272.

15. *Official Records*, 32, pt. 1, 113; Joseph Kargé to Robert F. Stockton, Jr., 6 March 1864, State Library of New Jersey, Trenton.

16. *Official Records*, 32, pt. 1: 264-65, 281.

17. Ibid.

18. Robert Underwood Johnson, ed., *Battles and Leaders of the Civil War* (New York: The Century Company, 1884-87), 4: 417.

19. *Official Records*, 32, pt. 2: 317; Henry, *"First with the Most" Forrest*, p. 219.

20. *Newark Daily Advertiser*, 7 March 1864; *Official Records*, 32, pt. 1: 282.

21. *Official Records*, 32, pt. 1: 171.

22. Waring, *Whip and Spur*, p. 109.

23. Ibid.; Mark M. Boatner III, *The Civil War Dictionary* (New York: David McKay Company, Inc., 1959), p. 776.

24. Boatner, *Civil War Dictionary*, p. 359.

25. *Official Records*, 32, pt. 2: 358.

26. Waring, *Whip and Spur*, p. 109.

27. James Larson, *Sergeant Larson, 4th Cav.* (San Antonio: Tex.: Southern Literary Institute, 1935), p. 217; *Official Records*, 32, pt. 1: 282.

28. *Official Records*, 32, pt. 1: 282.

29. Waring, *Whip and Spur*, p. 111

30. Ibid., pp. 112-13.

31. Ibid.

32. Larson, *Sergeant Larson, 4th Cav.*, p. 221.

33. *Official Records*, 32, pt. 1: 283; Joseph Kargé to Robert F. Stockton, Jr., 6 March 1864, State Library of New Jersey, Trenton.

34. Ibid.

35. *Official Records*, 32, pt. 1: 283.

36. Henry, *"First with the Most" Forrest*, p. 225.

37. Waring, *Whip and Spur*, p. 115; Wolcott, *Record of Services by Gen. B. H. Grierson*, p. 139.

38. *Official Records*, 32, pt. 2: 76, 251.

39. Joseph Kargé to Robert F. Stockton, Jr., 6 March 1864, State Library of New Jersey,

Trenton; and General S. D. Lee, "Sherman's Meridian Expedition and Sooy Smith's Raid to West Point," *Southern Historical Society Papers* 8 (February 1880): 55.

Sooy Smith learned of General Lee's movement to reinforce Forrest. Lee planned to join Forrest with some 3,500 cavalry on February 22. Nonetheless, Lee's and Forrest's combined force of 6,000 cavalry did not exceed Sooy Smith's 7,000.

40. Waring, *Whip and Spur*, p. 116; Henry, *"First with the Most" Forrest*, p. 233; *Official Records*, 32, pt. 1: 354.

According to the *Official Records*, Sooy Smith had twelve pieces of artillery.

41. *Official Records*, 32, pt. 1: 300.

42. Ibid., p. 283.

43. Larson, *Sergeant Larson, 4th Cav.*, p. 224; and *Official Records*, 32, pt. 1: 283.

44. *Official Records*, 32, pt. 1: 284.

45. Ibid., p. 257.

46. Ibid., p. 284; Joseph Kargé to Robert F. Stockton, Jr., 6 March 1864, State Library of New Jersey, Trenton. The Spencer carbine, a rifled "magazine" gun, held a tube of six metallic cartridges in the stock and one more cartridge in the barrel. Thus the cavalryman could fire seven quick shots, without losing time to reload or having to take his eyes off the target. The Spencer also possessed greater range and better handling qualities than the weapons of some of the other regiments—the Sharps and the Union carbines, which took paper cartridges one at a time.

47. *Official Records*, 32, pt. 1: 258; Waring, *Whip and Spur*, p. 119.

48. *Official Records*, 32, pt. 1: 268, 284.

49. *Newark Daily Advertiser*, 5 May 1864.

50. *Daily State Gazette and Republican* (Trenton), 12 March 1864; *Official Records*, 32, pt. 1: 270; Joseph Kargé to Robert F. Stockton, Jr., 6 March 1864, State Library of New Jersey, Trenton.

51. *Official Records*, 32, pt. 1: 268; Henry, *"First with the Most" Forrest*, pp. 229-30.

52. Waring, *Whip and Spur*, p. 123.

53. *Official Records*, 32, pt. 1: 269.

54. Henry, *"First with the Most" Forrest*, p. 232.

55. *Official Records*, 32, pt. 1: 285; and *Daily State Gazette and Republican* (Trenton), 11 March 1864.

56. *Official Records*, 32, pt. 1: 285; Joseph Kargé to Robert F. Stockton, Jr., 6 March 1864, State Library of New Jersey, Trenton.

57. *Official Records*, 32, pt. 1: 194.

58. Waring, *Whip and Spur*, p. 125.

59. *New York Times*, 5 March 1864; *Official Records*, 32, pt. 1: 257.

60. *Official Records*, 32, pt. 1: 257, 268; *State Gazette and Republican* (Trenton), 12 March 1864.

61. Joseph Kargé to Robert F. Stockton, Jr., 6 March 1864, State Library of New Jersey, Trenton.

62. *New York Times*, 2 March 1864.

63. *Official Records*, 32, pt. 1: 261.

64. Waring, *Whip and Spur*, p. 117; Johnson, *Battles and Leaders*, 4: 417; Wolcott, *Record of Services by Gen. B. H. Grierson*, p. 142.

65. *Official Records*, 32, pt. 1: 175, 181 and pt. 2: 363.

66. Waring, *Whip and Spur*, p. 117.

67. *Official Records*, 32, pt. 1: 182; General S. D. Lee, "Sherman's Meridian Expedition," *Southern Historical Society Papers* 8 (February 1880): 54.

68. *Official Records*, 32, pt. 1: 250 and pt. 2: 448.

69. Ibid., pt. 1: 189.

70. Johnson, *Battles and Leaders*, 4: 418; Wolcott, *Record of Services by Gen. B. H. Grierson*, pp. 143-44.

71. Boatner, *Civil War Dictionary*, p. 776.

72. Regimental Order Book, Second New Jersey Cavalry, National Archives.

73. *Newark Daily Advertiser*, 5 May 1864.

74. Joseph Kargé to Robert F. Stockton, Jr., 6 March 1864, State Library of New Jersey, Trenton.

75. Henry, *"First with the Most" Forrest*, p. 235.

Chapter 9: Kargé Beats Forrest

1. Henry, *"First with the Most" Forrest*, pp. 237-39, 241; *Official Records*, 32, pt. 3: 502.

2. *Official Records*, 52, pt. 2: 653.

3. Henry, *"First with the Most" Forrest*, p. 270.

4. *Official Records*, 32, pt. 3: 527.

5. Sherman, *Memoirs*, 2: 399.

6. *Official Records*, 32, pt. 3: 155, 165.

7. Ibid., p. 311 and pt. 1: 575-77.

8. Henry, *"First with the Most" Forrest*, p. 243; *Official Records*, 32, pt. 1: 582; Wolcott, *Record of Services by Gen. B. H. Grierson*, p. 147.

9. *Official Records*, 34, pt. 3: 184.

10. Ibid., 32, pt. 3: 288, 318.

11. Henry *"First with the Most" Forrest*, pp. 248, 250-51, 256.

12. *Official Records*, 32, pt. 3: 366-67, 462, 516.

13. Boatner, *Civil War Dictionary*, pp. 816, 892; Henry *"First with the Most" Forrest*, p. 272; *Official Records*, 32, pt. 3: 400.

14. *Official Records*, 32, pt. 3: 502; Wolcott, *Record of Services by Gen. B. H. Grierson*, pp. 153-54.

15. *Official Records*, 32, pt. 3: 484, 503, 529, 566.

16. Ibid., pt. 1: 695; 698-99, 702.

17. Ibid., p. 623. General Chalmers's congratulatory order was dated 20 April 1864.

18. Henry, *"First with the Most" Forrest*, p. 273.

19. Foster, *New Jersey and the Rebellion*, p. 594.

20. Robert Selph Henry, ed., *As They Saw Forrest: Some Recollections and Comments of Contemporaries* (Jackson, Tenn.: McCowat-Mercer Press, Inc., 1956), pp. 139, 155.

21. Henry, *"First with the Most" Forrest*, p. 275.

22. Henry, *As They Saw Forrest*, p. 156.

23. Thomas Jordan and J. P. Pryor, *The Campaigns of Lieut. Gen. N. B. Forrest, and of Forrest's Cavalry* (1868; reprint ed., Dayton, Ohio: Press of Morningside Bookshop, 1973), p. 457; Henry, *"First with the Most" Forrest*, p. 275.

24. Henry, *As They Saw Forrest*, p. 156; Foster, *New Jersey and the Rebellion*, p. 594.

25. *Official Records*, 32 pt. 1: 701; Jordan and Pryor, *Campaigns of Forrest*, p. 458. General Sturgis reported the Union loss as two killed and ten wounded. *Official Records*, 32, pt. 1: 699.

26. *New York Times*, 9 May 1864.

27. *Official Records*, 32, pt. 1, 694-95, 698, 700.

28. Ibid., p. 702.

29. *Civil War Times Illustrated*, July 1972, p. 7.

30. Some may consider Forrest's engagement at Parker's Crossroads, Tennessee, 31 December 1862, to be his first defeat. The engagement was a confused affair, in which Forrest first whipped a Union cavalry brigade under the command of Colonel Cyrus L. Dunham. While negotiating a surrender of Dunham's troops, Forrest was unexpectedly attacked from the rear by a Union brigade

led by Colonel John W. Fuller. Unprepared at the moment to fight a second antagonist, Forrest chose the only alternative open to him; he made a hasty retreat. John A. Wyeth, *That Devil Forrest: Life of General Nathan Bedford Forrest* (New York: Harper & Brothers, Publishers, 1959), pp. 112-13.

Chapter 10: *Battle of Brice's Cross-roads*

1. *Official Records*, 38, pt. 4, 294-95.
2. Ibid., 39, pt. 1: 86, 89-90.
3. Ibid., pp. 128, 131, 136; *Newark Daily Advertiser*, 23 June 1864.
4. *Official Records*, 39, pt. 1: 89-90, 103.
5. Ibid., pp. 85, 221-22.
6. Ibid., pp. 217-18.
7. Ibid., pp. 90, 95.
8. Ibid., pp. 90, 136, 139, 220; pt. 2: 79.
9. Henry, *As They Saw Forrest*, p. 246.
10. *Official Records*, 39, pt. 1: 207, 222; Wyeth, *That Devil Forrest*, p. 347.
11. *Official Records*, 39, pt. 1: 151; *Chicago Tribune*, 6 February 1882.
12. *Official Records*, 39, pt. 2: 83, 85, and pt. 1: 87-88, 90.
13. *Chicago Tribune*, 6 February 1882.
14. Ibid.; *Official Records*, 39, pt. 1: 91, 131, 134.
15. *Official Records*, 39, pt. 1: 88.
16. Ibid., pp. 91, 98; Wolcott, *Record of Services by Gen. B. H. Grierson*, p. 157. Grierson advised against continuing the march, encumbered and slowed down as it was by the large supply train.
17. Jerusha Wilcox Sturgis, "Family of General Samuel Davis Sturgis, 1822-1889," Microfilm in Manuscript Division, State Historical Society of Wisconsin, Madison, p. 6.
18. *Official Records*, 39, pt. 1: 149.
19. Ibid., pp. 98-99, 101; *Chicago Tribune*, 4 March 1882.
20. *Official Records*, 39, pt. 1: 91, 188.
21. Ibid., p. 129, 132. Relative to Kargé's whereabouts, the *Newark Daily Advertiser* reported 30 June 1864 that Kitchen commanded the regiment in place of Kargé, who had been "assigned to other duties." The newspaper did not provide any details. Kargé's absence from the regiment was temporary.
22. Willard Webb, ed., *Crucial Moments of the Civil War* (New York: Fountainhead Publishers, Inc., 1961), p. 282; *Official Records*, 39, pt. 1: 156-57.
23. *Official Records*, 39, pt. 1: 129, 132.
24. Henry, *"First with the Most" Forrest*, pp. 285-86.
25. *Official Records*, 39, pt. 1: 92.
26. Ibid., pp. 165, 208-9; and Bennett H. Young, *Confederate Wizards of the Saddle* (Boston: Chapple Publishing Co. Ltd., 1914; reprint ed., Kennesaw, Ga.: Continental Book Co., 1958), p. 12.
27. Henry, *"First with the Most" Forrest*, p. 293, *Official Records*, 39, pt. 1: 105.
28. *Official Records*, 39, pt. 1: 94, 211.
29. Ibid., pp. 94, 106, 211.
30. Ibid., pp. 94, 106, 146.
31. Ibid., 139, 171; Wm. Forse Scott, *The Story of a Cavalry Regiment* (New York: G. P. Putnam's Sons, 1893), p. 264.
32. Henry, *"First with the Most" Forrest*, p. 298; *Official Records*, 39, pt. 1: 133.

33. Foster, *New Jersey and the Rebellion*, p. 597; *Official Records*, 39, pt. 1: 171.

34. *Chicago Tribune*, 6 March 1882.

35. Ibid.; William R. Plum, *The Military Telegraph during the Civil War in the United States* (Chicago: Jansen, McClurg & Company, Publishers, 1882), 2: 193, 198.

36. *Chicago Tribune*, 6 March 1882.

37. *Official Records*, 39, pt. 1: 94; Scott, *Story of a Cavalry Regiment*, p. 267.

38. *Official Records*, 39, pt. 1: 95, 120.

39. Ibid., p. 116.

40. Ibid., pp. 109-110; Scott, *Story of a Cavalry Regiment*, p. 265.

41. *Official Records*, 39, pt. 1: 95, 133-34; Regimental Order Book, Second New Jersey Cavalry, National Archives; Stryker, *Record of Officers and Men of New Jersey*, pp. 1277, 1292, 1298, 1312, 1318.

George W. Green, Company G, became the seventh battle loss when he died in Memphis on 1 July 1864 of wounds received in action 10 June 1864.

Lieutenants Von Rudolphi and Von Braida, wounded by enemy fire in the right leg above the knee, became prisoners of war. Rudolphi was confined at Andersonville, Georgia, and Von Braida at Columbia, South Carolina (Military records of Julius von Rudolphi and pension records of Sigismund von Braida, National Archives).

Although Stryker lists Harrison as a "private," the regimental commander referred to him in correspondence as "sergeant."

42. *Official Records*, 39, pt. 1: 95-96.

43. Ibid., p. 130.

44. *Chicago Tribune*, 25 February 1882.

45. *Official Records*, 39, pt. 1: 96.

46. Ibid., p. 101; *State Gazette and Republican* (Trenton, New Jersey), 28 June 1864; *Chicago Tribune*, 25 February 1882.

47. General Carl von Clausewitz, *On War*, Colonel J. J. Graham, trans., with introduction and notes by Colonel F. N. Maude, C. B. (London: Kegan Paul, Trench, Trubner & Co., Ltd., 1940), 1: 280.

48. *Official Records*, 39, pt. 2: 121.

49. Ibid., pt. 1: 160.

50. Ibid., p. 202.

51. Ibid., p. 211.

52. *Chicago Tribune*, 25 February 1882.

53. Ibid., 2 March 1882; *Official Records*, 39, pt. 1: 170-71.

54. Boatner, *Civil War Dictionary*, p. 816.

55. *Official Records*, 39, pt. 1: 231.

Chapter 11: Higher Command and More Frustration

1. *State Gazette and Republican* (Trenton, New Jersey), 2 July 1864.

2. Stryker, *Records of Officers and Men of New Jersey*, p. 1255. The service record of P. Jones Yorke lists his age as twenty-one in 1864, when he received the promotion to lieutenant colonel. National Archives.

3. *Official Records*, 39, pt. 2: 115.

4. Scott, *Story of a Cavalry Regiment*, p. 281; *Official Records*, 39, pt. 2: 148-49, 166.

5. *Newark Daily Advertiser*, 9 July 1864; *Official Records*, 39, pt. 1: 246 and pt. 2: 163.

6. Charles Elihu Slocum, *The Life and Services of Major-General Henry Warner Slocum* (Toledo, Ohio: The Slocum Publishing Company, 1913), p. 196.

7. *Official Records*, 39, pt. 1: 242 and pt. 2: 150-51.

8. Ibid., pt. 2: 161.

9. Ibid., p. 160, and 34, pt. 3: 490-91.

10. Slocum, *Life and Services of Major-General Slocum*, pp. 196-97.

11. *Official Records*, 39, pt. 1: 246.

12. Ibid., p. 243.

13. *New York Herald*, 20 July 1864; *Official Records*, 39, pt. 1: 243, 246, 356.

14. *Official Records*, 39, pt. 1: 247, 356.

15. Ibid. General Slocum apparently did not prepare a report of his march from Vicksburg to Grand Gulf. Therefore the reason for his abrupt change in direction from the northeast (toward Canton) to the southwest remains unknown.

16. Byron Stinson, "Hot Work in Mississippi: The Battle of Tupelo," *Civil War Times, Illustrated* 11 (July 1972): 6.

17. Jordan and Pryor, *Campaigns of Lieut.-Gen. Forrest*, p. 501.

18. *Official Records*, 39, pt. 1: 250-53.

19. Ibid., pp. 249, 320 and pt. 2: 142, 204.

20. Ibid., pt. 2: 179, 184, 204.

21. Ibid., p. 202; Boatner, *Civil War Dictionary*, p. 384; Wolcott, *Record of Services by Gen. B. H. Grierson*, p. 164.

22. Scott, *Story of a Cavalry Regiment*, p. 292; *Official Records*, 39, pt. 1: 392.

23. *Official Records*, 39, pt. 2: 219, 222, 233.

24. Ibid., pt. 1: 386, 388, 392.

25. Henry, *"First with the Most" Forrest*, pp. 329-30; and *Official Records*, 39, pt. 2: 756.

26. *Official Records*, 39, pt. 1: 388-89.

27. Ibid. and pt. 2: 242.

28. Ibid., pt. 1: 387, 391.

29. Henry, *"First with the Most" Forrest*, pp. 333-40.

30. *Official Records*, 39, pt. 2: 282, 296.

31. Clifford Dowdey, *The Land They Fought For* (Garden City, N.Y.: Doubleday & Company, Inc., 1955), p. 350. Bruce Catton and Shelby Foote also say that the attack of Forrest on Memphis, 21 August, 1864, caused the recall of General A. J. Smith's expedition.

32. *Official Records*, 39, pt. 1: 469-70.

33. Ibid., p. 387, and pt. 2: 302.

34. Ibid., pt. 1: 387-88, 470.

35. Wolcott, *Record of Services by Gen. B. H. Grierson*, p. 166.

36. *Official Records*, 39, pt. 1: 471 and pt. 2: 347.

37. Ibid., pt. 1: 395.

38. Ibid., pt. 2: 233, 310, 318.

39. Scott, *Story of a Cavalry Regiment*, p. 309; *Official Records*, 41, pt. 1: 308-09. General A. J. Smith received orders to proceed as far toward Pilot Knob as he deemed compatible with certainty that his position would not be turned and the enemy get between him and St. Louis. Smith interpreted his orders with great caution.

40. Jay Monaghan, *Civil War on the Western Border* (Boston: Little, Brown and Company, 1955), pp. 311-13.

41. Scott, *Story of a Cavalry Regiment*, p. 309-10.

42. *Official Records*, 41, pt. 1: 327.

43. Scott, *Story of a Cavalry Regiment*, p. 312.

44. Ibid., pp. 312-42; L. R. Barnard to Major General Wm. L. Stryker, Adjutant General of New Jersey, 24 April 1875. Records of Second New Jersey Cavalry Regiment, State Library of New Jersey, Trenton.

45. *Official Records*, 41, pt. 1: 342-43.

46. *Newark Daily Advertiser*, 14 November 1864.

Chapter 12: Gallant Victory at Egypt Station

1. *Official Records*, 39, pt. 3: 161.
2. Stryker, *Record of Officers and Men of New Jersey in the Civil War*, p. 1255.
3. Records of Second New Jersey Cavalry Regiment, State Library of New Jersey, Trenton.
4. *Official Records*, 39, pt. 3: 64, 414-15.
5. Edward G. Longacre, *From Union Stars to Top Hat* (Harrisburg, Pa.: Stackpole Books, 1972), pp. 96-97, Boatner, *Civil War Dictionary*, p. 930.
6. *Official Records*, 39, pt. 3: 418, 609.
7. Ibid., pp. 661-62; 41, pt. 4: 624; 45, pt. 2: 61, 90, 173; Wolcott, *Record of Services of Gen. B. H. Grierson*, p. 175.
8. *Newark Daily Advertiser*, 12 December 1864.
9. Ibid., 19 December 1864.
10. *Official Records*, 39, pt. 3: 7; Esposito, *West Point Atlas of American Wars*, 1: 148, 150; J. B. Hood, *Advance and Retreat: Personal Experiences in the United States and Confederate States Armies* (Bloomington: Indiana University Press, 1959), pp. 264-68. President Jefferson Davis gave the command of the Army of Tennessee to General John Bell Hood, replacing General Joseph E. Johnston.
11. *Official Records*, 39, pt. 3: 202; Long, *Civil War Day by Day*, p. 596.
12. Esposito, *West Point Atlas of American Wars*, 1: 151-52; and *Personal Memoirs of U.S. Grant* (New York: Charles L. Webster & Company, 1885), 2: 380.
13. *Official Records*, 41, pt. 4: 782.
14. Esposito, *West Point Atlas of American Wars*, 1: 153.
15. *Official Records*, 41, pt. 4: 624, 799, 821.
16. Ibid., pp. 901-4.
17. Ibid., 45, pt. 1: 96.
18. Ibid., p. 845, and 41, pt. 4: 902-3.
19. Ibid., 45, pt. 1: 845, 848.
20. Ibid., pp. 846, 861.
21. Ibid., pp. 846, 849-50, 871; report of Lieutenant Colonel P. Jones Yorke to Lieutenant George A. Hewlett, Acting Assistant Adjutant General, First Cavalry Brigade, Cavalry Division, Department of the Mississippi, 12 January 1865. Regimental Order Book, Second New Jersey Cavalry, National Archives.
22. *Official Records*, 45, pt. 1: 863-64.
23. Ibid., pp. 849, 857, 860; Clement A. Evans, ed., *Confederate Military History* (Atlanta, Ga.: Confederate Publishing Co., 1899), 12 (*Mississippi*): 256. Colonel Kargé reported General Gholson mortally wounded, but Gholson survived the serious injury.
24. *Newark Daily Advertiser*, 25 January 1865.
25. Ibid., 17 January 1865; *Official Records*, 45, pt. 1: 849; Yorke to Hewlett, 12 January 1865. Regimental Order Book, Second New Jersey Cavalry, National Archives.
26. *Newark Daily Advertiser*, 25 January 1865; *Official Records*, 45, pt. 1: 849, 852, 857; Wolcott, *Record of Services of Gen. B. H. Grierson*, p. 179.
27. *New York Times*, 13 January 1865.
28. *Official Records*, 45, pt. 1, 847, 867.
29. Ibid., 2d ser., 8: 125.
30. *Natchez* (Mississippi) *Courier*, 20 January 1865. Reprinted from *Meridian* (Mississippi) *Clarion*, 5 January 1865.

31. *Official Records*, 45, pt. 1: 849, 851, 858.

32. Ibid., p. 868.

33. Ibid., pp. 846, 849, 858-59, 874-75.

34. Ibid., pp. 846-47. General Grierson summed up the destruction of property as follows: twenty thousand feet of bridges and trestle-work cut down and burned; ten miles of track rails bent and ties burned; twenty miles of telegraph poles cut down and wire destroyed; four serviceable locomotives and tenders and ten in process of repair; ninety-five railroad cars; more than three hundred army wagons and two caissons; thirty warehouses filled with quartermaster, commissary, and ordnance stores; large cloth and shoe factories, employing five hundred hands; several tanneries and machine shops; a steam pile-driver; twelve new forges; seven depot buildings; five thousand stand of new arms; seven hundred head of fat hogs; five hundred bales of cotton, marked "C.S.A."; immense amount of grain, leather, wool, and other government property, the value and quantity of which cannot be estimated.

35. *Official Records*, 41, pt. 1: 1000-1001.

36. Ibid., 45, pt. 2: 553, 566, 585-86; *New York Tribune*, 13 January 1865.

37. Scott, *Story of a Cavalry Regiment*, p. 362.

38. *Official Records*, 45, pt. 1: 866.

39. Scott, *Story of a Cavalry Regiment*, p. 362; *New York Tribune*, 13 January 1865.

40. *Official Records*, 45, pt. 1: 872.

41. Ibid., p. 847.

42. *Newark Daily Advertiser*, 17 January 1865.

43. L. R. Barnard to General William L. Stryker, Adjutant General of New Jersey, 24 April 1875. State Library of New Jersey, Trenton.

44. Boatner, *Civil War Dictionary*, p. 359; Kargé's Service Records, National Archives.

45. Foster, *New Jersey and the Rebellion*, p. 606.

Chapter 13: Alabama Campaign

1. Kargé's Service Records, National Archives; *Newark Daily Advertiser*, 24 January 1865.

2. *Official Records*, 48, pt. 1: 533-34, 1068, 1088, 1095, 1099; 45; pt. 2: 609-10, 614; Wolcott, *Record of Services by Gen. B. H. Grierson*, p. 188.

3. *Official Records*, 48, pt. 1: 786, 1056, 1083, 1109, 1196-97 and 49, pt. 1: 109.

4. Ibid., 49, pt. 1: 92, 593 and 48, pt. 1: 1092.

5. Ibid., 39, pt. 1: 403-4 and 49, pt. 1: 92.

6. Ibid., 48, pt. 1: 1234 and pt. 2: 49-50; Wolcott, *Record of Services by Gen. B. H. Grierson*, pp. 191-92.

7. *Official Records*, 49, pt. 1: 354; Wolcott, *Record of Services of Gen. B. H. Grierson*, pp. 182-84.

8. Frederick H. Dyer, *A Compendium of the War of the Rebellion* (New York: Thomas Yoseloff, 1959), 3: 1354; *Official Records*, 49, pt. 1: 92, 98-99.

9. *Official Records*, 49, pt. 1: 99 and pt. 2: 341; Wolcott, *Record of Services by Gen. B. H. Grierson*, pp. 195-96.

10. *Official Records*, 49, pt. 2: 358.

11. Ibid., pp. 374, 386-87.

12. Ibid., 48, pt. 2: 260.

13. Ibid., 49, pt. 1: 300.

14. Foster, *New Jersey and the Rebellion*, p. 607, *Official Records*, 49, pt. 1: 300 and pt. 2: 675.

15. Long, *The Civil War Day by Day*, p. 685; *Official Records*, 49, pt. 1: 100 and 48, pt. 2: 716.

16. *Official Records*, 49, pt. 1: 385 and pt. 2: 582-83, 795.

17. Ibid., pt. 2: 714, 887 and pt. 1: 301.

18. Ibid., pt. 2: 834.

19. Ibid., pt. 1: 301 and pt. 2: 714.

20. Long, *The Civil War Day by Day*, p. 690.

21. *Official Records*, 49, pt. 2: 948. General Orders No. 108, Adjutant General's Office, War Department, 2 June 1865.

22. *Official Records*, 49, pt. 1: 478, 513.

23. Ibid., pt. 2: 52, 891.

24. Ibid., 39, pt. 2: 333.

25. Ibid., 49, pt. 2, 697.

26. Kargé's Service Records, National Archives.

27. *Official Records*, 46, pt. 3: 1112; 48, pt. 2: 717; Foster, *New Jersey and the Rebellion*, p. 607; *Daily State Gazette and Republican* (Trenton, New Jersey), 15 July 1865; and Sheldon Sturgeon, Headquarters, Military Division of West Mississippi, New Orleans, to Governor of New Jersey, 3 July 1865, in which Sturgeon informed the governor that 622 men of the Second New Jersey Cavalry were mustered out July 2, 1865, at Vicksburg and departed for Trenton. Records of Second New Jersey, National Archives.

Although the Military Division of West Mississippi stated the number of mustered out men as 622, Foster gives 550 and the *Daily State Gazette* reported 580.

28. P. H. Sheridan, *Personal Memoirs* (New York: Charles L. Webster & Co., 1888), 2: 210; *Official Records*, 48, pt. 2: 648, 865-66, 917, 1087.

29. *Natchez* (Mississippi) *Courier*, 5 August 1865; Foster, *New Jersey and the Rebellion*, p. 608; *Daily State Gazette and Republican*, 19 August 1865.

30. *Official Records*, 48, pt. 2: 1087-88.

31. Brevet Major General Benjamin H. Grierson to Colonel Joseph Kargé, 28 July 1865. Kargé's Service Records, National Archives.

32. Colonel Joseph Kargé to Adjutant General, U.S. Army, 26 August 1865. Kargé's Service Records, National Archives.

33. *Natchez* (Mississippi) *Courier*, 2 September 1865.

34. Foster, *New Jersey and the Rebellion*, p. 608; Stryker, *Record of Officers and Men of New Jersey in the Civil War*, p. 1255.

35. Kargé to Major General Henry W. Slocum, 11 September 1865. Kargé's Service Records, National Archives; Foster, *New Jersey and the Rebellion*, p. 608; *Official Records*, 49, pt. 2: 1111; *Daily State Gazette and Republican*, 10 and 14 November 1865.

36. Field and Staff Muster-Out Roll, Kargé's Service Records, National Archives; *Daily State Gazette and Republican*, 14 November 1865. The returning captains were: Lambert L. Mulford, Albert H. Crump, William V. Scudder, Theodore W. Vandergrift, John N. Givens, Erich von Pannwitz, and Charles F. Fernald. The first lieutenants were: Carl F. Braune, George W. Johnson, Alexander D. Hamilton, Lewis Rainear, John Madigan, Frank T. Adams, and Jacob H. Hoffman. The second lieutenants were: Robert Hamilton, L. Henry Smith, Charles H. Rice, Charles Hawksworth, James H. O'Connor, and Mortimer von Strautz.

37. Major General Robert F. Stockton, Jr. to Brevet Brigadier General Joseph Kargé, 25 October 1865. Kargé's Service Records, National Archives.

Chapter 14: Soldier Turns Educator

1. Russell F. Weigley, *History of the United States Army* (New York: The Macmillan Company, 1967), pp. 266-67.

2. Joseph Kargé to Secretary of War Edwin M. Stanton, 15 August 1866. Kargé's Service Records, National Archives.

3. Former New Jersey Governor Peter D. Vroom et al. to Secretary of War Edwin M. Stanton, July 1866. Kargé's Service Records, National Archives.

4. Cortlandt Parker to Secretary of War Edwin M. Stanton, 31 July 1866. Kargé's Service Records, National Archives.

5. Governor Marcus Ward to Secretary of War Edwin M. Stanton, 6 August 1866; Joel Parker to President Andrew Johnson, 20 August 1866; General Lewis Perrine to Edwin M. Stanton, 20 August 1866. Kargé's Service Records, National Archives.

6. Joseph Kargé to Major General Edward Townsend, 7 June 1867; Joseph Kargé to Adjutant General, United States Army, 18 July 1867. Kargé's Service Records, National Archives.

7. Weigley, *History of the U.S. Army*, pp. 265, 267.

8. Theo. F. Rodenbough and William L. Haskin, eds., *The Army of the United States* (New York: Maynard, Merrill & Co., 1896), p. 269; Boatner, *Civil War Dictionary*, p. 669.

9. Kargé's Pension Records, National Archives.

10. Thomas Wren, *A History of the State of Nevada* (New York: The Lewis Publishing Co., 1904), pp. 295-96.

11. Ralph K. Andrist, *The Long Death* (New York: The Macmillan Co., 1964), pp. 24, 171; *Official Records*, 50, pt. 2: 1195.

12. Sidwa, *Proceedings of the New Jersey Historical Society* 81 (October 1963): 253.

13. First Lieutenant Joseph Kargé to Major John P. Sherburne, Assistant Adjutant General, Department of California, 2 December 1867. Records Group 393, Camp Winfield Scott, Nevada, Letters Sent, Volume 1 (1866-70), National Archives.

14. Wren, *History of Nevada*, p. 296; Rodenbough, *Army of the United States*, p. 270.

15. Rodenbough, *Army of the United States*, pp. 268-69.

16. Weigley, *History of the U.S. Army*, pp. 269-70, 272; Colonel George Ruhlen, "Early Nevada Forts," *Nevada Historical Society Quarterly* 7 (1964): 53-54.

17. Nevada State Historical Society, sponsor, *Nevada*, Writers' Program of the Work Projects Administration in the State of Nevada (Portland, Ore.: Binfords & Mort, Publishers, 1940), p. 216.

18. Sidwa, *Proceedings of the New Jersey Historical Society* 81 (October 1963): 253; Kargé's Service Records, National Archives.

19. Weigley, *History of the U.S. Army*, p. 267.

20. Kargé's Pension Records, National Archives.

21. Packard, *Joseph Kargé: A Memorial Sketch*, passim.

22. Ibid.

23. *The National Cyclopedia of American Biography* (New York: James T. White & Company, 1897), 7: 243.

24. *Polish American Journal* (Scranton, Pa.): 30 July 1960; *Princeton* (New Jersey) *Herald*, 27 May 1960.

25. Edwin Mark Norris, *The Story of Princeton* (Boston: Little, Brown and Company, 1917), pp. 207-8.

26. Packard, *Joseph Kargé: A Memorial Sketch*, p. 29.

27. Kargé's Pension Records, National Archives.

28. *New York Times*, 1 July 1875.

29. Kargé's Civil War Records, State Library of New Jersey, Trenton.

30. Packard, *Joseph Kargé: A Memorial Sketch*, pp. 29-30.

31. *New York Times*, 28 December 1892.

32. Packard, *Joseph Kargé: A Memorial Sketch*, p. 31; *The Trenton* (New Jerssey) *Times*, 31 December 1892.

33. Packard, *Joseph Kargé: A Memorial Sketch*, p. 31.

Epilogue

1. Records of Second New Jersey Cavalry Regiment, State Library of New Jersey, Trenton.

2. Victor A. Wojciechowski to author, 30 March 1961.

3. *Princeton* (New Jersey) *Herald*, 27 May 1960.

4. Professor Albert Elsasser to author, 11 December 1975.

5. Sidwa, "Joseph Kargé," *Proceedings of the New Jersey Historical Society* (October 1963): 255.

6. *Newark Star-Ledger*, 16 September 1963.

7. "A Civil War Centennial Tribute to Brig. General Joseph Kargé," September 21, 1963, a program brochure of the American-Polish Civil War Centennial Committee of Newark, New Jersey, listed in Donald A. Sinclair, *A Bibliography: The Civil War and New Jersey* (New Brunswick, N.J.: Published by the Friends of the Rutgers University Library for the New Jersey Civil War Centennial Commission, 1968), p. 30.

8. Printed program, "Closing Centennial Tribute to Brigadier General Joseph Kargé," held at New Jersey Historical Society, Newark, 9 November 1963, and sponsored by the American-Polish Civil War Centennial Committee; *Zgoda* (Chicago, Ill.), 15 January 1964 (official organ of the Polish National Alliance).

Bibliography

I. Primary Sources

1. *Government Documents*

Baldwin, Charles Candee. *Baldwin Genealogy, 1881*. National Archives.

Military Records of: Joseph Kargé, George D. Bayard, Benjamin F. Grierson, P. Jones Yorke, Marcus L. W. Kitchen, Peter D. Vroom, Erich von Pannwitz, Julius von Rudolphi, Frederick V. Dayton, and Philip L. Van Rensselacr. National Archives.

Pension Records of Joseph Kargé. National Archives.

Records of the First New Jersey Cavalry and of the Second New Jersey Cavalry Regiments. National Archives.

Records of the First New Jersey Cavalry and of the Second New Jersey Cavalry Regiments. State Library of New Jersey, Trenton.

Sinclair, Donald A. *A Bibliography: The Civil War and New Jersey*. New Brunswick, N.J.: Published by the Friends of the Rutgers University Library for the New Jersey Civil War Centennial Commission, 1968.

War of the Rebellion: A Compilation of the Official Records of the Union and Confederate Armies. 128 vols. Washington, D. C.: Government Printing Office, 1880-1901.

2. *Books and Articles*

Allan, Colonel William. "Jackson's Valley Campaign of 1862." *Southern Historical Society Papers* 7 (1879): 1-30.

Andrews, Edwin N. "The Chaplain's Address" to the Soldiers of the First Brigade, Second Division, Cavalry Corps at Memphis, Tennessee, July 1864. Library of Rutgers State University, New Jersey.

Bayard, Samuel J. *The Life of George Dashiell Bayard*. New York: G. P. Putnam's Sons, 1874.

Bouton, Edward. *Events of the Civil War, with a Sketch of the Author*. Los Angeles: Kingsley, Moles & Collins, 1906.

Brackett, Albert G. *History of the United States Cavalry, from the Formation of the Federal Government to the 1st of June, 1863*. New York: Harper & Brothers, 1865; reprint ed., Freeport, N. Y.: Books for Libraries Press, 1970.

Brown, J. Willard. *The Signal Corps, U. S. A., in the War of the Rebellion*. Boston: U.S. Veteran Signal Corps Association, 1896.

Clausewitz, Carl von. *On War*. 2 vols. Translated by Colonel J. J. Graham, with introduction and notes by Colonel F. N. Maude. London: Kegan, Trench, Trubner & Co., Ltd., 1940.

Cogley, Thomas S. *History of the Seventh Indiana Cavalry Volunteers*. Laporte, Ind.: Herald Company, Steam Printers, 1876.

Connolly, Major James A. "Diary and Letters." Illinois State Historical Society, *Transactions* (1928), pp. 215-438.

Cowles, Capt. Calvin D., comp. *Atlas to Accompany the Official Records of the Union and Confederate Armies*. Washington, D. C.: Government Printing Office, 1891-1895; reprint ed., *The Official Atlas of the Civil War*, with introduction by Henry Steele Commager. New York-London: Thomas Yoseloff, 1958.

Denison, Rev. Frederic. *Sabres and Spurs: The First Regiment Rhode Island Cavalry in the Civil War, 1861-1865*. Central Falls, R. I.: The First Rhode Island Cavalry Veteran Association, 1876.

————. "The Battle of Cedar Mountain: A Personal View." *Personal Narratives of Events in the War of the Rebellion*. Providence: Soldiers and Sailors Historical Society of Rhode Island, 1881.

Evans, Clement A., ed. *Confederate Military History*, vol. 12 (Alabama and Mississippi). Atlanta: Confederate Publishing Company, 1899.

Glazier, Willard. *Three Years in the Federal Cavalry*. New York: R. H. Ferguson & Co., 1874.

Grant, Ulysses S. *Personal Memoirs of U. S. Grant*. 2 vols. New York: Charles L. Webster & Company, 1885.

Henry, Robert Selph, ed. *As They Saw Forrest: Some Recollections and Comments of Contemporaries*. Jackson. Tenn.: McCowat-Mercer Press, Inc., 1956.

Hood, J. B. *Advance and Retreat: Personal Experiences in the United States and Confederate States Armies*. New Orleans, La.: Hood Orphan Memorial Fund, 1880; reprint ed., Bloomington: Indiana University Press, 1959.

Hopkins, E. M. "An Evening with Our Professor." *Nassau Literary Magazine* 43, nos. 4, 5, 6 (November 1887, December 1887, January 1888).

Johnson, Robert Underwood, ed. *Battles and Leaders of the Civil War*. 4 vols. New York: The Century Company, 1884-1887; reprint ed., New York-London: Thomas Yoseloff, 1956.

Jordan, General Thomas, and Pryor, J. P. *The Campaigns of Lieut.-Gen. N. B. Forrest and of Forrest's Cavalry*. New Orleans, Memphis, and New York: Blelock & Co., 1868; reprint ed., Dayton, Ohio: Press of Morningside Bookshop, 1973.

Larson, James. *Sergeant Larson, 4th Cav.* San Antonio, Tex.: Southern Literary Institute, 1935.

Lee, Stephen D. "Sherman's Meridian Expedition and Sooy Smith's Raid to West Point." *Southern Historical Society Papers* 8 (February 1880): 49-61.

Lloyd, William Penn. *History of the First Reg't Pennsylvania Reserve Cavalry*. Philadelphia: King & Baird, Printers, 1864.

Love, Wm. DeLoss. *Wisconsin in the War of the Rebellion: A History of All Regiments and Batteries.* 2 vols. Chicago: Church and Goodman, Publishers, 1866.

McDonald, Edward H. "Fighting under Ashby in the Shenandoah: A First-Person Account." *Civil War Times Illustrated* 5 (July 1966): 29-35.

Moore, James. *Kilpatrick and Our Cavalry.* New York: W. J. Widdleton, 1865.

National Cyclopedia of American Biography. vol. 7. New York: James T. White & Company, 1897.

Packard, William A. *Joseph Kargé: A Memorial Sketch.* New York: Anson D. F. Randolph and Co., Inc., 1893.

Palfrey, John C. "The Capture of Mobile, 1865." *Papers of the Military Historical Society of Massachusetts* 8 (1910): 531-57.

Preston, Noble D. *History of the Tenth Regiment of Cavalry, New York State Volunteers.* New York: D. Appleton and Company, 1892.

"Professor Joseph Kargé, Ph.D." *The Princeton College Bulletin* 5 (April 1893): 25-34.

Pyne, Henry R. *The History of the First New Jersey Cavalry.* Trenton, N. J.: J. A. Beecher, Publisher, 1871. (I used the 1871 edition exclusively, except for one reference to the reprint edition.)

Quaife, Milo M., ed. *From the Cannon's Mouth: The Civil War Letters of General Alpheus S. Williams.* Detroit, Mich.: Wayne State University Press, 1959.

Revised Regulations for the Army of the United States, 1861. By authority of the War Department. Philadelphia: J. G. L. Brown, Printer, 1861; reprint ed., Gettysburg, Pennsylvania: *Civil War Times Illustrated,* 1974.

Scott, Wm. Forse. *The Story of a Cavalry Regiment.* New York: G. P. Putnam's Sons, 1893.

Sheridan, P. H. *Personal Memoirs.* New York: Charles L. Webster & Co., 1888.

Sherman, W. T. *Memoirs of Gen. W. T. Sherman.* 2 vols. New York: Charles L. Webster & Co., 1891.

Stearns, Austin C. *Three Years with Company K* (Thirteenth Massachusetts Infantry). Edited by Arthur A. Kent. Rutherford, N. J.: Fairleigh Dickinson University Press, 1976.

Stryker, William S., Adjutant General. *Record of Officers and Men of New Jersey in the Civil War,* 1861-1865. Trenton, N.J.: John L. Murphy, Steam Book and Job Printer, 1876.

Sturgis, Jerusha Wilcox. "Family of General Samuel Davis Sturgis, 1822-1889." Microfilm in Manuscript Division, State Historical Society of Wisconsin, Madison.

Sypher, J. R. *History of the Pennsylvania Reserve Corps.* Lancaster, Pa.: Elias Barr & Co., 1865.

Taylor, Richard. *Destruction and Reconstruction: Personal Experiences of the Late War.* Edited by Richard B. Harwell. London-Toronto: Longmans, Green and Co., 1955.

Tobie, Edward P. *History of the First Maine Cavalry, 1861-1865*. Boston: Press of Emery & Hughes, 1887.

Waring, George E., Jr. *Whip and Spur*. New York: Doubleday and McClure Company, 1897.

Wilson, James Harrison. *Under the Old Flag*. 2 vols. New York and London: D. Appleton and Company, 1912.

Wolcott, E. L., comp. *Record of Services Rendered the Government by Gen. B. H. Grierson during the War*. Fort Concho, Tex.: pvt. pub., 1882.

Wood, Wales W. *A History of the Ninety-fifth Regiment, Illinois Infantry Volunteers*. Chicago: Tribune Company's Book and Job Printing Office, 1865.

Young, J. P. *The Seventh Tennessee Cavalry: A History*. South Nashville, Tenn.: M. E. Church, 1890; reprint ed., Dayton, Ohio: Press of Morningside Bookshop, 1976.

3. *Newspapers*

Chicago Tribune

Daily State Gazette and Republican (Trenton, New Jersey)

Natchez (Mississippi) *Courier*

New Brunswick (New Jersey) *Times*

Newark Daily Advertiser

Newark Daily Mercury

Newark Star-Ledger

New York Herald

New York Times

New York Tribune

Polish American Journal (Scranton, Pennsylvania)

Princeton (New Jersey) *Herald*

II. Secondary Sources

Books and Articles

Abdill, Geo. B. *Civil War Railroads*. New York: Bonanza Books, 1961.

Andrews, J. Cutler. *The North Reports the Civil War*. Pittsburgh, Pa.: University of Pittsburgh Press, 1955.

Andrist, Ralph K. *The Long Death*. New York: The Macmillan Company, 1964.

Army Information Digest, August 1961. Official Magazine of the Department of the Army. Special Civil War Centennial edition titled "The Lesson and the Legacy."

Ballard, Colin R. *The Military Genius of Abraham Lincoln*. Cleveland and New York: The World Publishing Company, 1952.

Bearss, Edwin C. *Decision in Mississippi: Mississippi's Important Role in the War between the States*. Jackson: Mississippi Commission on the War Between the States, 1962.

Boatner, Mark M. III. *The Civil War Dictionary*. New York: David McKay Company, Inc., 1959.

Brown, D. Alexander. *Grierson's Raid*. Urbana, Ill.: University of Illinois Press, 1954.

———. "The Battle of Brice's Cross Roads." *Civil War Times Illustrated* 7 (April 1968): 4-9, 44-48.

Castel, Albert. *General Sterling Price and the Civil War in the West*. Baton Rouge, La.: Louisiana State University Press, 1968.

Catton, Bruce. *The Centennial History of the Civil War*. 3 vols. *The Coming Fury, Terrible Swift Sword*, and *Never Call Retreat*. Garden City, N. Y.: Doubleday & Company, Inc., 1965.

———. Trilogy of the Army of the Potomac: *Mr. Lincoln's Army, Glory Road*, and *A Stillness at Appomatox*. Garden City, N. Y.: Doubleday & Company, Inc., 1954.

———. *This Hallowed Ground*. Garden City, N. Y.: Doubleday & Company, Inc., 1956.

Chambers, Lenoir. *Stonewall Jackson*. 2 vols. New York: William Morrow & Co., 1959.

Davis, Burke. *They Called Him Stonewall*. New York-Toronto: Rinehart & Company, Inc., 1954.

———. *Jeb Stuart: The Last Cavalier*. New York: Bonanza Books, 1957.

Donald, David, ed. *Why the North Won the Civil War: Essays*. Baton Rouge: Louisiana State University Press, 1960.

Dowdey, Clifford. *The Land They Fought For: The Story of the South as the Confederacy, 1832-1865*. Garden City, N. Y.: Doubleday & Company, Inc., 1955.

Dyer, Frederick H. *A Compendium of the War of the Rebellion*. 3 vols. New York-London: Thomas Yoseloff, 1959.

Esposito, Colonel Vincent J., chief ed. *The West Point Atlas of American Wars*. 2 vols. New York: Frederick A. Praeger, Inc., 1959.

Foote, Shelby. *The Civil War: A Narrative*. 3 vols. New York: Random House, 1958, 1963, 1974.

Foster, John Y. *New Jersey and the Rebellion*. Newark, N. J.: Martin R. Dennis & Co., 1868.

Freeman, Douglas Southall. *Lee's Lieutenants*. 3 vols. New York: Charles Scribner's Sons, 1942, 1943, 1944.

Haiman, Mieczyslaw (Miecislaus). *Historja Udzialu Polakow w Amerykanskiej Wojnie Domowej* [History of the Participation of Poles in the American Civil War]. Chicago: Drukiem Dziennika Zjednoczenia [Union's Daily Press], 1928.

———. *Polish Past in America, 1608-1865*. Chicago: Archives and Museum of the Polish Roman Catholic Union, 1939.

Henderson, G. F. R. *Stonewall Jackson and the American Civil War*. London-New York-Toronto: Longmans, Green and Co., 1898; reprint ed., New York: Van Rees Press, 1936.

Henry, Robert Selph. *"First with the Most" Forrest*. Indianapolis-New York: Bobs-Merrill Company, 1944; reprint ed., Jackson, Tenn.: McCowat-Mercer Press, Inc., Publishers, 1969.

Jurczynska, Sister Mary Patricia. "A Study of the Participation of the Poles in the American Civil War." M. A. thesis, St. John College of Cleveland, 1949.

Kerwood, John Richard. "His Daring Was Proverbial" (General Turner Ashby). *Civil War Times Illustrated* 7 (August 1968): 19-23, 28-30.

Lerski, George J. "The United States and the January Insurrection." *Polish American Studies* 30 (Spring 1973): 45-53.

Lewis, Lloyd. *Sherman: Fighting Prophet*. New York: Harcourt, Brace and Company, 1932.

Liddell Hart, B. H. *Sherman: Soldier, Realist, American*. New York: Dodd, Mead & Company, 1930.

———. "Sherman—Modern Warrior." *American Heritage* 13 (1962): 21-23, 102-6.

Long, E. B. *The Civil War Day by Day*. Garden City, N. Y.: Doubleday & Company, Inc., 1971.

Longacre, Edward G. *Mounted Raids of the Civil War*. South Brunswick and New York: A. S. Barnes and Company, 1975.

———. *From Union Stars to Top Hat: A Biography of the Extraordinary General James Harrison Wilson*. Harrisburg, Pa.: Stackpole Books, 1972.

Lonn, Ella. *Foreigners in the Union Army and Navy*. Baton Rouge: Louisiana State University Press, 1951.

———. *Foreigners in the Confederacy*. Gloucester, Mass.: Peter Smith, 1965.

Lord, Francis A. *Civil War Collector's Encyclopedia*. Harrisburg, Pa.: The Stackpole Company, 1963.

Lytle, Andrew Nelson. *Bedford Forrest and His Critter Company*. New York: Minton, Balch & Company, 1931.

Merrill, James M. *William Tecumseh Sherman*. Chicago-New York-San Francisco: Rand McNally Company, 1973.

Miers, Earl Schenck. *The General Who Marched to Hell: William Tecumseh Sherman and His March to Fame and Infamy*. New York: Alfred A. Knopf, 1951.

Miller, Francis Trevelyan, editor-in-chief. *The Photographic History of the Civil War*. New York: The Review of Reviews Co., 1911.

Monaghan, Jay. *Civil War on the Western Border, 1854-1865*. Boston and Toronto: Little, Brown and Company, 1955.

Nevada State Historical Society, Inc., sponsor. *Nevada*. Writer's program of the Works Projects Administration in the State of Nevada. Portland, Ore.: Binfords & Mort, Publishers, 1940.

Norris, Edwin Mark. *The Story of Princeton*. Boston: Little, Brown and Company, 1917.

O'Connor, Lieut. Charles M. "The Eighth Regiment of Cavalry," *The Army of the United States*, pp. 268-79. Edited by Theo. F. Rodenbough and William L. Haskin. New York: Maynard, Merrill & Co., 1896.

Peterson, Cyrus A., and Hanson, Joseph Mills. *Pilot Knob: The Thermopylae of the West*. N.p.: The Neale Publishing Company, 1914. Reprint ed., Cape Girardeau, Mo.: Ramfre Press, 1964.

Plum, William R. *The Military Telegraph during the Civil War in the United States*. 2 vols. Chicago: Jansen, McClurg & Company, Publishers, 1882.

Randall, J. G., and Donald, David. *The Civil War and Reconstruction*. Lexington, Mass.: D. C. Heath and Company, 1969.

Rhodes, James Ford. "Sherman's March to the Sea," *The American Historical Review* 6 (April 1901): 466-74.

Rodenbough, Theo. F., and Haskin, William L., eds. *The Army of the United States*. New York: Maynard, Merrill & Co., 1896.

Ropes, John Codman. *The Army under Pope*. New York: Charles Scribner's Sons, 1881.

Ruhlen, Colonel George. "Early Nevada Forts," *Nevada Historical Society Quarterly* 7 (1964): 52-55.

Sheppard, Captain Erich William. *Bedford Forrest, the Confederacy's Greatest Cavalryman*. London: H. F. & G. Witherby, 1930.

Sidwa, Anne H. "Joseph Kargé, 1823-1892." *Proceedings of the New Jersey Historical Society* 81 (October 1963): 247-55.

Siekaniec, Ladislas John. *The Polish Contribution to Early American Education, 1608-1865*. San Francisco, Calif.: R and E Research Associates, 1976.

Slocum, Charles Elihu. *The Life and Services of Major-General Henry Warner Slocum*. Toledo, Ohio: The Slocum Publishing Company, 1913.

Smith, George Winston, and Judah, Charles. *Life in the North during the Civil War*. Albuquerque: The University of New Mexico Press, 1966.

Smith, Raymond W. "Don't Cut! Signal Telegraph." *Civil War Times Illustrated* 15 (May 1976): 18-28.

Stackpole, Edward J. *From Cedar Mountain to Antietam*. Harrisburg, Pa.: The Stackpole Company, 1959.

Stinson, Byron. "Hot Work in Mississippi: The Battle of Tupelo." *Civil War Times Illustrated* 11 (July 1972): 4-9, 46-48.

Tanner, Robert G. *Stonewall in the Valley*. Garden City, N. Y.: Doubleday & Company, Inc., 1976.

Thomason, John W. *Jeb Stuart*. New York: Charles Scribner's Sons, 1930.

Webb, Willard, ed. *The Crucial Moments of the Civil War*. New York: Fountainhead Publishers, Inc., 1961.

Weigley, Russell F. *History of the United States Army*. New York: The Macmillan Company, 1967.

Wieczerzak, Joseph W. *A Polish Chapter in Civil War America: The Effect of the January Insurrection on American Opinion and Diplomacy*. New York: Twayne Publishers, Inc., 1967.

Williams, Kenneth P. *Lincoln Finds a General*. vol. 1. New York: The Macmillan Company, 1949.

Wilson, Edmund. "Uncle Billy." *The New Yorker* 34 (1958): 114-44.

Wren, Thomas. *A History of the State of Nevada*. New York-Chicago: The Lewis Publishing Co., 1904.

Wyeth, John A. *That Devil Forrest: Life of General Nathan Bedford Forrest*. New York: Harper & Brothers, Publishers, 1959.

Young, Bennett H. *Confederate Wizards of the Saddle*. Boston: Chapple Publishing Co., Ltd., 1914; reprint ed., Kennesaw, Ga.: Continental Book Co., 1958.

Index

Abbreviations of military rank:
Sgt., Sergeant
Lt., Lieutenant
Capt., Captain
Maj., Major
Lt. Col., Lieutenant Colonel
Col., Colonel
Brig. Gen., Brigadier General
Maj. Gen., Major General
Lt. Gen., Lieutenant General
Gen., General

Abbeville, Miss., 1976–77, 179, 181–82
Aberdeen, Miss., 125
Adams, Frank T., Lt., 256 n.36
Adams, Wirt, Brig. Gen., 190, 200, 202
Addonizio, Hugh J., 235
Alabama River, 207, 209, 211
Aldie, engagement at, 89–91
Aldie, Va., 88–89
Alexander, Julius H., Lt. Col., 30–31
Alexandria, Va., 30, 34, 108–10
Allen, Samuel H., Col., 64
American Museum of Natural History, 227
American-Polish Civil War Centennial
    Committee, 234–35
Anderson, Robert, Maj., 28
Andersonville, Ga., 252 n.41
Andrews, Edwin N., Chaplain, 107
Annandale, Va., 109–10
Antietam, Battle of, 81, 83, 140, 221
Anuszkiewicz, Benjamin T., Col., 235
Appleget, Adrian S., Lt., 164
Appomattox, Va., 212
Archacki, Henry, 234
Arkansas River, 184
Army of the Mississippi, 56
Army of the Potomac, 30, 33–34, 36–40, 56,
    83, 86–87, 89, 91–94, 98, 109, 140, 187,
    204, 217
Army of Tennessee(Confederate), 188, 203,
    254 n.10
Army of the Tennessee(Union), 110–11

Army of the Valley(Confederate), 41
Army of Virginia(Union), 56–57, 75, 81–82
Asbury, N. J., 100
Asch, Joseph P., Lt., 104
Ashby's Gap, 88
Ashby, Turner, Brig. Gen., 50–51, 54, 72, 91
Atlanta, Ga., 19, 87, 136
Auburn, Miss., 172
Augur, Christopher C., Brig. Gen., 66
Augusta, Ga., 210
Austin, Alanson, Lt., 67

Bailey's Cross Roads, Va., 82, 110
Baird, Absalom, Maj. Gen., 87
Baldwin, David Johnson Caleb, 240 n.5
Baldwin, James M., Capt., 107, 110, 216
Baldwyn, Miss., 155–57
Ballard, Colin R., Brig. Gen., 240 n.28
Baltic Sea, 26
Baltimore, Md., 110
Baltimore & Ohio RR, 111
Banks, Nathaniel, Maj. Gen., 41, 43, 58–60,
    64, 66–68, 86, 118
Bankston, Miss., 199
Barnett's Ford, 59, 64, 69
Barteau, Clark R., Col., 159
Barwis Clothing Store, Trenton, N. J., 100
Baton Rouge, La., 207
Bayard, George D., Brig. Gen., 39–40, 43–46,
    48–64, 66–67, 69–83, 87–88, 90–92,
    94–96, 217, 220, 241 n.14, 244 n.8, 245
    n.35
Bayard, Samuel J., 73
Bayard, William, Lt., 77, 80
Bayou Pierre, 172
Beaumont, Myron H., Maj., 33, 36, 38, 47,
    59–60, 62, 66, 71–74, 82, 91, 96
Beauregard, Pierre T., Gen., 28
Beckwith, Warren, Capt., 199
Beekman, Garrett, Lt., 67
Bellaire, Ohio, 111
Bellefontaine, Miss., 199
Belleville, N. J., 96–97, 206, 215

Bell, Tyree H., Col., 151, 153, 161
Benton, Miss., 200
Berlin, Prussia, 20–23, 25, 106
Bernard Mansion (Va.), 95
Big Black River, 170, 172, 213
Big Blue, Battle of, 184–85
Big Foot(Indian), 222
Blackfish Lake, 184
Black Warrior River, 211
Blakely, Ala., 210–11
Blenker, Louis, Brig. Gen., 34
Blue Ridge Mountains, 43–44, 83, 91
Boatner, Mark M., III, 13
Bolivar, Miss., 170
Bolivar, Tenn., 19, 113, 120, 142–46, 190;
    engagement at, 143–46
Booneville, Miss., 157, 192
Bordentown, N. J., 100
Bourdeau, Louis, 228
Bouton, Edward, Col., 148, 155, 159, 166
Boyd, Robert N., Capt., 35, 51, 63, 72
Brackett, Cyrus F., 227
Braida, Sigismund von, Lt., 106, 164, 246
    n.28, 252 n.41
Brandy Station, Va., 75, 77, 79; engagement
    at, 11, 77–81, 217
Braune, Carl F., Lt., 256 n.36
Breslau University, 24
Brice's Cross-Roads, Battle of, 155–62,
    165–66, 176, 193
Brick Presbyterian Church, New York, 29
Broderick, Virgil, Capt., 51, 72, 76, 78, 80–81
Brooke's Station, Va., 92
Brownsville, Ark., 184
Brownsville, Tex., 214
Buckland Mills, Va., 85
Buckland, Ralph P., Brig. Gen., 178
Buford, Abraham, Brig. Gen., 159, 161
Buford, John, Brig. Gen., 58–59, 86–87
Bull Run Mountains, 43
Burd, Stryker, Lt., 204, 237
Burke, Ross E., Lt. Col., 194–95, 197
Burlington, N. J., 100
Burns, John, Lt., 195, 204, 237
Burnside, Ambrose E., Maj. Gen., 92, 94
Burrsville, N. J., 100

Cahawba, Ala., 190, 199
Cairo, Ill., 139, 183, 189
Calkins, William H., Maj., 210
Camden, N. J., 100

Camp Bayard, Va., 96
Camp Custis, Va., 34, 38–39
Camp Halleck, Nev., 224
Camp Howard, Tenn., 186
Camp Kargé, Va., 96
Camp Mercer, Va., 30
Camp Parker, N. J., 102–4, 107–8, 110
Camp Perrine, N. J., 101
Camp Stockton, Va., 108–10
Camp Winfield Scott, Nev., 221–24
Canby, Edward R. S., Maj. Gen., 170–71,
    187, 189–90, 201, 206–13, 215
Canton, Miss., 134, 169, 172
Cantwell, James F., Maj. Gen., 235
Carroll, Samuel S., Col., 51
Cashtown, Pa., 98
Catlett's Station, Va., 43
Catton, Bruce, 253 n.31
Cavalry Bureau, War Department, 187
Cavalry Corps, Army of the Potomac, 110
Cavalry Corps, District of West Tennessee,
    107, 174–75, 177
Cavalry Corps, Military Division of the
    Mississippi, 186–87, 208
Cavalry Division, XVI Army Corps, 122
Cavalry Division, District of West Tennessee,
    140, 147, 168, 190
Cavalry Forces, Military Division of West
    Mississippi, 207
Cave's Ford, 58, 60–61, 69
Cedar Mountain, 63–64, 75
Cedar Mountain, Battle of, 63–64, 67, 69,
    71–72, 75, 86
Cedar Run, 62–64
Centerville, Ala., 211
Central Polish Committee of Paris, 24
Central Polish Committee in the United States,
    13
Centreville, Va., 83, 85, 90
Chalfin, Samuel F., Col., 215
Chalmers, James R., Brig. Gen., 143, 176–77
Chambersburg, Pa., 98
Chancellorsville, Battle of, 100
Chantilly, Va., 88
Charleston, S. C., 28
Charlottesville, Va., 58
Chattahoochie River, 209–11
Chattanooga, Tenn., 111, 137
Chicago, Ill., 234
Chicago Tribune, 165
Chrysler, Morgan H., Col., 213

Churchill Barracks, Nev., 224
Cincinnati, Ohio, 111
Citronelle, Ala., 211
Clarendon, Ark., 184
Clark, Henry, Capt., 51
Clark's Mountain, 75
Clausewitz, Carl von, 165
Cleveland, Grover, 234
Cleveland, Ohio, 234
Cluseret, Gustave P., Col., 51
Coggill, James C., Capt. 235
Coldwater River, 178, 182
Cole, J. C., Col., 195, 203
College de France, Paris, 24
College of New Jersey(Princeton), 226,
    228–29
Collierville, Tenn., 120–21, 125, 131, 133–34,
    148, 161–63, 165
Columbia, S. C., 252 n.41
Columbia, Tenn., 188
Columbus, Ga., 210
Columbus, Ky., 112–13, 120
Columbus, Miss., 147, 149, 175, 177, 179,
    201, 211
Confederate States of America, 16
Connolly, James A., Maj., 87, 245 n.29
Coon, Datus E., Maj., 127, 213
Cooper, Emanuel E., Sgt., 145
Corinth, Miss., 113, 148–49, 151–53, 164,
    185, 190, 192, 202–3
Cottonwood Creek, 224
Crawford, Samuel W., Brig. Gen., 58–60, 63,
    66, 68, 70
Crews, James M., Lt. Col., 138, 143–44
Cross Keys, Battle of, 51, 56
Crump, Albert H., Capt., 256 n.36
Culpeper, Va., 57–58, 60, 62–64, 68–70, 76,
    83, 137
Cummings, Alexander, Maj., 46
Curry, Amos P., Capt., 152
Curtin, Andrew G., 98
Custer, George A., Maj. Gen., 214

Dadeville, Ala., 209
Daily State Gazette and Republican (Trenton,
    N. J.), 99–103, 108, 118, 165, 214, 217
Daley, Richard J., 234
Dana, Napoleon J. T., Maj. Gen., 189–90,
    192, 201–3, 206
Danbury, Conn., 28
Danville, Miss., 151

Dauphin Island, 207
Davidson, John W., Brig. Gen., 206, 214, 216
Davies, Henry E., Brig. Gen., 110
Davis, Burke, 69
Davis, Jefferson, 137, 211, 254 n.10
Davis, Murray, Capt., 221
Dayton, Ferdinand V., Surgeon, 66, 68–69,
    107, 185
Dec, John, 235
Decatur, Stephen, 29
Decatur, Ala., 175
Denison, Frederic, Rev., 63
Dennis, Elias S., Brig. Gen., 172, 190
Department of Alabama, Mississippi, and East
    Louisiana(Confederate) 157, 173, 194, 211
Department of Arkansas, 170, 183
Department of the Gulf, 170, 190
Department of Louisiana and Texas, 238
Department of Mississippi, 189; Southern
    District, 214, 216
Department of Missouri, 183
Department of the Ohio, 140
Department of of the Tennessee, 111, 113, 179
Devin, Thomas C., Lt. Col., 221
District of Natchez, 206
District of St. Louis, 183
District of Nevada, 222
District of Vicksburg, 189, 204
District of West Tennessee, 139, 168
Dod, Charles H., Lt., 130, 135
Douglas, Stephen A., 28
Dresden Abend Zeitung, 35
Dresden, Tenn., 114, 116
Droga, Frederick, 164
Duckworth, William L., Col., 136
Duck River, 188
Duffié, Alfred N., Col., 64
Duffield, George, Lt. Col., 184
Dumfries, Va., 93
Dunham, Cyrus L., Col., 250 n.30

Early Grove, Tenn., 192
Eastport, Miss., 107, 110–11
Eaton, Charles G., Lt. Col., 163
Edinburg, Va., 48
Edward's Station, Miss., 172
Egypt Station, Miss., 100, 125, 194–96, 199;
    engagement at, 194–99, 202–3
Eighth U. S. Cavalry Regiment, 220–24
XI Corps(Union), 86

Elizabeth, N. J., 234
Ellett, Alfred W., Brig. Gen., 172
Elliott, Joel, Capt., 204, 238
Ellistown, Miss., 155
Elsasser, Albert, 230, 234
England, 27
Essex County, N. J., 215
Etienne, Claude, Capt., 242 n.30
Eufala, Ala., 210–11
Europe, 19–20, 24
Eutaw, Ala., 211
Ewell, Richard S., Maj. Gen., 44, 47, 51, 62, 66
Ewing, Thomas, Brig. Gen., 183

Fairfax Court Hours, Va., 86–87, 109–10
Falls, Richard I., Maj., 67, 79–80, 83
Falmouth, Va., 39, 43–44, 92
Farragut, David, Admiral, 173
Federation of Polish Societies of Newark, N. J., 235
Fernald, Charles F., Capt., 195, 256 n.36
Fine, Henry, 228
First(Nassau)Presbyterian Church, Princeton, N. J., 227, 230
First Volunteer Cavalry Brigade, 30, 33, 36
Fitzhugh, Norman, Maj., 75
Foote, Shelby, 253 n.31
Forrest, Jeffrey, Col., 130
Forrest, Nathan Bedford, Lt. Gen., 13, 19, 113–16, 118, 121, 126–27, 129–31, 133–38, 140, 142–49, 151–52, 154, 157–58, 161, 167–69, 172–79, 181–83, 185, 188, 190, 193, 201, 219, 250 n.30
Fort Anderson, Ky., 136
Fort Blakely, Ala., 207
Fort Gaines, Ala., 207
Fort Lyon, Va., 34
Fort Monroe, Va., 38–39
Fort Morgan, Ala., 208
Fort Moultrie, S. C., 28
Fort Pickering, Tenn., 178
Fort Pillow, Tenn., 138–39
Fort Scott, Kans., 185
Fort Sumter, S. C., 28
France, 14, 17, 219
Frankfort Diet, 34
Franklin, Miss., 200
Franklin(Tenn), battle of, 188
Franklin, Va., 43–44
Franklin, William B., Maj. Gen., 92, 94–95

Frazer, Donald, 164
Fredericksburg, Va., 39, 48, 58, 92, 114; Battle of, 94–95, 140, 221
Freeman, Douglas Southall, 64
Freeman's Ford, 91
Frémont, John C., Maj. Gen., 43–44, 46, 48, 51–52, 54
Front Royal, Va., 41, 44
Fuller, John W., Col., 250 n.30
Funke, Otto, Lt. Col., 193–94

Gainesville, Va., 83, 90
Gallagher, Michael, Capt., 100, 109–10, 143, 184, 194, 204, 237
"Galvanized Yankees," 198
Galveston, Tex., 212
Gamble, William, Maj., 221
Gardner, Franklin, Maj. Gen., 195–96, 198–99, 202–3
Garibaldi, Giuseppe, 38
Gaskell, Penn, Lt., 71, 80
Gayoso Hotel, Memphis, 154, 178
Georgetown, Ga., 211
Gerolt, Baron von, 106
Germany, 13
Gettysburg, Pa., 11, 97, 100
Gholson, Samuel J., Brig. Gen., 168, 196, 198–99, 254 n.23
Gilson, N. S., Col., 214
Givens, John N., Capt., 210, 256 n.36
Glogow, Prussian Poland, 22
Gordon, George H., Brig. Gen., 68
Gordonsville, Va., 57–58, 68
Gourlay, Private, 63
Grabowski, Arthur, Col., 28
Graham, John M., Maj., 181–82
Grand Gulf, Miss., 173
Grand Junction, Tenn., 190–92
Grant, Ulysses S., Lt. Gen., 111, 118, 121, 126, 135, 137–39, 142, 170, 172, 174, 179, 186–87, 189, 206–7, 212, 215–16, 220–21, 228
Graz, Austria, 246 n.28
Great Britain, 14
Green, Charles E., 228
Green, George W., 252 n.41
Greensborough, Ala., 211
Greenville, Ala., 210
Gregg, David McMurtrie, Maj. Gen., 230, 233
Gregg, John I., Col., 221, 224
Grenada, Miss., 149, 176, 200

Grierson, Benjamin H., Brig. Gen., 113, 115, 121, 123, 128, 133–34, 136–38, 140, 143, 147, 149, 151–59, 162–65, 168–69, 173–74, 177, 179, 181–82, 185–87, 189–90, 192–204, 207–15, 237–38, 255 n.34
Guntown, Miss., 155–56, 158–59, 193

Haggerty, James, Maj., 216
Haiman, Mieczyslaw, 246 n.28
Haines, Thomas, Capt., 50
Halleck, Henry, Maj. Gen., 183, 189–90, 201, 206, 208
"Halsted's Horse," 11, 29–30, 32–33, 38, 217
Halsted, Benjamin B., 32
Halsted, William, Col., 29–33, 35–38, 71
Hamburg, Germany, 27
Hamilton, Alexander D., Lt., 256 n.36
Hamilton, Robert, Lt., 256 n.36
Hanover Court House, Va., 41, 43
Hanson, E. Hunn, Capt., 155
Hardeman County, Tenn., 143
Harhaus, Otto, Maj., 83
Harman, Asher W., Col., 81
Harper's Ferry, Va., 83
Harris, Ira, Senator, 76
"Harris Light Cavalry," 76
Harrisburg, Miss., 193; Battle of, 174, 176
Harrisburg, Pa., 98
Harrison, Jessie L., Sgt., 164, 252 n.41
Harrisonburg, Va., 43–44, 49, 51–56, 72
Hatch, Edward, Brig. Gen., 174–77, 179, 181–82, 187
Hatch, John P., Brig. Gen., 57–58, 69
Hatchie River, 19, 119, 141–42, 144, 151–53, 158, 160, 166
Hawksworth, Charles, Lt., 256 n.36
Haymarket, Va., 43, 90
Hazen, William M., 62
Heintzelman, Samuel P., Maj. Gen., 33, 35–36, 38, 85–86, 97
Hencke, Theodore W., Capt., 204, 238
Hepburn, William P., Lt. Col., 125–27, 132
Hernando, Miss., 178, 181
Hess, Joseph C., Lt. Col., 119, 177
Hickahala Creek, 178
Hill, A. P., Maj. Gen., 66, 68
Hoboken, N. J., 103
Hoff, John, 164
Hoffman, Jacob H., Lt., 93–94, 107, 216, 256 n.36

Hoge, George B., Col., 148, 154, 158, 163
Holly Springs, Miss., 124, 131, 175–77, 179, 181–83, 190
Hood, John Bell, Gen., 188, 193, 198, 201–4, 206, 219, 237, 254 n.10
Hot Spring Mountains, Nev., 225
Houston, Miss., 199
Houston, Tex., 214
Howard, Oliver Otis, Maj. Gen., 179, 187–88
Howe, Oscar P., Capt., 129
Hughes, Richard J., 234–35
Humboldt County, Nev., 221
Hungarian Uprising of 1849, 86
Hunter, Pendleton, Lt., 222
Huntington, Tenn., 114, 116, 119
Hurlbut, Stephen A., Maj. Gen., 113, 121, 134, 137–39, 178
Hurricane Creek, 176–77
Huss, C. O., 228

Illinois State Journal, 165
Illinois units: Second Illinois Cavalry, 118, 129, 132; Third Illinois Cavalry, 148, 155; Fourth Illinois Cavalry, 193, 196, 200; Sixth Illinois Cavalry, 121; Seventh Illinois Cavalry, 148–49, 181; Ninth Illinois Cavalry, 148, 155; Eleventh Illinois Cavalry, 193, 199
Indiana units: Seventh Indiana Cavalry, 107, 118–19, 129, 131–32, 138, 148, 153, 155, 157, 175, 190, 193–95, 204, 213; Tenth Indiana Cavalry, 210–11; Twelfth Indiana Cavalry, 210; Thirteenth Indiana Cavalry, 210, 213
Iowa Units: Second Iowa Cavalry, 127; Third Iowa Cavalry, 148, 184, 198; Fourth Iowa Cavalry, 148, 160, 163, 187, 199, 201; Eighth Iowa Infantry, 187
Irving Block Prison, Memphis, 178
Irwinville, Ga., 211
Island No. 10, 56
Iuka, Miss., 111, 203
Ivey's Farm, Miss., 129–30; engagement at, 130–32

Jackson, Miss., 169–72
Jackson, Tenn., 113, 115–16, 119, 136, 188, 190
Jackson, Thomas J. (Stonewall), Lt. Gen., 31, 41, 44–53, 56–57, 60, 63–64, 66–70, 74
Jacksonville, Ill., 122

Janeway, Hugh H., Capt., 60–61
Jenkins, Micah, Brig. Gen., 98
Jersey City, N. J., 100, 103, 112, 228
Johnson, Andrew, 220
Johnson, George W., Lt., 256 n.36
Johnson, Gilbert M. L., Col., 210, 213
Johnston, Joseph E., Gen., 136–37, 210–11,
    254 n.10
Jones, Ivin D., Maj., 83
Jones, Own, Col., 53, 62
Jurczynska, Sister Mary Patricia, 246 n 28

Kane, Thomas L., Lt. Col., 45, 48, 50
Kansas unit: Seventh Kansas Cavalry, 138
Kargé, Joseph, Brevet Brig. Gen., introduction
    and early life: defeats Forrest, 19; officer in
    Prussian Royal Horse Guard, 20; joins
    People's Revolution in Berlin, 21;
    organizes battalion of Polish cavalry, 21;
    captured and abused by Prussians, 21–22;
    fights Prussian forces, 22; captured and
    court-martialed, 23; family background,
    23–24, escapes prison, 25–27; seeks
    asylum in England and meets brother, 27;
    sails for America, 27; becomes citizen,
    marries, fathers two sons, conducts
    language school, 28–29
—Service in the East, First New Jersey
    Cavalry: joins regiment as second in
    command, 29; competes for position, 30;
    trains regiment, 31–32; quarrels with
    commander, 32; orders inefficient officers
    before board, 33; meets Wladimir
    Krzyzanowski, 34; twice becomes target of
    court martial charges; 35–36; sick in
    Washington, 37; moves with regiment to
    Rappahannock, 39; makes feint toward
    Richmond, 39–41; marches to Shenandoah
    Valley, 43–44; scouts Strasburg for enemy,
    45; pursues Jackson up the Valley, 46;
    charges rebel battery, 47; struck by artillery
    shell, 48; fights at Woodstock, 48; stopped
    at Mount Jackson, 49; enters Harrisonburg
    and is ambushed, 50–51, 53–55; questions
    commander's decision, 53; gains Gen.
    Bayard's attention, 55; takes command,
    reorganizes regiment and performs grueling
    reconnaissance, 56–58; defends along
    Rapidan river, 59; makes daring strike
    behind enemy, 61–62; deploys at Cedar
    Mountain, 64; turns command to senior

    major, 66; engages in Battle of Cedar
    Mountain, 66–67; finds regiment
    exhausted, 69–70; acccused of cowardice,
    71; nature of charges, 72–73; Bayard
    defends Kargé, 73; charges withdrawn, 74;
    covers withdrawal of Pope's army from
    Rapidan, 75–77; clashes with Jeb Stuart's
    cavalry at Brandy Station, 77–80; suffers
    battle wound, 80; returns to duty, 82; leads
    brigade in reconnaissance missions for
    Army of Potomac, 83–85; recommended
    for promotion to one-star rank, 86–87;
    humorous camp incident, 87–88; scouts
    Gen. Lee's movements, 89; skirmishes
    with Stuart at Aldie, 89–90; returns to
    Rappahannock, 92; raids King George
    County, 92–93, Lt. Hoffman incident,
    93–94; asks for leave of absence for leg
    wound, 94; Battle of Fredericksburg, 94,
    grieves over death of Bayard, 95–96;
    resigns his commission, 96
—Service in the West, Second New Jersey
    Cavalry: testimonial dinner, 97; seeks to
    form own regiment, 97–98; appointed chief
    of cavalry of New Jersey Militia, 98; reverts
    to recruiting own regiment, 100; trains
    volunteers, 102; plagued with bounty
    jumpers and whiskey peddlers, 102–4;
    receives two Prussian officers, 106; selects
    only experienced officers, 106–7; conducts
    regimental review for governor, 107–8;
    departs with regiment for nation's capital,
    108; trains regiment in Virginia, 109–10;
    one company encounters Mosby's
    guerrillas, 109; moves regiment to
    Mississippi and then to Tennessee, 110–11;
    assigned to Sherman's Department of
    Tennessee, 112; pursues Forrest in West
    Tennessee, 114–16; moves to Collierville
    for Meridian campaign, 118–20; marches
    into Mississippi after Forrest, 121; ordered
    to retreat, 126; blocks Forrest's pursuit near
    Okolona, 128–30; retreats to Memphis and
    shows disgust with Sooy Smith, 130–32;
    refits the regiment and congratulates the
    men, 135; Kargé beats Forrest at Bolivar,
    Tenn., 142–46; marches in Sturgis
    expedition to destroy Forrest, 148–49;
    makes daring raid behind enemy lines,
    149–53; engages enemy at Brice's
    Cross-Roads, 155–61; fights off Forrest's

pursuit of defeated Federal army, 160–61; receives praise for rear guard action, 161; his regiment suffers heaviest losses in cavalry division, 163; promoted to brigade command, 168; leads brigade to Vicksburg for proposed raid on Mobile & Ohio RR, 169; Gen. Slocum countermands Kargé's planned raid, 170; takes part in Slocum's limited diversion, 172–73; marches in A. J. Smith expedition to bag Forrest, 175–83; takes command of cavalry division, 177; performance as division commander thwarted by Smith's insubordination, 181–83; sets off for Arkansas to stop Sterling Price, 184; becomes sick and is evacuated to Memphis, 184; evaluation of his leadership, 185; sees buildup of Second New Jersey Cavalry with draftees, 186; makes raid into Arkansas, 187; commands brigade in expedition to destroy Gen. Hood's lines of communication, 190; attacks rebels at Verona, Miss. and destroys vast quantities of supplies, 193; leads brigade in attack on entrenched enemy at Egypt Station, Miss., 194–99; captures 500 Confederates, 197; destroys rebel property across Mississippi, 199–201; his leadership contributes to successful mission, 202–3; recommended for promotion to brigadier general, 204; issues congratulatory order to brigade, 204–5; prepares for Gen. Canby's attack on Mobile, Ala., 207–8; in battle zone, 209; leads brigade across Alabama to Georgia, 210; learns of Lincoln's assassination, 210; returns to Mississippi after marching 700 miles, 211–12; Grierson again tries for Kargé's promotion, 213; commands post of Natchez, 214; promoted to brevet Brig. Gen., 215; mustered out of service and receives the thanks of State of New Jersey, 216–17; résumé of war service, 217–18
—Postbellum Life: spends Christmas of 1865 with family, 219; applies for Regular Army service in grade of major, 219–20; receives support of New Jersey citizens, 220; offered first lieutenancy and accepts, 220; his decision is a mistake, 220–21; assumes command of Camp Winfield Scott, Nev., 221; begins policy of evenhanded treatment of Indians, 222; finds frontier duty boring and stifling, 224; takes extended leave of absence after two years in Nevada, 225; offered Chair of Continental Languages at Princeton and accepts, 226; resigns army commission, 226; serves as college professor for 22 years, 226–29; first incumbent of Woodhull Professorship in Modern Languages, 227; awarded Doctor of Philosophy by Rutgers University, 227; dies suddenly of heart attack, 228; praised as faithful teacher with high ideals, 229

Kargé, Francis, Rev., 27, 239 n.7
Kargé, Jacob, 23
Kargé, Ladislaus, 29, 219, 228, 230, 240 n.6
Kargé, Maria, 29, 219, 240 n.5
Kargé, Romuald, 29, 219, 230, 240 n.6
Kargé, Veronica, 23, 227
Kerner, Otto, 234
Kester, John, Capt., 51, 72, 89
Kilpatrick, Judson, Brig. Gen., 76–77, 79–80, 111
King's Battery(Confederate), 195
King George County, Va., 92–93
King, Rufus, Maj. Gen., 58
Kingston, Ala., 211
Kingsley, John, Sgt., 63
King of Prussia, 21, 23
Kitchen, Marcus L. W., Lt. Col., 104, 106, 155, 168, 251 n.21
Knipe, Joseph F., Brig. Gen., 207–10, 213
Kosciusko, Miss., 134
Kosciuszko, Thaddeus, Brig. Gen., 14, 230
Kossuth, Louis, 86
Kossuth, Miss., 151
Krauter, John L., Surgeon, 164, 199, 216
Krzyzanowski, Wladimir, Brig. Gen., 13, 34–35

Lafayette, Marquis de, 14, 230
Lafayette(Rossville), Tenn., 147–48
Lafferty, John, Lt., 221–22
La Grange, Tenn., 169, 175, 181, 192
Lamar, Miss., 192
L'Anguille River, 184
Larson, James, Sgt., 125, 128
Lawler, Michael K., Brig. Gen., 190, 202
Lee, Robert E., Gen., 11, 39, 56–57, 74–75, 81, 88, 91, 98, 100, 104, 136, 212, 220
Lee, Stephen D., Lt. Gen., 137, 147–48, 157, 170, 172–74, 193, 248 n.39
Leedstown, Va., 93

Leesburg, Va., 83
Lehigh River, 44
Leski, Walter, Capt., 92
Lexington, Miss., 200, 202–3
Liberty Mills, Va., 69
Lincoln, Abraham, 28, 34, 39, 41, 43–44, 52, 56, 87, 92, 98, 110, 204, 210, 213, 215
Linden, Clarence, Lt., 109
Lipscomb, Thomas C., Col., 199
Little Humboldt River, 225
Little Rock, Ark., 183–84, 200
London, England, 27
Longstreet, James, Maj. Gen., 84, 88
Louisa Court House, Va., 75
Louisville, Miss., 134
Lucas, John H., Capt., 63, 80–81, 89–90, 93
Lucas, Thomas J., Brig. Gen., 207, 209–11, 213
Lunny, Robert M., 235
Luray, Va., 52
Luray Valley, 41, 51

Maas, Capt., 34, 240 n.25
Mabry's Cavalry(Confederate), 199
McArthur, John, Brig. Gen., 140
McClellan, George B., Maj. Gen., 30, 34–36, 38, 40–41, 52, 56–57, 75, 82–83, 92
McCosh, James, 226–27
McCrillis, Lafayette, Col., 125, 128, 132–33
McDonald's Battalion(Confederate), 143
McDowell, Irvin, Maj. Gen., 39–40, 43–46, 52, 57, 96–97
McKelway, George, 108
McMillen, William L., Col., 142, 148, 154, 158–60, 164–65
McPherson, James B., Maj. Gen., 121, 138, 140, 145, 169, 171, 187
Macon, Ga., 198–99, 209–10
Macon, Miss., 149, 169
Madigan, John, Lt., 256 n.36
Madison Court House, Va., 57–59, 69
Maine units: First Maine Battery, 48; First Maine Cavalry, 64, 75–77, 244 n.8
Manassas Gap, 44
Manassas Junction, Va., 56
Marais de Cygnes, Battle of, 184
Marion, Ala., 211
Martin Creek, 225
Mass, Bogumil, Capt., 240 n.25
Massanutten Mountains, 51
Maximilian, Emperor of Mexico, 214, 219

Meade, George Gordon, Maj. Gen., 98
Meeker, Carnot B., Lt., 130
Memphis, Tenn., 19, 107, 113, 118, 122, 130–34, 136, 138–41, 143, 145, 147–49, 154–55, 161–63, 165, 169, 173–74, 177–79, 181–87, 189–90, 192, 203, 206–8, 237, 253 n.31
Memphis & Charleston RR, 188, 192, 202
Mercer County, N. J., 102
Meridian, Miss., 118, 121, 125, 127, 135, 139–41, 213
Meridian Campaign, 118, 134–35, 139–41, 213
Meridian(Miss.) Clarion, 198–99
Merritt, Wesley, Maj. Gen., 214
Michigan units: First Michigan Cavalry, 70, 75; Third Michigan Cavalry, 138; Fourth Michigan Cavalry, 211
Mickiewicz, Adam, 24
Middleburg, Va., 88–90
Miers, Earl Schenck, 13
Military Division of the Gulf, 214
Military Division of the Mississippi, 121, 135, 186, 237
Military Division of the Southwest, 214
Military Division of West Mississippi, 170, 207, 243
Military Order of the Loyal Legion, 228, 230–33, 235
Minié, Claude Etienne, Capt., 242 n.30
Misiur, Matthew, 235
Mississippi Central RR, 169–70, 172, 175, 199
Mississippi River, 56, 118, 136–38, 170, 172–73, 184, 187–88, 208, 216
Mississippi units: First Mississippi Cavalry(Mounted Rifles, Union), 107, 172, 175, 190, 198
Mississippi Marine Brigade, 173
Missouri units: Fourth Missouri Cavalry, 107, 118–20, 129–32, 148, 153, 155, 184, 190, 195, 205; Tenth Missouri Cavalry, 142, 148–49, 151–52, 192
Mitchell, Richard D., Capt., 195
Mobile, Ala., 168, 173–74, 194, 206, 209–12
Mobile Bay, 207–8
Mobile & Ohio RR, 149, 152, 155, 169, 173, 185, 188–90, 192, 198–99, 203, 207
Monsoon (ship), 111
Montgomery, Ala., 206, 209–11, 213
Montgomery, Ebenezer, Lt., 130
Moore, Franklin, Capt., 129

Moore, Webster P., Lt. Col., 210
Moorefield, Va., 44
Moorman, George, Lt. Col., 200
Morristown, N. J., 100
Mosby, John, Col., 109
Moscow, Russia, 23
Moscow, Tenn., 120, 142, 192
Mount, Edward P., Capt., 102, 216
Mount Jackson, Va., 48–49
Mount Pinson, Tenn., 120
Mountville, Va., 90
Mower, Joseph A., Brig. Gen., 113, 115, 174, 176–77, 181, 183–84
Mulford, Lambert L., Lt., 166, 256 n.36
Murray, James O., 228–29
Myers, William C., Capt., 210

Napoleon Bonaparte, 23
Nashville, Tenn., 113, 137, 148, 183, 188–89; Battle of, 201
Natchez, Miss., 190, 206, 214, 216
Natchez (Miss.) *Courier*, 215
National Guard Association of the United States, 235
Nassau Literary Magazine, 12
Neet, Frederick R., Capt., 192
Newark, N. J., 100, 112, 185, 234–35
Newark Daily Advertiser, 97, 100, 110, 169, 185, 197, 206
Newark Daily Mercury, 57
New Albany, Miss., 124, 131
New Baltimore, Va., 83
New Brunswick, N. J., 100
New Brunswick Times, 38, 72
New Caledonia, Tenn., 114
New Jersey "Bobtails," 112, 118, 185, 192
New Jersey Civil War Centennial Commission, 234
New Jersey Dept. of Defense, 235
New Jersey Historical Society, 235
New Jersey State Assembly, 234
New Jersey units: First New Jersey Cavalry: mentioned, 11; organized by William Halsted, 29; becomes disorderly and inefficient, 30; Kargé, takes command and imposes discipline, 31–32; Halsted resumes charge, 32; assigned to Heintzelman's division, 33; the Capt. Boyd affair, 35–36; trouble between senior officers, 36–37; charges against chaplain, 38;

new commander, 38; assigned to Bayard's cavalry brigade, 39; advances toward Richmond, 39–41; ordered to Shenandoah Valley, 41; pursues Jackson, 45–49; ambushed and routed, 50–51, 54–55; Kargé takes command and rebuilds regiment, 56; holds Rapidan River line, 58–60; penetrates Jackson's army, 60–62; provides initial defense at Battle of Cedar Mountain, 64–67; runs efficient field hospital, 68–69; becomes exhausted by arduous campaign, 69–70; rebellion among officers, 71–74; covers Union withdrawal to Rappahannock River, 75–77; fights Jeb Stuart at Brandy Station, 77–80; welcomes Kargé back, 82; scouts Lee's army, 83–85; engages Jeb Stuart at Aldie, 89–90; displaces to Rappahannock River, 92; takes part in Battle of Fredericksburg, 94; grieves over death of Bayard, 95; commander resigns, 96
—Second New Jersey Cavalry: mentioned, 11; recruited, organized, and trained by Joseph Kargé, 100–10; receives two Prussian officers, 106; performs field training in Virginia, 108–110; assigned to Sherman's Army of the Tennessee, 110–12; marches against Forrest, 114–16; joins Gen. Sooy Smith's Meridian campaign, 118; marches into Mississippi, 121; ordered to withdraw, 126; blocks Forrest's pursuit near Okolona, 128–30; returns to Tennessee, 131–32; commended for performance, 135; marches to intercept Forrest, 140–42; defeats Forrest at Bolivar, 142–46; takes part in Sturgis expedition to bag Forrest, 148–49; makes daring raid to Rienzi and Corinth, 149–53; fights at Battle of Brice's Cross-Roads, 155–61; defends rear of defeated army, 160–63; suffers severe casualties, 163; wins praise for its performance, 164; takes part in Slocum's diversion near Vicksburg, 169–73; marches with Gen. A. J. Smith expedition to destroy Forrest, 175–83; frustrated by commander's inaction, 182; ordered to Arkansas to stop Sterling Price, 183–85; depleted ranks filled with draftees, 186; goes on Gen. Grierson's expedition into Mississippi, 189–92; destroys rebel supplies at Verona, 193; gains great victory at Egypt Station, 194–98; ends march at

Vicksburg, 200–1; congratulated by
brigade commander, 204–5; relocates to
Natchez, 106; moves to New Orleans for
Alabama campaign, 206; sails for Mobile,
209; departs for Montgomery, 210; shifts
march to Georgia, 210; marches at war's
end to Mississippi, 211–12; one-year men
depart for home, 213; serves at Natchez,
214; mustered out and returns to New
Jersey, 216–17
—First New Jersey Infantry, 106
New Madrid, Missouri, 58
New Market, Va., 49
New Orleans, La., 206–8, 211–14
New York, N. Y., 27–29, 103, 110, 228, 234
New York Herald, 172
New York Times, 54, 132–33, 144, 198, 228
New York Tribune, 53
New York units: Second New York Cavalry,
75–77, 79, 83, 88, 90, 92, 211; Fourth New
York Mounted Rifles, 49–50; Fifth New
York Cavalry, 59; Tenth New York
Cavalry, 88; 58th Regiment Infantry
("Polish Legion"), 34–36; 88th Regiment
Infantry, 100
Newning, Isaac, Sgt., 57, 83–84
Newsom, John F., Lt. Col., 152
Nicholson, John P., Lt. Col., 233
Noble, John W., Col., 176, 182, 198, 200
Norcross, James H., 116

Oakland, Tenn., 142
Obion River, 118–20
O'Connor, James H., Lt., 256 n.36
Ohio River, 118, 137
Ohio units: 13th Ohio Infantry Regiment, 121;
14th Battery, Ohio Light Artillery, 210;
72nd Ohio Infantry Regiment, 163
Okolona, Miss., 124, 126–28, 143, 145, 149,
193–94
Okolona, engagement at, 128–33
Old Town, Miss., 193
Old Town Creek, 193
Olden, Charles S., 38, 71, 82, 86, 97, 244 n.18
Opelika, Ala., 209
Opequon Creek, 83
Orange & Alexandria RR, 43
Orange Court House, Va., 59–60, 69
Ord, Edward, Maj. Gen., 43–44
Osage River, Battle of, 184–85

Osband, Embury D., Col., 190, 196–98, 200,
202–3, 212
Osborn, Henry F., 227
Osceola, Ark., 187
Oxford, Miss., 176–77, 179, 181–83, 190
Owyhee River, 222

Paducah, Ky., 111, 136–37
Palmer, Innis N., Brig. Gen., 37
Pannwitz, Erich von, Capt., 106, 129–30, 246
n.28, 256 n.36
Panola, Miss., 178–79, 181–82
Paradise Valley, Nev., 221–22, 224–25
Paris, France, 24
Paris, Tenn., 116
Parker, Cortlandt, 220
Parker, Crossroads, Tenn., 250 n.30
Parker, Joel, 11, 97–98, 100, 107–8, 220
Patton, Francis L., 228
Paxson, H. C., Capt., 102, 246 n.16
Payne, Maj., 84
Pearl River, 169–70
Pemberton, John C., Maj. Gen., 172
Peninsula Campaign, 75
Pennsylvania units: Pennsylvania
"Bucktails," 45–46, 48, 50–51, 241 n.14;
First Pennsylvania Cavalry, 39–40, 45, 48,
50, 53, 59–60, 62–64, 67, 70, 75–77, 80,
83, 88; Nineteenth Pennsylvania Cavalry,
107, 118–19, 133, 138, 148, 158, 170,
175, 177, 184, 190
Pensacola, Fla., 190, 208
Perrine, Lewis, Maj. Gen., 101, 104, 107, 220
Philadelphia, Miss., 134
Philadelphia, Pa., 108, 110, 230
Philadelphia Inquirer, 108
Phillips, William W. L., Surgeon, 37, 94, 233
Pickensville, Ala., 211
Pierce, Abial, Maj., 160
Pierson, J. Lacey, Maj., 104, 129, 185, 216
Pilot Knob, Missouri, 183
Plainfield, N. J., 230
Pleasonton, Alfred, Maj. Gen., 91–92, 110,
184–86
Poland, 13, 20, 23–24, 27, 34, 215
Polish American Veterans Association of
America, 235
Polish Government-in-Exile(London), 235
Polish Legion of American Veterans, 234–35
Polish Revolution of 1830, 34–35

Polish Revolutionary Committee, 21–22

Pontotoc, Miss., 127, 129, 131, 134, 155, 173, 176, 199

Pope, John, Maj. Gen., 56–58, 60, 63–64, 67–69, 75, 77, 81

Porter, Fitz John, Maj. Gen., 41

Port Conway, Va., 93

Port Gibson, Miss., 172, 214

Port Republic, Va., 49, 51; Battle of, 51–52, 56

Port Royal, Va., 93

Post of Brookhaven, Miss., 214

Post of Natchez, Miss., 214–15

Potockie Oledry, Poland, 239 n.2

Potomac River, 30, 41, 83, 85, 92, 108

Potsdam, Prussia, 22

Poznan, Poland, 13, 21–24, 239 n.2

Prairie Station, Miss., 125, 199

Price, Sterling, Maj. Gen., 183–85

Price, William R., Maj., 221

Princeton, N. J., 13, 100, 226

Princeton University, 13, 226–30, 234

Prospect, Tenn., 137

Provisional Brigade, District of Natchez, 206

Provisional Cavalry Division (Pleasonton), 184

Prussia, 13–14, 20

Prussians, 20–25, 88, 106

Pulaski, Casimir, Brig. Gen., 98n

Pulaski, Tenn., 188

Purdy, Tenn., 137, 141, 145

Pyne, Henry R., Chaplain, 38, 49, 60–61, 64, 68, 74, 76, 79, 80–81, 88, 90, 95, 241 n.10

Raccoon Ford, 59, 60, 76

Rainear, Lewis, Lt., 145, 164, 256 n.36

Raleigh, Tenn., 138, 190

Rapidan River, 58, 60, 62, 68–70, 75, 82, 87, 96

Rapidan Station, Va., 58–60, 63–64, 69, 75, 77

Rappahannock River, 39–40, 43, 45, 56–57, 75–76, 82, 87–88, 91, 93–94, 96, 244 n.8

Rawolle, William C., Capt., 165

Raymond, Miss., 172

Red River Campaign, 118, 134, 168

Reed, Charles E., 111

Reed, Thomas, 222, 224

Reiley, Charles C., Capt., 163

Reserve Corps, Military Division of West Mississippi, 190

Revere, Frederick B., Maj., 106

Revolution of 1848, 20, 25

Reynolds, John F., Maj. Gen., 95

Rhode Island units: First Rhode Island Cavalry, 63–64, 75–77, 89, 244 n.8

Rice, Charles H., Lt., 256 n.36

Richmond, Va., 38–39, 41, 43–44, 52, 56–57, 92, 110

Ricketts, James B., Brig. Gen., 44, 68

Rienzi, Miss., 149, 151–53, 164, 185

Riley, Thomas, 164

Rio Grande River, 214

Ripley, Miss., 144–45, 149, 152–53, 158, 160–61, 163, 173, 190, 192

Ripley, Tenn., 120

Roberts, Benjamin S., Brig. Gen., 64, 73

Robertson, Beverly H., Brig. Gen., 64, 77, 81

Robertson's River, 62, 75

Robertsville, S. C., 87

Robeson, George M., Gen., 107

Rock Creek, Washington, D. C., 29

Rockville, Md., 36

Rocky Springs, Miss., 172

Roddey, Phillip D., Brig. Gen., 111

Rodgers, F., 30

Rogers, John, 222

Rosecrans, William S., Maj. Gen., 183

Royal Horse Guard of Prussia, 20, 24–25

Rucker, Edmund W., Col., 151

Ruckersville, Miss., 148, 158

Rudolphi, Julius von, Lt., 106, 164, 246 n.28, 252 n.41

Rusling, James F., Gen., 228

Russellville, Ala., 148

Russia, 13–14, 23

Russians, 24, 34

Rutgers University, 227

St. Francis River, 184

St. Louis, Mo., 138, 183, 187

St. Matthews Church, Opalenica, Poland, 239 n.2

Salem, Miss., 148–49, 151, 160–61, 163, 192

Salem, N. J., 100

San Antonio, Tex., 214

Santa Rosa Mountains, 225

Sardinian army, 38

Saskatonchee River, 127

Saulsbury, Tenn., 163, 169

Savannah, Ga., 87

Sawyer, Henry W., Capt., 45–46, 79, 90

Sayreville, N. J., 234
Schofield, John M., Maj. Gen., 188
Schriver, Edmund, Col., 74
Schwartz, C. Stever, Lt., 130, 164
Schweitzer, George, 145
Scott, William B., 227
Scott, William Forse, Capt., 201
Scudder, William V., Capt., 102, 233, 256
    n.36
Search, Anthony T., Capt., 193
Second Bull Run Campaign, 71, 81–82
Selma, Ala., 127, 146, 206, 209–10
Senatobia, Miss., 178
Seven Days' Battles, 56
Seward, William H., 105–6
Shanks, John P. C., Col., 119, 212
Shannon Station, Miss., 192
Sharp's Ferry, Tenn., 118–19
Shelmire, John H., Capt., 50–51
Shenandoah Mountains, 49
Shenandoah River, 45, 48–49, 51–52
Shenandoah Valley, 41, 43–44, 51–52, 56–57,
    73
Sheridan, Phillip H., Maj. Gen., 214
Sherman, William T., Maj. Gen., 19, 87, 110,
    118, 120–21, 123, 126–27, 133–41, 145,
    147–48, 154, 165–70, 174–76, 179,
    182–83, 186, 188, 208, 210
Shields, James, Maj. Gen., 43–44, 51–52, 241
    n.10
Shorey, Samuel O., Maj., 172
Shreveport, La., 118
Sigel, Franz, Maj. Gen., 34, 57, 68, 75, 83, 86,
    97, 217
XVI Corps, Department of the Tennessee, 122
XVI Corps, Military Division of West
    Mississippi, 207, 209, 211
Slocum, Henry W., Maj. Gen., 169–74, 185,
    214, 216, 253 n.15
Smith, Andrew J., Maj. Gen., 112–16, 120,
    146, 168–69, 171–74, 176–79, 181–83,
    185, 193, 203, 107, 209–11
Smith, Edmund Kirby, Lt. Gen., 211–12
Smith, L. Henry, Lt., 164, 256 n.36
Smith, William F., Maj. Gen., 95
Smith, William Sooy, Brig. Gen., 118,
    120–27, 129–35, 140, 148, 202, 213, 248
    n.39
Snell, Fred W., 153, 161–62
Snickersville, Va., 89
Somerville Ford, 75

South Carolina unit: First Regiment of Infantry,
    28
South Mountain, Battle of, 140
Spanish Fort, Ala., 209
Spencer carbine, 129, 160, 206, 208, 249 n.46
Sperryville, Va., 57
Spring, Dr. Gardiner, 29
Spring Hill, Battle of, 188
Spring Peak, 225
Stafford Court House, Va., 92
Stahel, Julius, Brig. Gen., 48
Stanley, David S., Maj. Gen., 188
Stannardsville, Va., 58
Stanton, Edwin M., 43, 48, 98, 164–65, 179,
    187, 201, 204, 213, 215, 219–20
Starkville, Miss., 199
Steele, Frederick, Maj. Gen., 183–84, 207–9,
    211
Stettin, Prussia, 26
Stockton, Ala., 209
Stockton, Robert F., Commodore, 107
Stockton, Robert F., Jr., Maj. Gen., 98, 100,
    104, 107, 135, 145, 217, 235
Stoneman, George, Maj. Gen., 36–37, 89,
    108–10
Strange, John P., Maj., 144
Strasburg, Va., 41, 43–45
Strautz, Mortimer von, Lt., 106, 256 n.36
Struve, Gustav, Capt., 34
Stryker, William S., Maj. Gen., 228, 233
Stuart, Jeb, Maj. Gen., 75, 77, 89–91, 244 n.8
Stubbs's Farm, Miss., 155, 157, 159, 166
Sturgeon, Sheldon, Col., 256 n.27
Sturgis, Samuel D., Brig. Gen., 140–42,
    144–49, 151–60, 164–68, 174–75, 185,
    193, 202, 250 n.25
Sulphur Springs, Va., 75
Sumner, Edwin V., Maj. Gen., 221
Sumner, Edwin V., Jr., Capt., 221
Swallow, George R., Maj., 210

Talladega, Ala., 211
Tallahatchie River, 124, 131, 175–79, 181–83
Tallapoosa River, 209
Taylor, Richard, Lt. Gen., 194, 211
Tennessee River, 111–12, 136–37, 141, 145
Tennessee units: Second Tennessee Cavalry
    (Confederate), 159; Third Tennessee
    Cavalry (Union), 129; Seventh Tennessee
    Cavalry (Confederate), 136, 143–44
Tensas River, 207

Thimble Mountain, 225
XIII Corps, Military Division of West
    Mississippi, 209
Thomas, DeWitt C., Col., 161, 166
Thomas, George, Maj. Gen., 188–89, 201,
    206–7
Thomason, John W., Jr., Capt., 244 n.8
Thoroughfare Gap, 43, 83, 89
Tippah Creek, 124
Tishomingo Creek, 155, 159, 166
Todd, Galbraith Hall, 235
Todd, John R., Surgeon, 216
Tombigbee River, 193, 209
Townsend, Edward D., Maj. Gen., 219–20
Trans-Mississippi Department, 211–12
Trenton, N. J., 29, 57, 98, 100, 102, 108, 213,
    216–18, 228, 230
Troy, Ala., 210
Tulane, Paul, 234
Tulane University, 234
Tupelo, Miss., 145, 148–49, 151–52, 157,
    173–74, 190, 192–93, 201
Tupelo, Battle of, 146
Tuscumbia, Ala., 188
Tyler, Erastus B., Brig. Gen., 51

Union, Miss., 134
Union, Va., 91
Union City, Tenn., 112–14, 116, 118, 120, 136
Union Springs, Ala., 210
U. S. (Federal) units: Third U. S. Colored
    Cavalry, 200; Fourth U. S. Cavalry, 123,
    125, 128; Eighth U. S. Cavalry, 220–21,
    224; Ninth U. S. Infantry, 226
U. S. Military Academy, 40
U. S. Military Railroads, 111
U. S. Navy, 209
Upperville, Va., 88–89, 91
Uprising of 1830(Polish), 34
Upton, Emory E., Maj. Gen., 209
Utica, Miss., 172

Vaiden, Miss., 200
Vandergrift, Theodore W., 256 n.36
Van Rensselaer, Philip L., Maj., 168, 192
Veatch, James C., Brig. Gen., 137–38, 141
Vermont unit: First Vermont Cavalry, 59
Verona, Miss., 193, 219
Veteran Association of 2nd New Jersey
    Cavalry, 228, 230
Vicksburg, Miss., 97, 118, 121, 134, 140–41,
169–70, 173, 189–90, 200, 202, 211, 213,
    216
Vicksburg, Jackson, & Brandon RR, 170
Virginia units: Third Virginia Cavalry, 90;
    Fourth Virginia Cavalry, 90; Sixth Virginia
    Cavalry, 81; Seventh Virginia Cavalry, 60,
    81; Ninth Virginia Cavalry, 90; Twelfth
    Virginia Cavalry, 81; Seventeenth Virginia
    Cavalry, 77
Vroom, Peter D., Jr., Maj., 106, 110, 166,
    210, 216

Walker, James, Col., 61
Walker's Ford, 60
Walker's Mills, Miss., 123
War Department, 29–30, 33, 36–38, 52,
    86–87, 94, 96n, 97, 110–11, 179, 183,
    189, 212–16, 219–21, 226
Ward, Marcus L., 217, 220
Waring, George E., Jr., Col., 112–16, 118–21,
    123–28, 130–33, 138, 140, 142–43, 145,
    148, 155–58, 160, 166, 213
Warrenton, Va., 83–84, 91
Warsaw, Poland, 34
Washburn, Cadwallader C., Maj. Gen., 12,
    139–40, 145, 147–49, 153, 161–62,
    164–65, 168–75, 178–79, 181–83, 185,
    188–89, 201, 204, 213, 215
Washburn, Elihu, 140
Washburn, Israel, 140
Washington, D. C., 29, 36–37, 39, 56–57,
    68–69, 83, 85–86, 88, 104, 106, 108, 121,
    131, 164, 187, 189, 220
Waterford, Miss., 175
Webb, Charles H., 54–55
Weigley, Russell F., 221, 224
West, Joseph R., Brig. Gen., 209
West Point, Ga., 209
West Point, Miss., 124, 126–28, 132–34, 199
West Point(USMA), 40, 187
Westport, Battle of, 184
West Station, Miss., 200
White Plains, Va., 90
White's Station, Tenn., 162–63, 169, 175
Wier, William W., Col., 195–96
Wilkin, Alexander, Col., 148, 158, 163
Williams, Alpheus S., Brig. Gen., 66, 68
Williams, A. S., 240 n.5
Williams, Maria T., 28, 240 n.5
Wilson, James H., Maj. Gen., 127, 146,
    186–87, 190, 208, 210

Winchester, Va., 88

Winder, Charles S., Brig. Gen., 66, 68

Winona Station, Miss., 199–200

Winslow, Edward F., Col., 121, 134, 140–41,
148–49, 151, 156, 158–60, 166, 175–77,
183–84, 186–87, 189–90, 198–99, 202–3,
208, 212

Wisconsin units: First Wisconsin Cavalry, 211;
Fourth Wisconsin Cavalry, 201–11

Wittich, Capt., 34

Wojciechowski, Victor A., 230, 234

Wolf River, 142, 190

Woodhull Professorship in Modern Languages
(Princeton), 227

Wood, Ira W., 228

Wood, Robert C., Col., 200

Woods, William W., Capt., 163

Woodstock, Va., 46, 48

Woodward, Samuel L., Capt., 162

Wyndham, Sir Percy, Col., 38, 45–48, 50–51,
53–55, 71–73, 82–83

Yalobusha River, 176

Yard, Alexander A., Lt., 100, 102, 246 n.16

Yates, Richard, 105–6

Yazoo River, 118

Yocona River, 181

Yorke, P. Jones, Maj. and Lt. Col., 57, 106,
110, 128–30, 142–143, 168, 186–88,
194–95, 197, 199, 205, 210, 214, 216,
238, 252 n.2

Zagonyi, Charles, Col., 48

Zulinski, Mignon Bouget, 235